Circuits and Systems: Design and Applications

Volume III

Circuits and Systems: Design and Applications
Volume III

Edited by **Helena Walker**

CLANRYE INTERNATIONAL

New Jersey

Published by Clanrye International,
55 Van Reypen Street,
Jersey City, NJ 07306, USA
www.clanryeinternational.com

Circuits and Systems: Design and Applications
Volume III
Edited by Helena Walker

International Standard Book Number: 978-1-63240-099-4 (Hardback)

Printed in the United States of America.

Contents

Preface

At a very fundamental level, a circuit refers to an overall, complex arrangement of components such as resistors, conductors etc. which are connected in order to ensure a steady flow of current. It is only through circuits that signals or information is conveyed to the destination. Without a proper circuit system, the functional ability of any device becomes more or less redundant. The complexity and design of electronic circuits is ever increasing. Circuits are classified into analog circuits, digital circuits and mixed-signal circuits.

Circuits and systems in this book explain the handling of theory and applications of circuits and systems, signal processing, and system design methodology. The practical implementation of circuits, and application of circuit theoretic techniques to systems and to signal processing are the topics covered under this discipline. From radio astronomy to wireless communications and biomedical applications, the application of circuits and systems can be found across a varying range of subjects.

Circuits and Systems is an interesting discipline and is emerging as a coveted career option for many students. A lot of research, to develop more efficient systems is also being conducted.

I'd like to thank all the contributors for sharing their studies with us and make this book an enlightening read. I would also like to thank them for submitting their work within the set time parameters. Lastly, I wish to thank my family, whose support has been crucial for the completion of this book.

Editor

Novel Threshold-Based Standard-Cell Flash ADC

Marcel Siadjine Njinowa[1], Hung Tien Bui[1], François-Raymond Boyer[2]
[1]Department of Applied Sciences, Université du Québec à Chicoutimi, Chicoutimi, Canada
[2]Department of Computer Engineering, École Polytechnique de Montréal, Montréal, Canada

ABSTRACT

This paper introduces a novel standard-cell flash architecture for implementing analog-to-digital converters (ADC). The proposed ADC consists of several CMOS inverters all having their inputs connected to a common input node. The output of the ADC is a thermometer code generated by the inverter outputs. Depending on the relationship between the input signal and a given inverter's threshold voltage, the output will either be "0" or "1". By having many inverters with different threshold voltages, it is possible to create a 3-bit flash ADC. Even though the system is inherently non-linear, mathematical optimization has been done in order to improve its linearity. The proposed circuit dissipates 6.7 mW and uses in total 672 transistors of PMOS and NMOS types. This ADC is designed and simulated using TSMC's 0.18 μm CMOS and results show that the proposed circuit works as expected even in presence of process variations.

Keywords: Flash ADC; Standard Cells; Data Converters

1. Introduction

The aggressive technology scaling seen in recent years has helped improve the performance of many digital systems. Analog systems, on the other hand, have not benefited as much, as they are more sensitive to process variations which become more dominant with smaller technology nodes. In addition, reduction in feature size often entails reduction in supply voltage which can also cause problems in the design of analog circuits. These are some of the reasons why designers are interested in moving certain modules from the analog domain into the digital domain. Perhaps the most significant example is filters. Since passive components need certain physical dimensions in order to have the desired behavior, they do not scale down very well with node size reduction. That is the reason why many filters have migrated into the digital domain [1,2].

In order to convert analog modules into digital modules, ADC and digital to analog converters (DAC) are typically required to interface between the domains. The design of these components typically requires a certain level of expertise and they also require analog/mixed signal components. These two points typically increase the required design time and also increase the risk of having non-functional designs. It is therefore interesting to investigate ways to migrate these designs into more digital forms by using standard-cells [2-5]. Furthermore, a flash ADC which is mainly known for its high-speed conversion rate [6,7] consumes more power and occupies larger chip area in comparison to the other types of ADCs such as Successive Approximation and pipelined ADCs [8,9].

In this paper, we propose a flash ADC that can be fully implemented using only standard-cells. This approach helps to improve the high-speed conversion rate while maintaining comparable power consumption. This allows also the designer to stay within the mature digital design flow and effectively reduce risks and time-to-market. Other benefits of using this approach include higher speed and simpler design implementation.

The rest of the paper is divided as follows. Section 2 introduces the basic concept along with a first version of the proposed ADC. A second version with increased linearity and modularity is presented in Section 3. De- sign and simulation results of the implemented circuits are shown in Section 4 and conclusions are drawn in Section 5.

2. Initial Architecture

ADCs are an important building block in modern electronic systems. While numerous architectures exist [10-12], this work mainly focuses on the flash ADC whose structure is shown in **Figure 1(a)**.

The circuit in **Figure 1(a)** uses a string of resistors and comparators to generate a thermometer code in response to an analog input. The ADC shown in **Figure 1(a)** can be converted into a standard-cell form if the resistors and the comparators were substituted by logic gates **Figure**

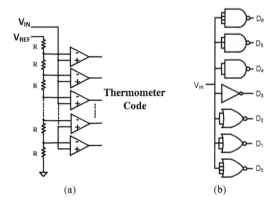

Figure 1. (a) Circuit of a flash ADC and of (b) the proposed architecture.

1(b). The proposed flash architecture uses logic gates configured as inverters that have different threshold voltages. The threshold voltage of the gates serves as the reference voltage to which is compared the input.

To explain the principle of operation, let us consider a 2-input NAND gate whose inputs are connected together. In such a configuration, the gate operates much like an inverter. The difference, however, lies within the threshold voltage of the gate. In a NAND gate, the NMOS network is in series whereas the PMOS network is in parallel. If the NMOS and the PMOS gates had identical V_{TH} and were sized to have identical μC_{OX} (W/L), the threshold of the NAND would be higher than that of the inverter. This is because, for the same V_{GS}, the PMOS network would generate more current since it has a parallel connection whereas the NMOS network has a series connection. For the currents to be equal, the NMOS transistors would need to have higher V_{GS} which explains the rise in gate's threshold voltage. A similar reasoning can be applied to a 2-input NOR gate and the conclusion would be that its threshold voltage is lower than that of the inverter.

To calculate the value of these threshold voltages, let us define the threshold voltage of a logic gate as being the input voltage at which the output voltage is $V_{DD}/2$. To simplify the analysis, we will assume that identical transistors in series can be considered as a single transistor whose channel is longer. Similarly, when identical transistors are in parallel, we assume that they can be seen as one transistor whose channel is wider.

For the purpose of this analysis, let us only consider inverters, NAND gates and NOR gates. Let M be the number of NMOS transistors connected in parallel. Knowing that static gates are complementary, the P-network will then have M transistors in series. The NMOS transistors can be replaced by a single transistor having a width that is M times that of that of the original transistor. Similarly, the PMOS transistors can be replaced by a single transistor having a length that is M times that of

that of the original transistor. This simplification facilitates the task of writing the current equation. However, equations cannot be written until the region of operation of these transistors is determined. Knowing that the threshold of a gate is the input voltage that generates an output of $V_{DD}/2$, it is mandatory that all PMOS and NMOS be conducting. This condition is satisfied when:

$$V_{TH} < V_G < V_{DD} - V_{TH} \qquad (1)$$

In addition, we know that the NMOS will be in saturation when $V_{DS} > V_{GS} - V_{TH}$. Since V_{DS} is equal to $V_{DD}/2$ at the threshold voltage, V_{GS} needs to be smaller than $V_{DD}/2 + V_{TH}$ for the transistor to be in saturation. Similarly, the PMOS is in saturation when V_{SD} is greater than V_{SG}-V_{TH}. Since V_{SD} is equal to $V_{DD}/2$ at the threshold voltage, the PMOS is in saturation when $V_{DD}/2 > V_{DD} - V_G - V_{TH}$. Thus, both networks will be in saturation if the following condition is satisfied:

$$\left(\frac{V_{DD}}{2} - V_{TH}\right) < V_G < \left(\frac{V_{DD}}{2} + V_{TH}\right) \qquad (2)$$

It can be shown that when $\dfrac{V_{DD}}{2} < 2V_{TH}$, both conditions in Equations (1) and (2) will be simultaneously satisfied. In this case, it means that, at the threshold voltage of the gate, all transistors will be in saturation. The technology used for this work meets all aforementioned conditions and therefore, the transistors will always be in saturation near the threshold voltage of the gate. Knowing the region of operation of these transistors, and knowing that their current is equal, it is possible to write the following equation:

$$\begin{aligned}(M)\frac{1}{2}\mu C_{OX}\left(\frac{W}{L}\right)\left(V_{GS} - V_{TH}\right)^2 \\ = \left(\frac{1}{M}\right)\frac{1}{2}\mu C_{OX}\left(\frac{W}{L}\right)\left(V_{SG} - V_{TH}\right)^2\end{aligned} \qquad (3)$$

When Equation (3) is solved for V_G, the threshold voltage of the gate (known as V_{GTH}) is obtained:

$$V_{GTH} = \frac{V_{DD} - V_{TH} + M \cdot V_{TH}}{M + 1} \qquad (4)$$

Equation (4) shows how the threshold voltage of a gate changes as a function of M. By using NAND and NOR gates with higher fan-ins, the value of M changes which, in turn, changes the threshold voltage of the gate. It is therefore possible to create a set of inverters having different threshold voltages to create a flash ADC using only standard cells.

To validate the functionality of the proposed architecture, a sample 3-bit ADC was created using a MATLAB model, version 2007. This architecture consists of NAND and NOR gates with two, three and four inputs along with an inverter (**Figure 1(b)**). Recall that M is the number of NMOS transistors connected in parallel. When these NMOS are connected in series, the value of M will be inverted. For instance, M will be equal to 1/4 for a 4-input NAND gate whereas it will be equal to four for a 4-input NOR gate. For the case of an inverter M will be equal to one.

By using TMSC's 0.18 m CMOS technology parameters in our MATLAB model, the different values of V_{GTH} have been plotted as function of M and the results are shown in **Figure 2**. The ideal ADC relationship between the input and output is also shown in the figure as a dotted line.

This figure shows that the relationship between M and threshold voltage is monotonic but clearly not linear. To quantify the linearity of the ADC, it is possible to use the sum of squared error between the real and ideal threshold voltages. In this sample implementation, the sum of squared error is calculated to be:

$$Error = \sum_n \left(V_{nIDEAL} - V_{nADC}\right)^2 = 8.9 \times 10^{-3}$$

In this equation, n is the index value representing M whereas V_{nIDEAL} and V_{nADC} are respectively the ideal and calculated threshold voltage.

3. Architecture with Improved Linearity

The previous section introduced a standard-cell flash ADC that works properly but lacks linearity. In this section, we propose a second design that is more modular and has improved linearity at the expense of a larger area and increased power consumption. The proposed architecture is shown in **Figure 3**. It consists of NAND and NOR gates of the highest fan-in in a given standardcell library. For the purpose of explaining the architecture, let us consider gates with a fan-in of four. The number of gates used in this structure will be equal to $(2^N - 2) * (2^N - 1)$, where N is the number of bits in the ADC. By progressively changing the number of NAND and NOR gates per output, it is possible to have threshold voltages that are more linearly spaced. An implementation with Q

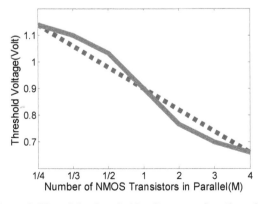

Figure 2. Plot of the threshold voltage as a function of m.

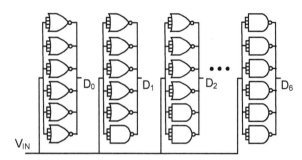

Figure 3. Architecture of the 3-bit ADC with $Q = 6$.

$= 6$ is shown in **Figure 3**, where Q and P are respectively the total number of gates and the number of NOR gates per output.

To calculate the linearity of the proposed ADC with Q equal to six, we must first calculate the threshold voltage of the different block of gates ($D0$ to $D6$). This is done by writing the current equations for the N-network and the P-network:

$$I_{DN} = P \frac{M}{2} \mu C_{OX} \left(\frac{W}{L}\right)\left(V_{GS} - V_{TH}\right)^2$$
$$+ (Q-P)\frac{1}{2M} \mu C_{OX} \left(\frac{W}{L}\right)\left(V_{GS} - V_{TH}\right)^2 \qquad (5)$$

$$I_{DP} = P \frac{1}{2M} \mu C_{OX} \left(\frac{W}{L}\right)\left(V_{SG} - V_{TH}\right)^2$$
$$+ (Q-P)\frac{M}{2} \mu C_{OX} \left(\frac{W}{L}\right)\left(V_{SG} - V_{TH}\right)^2 \qquad (6)$$

By equating (5) and (6) and by solving for V_G, we can find the threshold voltage of the different block of gates. The resulting equation for the threshold voltage is large and will therefore not be written here. Instead, its value has been calculated with the chosen process parameters and the results are plotted in **Figure 4**.

A comparison between **Figure 4(a)** and **Figure 4(b)** shows that the linearity has been improved. In order to quantify the improvement in linearity, the sum of squared error has been calculated:

$$Error = \sum_n \left(V_{nIDEAL} - V_{nADC}\right)^2 = 2.6 \times 10^{-3}$$

These results show that this new architecture is about three times more linear than the architecture proposed in the previous section.

3.1. Optimization

In order to further improve the linearity of the proposed solution, it is possible to increase Q to a value higher than $(2^N - 2)$. For instance, by doubling the value of Q while still keeping the number of bits equal to N, the result is a structure that has more threshold voltages than what is required. By selecting only the $(2^N - 1)$ required

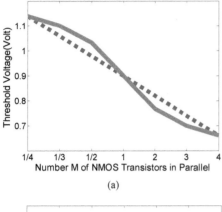

(a)

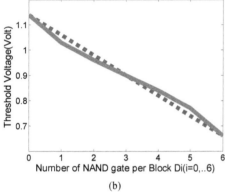

(b)

Figure 4. Threshold voltages of the design (a) in Figure 1(b) and (b) in Figure 3.

threshold voltages and by discarding the other possibilities, it is possible to improve the linearity of the ADC. The heuristic algorithm used for this process is described in the following pseudo-code:

NumberNAND(i) = 0   i
  For i = 0 to 7
    set NumberNAND(i) ∈ [0, 12]
    to minimize (idealvth(i) − adcvth(i, NumberNAND))²
End

To test the effectiveness of the proposed algorithm, it was applied to optimize the 3-bit ADC proposed in **Figure 3**. During this process, the squared errors were calculated and plotted for each of the associated block of gates in **Figure 3**. A sample plot is presented in **Figure 5** which shows the change in the sum of squared error as the number of NAND gates per block is changed. By using the number of NAND gates that minimizes the squared error for each block, it is possible to have a more linear ADC.

In **Figure 5**, it can be seen that, to minimize the error, the block of gates associated to $D2$ must contain three NAND gate. The other blocks were analyzed the same way to determine the number of NANDs to include.

Using this configuration, the threshold voltage of the proposed ADC was calculated and the results are shown in **Figure 6**. It shows a relation that is more linear than

that of **Figure 4**.

To quantify the linearity, we used the sum of squared error:

$$Error = \sum_{n} \left(V_{nIDEAL} - V_{nADC}\right)^2 = 8.1 \times 10^{-4}$$

This error is about 9.1% of its original value and validates the approach used during the optimization process.

3.2. Characterization

The proposed 3-bit ADC is designed in 180nm technology, characterized for parameters like differential non-linearity (DNL), integral non-linearity (INL) as shown in **Figure 7**. The results show that the ADC exhibits a maximum DNL of 0.4 LSB and INL of 0.2 LSB respectively.

4. Transistor-Level Design

To verify the functionality and the effectiveness of the proposed ADCs, these circuits were designed at the transistor level using 0.18 μm CMOS technology and simulated using Cadence's Spectre simulator. For the purpose of this test, two circuits were created: the original design (**Figure 1(b)**) and the design with improved linearity (**Figure 3**) that has also been optimized. The two circuits were evaluated by injecting a slow ramp at the input and observing the point at which the outputs toggle. The result

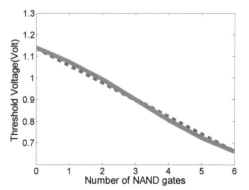

Figure 5. Sum of squared error for the D2 block.

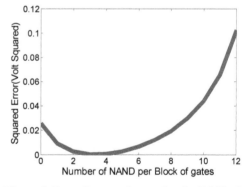

Figure 6. Threshold voltage of optimized blocks of gates.

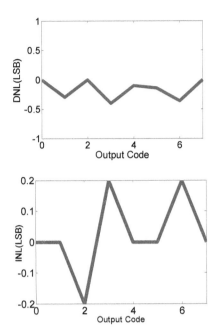

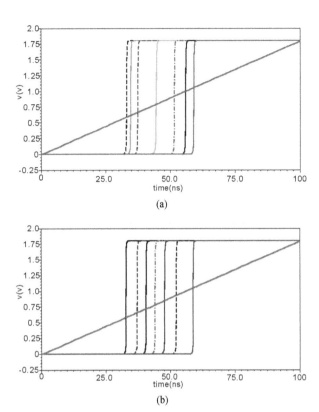

(a)

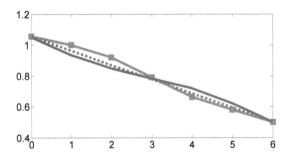

(b)

Figure 7. DNL and INL graphs of the proposed flash ADC.

Figure 8. Responses of the (a) Original and of the (b) Optimized ADCs.

of this simulation is shown in **Figure 8**. **Figure 8(a))** shows the output of the original 3-bit ADC whereas **Figure 8(b))** shows the output of the optimized design. These figures show that, as the input voltage increases, it eventually surpasses the value of the different reference voltages, which makes the gates transition to from "0" to "1". It confirms that the proposed ADCs operate as expected.

From these figures, it is also possible to see that the spacing between the transitions in **Figure 8(a)** is more uniform than the spacing from **Figure 8(a)**. This implies that the optimized design is more linear than the original one. To visualize the linearity of the proposed circuits, the simulation results have been measured and tabulated. These results were used to create **Figure 9**.

In this figure, the dotted line is the ideal response; the solid line with the markers is the original design whereas the remaining trace is the optimized design. It shows that the optimized design has a much more linear response.

To verify the proposed circuit's robustness to process variations, Monte Carlo analysis was run on the design for 100 cycles and no shown in this paper. The evaluated parameter in these simulations is the difference between adjacent reference voltages and. The simulation indicated that all the reference voltages typically change in the same direction in presence of process variations. Therefore, even in presence of process variations the difference in reference voltages varies minimally which ensures that the ADC will work even under process variations.

5. Conclusion

In this paper, we introduced a novel threshold-based standard-cell flash ADC. Its implementation is fully

Figure 9. Linearity of the proposed ADCs to a ramp input.

compatible with standard digital CMOS technology. The functionality of the proposed design was demonstrated using basic current equations. A new architecture with an enhanced linearity was also proposed. A linearization heuristic based on the sum of squared errors was introduced in order to improve its performance. It is shown that the resulting design is more linear. To validate the results, transistor-level simulations have been executed using Cadence's Spectre simulator while Monte Carlo simulations show that a 3-bit resolution is possible in 0.18 μm CMOS technology.

6. Acknowledgements

The authors would like to acknowledge financial support from NSERC and ReSMIQ.

REFERENCES

[1] S. Y. Sedra and K. C. Smith, "Microelectronic Circuits," Fourth Edition, Oxford University Press Inc., Oxford, 1998.

[2] T. Watanabe, T. Mizuno and Y. Makino, "An All-Digital Analog-to-Digital Converter with 12-μV/LSB Using Moving-Average Filtering," *IEEE Journal of Solid-State Circuits*, Vol. 38, No. 1, 2003, pp. 120-125.

[3] D. Lee, *et al.*, "Design Method and Automation of Comparator Generation for Flash A/D Converter," *ACM Portal*, No. 5, 2004, pp. 127-155.

[4] H. Farkhani, M. Meymandi-Nejad and M. Sachdev, "A Fully Digital ADC Using a New Delay Element with Enhanced Linearity," *IEEE International Symposium on Circuits and Systems, ISCAS*, 18-21 May 2008, pp. 2406-2409.

[5] M. A. Farahat, F. A. Farg and H. A. Elsimary, "Only Digital Technology Analog-to-Digital Converter Circuit," *International Midwest Symposium on Circuits and Systems, IEEE*, Vol. 1, 2003, pp. 178-181.

[6] B. Yu and W. Black Jr., "A 900 MS/s 6 b Interleaved CMOS Flash ADC," *IEEE Custom Integrated Circuits Conference*, Vol. 8, 2001, pp. 149-152.

[7] G. Geelen, "A 6 b 1.1 GSample/s CMOS A/D Con- ver-ter," *IEEE International Solid-State Circuits Confer- ence*, San Francisco, Vol. 2, 5-7 February 2001, pp. 128- 129.

[8] H. Chen, B. Song and K. Bacrania, "A 14-b 20-M Samples/s CMOS Pipelened ADC," *IEEE Journal of Solid-State Circuits*, Vol. 6, 2001, pp. 997-1001.

[9] Y. Park, S. Karthikeyan, F. Tsay and E. Bartolome, "A 10 b 100 M Samples/s CMOS Pipelined ADC with 1.8 V Power Supply," *IEEE International Solid-State Circuits Conference*, Vol. 8, 2001, pp. 130-131.

[10] J. Lin and B. Haroun, "An Embedded 0.8V/480μW 6b/22MHz Flash ADC in 0.13 μm Digital CMOS Process Using Nonlinear Double-Interpolation Technique," *IEEE Journal of Solid-State Circuits*, Vol. 37, No. 12, 2002, pp. 1610-1617.

[11] F. Munoz, A. P. VegaLeal, R. G. Carvajal, A. Torralba, J. Tombs and J. Ramirez-Angulo, "A 1.1 v Low-Power ΣΔ Modulator for 14-b 16 KHz A/D Conversion," *IEEE International Symposium on Circuits and Systems*, Vol. 1, 2001, pp. 619-622.

[12] B.-S. Song, "Analog Front-End Macro Circuit Design," *International Symposium on VLSI Technology Systems and Applications*, Taipei, 8-10 June 1999, pp. 223-226.

Characterization of a Novel Low-Power SRAM Bit-Cell Structure at Deep Sub-Micron CMOS Technology for Multimedia Applications

Rakesh Kumar Singh[1], Manisha Pattanaik[2], Neeraj Kr. Shukla[3]

[1]Department of E & CE, BT-Kumaon Engineering College, Dwarahat, India
[2]Department of Information Technology, VLSI Group, ABV-IIITM Gwalior, Gwalior, India
[3]Department of EECE, ITM University, Gurgaon, India

ABSTRACT

To meet the increasing demands for higher performance and low-power consumption in present and future Systems-on-Chips (SoCs) require a large amount of on-die/embedded memory. In Deep-Sub-Micron (DSM) technology, it is coming as challenges, e.g., leakage power, performance, data retention, and stability issues. In this work, we have proposed a novel low-stress SRAM cell, called as IP3 SRAM bit-cell, as an integrated cell. It has a separate write sub-cell and read sub-cell, where the write sub-cell has dual role of data write and data hold. The data read sub-cell is proposed as a pMOS gated ground scheme to further reduce the read power by lowering the gate and subthreshold leakage currents. The drowsy voltage is applied to the cell when the memory is in the standby mode. Further, it utilizes the full-supply body biasing scheme while the memory is in the standby mode, to further reduce the subthreshold leakage current to reduce the overall standby power. To the best of our knowledge, this low-stress memory cell has been proposed for the first time. The proposed IP3 SRAM Cell has a significant write and read power reduction as compared to the conventional 6 T and PP SRAM cells and overall improved read stability and write ability performances. The proposed design is being simulated at $V_{DD} = 0.8$ V and 0.7 V and an analysis is presented here for 0.8 V to adhere previously reported works. The other design parameters are taken from the CMOS technology available on 45 nm with $t_{OX} = 2.4$ nm, $V_{thn} = 0.224$ V, and $V_{thp} = 0.24$ V at T = 27°C.

Keywords: SRAM; Low-Power; Active Power; Standby Power; Gate Leakage; Sub-Threshold Leakage

1. Introduction

The Static Random Access Memory (SRAM) is a critical component in the modern Digital Systems-on-Chip (SoCs). As the demand for the portable multimedia rich applications is increasing, their role and need is also increasing day-by-day. As a result, SRAMs strongly impact the overall power, performance, stability and area requirements. In order to manage these constrained tradeoffs, they must be specially designed for target applications, e.g., portable multimedia products, implantable bio-medical devices, wireless sensor networks, etc. The highly power constrained systems demand more power for its active mode (read/write) operations. Also, the leakage power is coming as a big challenge in the DSM technologies, while the memory is in the standby mode, *i.e.*, it is just retaining the data. Advancement of semiconductor technology has driven the rapid growth of very large scale integrated (VLSI) systems for increasingly broad applications almost in all sphere of life, e.g., high-end computing, consumer electronics, medical electronics, and portable multimedia products, etc. Among embedded memories, six-transistor (6T)-based SRAM continues to play an important role in nearly all VLSI systems due to its superior speed and full compatibility with logic process technology. But as the technology scaling continues, SRAM design is facing severe challenge in maintaining sufficient cell stability margin under relentless area scaling with leakage power issues, both in dynamic and standby modes. Meanwhile, rapid expansion in mobile application, including new emerging application in sensor and medical devices, requires far more aggressive voltage scaling to meet very stringent power constraint [1]. According to the International Technology Roadmap (ITRS), 90% of the chip-area will be occupied by the memory core by 2014 [2]. This shows an increasing demand for more chips area for embedded memory with a commitment for low-power, standby data retention, stability, and less cell area. The power consumption in embedded SRAM memory is observed as active power (when device performing write/read switching action) and standby power (when device is in the ideal state). In the standby mode, there are several sources for the leakage current, e.g., the sub-threshold current due to low threshold voltage, etc., while in the dynamic mode, the gate leakage current due to very thin gate oxides, etc., [3]. The area and power consumption by the SoC devices, occupied by static random access memory, increase largely with the technology scaling. Thus they are the critical components in both high-performance processors and handheld applications [4]. As the CMOS process technology continues to scale to the nanometer regime, process variation and leakage current of transistors become more severe, which are further aggravated by the fluctuation of the operating conditions such as the variation of the supply voltage and/or the temperature leads to a higher chance of device malfunctioning [5]. A high-performance VLSI chip also demands ever increasing on-die SRAM to meet the performance needs. This pushes the SRAM scaling towards a more concern domain in today's VLSI design applications. The SRAM cell stability is further degraded by supply voltage scaling. The SRAM leakage power has also become a more significant component of total chip power as a large portion of the total chip transistors directly comes from on-die SRAM. Since the activity factor of a large on-die SRAM is relatively low. So, it is recommended by the researchers in the field to be more effective to put it in a power reduction mechanism dynamically, which modulates the power supply along the memory addressable unit or bank and the need for active/standby mode of operation. In this work, a novel IP3 SRAM cell structure is proposed to reduce the active and standby power, both. The proposed design has and integrated two sub-cell structure, one for write and other for read operation in the active mode. The drowsy technique [6] is utilized when the memory is in the standby mode to reduce standby power consumption. The subthreshold leakage is reduced by applying FBB scheme [7] while the cell is ideal. The read power is significantly reduced by the use of the pMOS gated structure at the read sub-cell along with the write power reduction. The data stability and data write ability, both are improved with a very less area penalty as the transistors used in the design are of minimum size.

The paper is organized as follows, the conventional 6T cell is presented in Section 2 and a brief review on the previous work is presented in Section 3. The Section 4 discusses the proposed IP3 SRAM cell structure followed by the simulation and conclusions in Section 5 and 6, respectively.

2. The Conventional 6T SRAM Bit-Cell—A Functional Approach

The Conventional SRAM (CV-SRAM) cell has Six MOS

transistors ("4" nMOS and "2" nMOS), **Figure 1**. Unlike DRAM it doesn't need to be refreshed as the bit is latched in. It can operate at lower supply voltages and has large noise immunity. However, the six transistors of an SRAM cell take more space than a DRAM cell made of one transistor and one capacitor thereby increasing the complexity of the cell [8].

2.1. The SRAM Bit Cell

The memory bit-cell has two CMOS inverters connected back to back (M1, M3, and M2, M4). Two more pass transistors (M5 and M6) are the access transistors controlled by the Word Line (WL), **Figure 1**. The cell preserves its one of two possible states "0" or "1", as long as power is available to the bit-cell. Here, Static power dissipation is very small. Thus the cell draws current from the power supply only during switching. But ideal mode of the memory is becoming the main concern in the deep-submicron technology due to its concerns in the leakage power and data retentation at lower operating voltages.

2.2. The Operation of SRAM Bit-Cell

Although the two nMOS and pMOS transistors of SRAM memory bit-cell form a bi-stable latch, there are mainly the following three states of SRAM memory cell, the Write, Read, and Hold states.

2.2.1. Standby Operation (Hold)
When WL = "0", M5 and M6 disconnect the cell from Bit-Lines (BL and BLB). The two cross-coupled inverters formed by M1-M4 will continue to reinforce each other as long as they are disconnected from the outside world. The current drawn in this state from the power supply is termed as standby current.

2.2.2. Data Read Operation
Read cycle starts with pre-charging BL and BLB to "1",

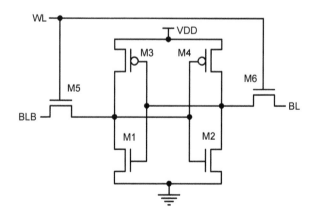

Figure 1. 6T-CMOS SRAM cell [8].

i.e., V_{DD}. Within the memory cell M1 and M4 are ON. Asserting the word line, turns ON the M5 and M6 and the values of Q and Q' are transferred to Bit-Lines (BL and BLB). No current flows through M6, thus M4 and M6 pull BL upto V_{DD}, *i.e.*, BL = "1" and BLB discharges through M1 and M5. This voltage difference is sensed and amplified to logic levels by sense amplifiers.

2.2.3. Data Write Operation

The value to be written is applied to the Bit lines. Thus to write data "0", we assert BL = 0, BLB = "1" and to write data "1", the BL = "1", BLB = "0", asserted when WL = "1".

3. The Related Work—A Brief Review

In [8], a P3 SRAM bit-cell structure at 45nm technology has been proposed for semiconductor memories with high activity factor based applications. It makes use of the series (in-line) connected pMOS transistor to create the stacking effects for power reduction. While in standby, the stacking transistors are kept off and on during the write/read operation. The pMOS pass transistors are used to lower the gate leakage currents [9] while full-supply body-biasing scheme is used to reduce the sub-threshold leakage currents. This structure achieved a significant reduction in the dynamic and standby power in compareson with the conventional 6T SRAM cell structure, at the cost of very small area penalty and issues with SNM.

In [9], a gate leakage current reduction technique based on the pMOS pass-transistor SRAM bit-cell structure as PP-SRAM Cell has been proposed at 45 nm technology and 0.8 V supply voltage. It has lower gate leakage compared to that of the conventional SRAM cell. In order to decrease the gate leakage currents of the SRAM cell, two nMOS pass transistors, are replaced by pMOS pass transistors. In it due to the use of the pMOS pass transistors, there is an increase in the dynamic power of the cell, which is consumed during read and write operation. By keeping a view on, the use of pMOS pass transistor, may lead to performance degradation due to different mobility coefficients for the nMOS and pMOS transistors. To overcome this problem, the width of pMOS pass transistor is selected as 1.8 times of that of the nMOS that may cause an area penalty.

4. IP3 SRAM Structure—The Proposed Low-Power SRAM Bit-Cell Structure

In the novel Improved P3 (IP3) SRAM Cell, an integrated approach of two separate sub-cells (write and read) structure is proposed with a pMOS gated ground and drowsy scheme to reduce the active and standby power without losing the cells' performance, **Figure 2**. The full-supply body biasing is used to further reduce the

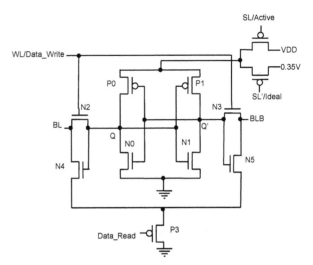

Figure 2. Proposed IP3 SRAM bit-cell.

sub-threshold leakage when the cell is in the standby mode. The data write and memory storage is being done at upper sub-cell while lower sub-cell is used for data-read operation, only. In the standby mode, the drowsy voltage (V_{DD} = 0.35 V) is being applied to the memory to retain the data in the upper memory sub-cell at very reduced power loss. The drowsy voltage can be applied through on board power supply or through an external power supply. In the active mode of operation, the cell is supplied with V_{DD}. In data write mode, the data read sub-cell is completely isolated from the data write sub-cell through BL's and vice-versa, which further improves the cell's stability.

4.1. Bit-Cell Analysis

A novel IP3-SRAM Cell structure with drowsy scheme and pMOS stacking with ground, e.g., pMOS gated ground, in the lower half cell half has been proposed. The basic objective for this design is to reduce the stress at 6T conventional SRAM cell in order to reduce the power consumption (active, leakage, and standby) without losing its performance. The area penalty in the new design is small as all the transistors used here are minimum sized transistors except transistor P3 which is about 1.8 times of the nMOS to meet the charge careers mobility [9] in nMOS and pMOS transistors. The proposed SRAM cell structure is comprises of two memory sub-cells, the write sub-cell (Pull Down Transistors: N0, N1; Access Transistors: N2, N3; Pull up Transistors: P0, P1) and the read-sub cell (Read Access Transistors: N4, N5; and a Gated pMOS transistor: P3). The write sub-cell performs the dual role, one as write data into memory and other holding the data in the memory. While writing data into the cell, the supply voltage V_{DD} is applied before making WL/Data_Write = HIGH, and data is being passed at the BL and BLB to write in the write sub-cell. Now, WL/Data_Write put on LOW by making the BLs HIGH to latch the data in the cell. Also, while the cell is not in use, *i.e.*, the cell in the standby, drowsy voltage 0.35 V is applied at the cell to retain the data in the cell. At this time, the stored information being available at the read sub-cell's gate for further read access operation, without disturbing the data in the write sub-cell. It is a unique feature of this cell to further improve its read performance. Now, to read the data from the read sub-cell, drowsy voltage is being switched to V_{DD} level and Data_Read signal is applied at P3 as LOW to put P3 ON and make lower sub-cell ready for read operation. Since, at this time only the read sub-cell is working, the read power reduced significantly without disturbing the stored data at the memory cell. Which further improves the cells read stability. As the write and read operations are performed in separate sub-cells, it improves the cells' write and read performance. In the standby mode, the memory cell is kept at the low-voltage drowsy mode to ensure the data retentation in the cell. The full supply body biasing voltge, further supports in the reduced subthreshold leakage power while the cell is ideal.

4.2. Bit-Cell Operation

The active mode (data write/read) and standby mode (data hold) operation of the cell is as follows,

4.2.1. Active Mode Operation
4.2.1.1. Write Mode
Make SL/Active = 0 to apply power supply V_{DD} at the cell. SL'/Ideal = 1, Data_Write = 1 to activate N2 and N3, and Data_Read = 1 to de-activate pMOS P3 to cut-off the lower sub-cell from the ground. Apply data to be stored in the cell at the BL and BLB to write into the upper sub-cell. After data write, to hold data, apply Data_Write = 0. This will cut-off the nMOS transistors N2 and N3 and cut the BL's from the upper sub-cell. This data will also be available at the gates of the nMOS transistors N4 and N5. Apply BL and BLB as HIGH. Now, the data is latched in the upper memory sub-cell. Keep Data_Read = 1, to keep the lower sub-cell cut-off from the ground through pMOS P3.

4.2.1.2. Read Mode
Make SL/Active = 1 and SL'/Ideal = 0 to apply drowsy supply voltage of V_{DD} = 0.35V at the upper sub-cell. Data_Write = 0 to de-activate the nMOS N2 and N3. This will disconnect the upper sub-cell from BL's and hold data in the cell. Apply Data_Read = 0 to activate pMOS P3 and connect the lower sub-cell to the ground for its normal read operation. This will bring the lower sub-cell in the data read mode. Put the upper sub-cell at low-power drowsy mode to retain data in the cell. This

stored data at Q and Q' is also available at the gates of N4 and N5 at the lower sub-cell, so the stored data is not disturbed at the upper sub-cell, this further improves the cells' read performance, *i.e.*, cells' stability improves. Now, to read the data, make BL and BLB HGH and access the stored data through the sense amplifier.

4.2.2. Standby Mode
Make SL/Active = 1, SL'/Ideal = 0 to apply drowsy voltage (V_{DD} = 0.35V) at the cell. This will reduce the standby power of the cell. Apply Data_Write = 0 to keep the access transistors cut-off from the memory cell. Apply Data_Read = 1 to put the read sub-cell separate from the ground to reduce the standby leakage from the read sub-cell. Put the upper sub-cell at low-power drowsy mode to retain data in the cell. The lower sub-cell also cut-off from the ground through pMOS gated transistor. This will reduce the sub-threshold leakage current and will reduce the standby power leakage of the cell.

5. Simulation

The simulation work is being performed for active power write/read for data "0/1" at supply voltage of 0.8 V and at Room Temperature (RT) of 27°C. The design parameters are, V_{thn} = 0.224, V_{thp} = 0.22V, t_{ox} = 2.4 nm and the standard nMOS and pMOS transistors to support chip fabrication process.

5.1. Performance Simulation and Analysis

5.1.1. Write Operation
The proposed IP3 cell demands 17.65% and 41.53% less power as compared to 6T and PP cells while performing the data write operation but costs 94% and 93% more power as compared to the P4 and P3 cell, **Figure 3**.

5.1.2. Read Operation
The IP3 cell is seen to be the best low-power cell among the 6T, PP, P3, P4, and P3 cells during read operation. It demands 99%, 99%, 90%, and 91% less read power as compared to the 6T, PP, P4, and P3 cell, respectively,

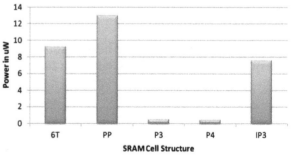

Figure 3. Active power (write) at V_{DD} = 0.8 V.

Figure 4. Because of this feature of the proposed cell, the cell is best suited for the applications where read operation has a greater activity factor, e.g., battery powered mobile multimedia applications.

5.1.3. Standby Leakage Power

The standby leakage power, when the memory is in the idle mode, it is observed that the IP3 cell is consuming 36% and 52% less power as compared to the 6T and PP cells while it takes 59% and 23% more power to P4 and P3 cells, **Figure 5**.

5.1.4. Stability

The read stability metrics, the SVNM and SINM is simulated here. The SVNM of IP3 is found no change with 6T cell while it is 55%, 52% improved with P4, P3 cells and 3% poor to PP cell. The SINM is 36% poor with 6T cell and 63%, 995, and 99% improved to PP, P4, and P3 cells, **Figures 6(a)** and **(b)**. The P4 and P3 cell have poor read stability while IP3 has improved read stability.

The WTV and WTI are the metrics for the write ability. The WTV for IP3 is same as that of 6T cell. The WTV for the IP3 is observed to be improved by 25%, 60%, and 62% by PP, P4, and P3 cells, **Figure 7(a)** The WTI is same as that of 6T and poor by 64% with PP cell while improved by almost 99% by P4, and P3 cell, **Figure 7(b)**. The P4, and P3 cells found to be the poor read ability while the IP3 cell has marginally improved write ability.

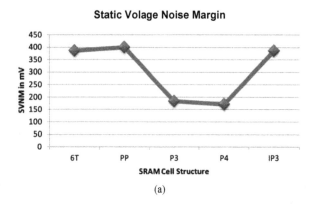

(a)

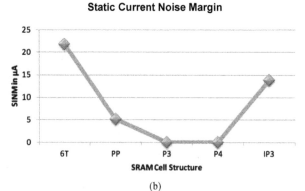

(b)

Figure 6. Read stability: Static Voltage Noise Margin (SVNM) at V_{DD} = 0.8 V.

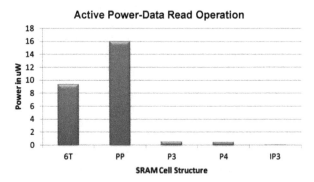

Figure 4. Active power (read) at V_{DD} = 0.8 V.

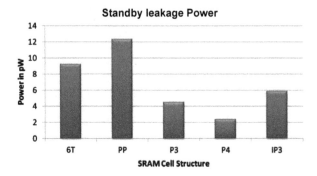

Figure 5. Standby leakage power at drowsy voltage V_{DD} = 0.35 V.

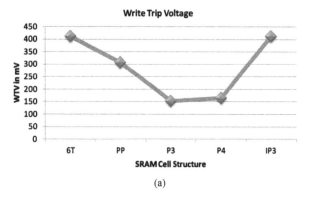

(a)

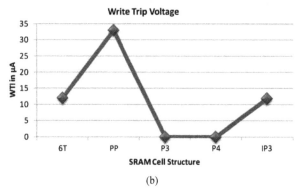

(b)

Figure 7. Write ability: Write Trip Voltage (WTV) at V_{DD} = 0.8 V.

5.1.5. Cell Area

The cell areas for the 6T, PP, P4, and P3 cells has less area by 47%, 26%, 2%, and 2% by the IP3 cell, **Figure 8**. The overall performance of the cell is improved as an area tradeoff.

6. Conclusion

In the proposed IP3 SRAM cell, at one time (write/read), only half of the cell is working, this reduces the power significantly during data write and data read operations. During standby mode, an appreciable power reduction is observed. The IP3 cell has 17.65% and 41.53% improved power as compared to 6T and PP cells while performing the data write operation 94% and 93% more power as compared to the P4 and P3 cell. The IP3 cell is seen to be the best low-power cell among the 6T, PP, P3, P4, and P3 cells during read operation. It demands 99%, 99%, 90%, and 91% less read power as compared to the 6T, PP, P4, and P3 cell, respectively. The standby leakage power, of the IP3 cell is 36% and 52% less as compared to the 6T and PP cells while it 59% and 23% more than the P4 and P3 cells. The SVNM of IP3 has no change with 6T cell while it is 55%, 52% improved with P4, P3 cells and 3% poor to PP cell. The SINM is 36% poor with 6T cell and 63%, 995, and 99% improved to PP, P4, and P3 cells, *i.e.*, it has overall improved read stability. The P4 and P3 cell have poor read stability while IP3 has improved read stability. The WTV for IP3 is same as that of 6T cell. The WTV for the IP3 is observed to be improved by 25%, 60%, and 62% by PP, P4, and P3 cells. The WTI is same as that of 6T and poor by 64% with PP cell while improved by almost 99% by P4, and P3 cell. The P4, and P3 cells found to be the poor read ability while the IP3 cell has marginally improved write ability. The cell areas for the 6T, PP, P4, and P3 cells has less area by 47%, 26%, 2%, and 2% by the IP3 cell. The overall performance of the cell is improved as an area tradeoff. Therefore, the proposed IP3 structure is good for the applications where the data is retrieve (read) operation is very high as compared to the data write, e.g., battery powered

and portable multimedia applications. The reduction is in standby leakage power, further supports for its low-power applications where the memory has low activity factor, *i.e.*, to hold data when the memory is not in use at area and performance tradeoff.

7. Acknowledgements

The authors are grateful to their respective organizations for their help and support.

REFERENCES

[1] K. Zhang (Ed.), "Embedded Memories for Nano-Scale VLSIs," Integrated Circuits and Systems Series, Springer, 2009.

[2] International Technology Roadmap for Semiconductors, 2003. http://www.publicitrs.net

[3] K. M. Kao, W. C. Lee, W. Liu, X. Jin, P. Su, S. K. H. Fung, J. X. An, B. Yu and C. Hu, "BSIM4 Gate Leakage Model Including Source-Drain Partition," *Proceedings of International Electron Devices Meeting*, San Francisco, 10-13 December 2000, pp. 815-818.

[4] L.-J. Zhang, C. Wu, Y.-Q. Ma, J.-B. Zheng and L.-F. Mao, "Leakage Power Reduction Techniques of 55 nm SRAM Cells," *IETE Technical Review*, Vol. 28, No. 2, 2011, pp. 135-145.

[5] C.-H. Lo and S.-Y. Huang, "P-P-N Based 10T SRAM Cell for Low-Leakage and Resilient Subthreshold Operation," *IEEE Journal of Solid-State Circuits*, Vol. 46, No. 3, 2011, pp. 695-704.

[6] K. Flautner, N. S. Kim, S. Martin, D. Blaauw and T. Mudge, "Drowsy Caches: Simple Techniques for Reducing Leakage Power," *Proceedings of 29th Annual International Symposium on Computer Architecture*, Anchorage, 25-29 May 2002, pp. 148-157.

[7] C. H. Kim, J.-J. Kim, S. Mukhopadhyay and K. Roy, "A Forward Body-Biased Low-Leakage SRAM Cache: Device, Circuit and Architecture Considerations," *IEEE Transaction on Very Large Scale Integration (VLSI) Systems*, Vol. 13, No. 3, 2005, pp. 349-357.

[8] N. Kr. Shukla, R. K. Singh and M. Pattanaik, "A Novel Approach to Reduce the Gate and Sub-threshold Leakage in a Conventional SRAM Bit-Cell Structure at Deep-Sub Micron CMOS Technology," *International Journal of Computer Applications (IJCA)*, Vol. 23, No. 7, 2011, pp. 23-28.

[9] G. Razavipour, A. Afzali-Kusha and M. Pedram, "Design and Analysis of Two Low-Power SRAM Cell Structures," *IEEE Transaction on Very Large Scale Integration (VLSI) Systems*, Vol. 17, No. 10, 2009, pp. 1551-1555.

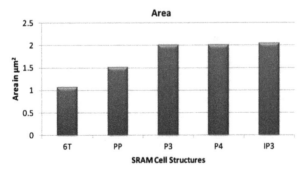

Figure 8. SRAM bit-cell area.

3

A Survey on the Stability of 2-D Discrete Systems Described by Fornasini-Marchesini Second Model

Manish Tiwari, Amit Dhawan

Electronics and Communication Engineering Department, Motilal Nehru National Institute of Technology, Allahabad, India

ABSTRACT

A key issue of practical importance in the two-dimensional (2-D) discrete system is stability analysis. Linear state-space models describing 2-D discrete systems have been proposed by several researchers. A popular model, called Fornasini-Marchesini (FM) second model was proposed by Fornasini and Marchesini in 1978. The aim of this paper is to present a survey of the existing literature on the stability of FM second model.

Keywords: 2-D Discrete Systems; FM Second Model; Asymptotic Stability; Lyapunov Methods

1. Introduction

There have been a continuously growing research interests in two-dimensional (2-D) systems due to their applications in various important areas such as multi-dimensional digital filtering, signal processing, seismographic data processing, thermal processes, gas absorption, water stream heating etc. [1-4]. In a 2-D discrete system, information propagates in two independent directions as a result of which the system dynamics may be represented as a function of two independent integer variables. Many researchers have made an attempt to describe the 2-D system dynamics in terms of linear state-space models for 2-D discrete systems [5-7]. The 2-D models that have received considerable attention are Roesser model [5], Fornasini-Marchesini (FM) first model [6] and FM second model [7].

Stability analysis and stabilization are the main issues in the design of any control system. Stability issues of 2-D systems have been considered by many researchers [8-18]. With the introduction of state-space models of 2-D discrete systems, various Lyapunov equations have emerged as powerful tools for the stability analysis and stabilization of 2-D discrete systems. Lyapunov based sufficient conditions for the stability of 2-D discrete systems have been studied in [19-26]. When the dynamics of practical systems are represented using state-space models, errors are inevitable as the actual system parameters would be different than the estimated system parameters, i.e., the model parameters. These errors arise due to the approximations made during the process modeling, differences in presumed and actual process operating points, change in operating conditions, system aging

etc. Control designs based on these models, therefore, may not perform adequately when applied to the actual industrial process and may lead to instability and poor performances. This has motivated the study of robust control for the uncertain 2-D discrete systems. The aim of robust control is to stabilize the system under all admissible parameter uncertainties arising due to the errors around the nominal system. Many significant results on the solvability of robust control problem for the uncertain 2-D discrete systems have been proposed in [27-33].

The issue in robust control design is twofold: first is to design a robust controller to ensure the stability of uncertain systems and the other is to guarantee a certain performance level under the presence of uncertainties. The latter is called as guaranteed cost control problem which has the advantage of providing an upper bound on the closed-loop cost function (performance index). Consequently, a guaranteed cost controller not only stabilizes the uncertain system but also guarantees that the value of closed-loop cost function is not more than the specified upper bound for all admissible parameter uncertainties. Based on this idea, many significant results have been obtained for the uncertain 2-D discrete systems [34-39].

Study and analysis of 2-D discrete systems under the presence of noise is another research area of great interest where it is usually necessary to estimate the state variables from the system measurement data. One of the celebrated approaches is Kalman filtering [40] which is based on two fundamental assumptions that the system under consideration is exactly known and a priori information on the external noises (like white noise, etc.). However, in many practical situations, these assumptions may be invalid. This has motivated the 2-D signal estimation using H_∞ filtering technique. The advantage of H_∞ filtering is that the noise sources can be arbitrary signals with bounded energy, or bounded average power instead of being Gaussian. Hence, H_∞ filtering tends to be more robust when there exist additional parameter disturbances in models and it is very appropriate in a number of practical situations [41]. The 2-D filtering approach with H_∞ performance measure has been developed in [41-47].

The linear matrix inequalities (LMIs) have been evolved as a powerful technique to formulate various control designs [48]. The advantage of LMI technique is that the problem of testing the stability of a system can be formulated in terms of existence of a certain LMI (e.g., see [49]). Since solving LMIs is a convex optimization problem, such formulations offer an efficient numerical method to deal with the problems that lack an analytical solution. These LMIs can be solved efficiently by Matlab LMI tool box [50].

In this paper, our main focus is on the FM second model which is one of the most investigated models for the study and analysis of 2-D discrete systems. A brief survey of the existing literature on the stability of the 2-D discrete systems described by FM second model has been presented in this paper. The paper is organized as follows: Section 2 presents the description of 2-D system described by FM second model. A brief survey and main results on the stability of FM second model has been discussed in Section 3. Finally, some concluding remarks are given in Section 4.

Throughout the paper the following notations are used: The Closed unit disc is represented by $\overline{U}$, $\partial \overline{U}$ represents the unit circle, U^2 denotes the closed unit bidisc. The superscript T stands for matrix transposition, R^n denotes real vector space of dimension n, $R^{n \times m}$ is the set of $n \times m$ real matrices, $\mathbf{0}$ denotes null matrix or null vector of appropriate dimension, I_n is the $n \times n$ identity matrix, diag (…) stands for a block diagonal matrix, $G > 0$ stands for the matrix G is positive definite, det (.) denotes determinant of a matrix, $\|.\|$ denotes induced matrix norm, $\rho(.)$ stands for spectral radius of a matrix, $\sigma(.)$ stands for spectrum of a matrix, for a matrix pair (A, B), $\sigma(A, B)$ denote the set of all its generalized eigenvalues i.e. $\sigma(A, B) := \{\lambda \in \mathbb{R} : \det(A - \lambda B) = 0\}$, where $\mathbb{R}$ is the set of complex numbers. Further, $|\mathbf{B}|$ stands for the matrix $\left[|b_{i,j}|\right]$, and $A \otimes B$ represents Kronecker product of the matrices A and B.

2. Description of FM Second Model

Consider the following 2-D discrete system represented by FM second model [7]:

$$x(i+1, j+1) = A_1 x(i, j+1) + A_2 x(i+1, j)$$
$$+ B_1 u(i, j+1) + B_2 u(i+1, j) , \tag{1a}$$

$$z(i, j) = Cx(i, j) + Du(i, j) , \tag{1b}$$

$$i \geq 0, j \geq 0 \tag{1c}$$

where $x(i, j)$ is an $n \times 1$ state vector, $A_1 \in R^{n \times n}$, $A_2 \in R^{n \times n}$, $u(i, j)$ is $m \times 1$ input vector, $B_1 \in R^{n \times m}$, $B_2 \in R^{n \times m}$ z is a scalar output, $C \in R^{1 \times n}$ and $D \in R^{1 \times m}$. It is understood that the above system has a finite set of initial conditions [2] i.e., there exist two positive integers r_1 and r_2 such that

$$x(i, 0) = \mathbf{0}, \; i \geq r_1, \; x(0, j) = \mathbf{0}, \; j \geq r_2 \tag{1d}$$

The equilibrium $x(i, j) = 0$ of system (1) is said to be globally asymptotically stable [2] if

$$\lim_{i \to \infty \; and/or \; j \to \infty} x(i, j) = \lim_{i+j \to \infty} x(i, j) = 0 \tag{2}$$

The transfer function of system (1) is given as

$$H(z_1, z_2) = C\left(I_n - z_1 A_1 - z_2 A_2\right)^{-1}$$
$$\times \left(z_1 B_1 + z_2 B_2\right) + D \tag{3}$$

If we define,

$$N(z_1, z_2) = \det\left(I_n - z_1 A_1 - z_2 A_2\right), \tag{4a}$$

then the state-space model (1) is asymptotically stable [7] if and only if

$$N(z_1, z_2) \neq 0 \text{ for all } (z_1, z_2) \in \overline{U}^2 \tag{4b}$$

where $\overline{U}^2 = \{(z_1, z_2) : |z_1| \leq 1, |z_2| \leq 1\}$.

3. A Brief Survey

The problem of asymptotic stability of system (1) has been studied by many researchers [51-59]. Lyapunov based sufficient condition for the stability of system (1) has been investigated in [51] and it is proposed that the system (1) is asymptotically stable if there exist an $n \times n$ symmetric matrix $P > 0$ such that

$$\begin{bmatrix} \alpha P & 0 \\ 0 & \beta P \end{bmatrix} - \begin{bmatrix} A_1 & A_2 \end{bmatrix}^T P \begin{bmatrix} A_1 & A_2 \end{bmatrix} > 0, \tag{5a}$$

provided

$$\alpha > 0, \beta > 0, \alpha + \beta = 1 \tag{5b}$$

Reference [52] presents a stability test for system (1) which states that

$$N(z_1, z_2) \neq 0 \text{ in } \overline{U}^2 \text{ if } \|A_1\| + \|A_2\| < 1, \tag{6}$$

where $N(z_1, z_2)$ is defined in (4a). Further, based on the 2-D Lyapunov equation approach, the problem of stability margin has also been studied in [52].

Studies in [53] has illustrated that there are a large

number of systems that are stable but their stability cannot be assured by (5). That is, no values of α and β can be found to satisfy (5) for a large number of systems to confirm their stability. The result proposed in [51] is made into more generalized form in [53] and it has been proposed that the system (1) is asymptotically stable if there exist $n \times n$ symmetric matrices $\boldsymbol{P} > 0$, $\boldsymbol{W_1} > 0$, $\boldsymbol{W_2} > 0$, $\boldsymbol{R} > 0$ such that

$$
\begin{bmatrix} \boldsymbol{P}^{T/2}\boldsymbol{W_1}\boldsymbol{P}^{1/2} & \boldsymbol{0} \\ \boldsymbol{0} & \boldsymbol{P}^{T/2}\boldsymbol{W_2}\boldsymbol{P}^{1/2} \end{bmatrix}
$$
$$
-\begin{bmatrix} A_1 & A_2 \end{bmatrix}^T \boldsymbol{P}^{T/2}\boldsymbol{R}\,\boldsymbol{P}^{1/2}\begin{bmatrix} A_1 & A_2 \end{bmatrix} > 0, \quad (7a)
$$

and

$$
(\boldsymbol{R} - \boldsymbol{W_1} - \boldsymbol{W_2}) \geq \boldsymbol{0}. \quad (7b)
$$

As noted in [53], (5) can be recovered as a special case of (7). It is also mentioned in [53], that without loss of generality $\boldsymbol{R}$ can be assigned to $\boldsymbol{I_n}$ and an equivalent condition of stability can be given as: The system (1) is asymptotically stable if there exist $n \times n$ symmetric matrices $\boldsymbol{P} > 0$, $\boldsymbol{W_1} > 0$ and $\boldsymbol{W_2} > 0$ such that

$$
\begin{bmatrix} \boldsymbol{P}^{T/2}\boldsymbol{W_1}\boldsymbol{P}^{1/2} & \boldsymbol{0} \\ \boldsymbol{0} & \boldsymbol{P}^{T/2}\boldsymbol{W_2}\boldsymbol{P}^{1/2} \end{bmatrix}
$$
$$
-\begin{bmatrix} A_1 & A_2 \end{bmatrix}^T \boldsymbol{P}\begin{bmatrix} A_1 & A_2 \end{bmatrix} > 0, \quad (8a)
$$

and

$$
(\boldsymbol{I_n} - \boldsymbol{W_1} - \boldsymbol{W_2}) \geq \boldsymbol{0}. \quad (8b)
$$

In [54], sufficient conditions to guarantee the asymptotic stability of system (1) are presented. The first criterion states that for system (1) to be asymptotically stable it is sufficient that

1) $\quad \det\left(\boldsymbol{I_n} - e^{j\omega_1}A_1 - e^{j\omega_2}A_2\right) \neq 0$, $\quad (9a)$

and

2) there exist an $n \times n$ symmetric matrix $\boldsymbol{P} > 0$ such that

$$
\begin{bmatrix} \alpha\boldsymbol{P} & \boldsymbol{0} \\ \boldsymbol{0} & \beta\boldsymbol{P} \end{bmatrix} - \begin{bmatrix} A_1 & A_2 \end{bmatrix}^T \boldsymbol{P}\begin{bmatrix} A_1 & A_2 \end{bmatrix} \geq \boldsymbol{0}, \quad (9b)
$$

provided

$$
\alpha > 0, \beta > 0, \alpha + \beta = 1.
$$

Here ω_1 and ω_2 are the horizontal and vertical radian frequencies, respectively.

The second criterion states that the system (1) is asymptotically stable if there exist $n \times n$ symmetric matrices $\boldsymbol{P} > 0$, $\boldsymbol{W_1} > 0$ and $\boldsymbol{W_2} > 0$ such that

$$
\begin{bmatrix} \boldsymbol{P}^{T/2}\boldsymbol{W_1}\boldsymbol{P}^{1/2} & \boldsymbol{0} \\ \boldsymbol{0} & \boldsymbol{P}^{T/2}\boldsymbol{W_2}\boldsymbol{P}^{1/2} \end{bmatrix}
$$
$$
-\begin{bmatrix} A_1 & A_2 \end{bmatrix}^T \boldsymbol{P}\begin{bmatrix} A_1 & A_2 \end{bmatrix} \geq \boldsymbol{0} \quad (10a)
$$

and

$$
(\boldsymbol{I_n} - \boldsymbol{W_1} - \boldsymbol{W_2}) > \boldsymbol{0}. \quad (10b)
$$

At this point, readers are advice to observe the differences between (8) and (10). Furthermore, the relationship between 2-D Lyapunov approach and stability margin has also been investigated in [54].

Another 2-D Lyapunov equation, which is in a more general form, for asymptotic stability of system (1) has been presented in [55]. According to [55], the system (1) is asymptotically stable provided there exist $n \times n$ symmetric matrices $\boldsymbol{R_1} > 0$, $\boldsymbol{R_2} > 0$ such that

$$
\begin{bmatrix} \boldsymbol{R_1} & \boldsymbol{0} \\ \boldsymbol{0} & \boldsymbol{R_2} \end{bmatrix} - \begin{bmatrix} A_1 & A_2 \end{bmatrix}^T (\boldsymbol{R_1} + \boldsymbol{R_2})\begin{bmatrix} A_1 & A_2 \end{bmatrix} > 0. \quad (11)
$$

Further, it has been shown that the Lyapunov matrix Inequality (11) can be expressed in a succinct form using parallel addition of positive definite matrices and an equivalent condition of stability can be given as: The system (1) is asymptotically stable if there exist a pair of $n \times n$ positive definite matrices $\boldsymbol{P_1}$, $\boldsymbol{P_2}$ such that

$$
\boldsymbol{P_1} : \boldsymbol{P_2} - A_1\boldsymbol{P_1}A_1^T - A_2\boldsymbol{P_2}A_2^T > 0, \quad (12)
$$

where $\boldsymbol{P_1} : \boldsymbol{P_2} = \left(\boldsymbol{P_1}^{-1} + \boldsymbol{P_2}^{-1}\right)^{-1} = \boldsymbol{P_1}\left(\boldsymbol{P_1} + \boldsymbol{P_2}\right)^{-1}\boldsymbol{P_2}$, $\boldsymbol{P_1} = \boldsymbol{R_1}^{-1}$, $\boldsymbol{P_2} = \boldsymbol{R_2}^{-1}$ and $\boldsymbol{P_1} : \boldsymbol{P_2}$ is known as parallel addition of $\boldsymbol{P_1}$ and $\boldsymbol{P_2}$. It is interesting to note that as a rough approximation, the terms $A_1\boldsymbol{P_1}A_1^T$ and $A_2\boldsymbol{P_2}A_2^T$ makes out the next time energy along the one-dimensional dynamics; it then follows that the sum of total next time energy should be less than the modified present energy represented by $\boldsymbol{P_1} : \boldsymbol{P_2}$ for the 2-D system (1) to be asymptotically stable. It has been further illustrated that in spite of its outward beauty, the Inequality (12) is rather complicated even for smaller values of n.

In [56], the estimation of stability robustness for the FM second model has been studied and it is mentioned that the use of the stability bounds through the 2-D Lyapunov approach is limited in application. Studies in [57] explore numerically efficient stability test methods for 2-D discrete systems based on matrix pencil approach. The necessary and sufficient conditions for the stability 2-D system have been formulated as a problem of solving the generalized eigenvalues of a constant matrix pair. As stated in [57], the system (1) is stable if and only if

$$
N(z_1, 0) \text{ is stable} \quad (13a)
$$

and

$$
N(z_1, z_2) \neq 0 \text{ for all } z_1 \in \partial\mathrm{U}, z_2 \in \overline{\mathrm{U}} \quad (13b)
$$

Here the stability of $N(z_1, 0)$ is equivalent to $\rho(A_1) < 1$. If we define the matrices

$$
\boldsymbol{K_0} = A_1 \otimes A_2^T, \quad (14a)
$$

$$K_1 = A_1 \otimes A_1^T + A_2 \otimes A_2^T - I_n, \tag{14b}$$

$$K_2 = A_2 \otimes A_1^T, \tag{14c}$$

then, the necessary and sufficient condition for the stability is as follows: The 2-D system (1) is stable if and only if $\rho(A_1) < 1$ and additionally one of the following conditions holds:

1) $\rho(A_1 + z_2 A_2) < 1$, for all $z_2 \in \overline{U}$. $\qquad$ (15a)

2) $\rho(A_1 + e^{j\theta} A_2) < 1$, for all $\theta \in [0, 2\pi]$. $\qquad$ (15b)

3) $\sigma(A_1 + z_2 A_2) \cap \partial \overline{U} = \varnothing$, for all $z_2 \in \partial \overline{U}$

and

$$\rho(A_1 + A_2) < 1. \tag{15c}$$

4) $\rho(A_1 + A_2) < 1$

and

$$\sigma(U, V) \cap \partial \overline{U} = \varnothing, \tag{15d}$$

where

$$U := \begin{bmatrix} 0 & I_n \\ -K_0 & -K_1 \end{bmatrix},$$

and

$$V := \begin{bmatrix} I_n & 0 \\ 0 & K_2 \end{bmatrix}.$$

Further, the authors in [57] have also claimed that the above stability tests tend to provide high computational accuracy.

An LMI based necessary and sufficient condition for the positive FM second model has been presented in [58]. If all the elements of system matrices A_1 and A_2 are positive then the system (1) will be asymptotically stable if and only if one of the following equivalent conditions holds:

1) The LMI

$$block\ diag\left[2P - \sum_{k=1}^{2}\left(A_k^T P + P A_k\right),\ P \right] > 0, \tag{16a}$$

is feasible with respect to the diagonal matrix P.

2) The LMI

$$block\ diag\left[P - \sum_{k=1}^{2}\sum_{l=1}^{2}\left(A_k^T P A_l\right),\ P \right] > 0, \tag{16b}$$

is feasible with respect to the diagonal matrix P.

The Lyapunov based sufficient condition for the stability of system (1) under shift delays has been discussed in [59]. It has been proposed that system (1) under shift delays is asymptotically stable if there exist $n \times n$ symmetric matrices $P > 0$, $Q > 0$, $Q_1 > 0$, $Q_2 > 0$ such that

$$\begin{bmatrix} A_1 & A_{1d} & A_2 & A_{2k} \end{bmatrix}^T P \begin{bmatrix} A_1 & A_{1d} & A_2 & A_{2k} \end{bmatrix}$$
$$- \begin{bmatrix} P - Q - Q_1 - Q_2 & 0 & 0 & 0 \\ 0 & Q & 0 & 0 \\ 0 & 0 & Q_1 & 0 \\ 0 & 0 & 0 & Q_2 \end{bmatrix} < 0, \tag{17}$$

where $A_{1d} \in R^{n \times n}$ and $A_{2k} \in R^{n \times n}$ are delay matrices. Based on condition (17), the problem of robust stability and stabilization of 2-D discrete shift-delayed system described by the FM second model has also been addressed.

In [60], the problem of robust guaranteed cost control for 2-D discrete system under shift delays has been considered and sufficient condition for the existence of robust guaranteed cost controller via static-state feedback has been derived.

In [61], some technical errors that have occurred in the main results of [60] are pointed out and corrected.

4. Concluding Remarks

A review on the stability of 2-D discrete systems described by FM second model has been presented in this paper. The Lyapunov based approach has emerged as a popular approach to study the stability properties of such systems. The 2-D Lyapunov based stability conditions discussed so far in literature are only sufficient conditions. The Lyapunov based necessary and sufficient condition for the stability of 2-D discrete systems remains an open and challenging problem.

5. Acknowledgements

The authors wish to thank the associate editor and the anonymous reviewers for their constructive comments and suggestions.

REFERENCES

[1] N. K. Bose, "Applied Multidimensional System Theory," Van Nostrand Reinhold, New York, 1982.

[2] T. Kaczorek, "Two-Dimensional Linear Systems," Springer-Verlag, Berlin, 1985.

[3] W.-S. Lu and A. Antoniou, "Two-Dimensional Digital Filters," Marcel Dekker, Electrical Engineering and Electronics, Vol. 80, New York, 1992.

[4] R. N. Bracewell, "Two-Dimensional Imaging," Prentice-Hall Signal Processing Series, Prentice-Hall, Englewood Cliffs, 1995.

[5] R. P. Roesser, "A Discrete State-Space Model for Linear Image Processing," *IEEE Transactions on Automatic Control*, Vol. 20, No. 1, 1975, pp. 1-10.

[6] E. Fornasini and G. Marchesini, "State-Space Realization Theory of Two Dimensional Filters," *IEEE Transactions*

on *Automatic Control*, Vol. 21, No. 4, 1976, pp. 484-492.

[7] E. Fornasini and G. Marchesini, "Doubly Indexed Dynamical Systems: State-Space Models and Structural Properties," *Mathematical Systems Theory*, Vol. 12, No. 1, 1978, pp. 59-72.

[8] R. Gnanasekaran, "A Note on the New 1-D and 2-D Stability Theorems for Discrete Systems," *IEEE Transactions on Acoustics, Speech, & Signal Processing*, Vol. 29, No. 6, 1981, pp. 1211-1212.

[9] T. Bose and D. A. Trautman, "Two's Complement Quantization in Two-Dimensional State-Space Digital Filters," *IEEE Transactions on Signal Processing*, Vol. 40, No. 10, 1992, pp. 2589-2592.

[10] P. Agathoklis, E. I. Jury and M. Mansour, "Algebraic Necessary and Sufficient Conditions for the Stability of 2-D Discrete Systems," *IEEE Transactions on Circuits and Systems II: Analog and Digital Signal Processing*, Vol. 40, No. 10, 1993, pp. 251-258.

[11] T. Bose, "Stability of 2-D State-Space System with Overflow and Quantization," *IEEE Transactions on Circuits and Systems II*, Vol. 42, No. 6, 1995, pp. 432-434.

[12] Y. Su and A. Bhaya, "On the Bose-Trautman Condition for Stability of Two-Dimensional Linear Systems," *IEEE Transactions on Signal Processing*, Vol. 46, No. 7, 1998, pp. 2069-2070.

[13] T. Fernando and H. Trinh, "Lower Bounds for Stability Margin of Two-Dimensional Discrete Systems Using the MacLaurine Series," *Computer and Electrical Engineering*, Vol. 25, No. 2, 1999, pp. 95-109.

[14] R. Thamvichai and T. Bose, "Stability of 2-D Periodically Shift Variant Filters," *IEEE Transactions on Circuits and Systems II*, Vol. 49, No. 1, 2002, pp. 61-64.

[15] Y. Bistritz, "Testing Stability of 2-D Discrete Systems by a Set of Real 1-D Stability Tests," *IEEE Transactions on Circuits and Systems I*, Vol. 51, No. 7, 2004, pp. 1312-1320.

[16] G.-D. Hu and M. Liu, "Simple Criteria for Stability of two-Dimensional Linear Systems," *IEEE Transactions on Signal Processing*, Vol. 53, No. 12, 2005, pp. 4720-4723.

[17] T. Kaczorek, "New Stability Tests of Positive Standard and Fractional Linear Systems," *Circuits and Systems*, Vol. 2, No. 4, 2011, pp. 261-268.

[18] T. Liu, "Stability Analysis of Linear 2-D Systems," *Signal Processing*, Vol. 88, No. 8, 2008, pp. 2078-2084.

[19] E. Fornasini and G. Marchesini, "Stability Analysis of 2-D Systems," *IEEE Transactions on Circuits and Systems*, Vol. 27, No. 12, 1980, pp. 1210-1217.

[20] W.-S. Lu and E. B. Lee, "Stability Analysis for Two-Dimensional Systems via a Lyapunov Approach," *IEEE Transactions on Circuits and Systems*, Vol. 32, No. 1, 1985, pp. 61-68.

[21] P. Agathoklis, "The Lyapunov Equation for *n*-Dimensional Discrete Systems," *IEEE Transactions on Circuits and Systems*, Vol. 35, No. 4, 1988, pp. 448-451.

[22] P. Agathoklis, E. I. Jury and M. Mansour, "The Discrete-Time Strictly Bounded-Real Lemma and the Computation of Positive Definite Solutions to the 2-D Lyapunov Equation," *IEEE Transactions on Circuits and Systems*, Vol. 36, No. 6, 1989, pp. 830-837.

[23] D. Liu and A. N. Michel, "Stability Analysis of State-Space Realizations for Two-Dimensional Filters with Overflow Nonlinearities," *IEEE Transactions on Circuits and Systems I*, Vol. 41, No. 2, 1994, pp. 127-137.

[24] C. Xiao, D. J. Hill and P. Agathoklis, "Stability and the Lyapunov Equation for *n*-Dimensional Digital Systems," *IEEE Transactions on Circuits and Systems I*, Vol. 44, No. 7, 1997, pp. 614-621.

[25] H. Kar and V. Singh, "Stability of 2-D Systems Described by Fornasini-Marchesini First Model," *IEEE Transactions on Signal Processing*, Vol. 51, No. 6, 2003, pp. 1675-1676.

[26] H. Kar and V. Singh, "Stability Analysis of 2-D Digital Filters with Saturation Arithmetic: An LMI Approach," *IEEE Transactions on Signal Processing*, Vol. 53, No. 6, 2005, pp. 2267-2271.

[27] W.-S. Lu, "Some New Results on Stability Robustness of 2-D Digital Filters," *Multidimensional Systems and Signal Processing*, Vol. 5, No. 4, 1994, pp. 345-361.

[28] W.-S. Lu, "On Robust Stability of 2-D Discrete Systems," *IEEE Transactions on Automatic Control*, Vol. 40, No. 3, 1995, pp. 502-506.

[29] L. Xie, "LMI Approach to Output Feedback Stabilization of 2-D Discrete Systems," *International Journal of Control*, Vol. 72, No. 2, 1999, pp. 97-106.

[30] C. Du and L. Xie, "Stability Analysis and Stabilization of Uncertain Two-Dimensional Discrete Systems: An LMI Approach," *IEEE Transactions on Circuits and Systems I*, Vol. 46, No. 11, 1999, pp. 1371-1374.

[31] K. Galkowski, J. Lam, S. Xu and Z. Lin, "LMI Approach to State-Feedback Stabilization of Multidimensional Systems," *International Journal of Control*, Vol. 76, No. 14, 2003, pp. 1428-1436.

[32] Z. Wang and X. Liu, "Robust Stability of Two-Dimensional Uncertain Discrete Systems," *IEEE Signal Processing Letters*, Vol. 10, No. 5, 2003, pp. 133-136.

[33] H. Kar and V. Singh, "Corrections to Robust Stability of Two-Dimensional Uncertain Discrete Systems," *IEEE Signal Processing Letters*, Vol. 10, No. 8, 2003, p. 250.

[34] X. Guan, C. Long and G. Duan, "Robust Optimal Guaranteed Cost Control for 2D Discrete Systems," *IEE Pro-*

ceedings—*Control Theory & Applications*, Vol. 148, No. 5, 2001, pp. 355-361.

[35] A. Dhawan and H. Kar, "Comment on Robust Optimal Guaranteed Cost Control for 2-D Discrete Systems," *IEE Proceedings—Control Theory & Applications*, Vol. 1, No. 4, 2007, pp. 1188-1190.

[36] A. Dhawan and H. Kar, "LMI-Based Criterion for the Robust Guaranteed Cost Control of 2-D Systems Described by the Fornasini-Marchesini Second Model," *Signal Processing*, Vol. 87, No. 3, 2007, pp. 479-488.

[37] A. Dhawan and H. Kar, "Optimal Guaranteed Cost Control of 2-D Discrete Uncertain Systems: An LMI Approach," *Signal Processing*, Vol. 87, No. 12, 2007, pp. 3075-3085.

[38] A. Dhawan and H. Kar, "An LMI Approach to Robust Optimal Guaranteed Cost Control of 2-D Discrete Systems Described by the Roesser Model," *Signal Processing*, Vol. 90, No. 9, 2010, pp. 2648-2654.

[39] A. Dhawan and H. Kar, "An Improved LMI-Based Criterion for the Design of Optimal Guaranteed Cost Controller for 2-D Discrete Uncertain Systems," *Signal Processing*, Vol. 91, No. 4, 2011, pp. 1032-1035.

[40] W. A. Porter and J. L. Aravena, "State Estimation in Discrete M-D Systems," *IEEE Transactions on Automatic Control*, Vol. 31, No. 3, 1986, pp. 280-283.

[41] C. Du, L. Xie and Y. C. Soh, " H_∞ Filtering of 2-D Discrete Systems," *IEEE Transactions on Signal Processing*, Vol. 48, No. 6, 2000, pp. 1760-1768.

[42] C. Du and L. Xie, " H_∞ Control and Filtering of Two Dimensional Systems," Springer-Verlag, Berlin, 2002.

[43] M. Sebek, " H_∞ Problem of 2-D Systems," *Proceeding of the European Control Conference*, Groningen, Netherlands, 28 June-1 July 1993, pp. 1476-1479.

[44] H. D. Tuan, P. Apkarian, T. Q. Nguyen and T. Narikiyo, "Robust Mixed H_2/H_∞ Filtering of 2-D Systems," *IEEE Transactions on Signal Processing*, Vol. 50, No. 7, 2002, pp. 1759-1771.

[45] L. Xie, C. Du, C. Zhang and Y. C. Soh, " H_∞ Deconvolution Filtering of 2-D Digital Systems," *IEEE Transactions on Signal Processing* Vol. 50, No. 9, 2002, pp. 2319-2331.

[46] C. Du, L. Xie and C. Zhang, " H_∞ Control and Robust Stabilization of Two Dimensional Systems in Roesser Models," *Automatica*, Vol. 37, No. 2, 2001, pp. 205-211.

[47] E. de Souza, L. Xie and D. F. Coutinho, "Robust Filtering for 2-D Discrete-Time Linear Systems with Convex-Bounded Parameter Uncertainty," *Automatica*, Vol. 46, No. 4, 2010, pp. 673-681.

[48] S. Boyd, L. El Ghaoui, E. Feron and V. Balakrishnan, "Linear Matrix Inequalities in System and Control Theory," SIAM, Philadelphia, 1994.

[49] B. Dumitrescu, "LMI Stability Tests for the Fornasini-Marchesini Model," *IEEE Transactions on Signal Processing*, Vol. 56, No 8, 2008, pp. 4091-4095.

[50] P. Gahinet, A. Nemirovski, A. J. Laub and M. Chilali, "LMI Control Toolbox—For Use with Matlab," The MATH Works Inc., Natick, 1995.

[51] T. Hinamoto, "2-D Lyapunov Equation and Filter Design Based on the Fornasini-Marchesini Second Model," *IEEE Transactions on Circuits and Systems I*, Vol. 40, No. 2, 1993, pp. 102-110.

[52] A. Kanellakis, "New Stability Results for 2-D Discrete Systems Based on the Fornasini-Marchesini State Space Model," *IEE Proceedings Circuits, Devices & Systems*, Vol. 141, No. 5, 1994, pp. 427-432.

[53] W.-S. Lu, "On a Lyapunov Approach to Stability Analysis of 2-D Digital Filters," *IEEE Transactions on Circuits and Systems I*, Vol. 41, No. 10, 1994, pp. 665-669.

[54] T. Hinamoto, "Stability of 2-D Discrete Systems Described by Fornasini-Marchesini Second Model," *IEEE Transactions on Circuits and Systems I*, Vol. 44, No. 3, 1997, pp. 254-257.

[55] T. Ooba, "On Stability Analysis of 2-D Systems Based on 2-D Lyapunov Matrix Inequalities," *IEEE Transactions on Circuits and Systems I*, Vol. 47, No. 8, 2000, pp. 1263-1265.

[56] T. Ooba, "On Stability Robustness of 2-D Systems Described by the Fornasini-Marchesini Model," *Multidimensional Systems and Signal Processing*, Vol. 12, No. 1, 2001, pp. 81-88.

[57] P. Fu, J. Chen and S.-I. Niculescu, "Generalized Eigenvalue-Based Stability Tests for 2-D Linear Systems: Necessary and Sufficient Conditions," *Automatica*, Vol. 42, No. 9, 2006, pp. 1569-1576.

[58] T. Kaczorek, "LMI Approach to Stability of 2D Positive Systems," *Multidimensional Systems and Signal Processing*, Vol. 20, No. 1, 2009, pp. 39-54.

[59] W. Paszke, J. Lam, K. Galkowski, S. Xu and Z. Lin, "Robust Stability and Stabilization of 2D Discrete State-Delayed Systems," *Systems & Control Letters*, Vol. 51, No. 3-4, 2004, pp. 277-291.

[60] S. Ye, W. Wang and Y. Zou, "Robust Guaranteed Cost Control for a Class of Two-Dimensional Discrete Systems with Shift-Delays," *Multidimensional Systems and Signal Processing*, Vol. 20, No. 3, 2009, pp. 297-307.

[61] M. Tiwari and A. Dhawan, "Comment on 'Robust Guaranteed Cost Control for a Class of two-Dimensional Discrete Systems with Shift-Delays'," *Multidimensional Systems and Signal Processing*, 2011.

4

A C-Based Variable Length and Vector Pipeline Architecture Design Methodology and Its Application

Takashi Kambe[1], Nobuyuki Araki[2]

[1]Department of Electrical and Electronic Engineering, Kinki University, Higashi-Osaka, Japan
[2]Graduate School of Science and Technology, Kinki University, Higashi-Osaka, Japan

ABSTRACT

The size and performance of a System LSI depend heavily on the architecture which is chosen. As a result, the architecture design phase is one of the most important steps in the System LSI development process and is critical to the commercial success of a device. In this paper, we propose a C-based variable length and vector pipeline (VVP) architecture design methodology and apply it to the design of the output probability computation circuit for a speech recognition system. VVP processing accelerated by loop optimization, memory access methods, and application-specific circuit design was implemented to calculate the Hidden Markov Model (HMM) output probability at high speed and its performance is evaluated. It is shown that designers can explore a wide range of design choices and generate complex circuits in a short time by using a C-based pipeline architecture design method.

Keywords: Variable Length and Vector Pipeline Architecture; C-Based Design; System LSI; Speech Recognition

1. Introduction

The size and performance of a System LSI depend heavily on the architecture which is chosen. As a result, the architecture design phase is one of the most important steps in the System LSI development process and is critical to the commercial success of a device. Architectural design means determining an assignment of the circuit functions to resources and their interconnection, as well as the timing of their execution. The macroscopic figures of merit of the implementation, such as circuit area and performance, depend heavily on this step [1]. Recently, three types of architecture design style are used for System LSI design.

The first is processor based architecture design. This is based on specific computing architectures such as DSP [2], ASIP [3], heterogeneous systems on chip [4], MPSoC [5], network on chip [6], and so on. Such a method is suitable for large scale designs, but suffers the drawback that it is difficult to choose and/or change the type of processor to implement each application.

The second is architecture design based on specific architecture description languages such as LISA [7], EXPRESSION [8], and so on. Various architectures can be generated automatically using these languages, but they are restricted to pre-prepared architecture templates and limited by the language semantics.

The third is C-based architecture design. A C-based architecture design methodology offers the following advantages:

1) A C-based language with untimed semantics is suitable for large-scale architecture design.

2) A C level simulator handles bit-accurate operations and is 10 - 100 times faster than HDL simulators.

3) A High level synthesizer can compile a program (written in C) describing the untimed behavior of hardware into RTL VHDL. It can also automatically generate interface circuits for inter-process data transfer.

In this paper, we use the *Bach* system [9-12] for C-based architecture design. *Bach*'s input language, *Bach C*, is based on standard ANSI C with extensions to support explicit parallelism, communication between parallel processes, and the bit-width specification of data types and arithmetic operation. Circuits synthesized using *Bach* consist of a hierarchy of sequential threads, all running in parallel and communicating via synchronized channels and shared variables. Using the *Bach* system, designers can develop parallel algorithms, explore the architecture design space and generate complex circuits in a much shorter time than using conventional HDL based design methodologies.

In our investigation, we focused on C-based pipelining architecture design because compared to data oriented parallel processing, a pipelining architecture can achieve higher speed without increasing the circuit size. Especially we propose a C-based variable length and vector pipelining (VVP) architecture design methodology and show how the performance can be improved by the use of loop optimizations, speeding up memory access and by creating application-specific arithmetic circuits.

The rest of this paper is organized as follows. Section 2 describes the C-based VVP architecture design methodology. In Section 3, the speech recognition algorithm is briefly explained. Section 4 describes the VVP architecture design to accelerate the output probability computation. Section 5 compares and evaluates the performance of each architecture design. Finally, Section 6 summarizes the work.

2. C-Based VVP Architecture Design Methodology

In this section, the VVP architecture design methodology and its acceleration by memory access method and application-specific arithmetic circuit design are described. And its design flow is also proposed.

2.1. Variable Length Pipelining

In *Bach* C-based design, parallelization can be applied at both the functional level and the loop structure level. The functional level pipeline processing is controlled only by the control signals among the functional modules. When the processing of one pipeline stage is complete, a signal is sent to the next stage. The next stage starts when this signal is received. Using this method, C-based functional level pipeline design permits different processing times for each stage, while conventional pipeline processing needs to maintain the same processing time for each stage. Therefore, variable length processes such as memory access conflict handling and recursion based calculations can be included in the pipeline.

Two kinds of *pragma* are used in the *Bach* system to accelerate loop calculations. The *unroll pragma* expands the specified for loop with fixed iteration number and computes as much of each step in parallel as possible. The *throughput pragma* automatically generates a loop pipelining structure with the specified throughput.

2.2. Memory Access Optimization

For many applications, memory access is often the major bottleneck. The simplest way to access large amounts of data at high speed is to store all the data in on-chip memory, but this increases chip size and is expensive. The following optimizations are applied depending on the type of data access.

1) When accessing large data multiple-times, small on-chip SRAM or registers are used to hold the most frequently accessed data and reduce the number of off-chip memory accesses.

2) When data is accessed sequentially, pipelining of the memory accesses and arithmetic calculations is effective. During internal data processing, the next data can be read into the on-chip memory. Thus only the data required for each calculation is placed in on-chip memory.

3) When accessing large off-chip memory, the memory is divided into separate *bank*s to avoid access conflicts.

4) When accessing several small off-chip memories, related data can be merged to reduce the number of memory accesses.

2.3. Application-Specific Arithmetic Circuit Design

In many cases, the processing overhead which occurs when arithmetic calculations are performed multiple times is another bottleneck in the system. The circuit size and processing time for multiplication, division and other basic functions are often especially large. In C-based design, the application-specific arithmetic hardware circuit is designed using the following procedure.

1) Select the target arithmetic block to be accelerated from the software.

2) Modify the software algorithm to facilitate implementation in hardware. For example, convert time-consuming operations, such as division, into simple and equivalent calculations.

3) Use a hardware algorithm which matches the required calculation. For example, a high order polynomial can be calculated using various shifter and adder approximations.

4) Use the *preserve pragma* of *Bach* C to ensure that the resource is not shared by other circuits.

A software implementation often uses floating-point arithmetic. However, because implementing floating-point arithmetic in hardware has a large area overhead, fixed-point arithmetic is most suitable. In addition, when minimizing the bit length of each fixed-point variable, the overflow and underflow for each calculation have to be considered. The *Bach* system's bit-accurate C level simulator enables the results of these calculations to be verified using real data with the specified bit lengths.

2.4. The C-Based VVP Architecture Design Flow

The C-based VVP architecture design flow, including memory access optimization and application-specific arithmetic circuit design, consists of the following steps.

1) The target specification such as clock frequency, processing time, and gate size of the circuit are specified.

2) The *Bach compiler* calculates the cycle number of the processing for every function in the hardware portion described by *Bach* C.

3) If (the cycle number of the *dominant stage*) <

(target cycle number), the function based variable pipeline architecture is adopted. The *dominant stage* means that its cycle number is maximum among all pipeline stages

4) Otherwise, the following four methods are applied repeatedly until achieving the target specification. The methods of which the cycle number of the *dominant stage* is reduced maximally and its circuit size is increased minimally are chosen.

(a) Vector pipeline architecture [13] is applied to the dominant stage using the plural pipelines. The number of the pipeline is given by the following equation.

$$NoP = \lfloor Cd/Tcn \rfloor \qquad (1)$$

where *NoP* denotes the number of the pipeline, *Cd* denotes the cycle number of the *dominant stage*, and *Tcn* denotes the target cycle number.

(b) The *unroll* and *throughput pragma*s are applied to the for loop structure.

(c) The memory access optimization of Subsection 2.2 is applied.

(d) The application-specific arithmetic circuit design of Subsection 2.3 is applied.

The cycle number of each stage is estimated using the high-level synthesized result. In many cases, two or more methods are mixed to accelerate the architecture effectively.

3. Speech Recognition Application

We applied this C-based VVP architecture design methodology to large vocabulary continuous speech recognition using the open-source software Julius [14]. The most popular acoustic model for speech recognition is a Hidden Markov Model (HMM), where speech signals are modeled as time-sequential automata that compute output probabilities for the given speech segment (frame) and also have a probabilistic transition.

The spectrum of a fixed width speech frame is analyzed and its acoustic features are extracted. Julius extracts 25 ms frames at 10 ms intervals. The output probability is computed using the HMM algorithm and the acoustic features are extracted from the input speech frame. The acoustic features of each frame are expressed by a *p*-dimensional vector. The output probability of HMM is expressed as a Gaussian mixture distribution. Gaussian distribution calculation for state *i* and mixture *m* is given by the following expression.

$$\log b_{im}\left(o_t\right) = \omega_i - \frac{1}{2}\sum_{p=1}^{P}\frac{1}{\sigma_{imp}^2}\left(o_{tp} - \mu_{imp}\right)^2 \qquad (2)$$

where o_{tp} denotes the p-dimensional input vector for frame *t*, ω_i denotes the mixture weight coefficient, μ_{imp} denotes the average vector and σ_{imp}^2 denotes the variance vector. The output probability b_i of M Gaussian mixture distributions is given by the following expression.

$$\log b_i\left(o_t\right) = \log\sum_{m=1}^{M}\exp\left(b_m\right) \qquad (3)$$

Some researchers [15-18] have adopted a Simultaneous Multi-threading or Symmetric Multiprocessing architecture using a 32 bit RISC processor with some kind of co-processor to realize real-time and low-power large vocabulary speech recognition. Another researcher [19] has developed a hardware accelerator architecture for the Gaussian mixture distribution calculation to achieve real-time processing. Nevertheless, it still required a 32 bit RISC processor to implement the remaining functions. Therefore, the size of these systems is very large.

4. Pipeline Architecture Design of Output Probability Computation

This section discusses the architecture of the output probability computation circuit as an example of C-based VVP architecture design. There is a trade-off between speed and cost. In this paper, the goal of the output probability computation circuit design is to minimize the total gate count while maintaining the required performance.

4.1. VVP Architecture for the Output Probability Computation

Although the output probability can be computed in parallel for mixtures, memory access, Gaussian distribution, exponential and logarithmic (*EL*) calculations have to be processed sequentially. To accelerate the output probability computation, we applied the VVP architecture for memory access, Gaussian distribution, exponential and logarithmic calculations. Our phoneme-HMM model has 1012 states and four mixtures to recognize large vocabulary continuous speech.

Because the processing time of Gaussian mixture distribution calculation for one state and one mixture is 5731 ns from **Table 1** and the target processing time of the output probability calculation is under 10 ms, the calculation result of the Equation (1) is as follows.

$$\lfloor(5731\text{ns} \times 1012 \times 4)/10\text{ms}\rfloor = 3 \qquad (4)$$

The number of pipeline is four from this result and the number of mixture in this case.

4.2. The Arithmetic Circuit Design for Output Probability Computation

By experimenting with various numbers of bits in **Table 2**, the minimum number of integer and decimal bits which have no overflow and underflow in the output probability

Table 1. The processing time(ns) of each stage in the pipelining.

No.	buffering	Gaussian	EL cal.
(A)		*5731	290
(B)		*5333	228
(C)	3391	*4835	214
(D)	1070	*4820	228
(E)		*4851	228
(F)	*3357	1344	290
(G)		*1135	228
(H)	1070	*1115	228

*: the dominant stage.

Table 2. The number of bits of fixed-point arithmetic.

No. of integer bits	Recognition rate (%)	No. of decimal bits	Recognition rate (%)
floating point	94.72	floating point	94.72
11	0.55	15	4.36
12	0.55	16	13.54
13	13.42	17	18.51
14	94.72	18	94.72
15	94.72	19	94.72
16	94.72	20	94.72

(left group labeled "20 decimal bits"; right group labeled "14 integer bits")

calculation were selected. It was found that when 14 integer bits and 18 decimal bits are used, the recognition rate is similar to that of the floating point arithmetic implementation in *Julius* system. In this experiment, five kinds of acoustic samples which have high recognition rate by Julius software[14] were used.

Two *EL* calculation circuits based on the continued fraction and on the *Faster Shift and Add* (FSA) algorithm [20] were also designed and their performances compared. Though the continued fraction has many divisions, *FSA* algorithm has simple calculation such as shift and addition. The processing time of the circuit for Continued fraction and FSA algorithm are 21.864 ms and 20.241 ms, respectively. The circuit area are 62,812 and 48,386 gates. The FSA algorithm is about 14% faster than the continued fraction algorithm for output probability computation.

4.3. Memory Access Optimization Methods and Loop Unrolling

To improve the memory access speed, we propose two kinds of memory access optimizations. One is to use two buffers to access the HMM parameters for each mixture.

The size of each buffer is 208 bytes. HMM parameters for the next Gaussian distribution calculation is read into buffer 2(1) while the Gaussian distribution calculation circuit is accessing buffer 1(2). The other is HMM memory separation. In the pipelining, the data access to HMM RAM by Gaussian distribution calculation circuits often has conflicts. By separating HMM RAM, each Gaussian distribution calculation circuit can access HMM RAM at the same time (*memory separation*).

The 25 dimensional Gaussian distribution calculation is accelerated by utilizing *Bach* system's unroll command.

5. Design Results and Its Productivity

In this section, the design results for each architecture are compared (**Table 3**). All architectures in this section adopt the *EL* calculation based on the FSA algorithm. To evaluate the performance of the pipeline architecture, we also implemented sequential processing. **Table 3** shows the processing time of each pipeline stage in each architecture. These numbers are the average of processing time of four mixtures. In this investigation the gate level circuits are synthesized from RT level HDL using Design Compiler provided by VDEC and mapped to Hitachi 0.18 micron CMOS library cells and the clock frequency of all circuits is 100 MHz.

The following equation calculates the processing time of each architecture from that of the dominant stage.

$$Mix/Pipe \times St \times TD = TT \qquad (5)$$

where *Mix* denotes the number of mixtures, *Pipe* denotes the number of pipeline stages, *St* denotes the number of states, *TD* denotes the processing time of the dominant stage in **Table 1** and *TT* denotes the processing time of the architecture in **Table 3**. For example of the archi-

Table 3. The comparison of each architecture.

arch.	mem. separ.	buffer	unroll	area (gates)	time (ms)
soft					55,300
Seq.	no	no	no	48,385	20.341
(A)	no	no	no	171,968	5.826
(B)	yes	no	no	170,813	5.396
(C)	no	yes	no	294,579	4.906
(D)	yes	yes	no	293,706	4.891
(E)	no	no	yes	316,725	5.127
(F)	no	yes	yes	547,231	4.345
(G)	yes	no	yes	439,783	1.226
(H)	yes	yes	yes	546,080	1.127

tecture (C), the result of the equation (4893 ms) is almost equal to 4906 ms in **Table 3**.

$$4/4 \times 1012 \times 4835 = 4893 \text{ ms} \qquad (6)$$

The error of Equation (6) is small and it is because there are variations of the acoustic data and the convergence of EL calculation.

The vector pipelining circuit (A) is about four times faster than the sequential circuit. The processing time of the Gaussian distribution calculation in this architecture includes the memory access resolving time.

The results for architecture (B), (C), and (D) show the following points. The data buffering and the HMM RAM separation reduce the memory access time from the processing time of the dominant stage, but the data buffering requires additional gates for the buffers. The HMM RAM separation with data buffer implementation is best for speeding-up memory access, but the improvement is 16% or less. Because the data buffering in (C) and (F) has memory access conflicts, these processing times are larger than ones in (D) and (H).

The architectures with loop unrolling such as (F), (G), and (H) are faster than the ones without it. However, because there are memory access conflicts, architecture (E) is slower than the others. Resolving access conflicts by using the memory access methods, the architecture (H) achieves the highest performance.

These results also show that VVP processing permits different processing time of each stage such as memory access conflict and the convergence variation of EL calculation.

For real-time processing one frame must be handled in less than 10ms and these architectures are able to achieve real-time processing of the output probability computation and the architecture (F), (G), and (H) can use lower clock frequency to reduce their power consumption.

The architecture (H) in **Figure 1** has the following behaviors. For each mixture, the Gaussian distribution calculation circuit reads the acoustic features from registers and HMM parameters from data buffers, and computes a 25 dimensional Gaussian distribution. The result is sent to EL calculation circuit. The EL calculation circuit receives the results of EL calculations and Gaussian distributions from the previous mixtures and adds to the output probability of the current mixture. The result of the EL calculation at the final mixture is the output probability. The *Bach C* description of this architecture is shown briefly in **Figure 2**. This architecture is described by four functions and the communication among them using primitives such as *send*() and *receive*() to control the VVP process.

Table 4 shows the number of lines used in the *Bach C* description and the design time to change the architecture

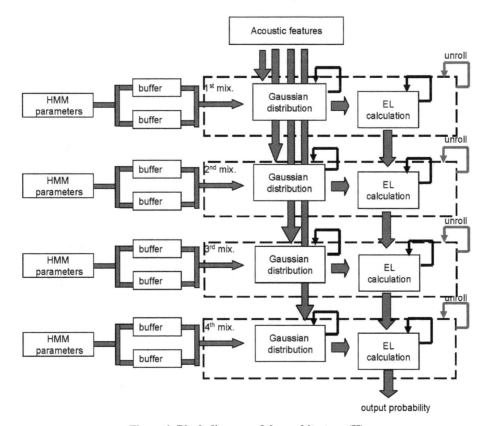

Figure 1. Block diagram of the architecture (H).

```
void gprune_none()  // VVP control
{
//parallel contruct
  par{
//data buffering
    buffer_f0(buffer_s0, buffer_s1, sw0);
//Gaussian calculation
    compute_g_base_0(       sw0, st_in,st_a,pr0);
  //EL calculation
    addlog(logzero,               pr0,logout0);
//data buffering
    buffer_f1(buffer_s1,buffer_s2,sw1);
//Gaussian calculation
    compute_g_base_1(   sw1, st_a,st_b,  pr1);
  //EL calculation
    addlog(logout0,               pr1,logout1);
//data buffering
    buffer_f2(buffer_s2, buffer_s3, sw2);
//Gaussian calculation
    compute_g_base_2(   sw2, st_b,st_c,  pr2)
  //EL calculation
    addlog(logout1,               pr2,logout2);
//data buffering
    buffer_f3(buffer_s3,buffer_s4,sw3);
//Gaussian calculation
    compute_g_base_3(   sw3, st_c,st_t,  pr3);
  //EL calculation
    addlog(logout2,               pr3,logout3);
  }
}

void addlog_2( ··· )  //EL calculation
{
  while(1){
      y = receive(probin);
      x = receive(logprobin);

      send(logprobout,calc_out);
  }
}

void compute_g_base_0(···)  //Gaussian calculation
{
  while(1){
    sw_tmp = receive(sw0);

    send(probout,prob);
  }
}

void buffer_func0()  //data buffering
{
  while(1) {
    receive(buffer_in);

    for(i=0; i<BUFFER_N; i++){
      send(sw0,0);

    }
  }
}
```

Figure 2. The Bach C description of Figure 1.

from the previous one.

6. Concluding Remarks

In this paper, we proposed a C-based VVP architecture design methodology and VVP architectures accelerated by application-specific circuit design, memory access me-

Table 4. The number of the descriptions and the design time.

arch.	Bach C (lines)	Design time (days)
(S)	143	10
(A)	283	8
(B)	306	4
(C)	481	4
(D)	505	4
(E)	283	4
(F)	481	4
(G)	306	4
(H)	503	5

thod, and loop unrolling were implemented to calculate the Hidden Markov Model (HMM) output probability at high speed and the implementation performances were evaluated. It was demonstrated that designers can explore a wide range of design choices and generate complex circuits in a short time by using a C-based architecture design methodology.

7. Acknowledgements

The authors would like to thank the *Bach* system development group in SHARP Corporation Electronic Components and Devices Development Group, for their help in hardware design using the *Bach* system. This work is supported by the VLSI Design and Education Center (VDEC), the University of Tokyo in collaboration with Synopsys Corporation.

REFERENCES

[1] G. D. Micheli, "Sythesis and Optimization of Digital circuits," McGraw-Hill, New York, 1994.

[2] F. Catthoor and H. J. De Man, "Application-Specific Architectural Methodologies for High-Throughput Digital Signal and Image Processing," *IEEE Transactions on Acoustics, Speech, and Signal Processing*, Vol. 38, No. 2, 1990, pp. 339-349.

[3] S. Kobayashi, K. Mita, Y. Takeuchi and M. Imai, "Design Space Exploration for DSP Applications Using the ASIP Development System PEAS-III," *Proceedings of the Acoustics, Speech, and Signal Processing*, Vol. 3, 13-17 May 2002, pp. 3168-3171.

[4] H. Blume, H. Hubert, H. T. Feldkamper and T. G. Noll. "Model-Based Exploration of the Design Space for Heterogeneous Systems on Chip," *Journal of VLSI Signal Processing Systems*, Vol. 40, No. 1, 2005, pp.19-34.

[5] S. Pasricha and N. Dutt, "COSMECA: Application Specific Co-Synthesis of Memory and Communication Ar-

chitectures for MPSoC," *Proceedings of the Conference on Design, Automation and Test in Europe*, 6-10 March 2006, pp. 700-705.

[6] M. P. Vestias and H. C. Neto, "Co-Synthesis of a Configurable SoC Platform Based on a Network on Chip Architecture," *Asia and South Pacific Conference on Design Automation*, Yokohama, 24-27 January 2006, pp. 48-53.

[7] O. Schliebusch, A. Hoffmann, A. Nohl, G. Braun and H. Meyr, "Architecture Implementation Using the Machine Description Language LISA," *Proceeding of the Asia and South Pacific Design Automation*, Bangalore, 7-11 January 2002, pp. 239-244.

[8] A. Halambi, P. Grun, V. Ganesh, A. Khare, N. Dutt and A. Nicolau, "Expression: A Language for Architec- ture Exploration through Compiler/Simulator Retarge- tability," *The Proceeding of Design, Automation and Test in Europe Conference and Exhibition*, 9-12 March 1999, pp. 485-490.

[9] K. Okada, A. Yamada and T. Kambe: "Hardware Algorithm Optimization Using Bach C," *IEICE Transactions on Fundamentals*, Vol. E85-A, No. 4, 2002, pp. 835-841.

[10] T. Kambe, A. Yamada, K. Okada, M. Ohnishi, A. Kay, P. Boca, V. Zammit and T. Nomura, "A C-Based Synthesis System, Bach, and Its Application," *Proceeding of the Asia and South Pacific Design Automation*, 30 January-02 February 2001, pp. 151-155.

[11] T. Kambe, H. Matsuno, Y. Miyazaki and A. Yamada, "C-Based Design of a Real Time Speech Recognition System," *Proceeding of IEEE International Symposium on Circuits and Systems*, Island of Kos, 21-24 May 2006, pp. 1751-1755.

[12] K. Jyoko, T. Ohguchi, H. Uetsu, K. Sakai, T. Ohkura and T. Kambe, "C-Based Design of a Particle Tracking System," *Proceeding of the 13th Workshop on Synthesis and System Integration of Mixed Information Technologies*, 2006, pp. 92-96.

[13] H. Cheng, "Vector Pipeling, Chaining and Speed on the IBM 3090 and Cray X-MP," *IEEE Computer*, Vol. 22, No. 9, September 1989, pp. 31-42, 44, 46.

[14] K. Shikano, K. Itoh, T. Kawahara, K. Takeda and M. Yamamoto, "IT TEXT Speech Recognition System," Ohomu Co., May 2001 (in Japanese).

[15] T. Anantharaman and B. Bisiani, "A Hardware Accelerator for Speech Recognition Algorithms," *Proceedings of the 13th Annual International Symposium on Computer Architecture*, Vol. 14, No. 2, 1986, pp. 216-223.

[16] S. Chatterjee and P. Agrawal, "Connected Speech Recognition on a Multiple Processor Pipeline," *Proceedings of International Conference on Acoustics, Speech, and Signal Processing*, Vol. 2, 23-26 May 1989, pp. 774-777.

[17] H. Hon, "A Survey of Hardware Architectures Designed for Speech Recognition," Technical Report CMU-CS-91-169, August 1991.

[18] S. Kaxiras, G. Narlikar, A. Berenbaum and Z. Hu, "Comparing Power Consumption of an SMT and a CMP DSP for Mobile Phone Workloads," *Proceedings of the International Conference on Compilers, Architecture, and Synthesis for Embedded Systems*, November 2001, pp. 211-220.

[19] B. Mathew, A. Davis and Z. Fang, "A Low-Power Accelerator for the SPHINX 3 Speech Recognition System," *Proceedings of International Conference on Compilers, Architecture and Synthesis for Embedded Systems*, 2003, pp. 210-219.

[20] J. M. Muller, "Elementary Functions," Birkhauser, Boston, 1997.

5

A New Approach to Complex Bandpass Sigma Delta Modulator Design for GPS/Galileo Receiver

Nima Ahmadpoor, Ebrahim Farshidi
Department of Electrical Engineering, Shahid Chamran University, Ahvaz, Iran

ABSTRACT

In this paper, new complex band pass filter architecture for continuous time complex band pass sigma delta modulator is presented. In continuation of paper the modulator is designed for GPS and Galileo receiver. This modulator was simulated in standard 0.18 µm CMOS TSMC technology and has bandwidth of 2 MHz and 4 MHz for GPS and Galileo centered in 4.092 MHz. The dynamic range (DR) is 56.5/49 dB (GPS/Galileo) at sampling rate of 125 MHz. The modulator has power consumption of 4.1 mw with 3 V supply voltage.

Keywords: Continuous Time; Quadrature; Sigma Delta; MOS; Modulator; OTA

1. Introduction

IN recent years, continuous time (CT) sigma delta modulators have attracted increasingly due to low power consumption, low supply voltage, high sampling frequency and high bandwidth in comparison with similar discrete time sigma delta modulators [1-3]. Moreover, because of placing sampler inside loop filter, charge injection effect and nonlinear sampling switched on resistances are significantly suppressed. In addition, the continuous time loop filter attenuating out of band high frequency interferers before sampling act as an anti-alias filter. The CT sigma delta converters have found in such applications as wireless communications systems (zero and low-IF receivers), signal processing, readouts powerless biological signal, in micromachined consumer and professional audio, industrial weight scales and precision measurement devices. Low-IF receivers often use quadrature mixer with complex signals (I/Q) as shown in **Figure 1**. In the conventional low-IF receivers, analog signal convert to digital by use of two lowpass ADCs, the structure of lowpass ADCs in these receivers lead to interference problems that performed by 1/f noise and DC offset. Even, use of the real bandpass ADC structures in low-IF receivers can be problematic for demanding image rejection requirements and low power consumption although the interferences can be fall outside the signal band. Hence, the quadrature sigma delta modulator is state of the art alternative for the complex analog to digital conversion of quadrature signals in low-IF receivers. In the recent years several successful literatures have been presented, that illustrate the new methods in quadrature

bandpass sigma delta design [4,5]. This paper proposes novel design architecture in a bandpass quadrature sigma delta modulator with a lower order and a lower frequency sampling, resulting in low power consumption, the prevention of susceptibility to instability and for goal of smaller chip area. The proposed sigma delta is realized by replacing the lowpass loop filter by complex band pass filter in a lowpass sigma delta, which has been implemented in chain of integrators with feed forward summation (CIFF) topology. The lossy integrators of the design have OTA-C structure with improvement in OTA circuit.

2. Basic Principle of Proposed Complex Filter

Single loop sigma delta architecture often use of several topologies for loop filter, such as chain of integrators with weighted feedforward summation (CIFF) [6], and chain of integrators with distributed feedback (CIFB) [7], resulting in stability and realization considered transfer functions. CIFF topology has several benefits in compared to CIFB. In the CIFF topology the swing of output integrators is lower than CIFB. Consequently, it is better

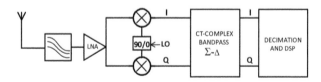

Figure 1. Low-IF receiver structure using complex sigma-delta.

selection for low power, low voltage and wideband modulator implementation. On the other hand, this feature cause to increasing input resistance of integrators, then the unpleasant gain bandwidth effect can be reduced in modulator. Also the CIFF topology have single feedback DAC, which is due to degradation in excess loop delay and clock jitter effects in compared with CIFB. In the proposed design CIFF topology is selected for the complex loop filter architecture of quadrature sigma delta. The transfer function of complex filter is output current to input voltage ratio. So it is transconductance transfer function. For realizing the novel transfer function of complex filter design, one of method is transferring of lowpass filter characteristics from DC to determined center frequency by crass coupling two lowpass filters. So in the first steps we establish the lowpass filter structure. **Figure 2** shows the selected lowpass filter with CIFF topology. At the output node, the summation of output feedforward paths is formed with no extra active component circuit. Use of current summation at output node lead to degradation of power consumption and be rising linearity. In the **Figure 2**, as shown, the output current is collected by summation of transconductance feedforward branches are denoted as gmi (gm1 and gm2). In addition, just as said, the conventional method too

shifting transfer function of low pass filter to new center frequency is crass coupling integrators in quadrature paths (I/Q), which is realized the complex filter as shown in **Figure 3**.

Figure 3 is half structure of the proposed complex filter. As exhibited in **Figure 3**, crass coupling branches are implemented by transconductances that are denoted as gci, and the basic duty of them is movement poles to center frequency. Furthermore, for the goal of wideband conversion, zeroes of transfer function must be moved to around of center frequency too. This work can be accomplished by feedforward summation coefficients (gmi). In order to optimization of zeros placement, local feedback transconductances are applied, that are named by gbi in **Figures 2-3**.

3. Implementation

3.1. Operational Transconductance Amplifier (OTA)

Figure 4 shows the optimized OTA from [8]. It can operate in both weak and strong inversion regions and has several benefits, wide common-mode input range, high CMRR and wide linearity limits.

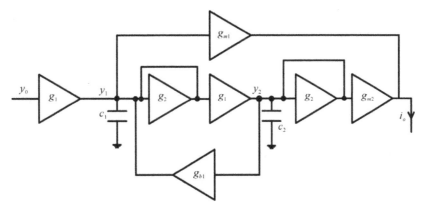

Figure 2. Low-pass filter scheme with CIFF topology.

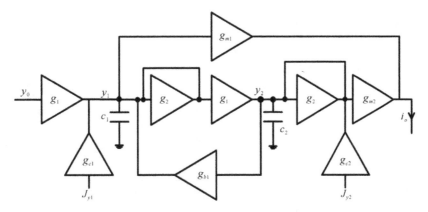

Figure 3. The half structure of the proposed complex filter.

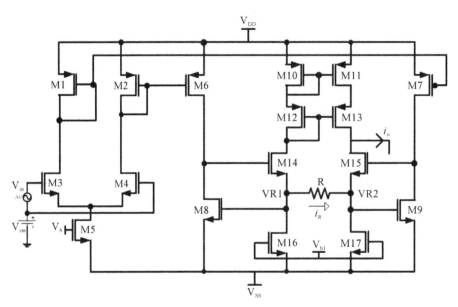

Figure 4. Circuit diagram of the employed OTA.

As shown in **Figure 4**, input common-mode (V_{cm}) and differential signals (V_{in}) can be transfer to sides of resistor (R) by transistors M1-M9 with following equations [8]:

$$VR1 = V_{CM} - V_s + \frac{V_{in}}{2} \qquad (1)$$

$$VR2 = V_{CM} - V_s - \frac{V_{in}}{2} \qquad (2)$$

where V_s is voltage of source M1 and M2. From (1) and (2), i_R can be obtained by

$$i_R = \left(\frac{1}{R}\right) V_{in} \qquad (3)$$

In circuit schematic of OTA in **Figure 4**, M10-M13 are operating as current mirrors. Thus, the output current is given by

$$i_o = 2i_R = \left(\frac{2}{R}\right) V_{in} \qquad (4)$$

Above equation indicates the inverse relation between transconductance of OTA and resistor values. Therefore, we can change the transconductor by switching the resistor. This advantage can able us for multi-mode implementation by use of digital calibration logic and external pins.

3.2. Proposed Complex Filter for GPS/Galileo Receivers

The proposed complex sigma delta modulator can be switched between two satellite navigation systems, for GPS and Galileo. In this receivers, the ADC must support a bandwidth of 2/4 MHz (GPS/Galileo) and the

minimum signal to noise ratio (SNR) of 42 dB with an OSR = 64/32 (GPS/Galileo). The center frequency must be tuned in f_c = 4.092 MHz. **Figure 5** shows the proposed two order complex filter schematic for the GPS/Galileo modulators, which is useful to low power, low resolution and low data rate. As can be seen in **Figure 5**, the OTA-C lossy integrators are used for degradation in excess loop delay and mismatch loop delay sensitivity [9]. Furthermore the lossy integrators are used for securing of stability. In this figure Y_0 and Q_0 are input voltages of complex filter in the quadrature lines, also i_o and i_Q are output currents of complex filter in the quadrature lines. If $g_{c1} = g_{c2}$, the transfer function is:

$$H_{CF} = \frac{kw_0\sqrt{A}\left(S + \frac{w_0}{Q} - jw_C\right) + Aw_0^2}{\left(S + \frac{w_0}{Q} - jw_C + jw_0\right)\left(S + \frac{w_0}{Q} - jw_C - jw_0\right)} \qquad (5)$$

where $w_0 = \frac{\sqrt{g_1 g_{b1}}}{C}$, $w_C = \frac{g_{c1}}{C}$, $Q = \frac{\sqrt{g_1 g_{b1}}}{g_2}$, $A = \frac{g_{m2} g_1}{g_{b1}}$

and $k = \sqrt{\frac{1}{g_{m2}}} g_{m1}$, Parameters of complex filter can be

distinguished from the specification the quadrature sigma delta in GPS/Galileo receiver. So the placement of pols of complex filter can be introduced by zeros of the equivalent noise shaping transfer function (NTF). In addition, the crass coupling coefficients can be determined from center frequency of the GPS/Galileo center frequency, and finally the required bandwidth for the GPS/Galileo sigma delta corresponds to bandwidth and order of complex filter. So the imaging of pols can be determined by $w_C \pm w_0 = w_C \pm 0.5w_B$, this relation results:

$$\frac{\sqrt{g_1 g_{b1}}}{C} = 0.5 w_B \qquad (6)$$

The fully proposed circuit of complex filter for GPS/Galileo bandpass quadrature sigma delta has been shown in **Figure 5**. That is determined the transconductors and capacitances according to **Table 1**.

3.3. Quantizer

Figure 6 shows circuit diagram of the applied quantizer. The quantizer consists of a one bit comparator, followed by a D-latch [9]. Two differential amplifiers with diode loads by transistors M1-M10 are used as pre-amplifier and front-end of comparator. Also cross coupled amplifier as a track-and-latch (by transistors M11-M16) is employed for back-end of clocked regenerative comparator. **Figure 7** shows circuit diagram of D flip-flap that composed by two back-to-back not gate (transistors M1-M4) for memory cell and another not gate for voltage compatibility of the output (transistors M5, M6). In this Figure q and $\bar{q}$ are output nodes.

3.4. Dac

Figure 8 shows the 1 bit D/A converter that employs two voltage sources and two switches, whose voltages are directed via switches that are controlled by the output of the quantizer. When the switch q turns on, the positive reference voltage connects to the output node and when switch q turns off, the negative reference voltage connects to the output node. In this Figure q and $\bar{q}$ are input nodes and $V_{D/C}$ is output node.

4. Simulation Result

The proposed second order complex bandpass sigma-delta modulator circuit was simulated by HSPICE in 0.18 μm CMOS TSMC technology. $V_{dd} = 1.5$ V, $V_{ss} = -1.5$ V and $V_{ref} = \pm 0.9$ V was chosen. Two sinusoidal quadrature signals with amplitude of 0.5 V_{ref} and frequency of 4 MHz were applied for input of modulator. The sampling frequency was set 125 MHz the oversampling ratios (OSR), are 64/32(GPS/Galileo). The bandwidth is switched for GPS/Galileo by change of transcondutor values in local feedback loop and lossy integrators, as shown in **Table 1**, as well as the bandwidth can be tuned by switchable integrating capacitors and center frequency can be tuned by crass coupling transcondutor values, which can be change by replacing resistor of proposed OTA whit logic switches and external pins. The output data of the modulator were collected, and then 50 kHz fast Fourier transformation (FFT) with hanning window was used to evaluate SNR and power spectral density (PSD). **Figure 9** shows the power spectrum of the GPS modulator and **Figure 10** shows Signal-to-Noise vs. input amplitude for the GPS/Galileo receiver, this figure

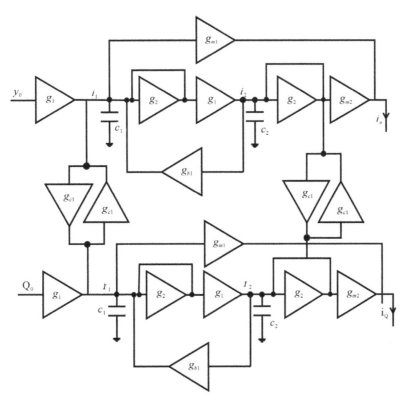

Figure 5. Fully schematic of the proposed complex filter.

Table 1. Component values of the proposed complex filter.

GPS	Galileo
$g_1 = 36\ \mu$	$g_1 = 72\ \mu$
$g_2 = 3.5\ u$	$g_2 = 7\ u$
$g_{m1} = 148\ \mu$	$g_{m1} = 148\ \mu$
$g_{m2} = 90\ \mu$	$g_{m2} = 45\ \mu$
$g_{b1} = 1.08\ \mu$	$g_{b1} = 4.32\ \mu$
$g_{c1} = 51\ \mu$	$g_{c1} = 51\ \mu$
$C = 2\ pf$	$C = 2\ pf$

shows that the maximum SNR (including distortion) for the GPS and Galileo modulators are 52 dB and 47 dB respectively, therefore the bit resolution of proposed modulator is 8.3 bit and 7.5 bit respectively. Furthermore we can determine the dynamic range of modulators from **Figure 10**; these values are 56.5 dB and 49 dB for the GPS and Galileo modulator respectively. Simulation results showed the power consumption of less than 4.1mW. The characteristics of the modulator for the GPS/Galileo are summarized in **Table 2**. Also this design compare with two same recent works too. As seen in the last row of table, the figure of merit was used for comparison of

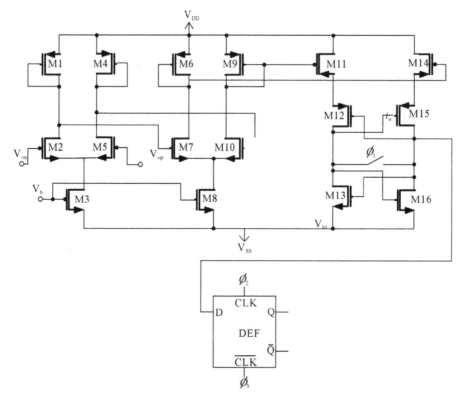

Figure 6. Circuit diagram of the applied quantizer.

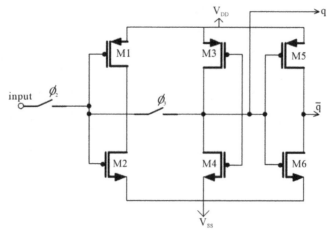

Figure 7. Circuit diagram of D flip-flap.

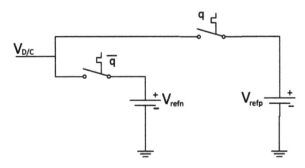

Figure 8. Circuit diagram of the 1bit D/A converter.

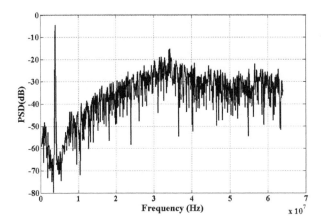

Figure 9. Power spectrum of the modulator.

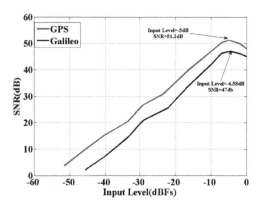

Figure 10. Signal-to-Noise vs. input amplitude of the modulator.

performances that is certifying to preference of this design. This figure of merit is calculated by following formula:

$$FOM = \frac{Power}{2^{\frac{SNDR-1.76}{6.02}} \times 2BW} \qquad (7)$$

5. Conclusion

A new continuous time complex bandpass sigma delta modulator for using multi-mode receiver (GPS/Galileo) is presented. The modulator was realized in new structure

Table 2. Circuit charactristic.

parameter	Henkel [10]	Song-Bok Kim [4]	This Design
Input IF	1 MHz	4.092 MHz	4.092 MHz
Bandwidth	1 MHz	2/4 (GPS/Galileo)	2/4 (GPS/Galileo)
Peak SNR	56.7 dB	52.9/48.4 dB (GPS/Galileo)	51.2/47 dB (GPS/Galileo)
Input DR	63.8 dB	57.5/50.2 dB (GPS/Galileo)	56.5/49 dB (GPS/Galileo)
Input Range	2 V_{p-p}	1.8 V_{p-p}	1.8 V_{p-p}
Power dissipation	21.8 mW	20.5 mW	4.1 mW
Technology	0.65 μm BiCMOS	0.25 μmCMOS	0.18 μm CMOS
FOM	19.5e–12	14.2e–12/11.9e–12 (GPS/Galileo)	3.5e–12/2.8e–12 (GPS/Galileo)

with CIFF topology and transconductance transfer function. So it was designed for the low power consumption. The proposed complex modulator has 4.1 mw power consumption at ±1.5 supply voltage. It can provide the peak SNR 51.2 dB and 47 dB and a dynamic range of 56.5 dB and 49 dB at Fs = 125 MHz for the GPS and Galileo respectively.

REFERENCES

[1] E. D. Gioia and H. Klar, "A 11-bit, 12.5 MHz, Low Power Low Voltage Continuous-Time Sigma-Delta Modu-lator," *Proceedings of the* 17*th International Conference on Mixed Design of Integrated on Circuits and Systems* (*MIXDES*), Warsaw, 24-26 June 2010, pp. 176-181.

[2] G. Mitteregger, C. Ebner, C. Mechnig, T. Blon, C. Holui-gue, E. Romani, A. Melodia and V. Melini, "A 14b 20 mW 640 MHz CMOS CT/spl Delta//spl Sigma/ADC with 20 MHz Signal Bandwidth and 12b ENOB," *Solid-State Circuits Conference* (*ISSCC*), *Digest of Technical Papers IEEE International*, San Francisco, 6-9 February 2006, pp. 131-140.

[3] E. Prefasi, L. Hernandez, S. Paton, A. Wiesbauer, R. Gaggl and E. Pun, "A 0.1 mm, Wide Bandwidth Continuous-Time ADC Based on a Time Encoding Quantizer in 0.13

m CMOS," *IEEE Journal of Solid-State Circuits*, Vol. 44, No. 10, 2009, pp. 2745-2754.

[4] S. B. Kim, S. Joeres, N. Zimmermann, M. Robens, R. Wunderlich and S. Heinen, "Continuous-Time Quadrature Bandpass Sigma-Delta Modulator for GPS/Galileo Low-IF Receiver," *IEEE International Workshop on Radio-Frequency Integration Technology* (*RFIT* 007), Rasa Sentosa Resort, 9-11 December 2007, pp. 127-130.

[5] J. Arias, P. Kiss, V. Prodanov, V. Boccuzzi, M. Banu, D. Bisbal, J.S. Pablo, L. Quintanilla and J. Barbolla, "A 32-mW 320-MHz Continuous-Time Complex Delta-Sigma ADC for Multi-Mode Wireless-LAN Receivers," *IEEE Journal of Solid-State Circuits*, Vol. 41, No. 2, 2006, pp. 339-351.

[6] F. Esfahani, P. Basedau, R. Ryter and R. Becker, "A Fourth Order Continuous-Time Complex Sigma-Delta ADC for Low-IF GSM and EDGE Receivers, in VLSI Circuits," *Symposium on Digest of Technical Papers*, 12-14 June 2003, pp. 75-78.

[7] M. Ortmanns, F. Gerfers and Y. Manoli, "A Continuous-Time Sigma-Delta Modulator with Switched Capacitor Controlled Current Mode Feedback," *Proceedings of the* 29*th European Solid-State Circuits Conference* (*ESSCIRC'* 03), 16-18 September 2003, pp. 249-252.

[8] K. Tanno, H. Tanaka, R. Miwa and H. Tamura, "Wide-Common-Mode-Range and High-CMRR CMOS OTA Operable in Both Weak and Strong Inversion Regions," *IEEE Asia Pacific Conference on Circuits and Systems* (*APCCAS*), Macao, 30 November-3 December 2008, pp. 1180-1183.

[9] S. B. Kim, S. Joeres and S. Heinen, "A Compensation Method of the Excess Loop Delay in Continuous-Time Complex Sigma-Delta Modulators," 18*th European Conference on Circuit Theory and Design* (*ECCTD*), Seville, 27-30 August 2007, pp. 140-143.

[10] F. Henkel, U. langmann, A. Hanke, S. Heinen and E. Wagner, "A 1-MHz-Bandwidth Second-Order Continuous-Time Quadrature Bandpass Sigma-Delta Modulator for Low-IF Radio Receivers," *IEEE Journal of Solid-State Circuits*, Vol. 37, No. 12, 2002, pp. 1628-1635.

6

The Effects of Fabrication Parameters and Electroforming Phenomenon on CdTe/Si (p) Heterojunction Photovoltaic Solar Cell

Wagah F. Mohammad
Communications & Electronics Department, Faculty of Engineering, Philadelphia University, Amman, Jordan

ABSTRACT

The In-doped CdTe/Si (p) heterostruture was fabricated and its electrical and photoelectrical properties were studied and interpreted. During the fabrication processes of CdTe/Si heterojunction, some practical troubles were encountered. However, the important one was the formation of the SiO_2 thin oxide layer on the soft surface of the Si during the formation of the back contact. The silicon wafer was subjected to different chemical treatments in order to remove the thin oxide layer from the silicon wafer surfaces. It was found that the heterojunction with Si (p+) substrate gave relatively high open circuit voltage comparing with that of Si (p) substrate. Also an electroforming phenomenon had been observed in this structure for the first time which may be considered as a memory effect. It was observed that there are two states of conduction, non-conducting state and conducting state. The normal case is the non-conducting state. As the forward applied voltage increased beyond threshold value, it switches into the conducting state and remains in this state even after the voltage drops to zero.

Keywords: CdTe Solar Cells; CdTe/Si Heterojunction; In-Doped CdTe

1. Introduction

In recent years much attention had been paid to the heterojunction devices research [1]. The success of heterojunctions is fully established in electronic devices including solar cells high quality lasers, and optical detectors [2]. Heterojunctions which consist of CdTe as one of the junction sides had been under investigation for many years. Mohamed *et al.* [3] also studied the electrical properties of post-deposition annealed and as-deposited In-doped CdTe thin films, it was observed that the CdTe film was of modified Poole-Frenkel conduction mechanism and the resistivity of the film could be lowered by more than one order of magnitude due to indium doping. Also, considerable amount of work had been paid to develop the CdS/CdTe solar cells over the last ten years [4,5]. Levi [6] also studied the electrical, photo-electrical, and structural properties of CdS/CdTe heterostruture. High efficiency solar cells of efficiencies up to 12.5% were developed with a CdTe low temperature (>450°C) process [7]. Efficient solar cell performance requires minimizing the forward recombination current and maximizing the light generated current. Collection losses can be minimized in thin film of high absorption and short diffusion length. Voltage dependent photocurrent collection losses in CdTe films

were observed [8]. The voltage dependence of photo current of CdTe/CdS solar cells was characterized by separating the forward current from the photocurrent

2. CdTe/Si Heterojunctions Properties

Mohamed *et al.* [9] have studied the photovoltaic properties of In-doped CdTe (p) homojunction structure. It was revealed that the In-doped CdTe thin film is of high bulk resistivity, which affects its photovoltaic properties. The deteriorative effect of high bulk resistivity increases by increasing the light intensity which in turn limits the benefit of using higher light intensity that improves the conversion efficiency. A new factor denoted as "S" was devised to measure how the series resistance affects the short circuit current versus light intensity characteristics of the new structure and generalized conclusions were put forward to cover all types of the conventional solar cells. The In-doped CdTe (p) thin film is of high bulk resistivity which largely affects its photovoltaic properties particularly the short circuit current. It was noted that, the deteriorative effect of the high bulk resistivity increases by increasing the light intensity, which in turn limits the benefit of using light concentrators that improve the short circuit current. Birkmanm and Alamri [10] found that the use of post deposition heat treatment would probably reduce the bulk resistance and possibly improves contact performance. It was proved previously [4] that the polarity of the applied voltage had almost no effect on the I-V characteristics of Al-In doped-CdTe-Al structure annealed at 100°C, which means that the contacts are ohmic. Variation of bulk resistivity with the diffusion temperature is shown in **Figure 1**. It can be observed that the bulk conductivity of the doped (diffused) films is about one order higher than that of the undoped CdTe films. This is due to the incorporation of Indium atoms that acts as donor sites, which in turn increases the carrier concentration. This will decrease the barrier height at the grain boundaries, resulting in less impedance to the carrier transport [11]. Also it was found that the maximum bulk conductivity is occurred at 100°C diffusion temperature.

There is intensive interest to develop high efficiency multi-junction solar cells including the exploration of using silicon (Si) substrate. Heterojunction devices have been realized by depositing phosphorus-doped silicon (Si) (n-type) on a p-type crystalline silicon substrate. The open circuit voltage increases proportionally to the band gap, whereas the number of absorbed photons, *i.e.*, the current decreases with broadening the band gap. The resulting power, as the product of voltage and current, has a maximum value at 1.3 eV. Silicon with the band gap of 1.1 eV and CdTe with 1.5 eV are close to this optimal value. Consistent growth of laterally uniform CdTe (CT) on Si substrate by molecular beam epitaxy has been reported, which indicates that II-VI semiconductor alloys based on CdTe and grown on Si substrates may give good cell performance [12]. Recent nanostructures materials (nanocrystal incorporated in isolators) are used for windows. Electrons can migrate in these structures from one nanocrystal (nc) to adjacent nc and to electrode by tunnel effect, therefore such materials are conductive. Usually nc of the same material as in solar is used for window. Thus, CdTe nc can be used for CdTe solar cell window. Then n-type Si nc on p-type bases is a possible perspective [13].

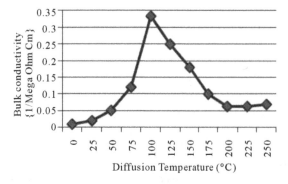

Figure 1. Bulk conductivity vs. diffusion temperatures of In-doped CdTe thin films.

3. Laboratory Preparation

The samples that will be discussed in this paper are of common evaporation conditions. Few samples of CdTe thin films were prepared by thermal evaporation and deposited on Si substrate. The deposition parameters and the sequence of fabricating In-doped CdTe/Si (p) structure are as follow (see **Figure 2**):

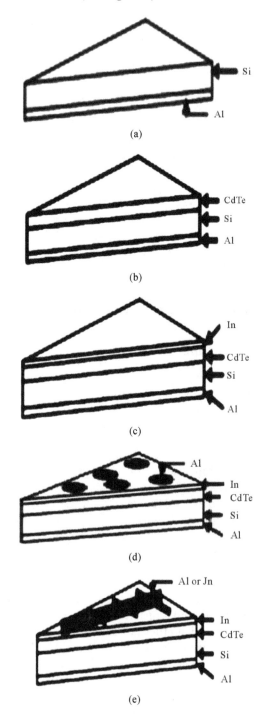

Figure 2. The sequence of preparing In (Al)-In-doped CdTe/Si-Al structure.

The Effects of Fabrication Parameters and Electroforming Phenomenon on CdTe/Si (p) Heterojunction
Photovoltaic Solar Cell

35

(a) Deposition of Al back contact 2000 Å on the back surface of the silicon wafer.

(b) Deposition of CdTe layer of 4000 Å thickness (since the photosensitivity of the evaporated CdTe shows a relatively high value at this thickness [14]) with 8 Å/s rate of deposition and at 25°C substrate temperature. The next step is annealing process at 200°C (under vacuum) for an hour in order to anneal the CdTe layer and to support back contact formation.

(c) Deposition of indium layer with 100 Å thickness, on top of the CdTe layer followed by Indium diffusion in CdTe by heating process at 100°C under vacuum for an hour.

(d) and (e) deposition of aluminum or indium top contact.

In this paper different structures will be studied. So, for the sake of simplicity, some symbols will be used so that one can easily recognize the different structures. These symbols will be used as superscript incorporated on the letters that describe different structure layers. For instance, the structure $In^*-In^{\sim*}$ CdTe/Si (p) indicates and from right to left that: a silicon wafer (p-type) on which a CdTe layer is deposited, $In^{\sim*}$ denotes an indium layer diffused in the CdTe layer in dot-shaped form, so the superscript ($\sim$) represents a diffused layer followed by the superscript (*) denotes the shape of the diffused layer in dot- shaped form. In^* denotes indium top contact in dot-shaped form. In this paper the following superscripts will be used: (*): denotes a dot shape, ($\sim$): denotes a diffused layer and ($^\#$): denotes a grid shape, usually used for top contacts.

During the fabrication processes of CdTe/Si heterojunction, some practical troubles were encountered. However, the important one is the formation of the SiO_2 thin oxide layer on the soft surface of the Si during the formation of the back contact. The silicon wafer is subjected to different chemical treatments in order to remove the thin oxide layer from the silicon wafer surfaces. Then the sequence of fabrication the on Al-CdTe/Si (p)-Al structure is as follow:

1) Deposition of Al back contact.

2) Formation of the back contact by annealing process at 200°C for an hour (under vacuum).

3) Deposition of CdTe layer.

4) Deposition of Al top contact.

During the formation of the back contact, a thin oxide layer (SiO_2) is grown undeliberately. The existence of this layer is investigated practically by fabrication of Al-Si-Al structure with back contact formation as in steps 1 and 2 above, after which a top contact Al is deposited. **Figure 3** illustrates the (I-V) characteristics of the device, which exhibits a diode effect that consequently indicates the formation of a MOS diode (Al-SiO_2-Si-Al). The existence of the oxide layer badly

affects the (I-V) characteristics of the structure Al-CdTe/Si (p)-Al.

Figure 4 depicts the (I-V) characteristics of the CdTe/Si with the interfacial oxide layer with different CdTe thicknesses. It can be deduced that the characteristics are not of a PN junction (no rectification effect) due to the interfacial oxide layer which prevents the establishment of heterojunction between CdTe and Si. Evidently the introduction of oxide layer increases the total absorption depth. This in turn utilizes the wasted portion of the solar spectrum, consequently increases the short circuit current [15,16].

4. The Effect of Top Contact Material

Two metals are used as top contacts they are, indium and aluminum. **Figure 5** illustrates the dark (I-V) characteristics of the structure $In^\sim$-CdTe/Si (p) with two top contact materials: indium and aluminum in dot-shaped form. The two devices are fabricated under the same evaporation conditions and for the same time. It is observed that the device with indium top contact has a good rectification characteristic comparing with that of the aluminum top contact. Since the bending of the forward dark (I-V) characteristic towards the voltage axis is indicative of high series resistance [17], the conclusion that aluminum metal shows a high ohmic contact resistance to the $In^\sim$-CdTe (In-doped CdTe) is valid. The two devices had

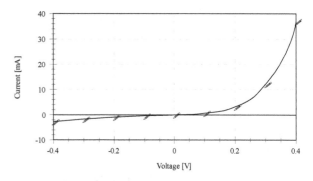

Figure 3. I-V characteristics of Al-Si (p)-Al.

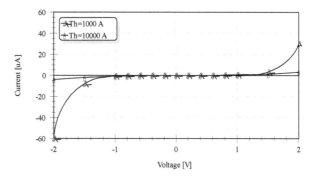

Figure 4. I-V characteristics of CdTe/Si (p) with interfacial oxide layer for different CdTe thicknesses.

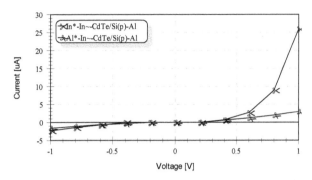

Figure 5. I-V characteristics of In-doped CdTe/Si (p) for In and Al top contacts in dot-shaped form.

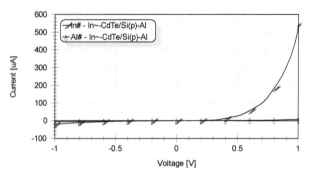

Figure 6. I-V characteristics of In-doped CdTe/Si (p) for In and Al top contacts in grid form.

equal open circuit voltage of about 20 mV at 75 mW/cm^2 light intensity with very low short circuit current.

Figure 6 depicts the dark (I-V) characteristics of the same structure but with indium and aluminum top contacts in grid form. It is noted that the device with indium top contact has also a good rectification characteristic supporting the conclusion that indium metal shows better ohmic contact comparing to aluminum metal.

5. The Effect of Device Area

Figure 7 illustrates a comparison between the dark (I-V) characteristics of device areas 1 cm^2 and 3 mm^2. Indium was used as a top contact in grid form in the large area device, and in dot-shaped form in the small area one. It is clear that the increase in the top contact area increases the current flowing in the device due to the relatively low bulk resistance. It was found that the large area device showed an open circuit voltage greater than that of the small area, 36 mV and 20 mV respectively at 75 mW/cm^2 light intensity. The slight increase in the open circuit voltage due to area increase of the device may be attributed to the increase in the photo generated current by increasing the device area, this in turn increases the open circuit voltage.

6. The Effect of Silicon Concentration

The dark (I-V) characteristics of the two structures In$^\sim$-CdTe/Si (p+) and In$^\sim$-CdTe/Si (p) are discussed. **Figure 8** shows that the leakage current in the former structure is more than in the latter. This effect can be explained in terms of silicon concentration as follows: in the case of Si (p+), the depletion region is narrow due to the high holes concentration in the silicon, while in the case of Si (p) the low holes concentration results in a wider depletion region and consequently the low leakage current. The device with Si (p+) showed an open circuit voltage of 100 mV at 75 mW/cm^2 light intensity due to the increase in the holes concentration in the silicon, this, in turn increased the junction abruptness that increase the open circuit voltage.

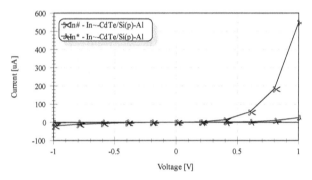

Figure 7. I-V characteristics of In-doped CdTe/Si (p) for In top contacts in dot-shaped and grid forms.

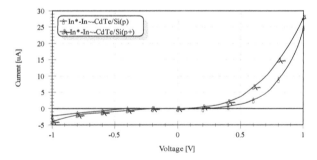

Figure 8. I-V characteristics of In-doped CdTe/Si (p) and In-doped CdTe/Si (p+) structures.

7. Electro Forming Phenomenon

It was found that in high electric field the (I-V) characteristics exhibited unusual behaviors as shown in **Figure 9**. It was observed that there were two states of conduction, non-conducting state represented by the curve AB and conducting state represented by the curve CD. The normal case is the non-conducting state. As the forward applied voltage was increased beyond the threshold value (7 V), it switched to the conducting state and remained in this state even after the voltage dropped to zero.

This behavior is similar to the electroforming phenomenon observed in metal-insulator-metal structure that is explained in terms of filamentary conduction model [18]. In this model, the conduction takes place through

The Effects of Fabrication Parameters and Electroforming Phenomenon on CdTe/Si (p) Heterojunction
Photovoltaic Solar Cell

37

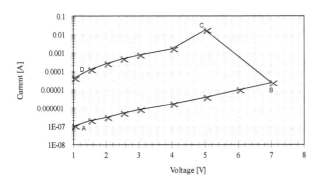

Figure 9. Forming effect in CdTe/Si (p) with interfacial oxide layer with CdTe thickness of 5740 Å.

highly conductive filaments that are created during the Forming process, that bridge the insulating layer between the electrodes. Here the insulating layer consists of two sub-layers, the oxide layer and the semi-insulating CdTe layer. It is observed that when the samples remain under conducting state for several minutes, during which high current flows through the sample, the samples drops to its non-conducting state suddenly. This may be attributed to the rupturing of the conductive filaments due to the relatively high local temperature arises from high current flow. This phenomenon is observed for several samples prepared with different CdTe thicknesses.

8. Conclusions

The heterojunction structure In-doped CdTe/Si (p) has poor photovoltaic properties due to the high resistivity of CdTe film and due to the large mismatch between CdTe and Si. It is observed that the Indium metal makes a good ohmic contact to the In-doped CdTe thin film comparing with the Aluminum metal. The heterojunction In-doped CdTe/Si (p+) has shown a relatively high open circuit voltage comparing with that of the Si (p) substrate due to higher junction abruptness that improve the photovoltaic action in the structure. Finally, an electroforming phenomenon has been observed in the CdTe/Si (p) heterojunction which may be considered as a memory effect.

REFERENCES

[1] L. M. Woods, D. H. Levi, V. Kaydonov, G. Y. Robinson and R. K. Ahrenkiel, "Electrical Characterization of CdTe Grain Boundary Properties from as-Processed CdTe/CdS Solar Cells," *2nd World Conference and Exhibition on Photovoltaic Solar Energy Conversion*, Vienna, 6-10 July 1998, pp. 1043-1049.

[2] P. Fernández, J. Solisa and J. Piqueras, "Pulsed Laser Annealing of CdTe Single Crystals," *Journal of Opto-electronics and Advanced Materials*, Vol. 2, No. 3, 2000, pp. 235-240.

[3] W. F. Mohamed and M. A. Shehathah, "The Electrical Properties of Post-Deposition Annealed and As-Depo-

sited In-doped CdTe Thin Films," *Renewable Energy Journal*, Vol. 26, 2002, pp. 285-294.

[4] X. Mathew, J. P. Enriquez, A. Romeo and A. N. Tiwari, "CdTe/CdS Solar Cells on Flexible Substrates," *Solar Energy Journal*, Vol. 77, 2004, pp. 831-838.

[5] T. Potlog, "Development of New Techniques of CdS/CdTe Solar Cell Enhancement," *International Semiconductor Conference*, Sinaia, 27-29 September 2006, pp. 171-174.

[6] D. H. Levi, L. M. Woods, D. S. Albin and T. A. Gessert,, "The Influence of Grain Boundary Diffusion on the Electro-Optical Properties of CdTe/CdS Solar Cells, Austria," *6-2nd World Conference and Exhibition on Photovoltaic Solar Energy Conversion*, Vienna, 10 July 1998. pp. 1057-1062.

[7] G. Khrypunov, A. Romeo, F. Kurdesau, D. Batnzer, H. Zogg and D. L. Tiwari, "Recent Development in Evaporated CdTe Solar Cells," *Solar Energy Material and Solar Cells*, Vol. 90, 2006, pp. 664-677.

[8] S. Hegedus, D. Desai and C. Thompson, "Voltage Dependent Photocurrent Collection in CdTe/CdS Solar Cells," *Progress in Photovoltaics: Research and Applications*, Vol. 15, No. 7, 2007, pp. 587-602.

[9] W. F. Mohamed and M. A. Shehathah, "The Effect of the Series Resistance on the Photovoltaic Properties of In-Doped CdTe (p) Thin Film Homojunction Structure," *Renewable Energy Journal*, Vol. 21, No. 2, 2000, pp. 141-152.

[10] A. W. Brinkman and S. M. Al-Amri, "Thin Film CdTe Based Solar Cell," *Proceedings of the Sixth Arab International Solar Energy Conference*, Muscat, Sultanate of Oman, 29 March 1998, p. 752.

[11] W. Huber and A. Lopez, "The Electrical Properties of CdTe Films Grown by Hot Wall Epitaxy," *Thin Solid Films*, Vol. 58, 1979, pp. 21-27.

[12] Y. G. Xiao, Z. Q. Li, M. Lestrade and Z. M. Simon Li, "Modeling of CdZnTe/CdTe/Si Triple Junction Solar Cells," *37th IEEE Photovoltaic Specialists Conference PVSC*, No. 604, 2011, pp. 14-16.

[13] S. Park, E. Cho, D. Song, G. Conibeer and M. Green, "n-Type Silicon Quantum Dots and p-Type Crystalline Silicon Heteroface Surface Solar Cells," *Solar Energy Materials & Solar Cells*, Vol. 93, No. 6-7, 2009, pp. 684-690.

[14] S. Saha, U. Pal, B. K. Samantaray, A. K. Chaudhuri and H. D. Banerjee, "Structural Characterization of Thin films Cadmium Telluride," *Thin Solid Films*, Vol. 164, 1988. pp. 85-89.

[15] W. F. Mohamad and A. M. Mustafa, "The Influence of Defects on Short Circuit Current Density in p-I-n Silicon Solar Cell," *Renewable Energy Journal*, Vol. 30 No. 2, 2005, pp. 187-193.

[16] W. F. Mohamad, A. Abuhajar and A. N. Saleh, "Effect of

Oxide Layers and Metals on Photoelectric and Optical Properties of Schottky Barrier Photo Detector," *Renewable Energy Journal*, Vol. 31, No. 10, 2006, pp. 1493-1503.

[17] A. M. Al-Dhafri, "Photovoltaic Properties of CdTe/Cu$_2$Te," *Renewable Energy Journal*, Vol. 14, No. 1-4, 1998, pp. 141-147.

[18] W. F. Mohamad and L. S. Ali, "Digital and Analogue storage Capability of Al/SiO$_2$/Si Structures," *Asian Journal of Information technology*, Vol. 5, No. 1, 2006. pp. 1-5.

7

Thermodynamical Phase Noise in Oscillators Based on *L-C* Resonators (Foundations)[*]

Jose-Ignacio Izpura, Javier Malo

Group of Microsystems and Electronic Materials (GMME-CEMDATIC), Universidad Politécnica de Madrid (UPM), Madrid, Spain

ABSTRACT

By a Quantum-compliant model for electrical noise based on Fluctuations and Dissipations of electrical energy in a Complex Admittance, we will explain the phase noise of oscillators that use feedback around *L-C* resonators. Under this new model that departs markedly from current one based on energy dissipation in Thermal Equilibrium (TE), this dissipation comes from a random series of discrete Dissipations of previous Fluctuations of electrical energy, each linked with a charge noise of one electron in the Capacitance of the resonator. When the resonator out of TE has a voltage between terminals, a discrete Conversion of electrical energy into heat accompanies each Fluctuation to account for Joule effect. This paper shows these Foundations on electrical noise linked with basic skills of electronic Feedback to be used in a subsequent paper where the aforesaid phase noise is explained by the new Admittance-based model for electrical noise.

Keywords: Admittance-Based; Noise Model; Energy Dissipation; Energy Conversion into Heat; Phase Noise

1. Introduction

As it is well known, no voltage V_0 set on a capacitor of capacitance C can remain constant with time t. The first reason is a self-discharge of C through its resistance R, because capacitors offering a pure capacitance at $T > 0$ do not exist [1]. This leads to an exponential decay with time constant $\tau = RC$ of any $V_0 \neq 0$ set in C that ends with a null V_0 only on average: $\langle V_0 \rangle = 0$, because the thermal fluctuation $kT/2$ J per degree of freedom sets an ac voltage noise in C whose spectral density is shaped by R to give a mean square noise voltage kT/C V^2 on C. This last sentence summarizes the new model for electrical noise used recently to explain the flicker noise found in vacuum devices [1] and the *1/f* excess noise of Solid State ones [2]. This new model considers that the noise of resistors and capacitors is born in their capacitance C between terminals and that their conductance $G = 1/R$ shunting C only shapes the noise spectrum to accomplish Equipartition as it can be deduced from [3]. The complex Admittance this new model uses allows to handle *Fluctuations and Dissipations* of electrical energy in time [4], thus excelling today's model based on Real Conductance that neither considers Fluctuations of this energy, nor distinguishes Dissipation of electrical energy from its Conversion into heat as we will do.

Shunting the *R-C* parallel circuit of a capacitor by a finite inductance $L \neq 0$, an *L-C-R* parallel resonator of resonance frequency f_0 appears. The role of this L can be seen as a feedback current that being proportional to the voltage $v(t)$ on C, has –90° phase lag under sinusoidal regime (SR). This feedback *in quadrature* with $v(t)$ that affects f_0, leads to the feedback-induced phase noise that we showed for oscillators based on resonant microcantilevers in [5]. This *Technical* phase noise due to a deficient phase control of the feedback adds to the non technical, but *Thermodynamical* phase noise we will explain for oscillators with perfect loops where current feedback to the resonator is exactly in-phase with its voltage $v(t)$ for Positive Feedback (PF) or exactly at ±180° for Negative Feedback (NF). This prevents the addition of Technical phase noise to the Thermodynamical one sketched in [6] that we will explain, which is linked with resonator's *losses* represented by its R and with noise added by the feedback electronics, both considered by the noise figure F of Leeson's pioneering work [7]. We will show the theory behind Leeson's empirical formula and behind the Line Broadening that these oscillators show around their mean oscillation frequency f_0 [8]. The general theory on phase noise of [9,10] and the references therein are valuable introductions on this topic that we will define as: *the impossibility to achieve a periodic Fluctua-*

[*]Work supported by the Spanish CICYT under the MAT2010-18933 project, by the Comunidad Autónoma de Madrid through its IV-PRICIT Program, and by the European Regional Development Fund (FEDER).

tion of charge in L-C resonators.

Although phase noise means that the energy of the oscillator's output signal is spread around f_0 (e.g. its spectrum is not a $\delta(f-f_0)$ function or "line"), the amount of this spreading due to each feedback of the oscillator is not obvious. Hence the reason to start with a "special oscillator" giving a signal of frequency $f \to 0$ whose phase noise can't be defined because this signal doesn't change phase in a finite time interval, but where Dissipations of electrical energy enhanced by a Clamping Feedback can be shown easily, as well as the Pedestal of electrical noise that results when this feedback is confused by noise not in phase with the output signal it tracks. This paves the way towards actual oscillators of $f_0 \neq 0$ that we will study in a subsequent paper under the same title, where Fluctuations and Dissipations of energy will produce, respectively, the Line Broadening of the output spectrum and the Pedestal far from f_0, both sketched in [6]. Our results will show that *L-C* oscillators show phase noise because they are Charge Controlled Oscillators for an unavoidable *charge noise power* of $4FkT$ C^2/s [4] that disturbs their otherwise periodic fluctuation of charge expected from the exchange of energy between their opposed susceptances due to *L* and *C*.

This paper is organized as follows. In Section 2 we consider Fluctuation, Dissipation and Feedback around a capacitor to show their basic interaction. Section 3 shows the difference between Dissipation of electrical power in Thermal Equilibrium (TE) and its Conversion into heat in capacitors and resistors out of TE that allows to understand why electrical noise doesn't depend noticeably on the power being converted into heat out of TE when the temperature rising is low, although this Converted power can be millions of times larger that the electrical power Dissipated in TE following to [4]. Some relevant conclusions used to explain phase noise in a subsequent paper under the same title, are summarized the end.

2. Fluctuation, Dissipation and Feedback around a Capacitor

The circuit of **Figure 1(a)** shows the equivalent circuit of a capacitor of capacitance *C* or resistor of resistance *R* at low *f*. This circuit allowing Fluctuations of electrical energy as fast displacements currents in *C*, each triggering a subsequent Dissipation of energy by a conduction current through *R*, is a physically cogent circuit for electrical noise [4]. At its cut-off frequency $f_C = 1/(2\pi RC)$ the current $i_Q(t)$ through *C* and the current $i_P(t)$ through *R* have equal magnitude under SR. This f_c separates the low-*f* region $(f \ll f_C)$, where the active power dissipated in *R* surpasses the reactive power fluctuating in *C*, from the high-*f* region $(f \gg f_C)$ where the situation is the opposed one. This device is a good resistor when its

ratio $Q = i_Q(t)/i_P(t)$ is low (e.g. at $f \ll f_C$) because it mostly *dissipates* electrical energy. At high *f*, however, it is a good capacitor where electrical energy mostly *fluctuates* because the ratio *Q* is high. Thus, the quality factor *Q(f)* sets the dissipative or reactive character of this device. **Figure 1(b)** shows the time evolution of a voltage V_0 existing at $t = 0$ on *C*. This voltage endures an energy $U_0 = CV_0^2/2$ J stored in *C* out of TE that can be converted into heat "in *R*". This gives the exponential decay of $v(t)$ with time constant $\tau = RC$ whereas the stored energy decays with a time constant $\tau_U = RC/2$.

Let's consider an spectrum analyzer sampling $v(t)$ from $t = 0$ to $t_{end} \gg \tau$ (e.g. $t_{end} = 100\tau$) to obtain its Fast Fourier Transform (FFT). Because the energy content of $v(t)$ after t_{end} is small, this FFT analyzer having recorded nearly all the energy U_0 of this Signal would give a Lorentzian spectrum $S_{VS}(f)$ like that of **Figure 1(c)**.

This $v(t)$ signal, viewed as a single decay born in $t = 0$ and its Fourier transform are:

$$v(t) = V_0 \times \exp\left(\frac{-t}{\tau}\right) \times u(t) \quad [\text{V}] \quad \leftrightarrow$$

$$Y(f) = V_0 \times \frac{\tau}{1 + j\dfrac{f}{f_C}} \quad [\text{V/Hz}] \tag{1}$$

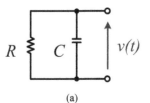

(a)

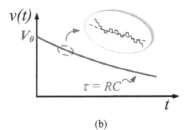

(b)

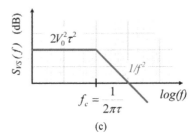

(c)

Figure 1. (a) Noise circuit of resistors and capacitors; (b) Time evolution $v(t)$ of a voltage V_0 stored in C at $t = 0$; (c) Unilateral spectrum of $v(t)$ (see text).

thus giving this unilateral Lorentzian spectrum for $v(t)$:

$$S_{VS}(f) = 2\frac{V_0^2 \tau^2}{1+\left(\dfrac{f}{f_C}\right)^2} \quad \left[\text{V}^2\text{s/Hz}\right] \qquad (2)$$

Integrating (2) from $f \to 0$ to $f \to \infty$ by its equivalent Bandwidth $BW_{eq} = (\pi/2)f_C$, we obtain: $M = V_0^2 \times (\tau/2)$ $\text{V}^2 \times$ s, a value that also appears by integrating the square of the decay (1) from $t = 0$ to $t \to \infty$ (Parseval's Theorem). Thus, M is not the electrical energy U_{DS} converted into heat by $v(t)$ driving R from $t = 0$ to $t \to \infty$. This energy is: $U_{DS} = M/R$ J, thus suggesting that $G = 1/R$ will contain some *rate factor* λ (s^{-1}) to cancel the time unit of (2) as well as a *capacitive factor* to convert V^2 into J. This paves the way to see Conductance $G = 1/R$ as a rate of discrete chances to exchange electrical energy [4] that makes easier the understanding of phase noise. Added to the Signal spectrum (2) there will be a small Noise spectrum due to the thermal charge noise of C viewed as the kT/C noise of this capacitor or as the Johnson noise "of its R". This noise comes from a random series of Thermal Actions (TA) on C, each being an impulsive charge variation of one electron between its plates, which are the terminals of R [4]. Each TA sets a voltage step of q/C V in C that decays with time constant τ as C discharges through R. These decays called Device Reactions (DR) in [4] are sketched in **Figure 1(b)**. Each DR endures a slower charge noise of one electron with opposed sign to that of its preceding TA. This random series of DRs with zero mean (e.g. the number of positive and negative DR's is equal on average) keeps the native spectrum of its basic impulse (Carson's Theorem). The charge noise due to these (TA-DR) pairs has an average *power* $4kT/R$ C^2/s that gives a noise $v_n(t)$ whose mean density is [4]:

$$S_{VN}(f) = \frac{4kTR}{1+\left(\dfrac{f}{f_C}\right)^2} \quad \left[\text{V}^2\text{/Hz}\right] \qquad (3)$$

where k is Boltzmann constant and T temperature. It's worth noting that replacing C by αC in **Figure 1(a)** the amplitude of these DRs will change from q/C V to $q/(\alpha C)$ V and their time constant from τ to $\alpha\tau$, thus keeping the amplitude of (2) and (3), *but shifting their cut-off frequency to* f_c/α. This way, electrical noise obeying Equipartition keeps $kT/2$ J as the Thermal fluctuation in C [4]. This change in C will appear later as an effect due to a feedback acting on the circuit of **Figure 1(a)**.

Since the FFT analyzer considers that the Signal (2) repeats each $t_{end} = 100\tau$ seconds (otherwise the mean Signal power would be null), we have to multiply (2) by the rate $\lambda_{FFT} = 1/(100\tau)$ to have some *Signal power*

sustained in time to compare with the mean *Noise power* that thermal activity sustains in time. This way the unit of time (s) disappears in (2), which acquires the familiar units V^2/Hz of "power density on 1 Ω". This allows comparing the two Lorentzian spectra "seen" by the FFT analyzer: the big one of the "repetitive" Signal given by (2) in V^2/Hz units and the small Noise spectrum of (3). Let's have some figures at room T with $V_0 = 1$ V for $C = 10$ pF and $R = 1$ GΩ ($\tau = 0.01$ s). From (2) and (3) the Signal/Noise ratio of the above spectra is higher than 10^7, thus meaning that the Lorentzian noise spectrum would be buried by the Signal one of equal shape, or buried in its "roughness" coming from mathematical rounding in the FFT algorithm, quantization noise, etc.

For its utility to start oscillators, let's use *electronic feedback to generate* a voltage V_0 in the capacitor of **Figure 1** *from its own thermal noise and to sustain it in time* as close as possible to a dc reference V_{Ref}. **Figure 2** shows a PF adding a resistance $-R$ in parallel with C by feeding-back a current $i_{FB}(t) = -v(t)/R$, proportional to the voltage sampled by the feedback network of transconductance $\beta_Y = -1/R$ A/V. This PF aims at compensate losses of electrical energy taking place by R when C stores an energy that differs from its value in Thermal Equilibrium (TE). Thus, *this PF doesn't remove losses in R: it only compensates them.* This β_Y leading to a loop where power lost in R and power delivered by the PF are equal (Gain = Losses condition) does not mean that this PF removes the losses of this "resonator of $f_0 \to 0$". Contrarily, *this PF sustains in time resonator's losses* by injecting the same power it loses through R, thus sustaining in t a Conversion of electrical energy into heat in this resonator that having a non null voltage V_0, is thus out of TE. This distinction between *Dissipation* of electrical energy [4] and *Conversion of electrical energy into heat* that occurs out of TE will be clarified later.

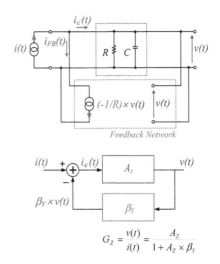

Figure 2. Feedback scheme allowing to compensate losses of energy in R without changing the value of C.

With $v(t) = 10$ V and $R = 10$ MΩ, the circuit of **Figure 2** would convert electrical energy into heat at a rate of 10 μJ per second (10 μW) that its PF would inject continuously. The transfer of this heat power to its environment in steady state requires a temperature gradient with this capacitor out of TE being at temperature T^* higher than that of its environment T. This warming effect that will be low for high-Q resonators, can be accounted for inadvertently (e.g. not by a different noise temperature $T^* > T$) by using a noise figure $F > 1$ like that of [7] because a quiet electronics ($F = 1$) around a capacitor at $T^* = 1.3\,T$ or a noisy electronics ($F = 1.3$) around a capacitor at T, are numerically equivalent in **Figure 2**. Only the need for $T^* > T$ to evacuate heat from the resonator and the $F > 1$ of any actual electronics suggest that the situation is a mix of the above two (e.g. $T < T^* < 1.3T$ and $F > 1$). This need to evacuate the generated heat leads to consider the energy *Conversion into heat* out of TE, whereas in TE we will speak about energy *Dissipation* following each *Fluctuation* of energy [4] because no heat is generated. After this reflection about $T^* > T$ let's consider the feedback loop of **Figure 2**. Using $\beta_Y = -1/R_{FB}$ and its transfer function G_Z, its gain $G_Z(j\omega) = v(j\omega)/i(j\omega)$ is:

$$G_Z(j\omega) = \frac{v(j\omega)}{i(j\omega)} = \frac{A_Z = \dfrac{R}{1 + j\omega RC}}{1 + A_Z \beta_Y}$$
$$= \frac{RR_{FB}}{(R_{FB} - R) + j\omega C(RR_{FB})} \tag{4}$$

that for $R_{FB} = R$ (Gain = Losses condition) gives:

$$G_Z(j\omega) = \frac{1}{j\omega C} \Rightarrow G_Z(s) = \frac{1}{sC} \tag{5}$$

Therefore, the Gain = Losses condition converts the lossy capacitor of capacitance C into a lossless one of the same C because this feedback *in-phase* with $v(t)$ doesn't vary C [5]. Using $s = \sigma + j\omega$, the inverse Laplace transform of $G_Z(s)$ will be the time response of the system of **Figure 2** to an impulsive driving current $i(t)$ like those TAs occurring in C [4]. The $G_Z(s)$ of (5) indicates that a current impulse of weight q (a charge q displaced in C in a vanishing time interval) will set a voltage step $\Delta v = q/C$ V in C that will remain forever. These voltage steps appearing randomly in time and with random signs have been sketched in **Figure 3** to show their null mean value $\langle v(t) \rangle = 0$. Thus, this PF won't "build" a voltage in C like the V_0 we are looking for and moreover: the $1/R_{FB} = 1/R$ condition at each instant t can not be met because the random drift with time of R in this capacitor can't be compensated for by the feedback network having its own, small drift with time.

To generate a noticeable voltage in C we need to have:

Figure 3. Output signal of the feedback loop of Figure 2.

$1/R_{FB} > 1/R$ or $R_{FB} < R$. This is the *Gain > Losses* condition meaning that (4) in s domain has a pole with positive real part (e.g. $s_p = \sigma + j0$ with $\sigma > 0$). In this case the steps of **Figure 3** no longer are flat, but exponential risings. For the *particular* case $R_{FB} = R/2$ (e.g $\beta_Y = -2/R$), the resistance shunting C is: $R_{Eff} = -R$ because $R_{Eff} = R \times (-R/2)/(-R/2 + R)$ and we obtain:

$$G_Z(j\omega) = \frac{1}{-1 + j\omega RC} \Rightarrow G_Z(s) = \frac{1}{C} \times \frac{RC}{sRC - 1} \tag{6}$$

Equation (6) means that an impulsive current of weight q will create a voltage q/C V in C that will rise exponentially with time constant $\tau = RC$ for this particular β_Y. For $C = 10$ pF and $R = 1$ GΩ used previously we have: $\tau = 10$ ms and a small voltage step $q/C \approx 16$ nV growing in this way would reach 1 V in $t_{start} \approx 180$ ms. For cuasi-dc signals as the aimed V_0, this t_{start} seems a fast enough starting time that would be lower for higher β_Y values. Due to the random sign of the DRs (note that a DR is a voltage decay $v(t)$ in **Figure 4** coming from an impulsive current $i(t)$ of one electron) we have to amplify only those DRs whose polarity is that of the aimed V_0. This is done in **Figure 4** by the rectifiers D_1 and D_2, taken as ideal ones to simplify. Due to the blocking action of D_1, a voltage step $\Delta v = -q/C$ V appearing in $v(t)$ wouldn't feedback current to the input whereas a positive $\Delta v = +q/C$ would do it.

This positive Δv would give a $v(t) > 0$ rising with time as explained. Due to the blocking action of D_2, a voltage $v(t) < V_{Ref}$ wouldn't feedback current, but for $v(t)$ surpassing V_{Ref}, this NF loop will feedback a current i_{ALC} to counterbalance the excess of PF that existed during t_{start}, thus passing to sustain a voltage $v(t)$ close to V_{Ref} that the PF has "built" in C. Thus, this NF called Clamping Feedback (CF) is necessary to recover first and *to keep continuously* next, the $1/R_{FB} = 1/R$ condition that during t_{start} was: $1/R_{FB} > 1/R$ This CF implicit in the action of Automatic Level Control (ALC) systems or amplitude limiters used in oscillators, works when $v(t)$ surpass V_{Ref}, thus generating *the error signal it needs* to be driven, which is $v_\varepsilon(t) = (v(t) - V_{Ref}) > 0$.

When $v(t)$ surpasses V_{Ref}, this CF has to feedback enough current to counterbalance the excess of PF used to start the system. With $R_{FB} = R/2$, the system starts with loop gain $T_{start} = 2$ because $\beta_Y = 2/R$. Note that the sign of $-2/R$ in the PF generator of **Figure 2** disappears if its arrow is reversed to follow the path allowed

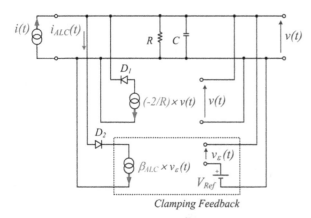

Figure 4. Electrical circuit with positive feedback and negative clamping feedback loops to generate first, and to sustain next, a positive voltage V_0 in C (see text).

by D_1. This β_Y shunting C by $R_{FB} = -R/2$, needs to be counterbalanced in some extent by the CF when $v(t)$ approaches V_{Ref} in order to leave C shunted by $R_{Sus} = -R$ and by its own R. In this case the CF has to shunt C with a resistance $R_{ALC} = +R$ to counterbalance the 50% of $\beta_Y = 2/R$ in order to recover the *Gain = Losses* condition or a loop gain $T_L = 1$. This requires a current $i_{ALC}(t) = v(t)/R$ coming from $v_\varepsilon(t) = (v(t) - V_{Ref})$, not from $v(t)$, thus meaning that *the CF has to be very strong* because it is driven by a signal of amplitude much smaller than the one it keeps in time, which is the output amplitude driving continuously the PF loop whose excess of feedback has to be counterbalanced by the CF.

Thus, any small signal as DRs (noise) appearing in $v(t)$ when it is close to V_{Ref} will be strongly damped by this NF. If we define the Clamping Factor (CL) as: $CL = V_{Ref}/\langle v_\varepsilon(t)\rangle$ we have: $\langle v(t)\rangle = \langle v_\varepsilon(t)\rangle + V_{Ref}$. Thus, the CF driven by $v_\varepsilon(t)$ will be $(CL + 1)$ times stronger than the PF driven by $v(t)$ to feedback a similar current with regard the excess of PF that the CF has to counterbalance. This excess of PF is:

$$\Delta\beta_Y = \frac{1}{R_{FB}} - \frac{1}{R} = \frac{(R - R_{FB})}{(R \times R_{FB})} \tag{7}$$

that for $R_{FB} = R/2$ gives: $\Delta\beta_Y = 1/R$.

Since $i_{ALC}(t)$ is generated from $v_\varepsilon(t)$ that is $(CL + 1)$ times lower than $v(t)$ and it has to counterbalance a current $\Delta\beta_Y \times v(t) = v(t)/R$, the transconductance β_{ALC} thus required will be:

$$\beta_{ALC} = (CL + 1) \times \Delta\beta_Y = (CL + 1) \times \frac{R - R_{FB}}{R \times R_{FB}} \tag{8}$$

Taking a 0.1% excess over V_{Ref} as error signal we have: $\langle v_\varepsilon(t)\rangle = (V_0 - V_{Ref}) = 0.001 V_{Ref}$. In our particular case with $R_{FB} = R/2$, (8) gives $\beta_{ALC} = 1001/R$ A/V. Thus, for small departures of $v(t)$ from its mean value $\langle v(t)\rangle = 1.001 V_{Ref}$ this CF will react as a resistance

$R_{DIF} = R/1001$ Ω shunting C. Since this reaction is driven by $v_\varepsilon(t)$, any small voltage like noise added to its mean value $\langle v_\varepsilon(t)\rangle = V_{Ref}/CL$ will feel this R_{DIF}. For $V_{Ref} = 1$V the error signal driving the CF will be the dc signal $\langle v_\varepsilon(t)\rangle = 1$ mV accompanied by the ac noise due to DRs being modified by the CF that dominates the circuit after t_{start}. Hence the reason to distinguish $v_\varepsilon(t)$ from its average value (1 mV) that gives the conductance $G_{ALC} = \beta_{ALC} \times 1\text{mV} = +1/R$ A/V that *counterbalances at each instant* the excess of PF used during t_{start}. **Figure 5** shows the output voltage $V_0 = V_{Ref} + 1\text{mV}$ in our case, together with some DRs coming from TAs taking place in C, which would form the $i(t)$ of **Figure 4**.

The CF is thus driven by a dc voltage $\langle v_\varepsilon(t)\rangle = 1$ mV and by the ac noise of C, both feedback by β_{ALC}. The feedback of $\langle v_\varepsilon(t)\rangle$ performs the aimed clamping function and *the feedback of the noise changes its spectrum* as shown by curve b) of **Figure 6**. For $\beta_{ALC} = 1001/R$ A/V, the low R_{DIF} shunting C for $t > t_{start}$ means that the DRs of **Figure 5** won't decay with the native τ of **Figure 1(b)**, but 1001 times faster. This is a known result coming from the Gain×Bandwidth product conservation in systems like this one where a flat NF is applied to a first-order, low-pass, forward gain (see Chapter 5 of [11]). Since the rate λ of DRs is unaffected by this NF, the noise spectrum found in the voltage $v(t)$ of **Figure 4** will be that of curve b) of **Figure 6**, where the native spectrum of (3) has been *broadened in frequency by* $1001 \approx 10^3$ *and attenuated by* $(1001)^2 \approx 10^6$ due to the quadratic dependence of (2) with τ, because the amplitude q/C of these "*accelerated DRs*" won't change since C is not affected by this feedback in-phase [5]. Thus, the noise spectrum will be:

$$S_{VNP}(f) = \frac{4kTR}{(1001)^2} \times \frac{1}{1 + \left(\dfrac{f}{1001 f_c}\right)^2} \left[\text{V}^2/\text{Hz}\right] \tag{9}$$

whose $\approx 10^6$ lower amplitude comes from the action of the CF on each DR, increasing its conduction current by 1001. Thus, this CF not only keeps the output amplitude close to V_{Ref}, but also damps heavily the noise it finds on the output amplitude in the form of DRs. A higher CL to

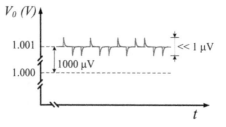

Figure 5. Detail of the voltage $V_0 = 1.001$ V kept in C by the feedback system of Figure 4 together with its electrical noise (see text).

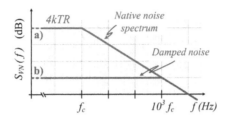

Figure 6. Noise damping in the feedback system of Figure 4.

clamp $v(t)$ more closely to V_{Ref} would give a higher attenuation and broader bandwidth in **Figure 6(b)**, whence it can be found the reason for the name High Damping (HD) we will give to this effect due to the CF that underlies limiters and ALC systems of oscillators. This HD effect agrees with the action one expects for an ALC system that, *unable to avoid the appearance* of DRs in C, tries to remove them quickly once they have appeared.

It's worth noting that this NF *in-phase* with $v(t) = V_0$ is possible because we have a "resonator of $f_0 \rightarrow 0$" whose output amplitude is a constant V_0 allowing to consider that its output signal $v(t)$ is at its top or with zero-phase for this signal being: $v(t) = V_0 \times \cos(2\pi f_0 t)$ with $f_0 \rightarrow 0$. Despite its simplicity, this model gives a good picture about the way the CF will work in actual oscillators with $f_0 \neq 0$ that we will study in the subsequent paper under this same title. To pass from this "dc approach with $f_0 \rightarrow 0$" to an ac one with $f_0 \neq 0$, we could discuss about the way to clamp negative semi periods in **Figure 4** by adding a new feedback box with a third diode D_3 injecting current towards the anode of D_2 to allow an $i_{ALC}(t)$ of opposed sense coming from a $v_\varepsilon(t)$ of opposed polarity, obtained from the sampling of $v(t)$ minus a V_{Ref} with proper sign. The two feedback boxes containing D_2 and D_3 would have to be driven by a time-varying reference signal $V_{Ref}(t) = V_{Ref} \times \cos(2\pi f_0 t)$ that they would use to clamp the output signal $v(t)$ close to this $V_{Ref}(t)$. The problem, however, is that this $V_{Ref}(t)$ is not available because it requires to have in advance, at each instant of time, the signal the oscillator is going to generate. An approach to avoid this unavailable requirement is to sample the peak value of $v(t)$ each period and to compare it with a dc reference V_{Ref} to generate the proper β_{ALC} to be used next. Although it works quite well, this approach has a drawback however, because it converts the ALC system or its implicit CF into a sampled system whose sampling rate f_0 (or $2f_0$ by sampling the positive and negative peaks of the output signal), we will consider as appropriate in this introductory paper to simplify.

What we will study more carefully is *the noise due to this solution that locks in phase the CF and the carrier* of frequency f_0 whose amplitude V_0 it keeps in time close to V_{Ref}. We refer to the noise generated by this locked CF *when it is confused by the noise it samples in quadrature with the carrier* it tracks, because its heavy attenuation

on the noise it samples in phase is clear from **Figure 6** or by (9). To study this collateral effect that appears when the carrier has a non null frequency $f_0 \neq 0$, let's consider that the NF of the ALC system or limiter is phase-locked to the carrier that is the big arrow (phasor) rotating at f_0 times per second in **Figure 7**, where the noise coming from random DRs is the small arrow $V_N(t)$ at its end whose mean square voltage is kT/C V^2.

Since $V_N(t)$ points randomly respect to the carrier, we will consider its *component* along the carrier and that *orthogonal* to it. This endures a *noise partition* where the mean square voltage of noise sampled *in-phase* and that sampled in quadrature both are equal: $kT/(2C)$ V^2 and their sum is kT/C V^2 (e.g. the sum in power of these two uncorrelated noises). With this partition, which acquires its proper meaning when phase can be defined for $f_0 \neq 0$ as we will see in actual oscillators, let's redrawn **Figure 6** where all the noise of C was sampled in-phase. This is shown in **Figure 8** where curve a) is the noise spectrum of the resonator without feedback and where curve b) is the noise spectrum coming from the 50% noise of C being feedback in phase with the carrier, thus 3 dB less than curve b) of **Figure 6**. Concerning the +90° or –90° phase of the 50% noise power feedback in quadrature, let's recall that the zero-phase reference is the current injected by the PF because it follows the amplitude of the carrier in oscillators of $f_0 \neq 0$. Because C stores energy as it builds voltage from the current it integrates in time, any noise *current i(t)* will *create* voltage components in $v(t)$ at 0° (in-phase) and at –90° (in quadrature) respect to $i(t)$ under SR. Since $i(t)$ (Cause [4]) represents random TAs with any phase respect to the reference carrier, it will produce noise voltages (Effect [4]) both at –90° as well as at +90°° in the error signal $v_\varepsilon(t)$ driving the CF.

A noise voltage at –90° in the error signal $v_\varepsilon(t)$ driving this NF means a current at –90° absorbed from the resonator following the arrow of i_{ALC} in **Figure 4**. This is equivalent to current at +90° arriving to the top node of the resonator that *compensates current at +90° leaving it through C*. Thus, DRs having in-quadrature components at –90° respect to the carrier being generated will find a lower capacitance than C (e.g. αC with $\alpha < 1$) in the resonator due to this NF. This will give voltage steps of amplitude $q/(\alpha C) > q/C$ with α times faster decay than those in TE without feedback, *thus broadening their*

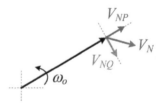

Figure 7. Phasor Hz whose real part represents the output signal $v(t)$ of an oscillator, disturbed by additive noise V_N.

noise spectrum while keeping its amplitude as we wrote below (3). Dually, DRs with in-quadrature components at +90° respect to the carrier being generated, will find more capacitance than C in the resonator (e.g. αC with $\alpha > 1$) thus giving a voltage steps of $q/(\alpha C) > q/C$ V with α times slower decay than those in TE without feedback. This will narrow their noise spectrum *while keeping unaffected its amplitude* because none of these feedbacks in quadrature modifies R [5]. Hence, the CF confused by noise in-quadrature will broaden the native noise spectrum while keeping its $2kTFR$ V²/Hz amplitude and this will give *a noise Pedestal of $2kTFR$ V²/Hz due to the 50% noise power the CF finds in quadrature.*

To compare this noise with its corresponding noise sampled in phase, curve b) of **Figure 8**, let's take a feedback factor of equal magnitude to the one we have used for curve b): $|-j\beta_{ALC}| = 1001/R$, for j being the imaginary unit meaning +90° phase shift. Let's take a resonator with $Q(f_0) = 1002$ where the current through C at f_0 is 1002 times higher than that through R. In this case, the $|\beta_{ALC}| = 1001/R$ A/V of the CF would compensate 1001 parts of the 1002 parts of current flowing through C at f_0.

Although this reasoning in SR requires an $f_0 \neq 0$, let's continue as if currents in the resonator had a non null $f_0 \to 0$ allowing the aforesaid noise partition. The capacitive current at $f_0 \to 0$ demanded by the resonator with this feedback would be only 1/1002 times the current of C, while its R would be unaffected. Thus, each DR of q/C V amplitude and time constant τ in TE would pass to have amplitude $1002(q/C)$ V and time constant $\tau_{Pdl} = \tau/1002$. The spectrum of these DRs sampled and feedback in quadrature would have ≈ 1000 times higher bandwidth but the same amplitude $2kTFR$ V²/Hz of the 50% noise spectrum found in quadrature by the CF, as it is shown by curve c) in **Figure 8**. It would be:

$$S_{VNQ}(f) = \frac{\dfrac{4kTR}{2}}{1 + \left(\dfrac{f}{1002 f_c}\right)^2} = \frac{2kTR}{1 + \left(\dfrac{f}{1002 f_c}\right)^2} \left[V^2/Hz\right] \quad (10)$$

where the 2 below the Johnson noise $4kTR$ V²/Hz recalls

the orthogonal partition of the noise in C. Following [4], an equivalent Noise Figure F like that of [7] means that the rate λ of TAs and DRs is F times higher than the average rate $\lambda = 2kT/(q^2 R)$ of thermal TAs associated to R in TE at T. If the resonator of $f_0 \to 0$ we are using had a temperature $T^* > T$ due to the power it is *Converting into heat* (V_0^2/R watts in dc, see next section), the extra noise due to $T^* > T$ and the noise added by the feedback electronics could be taken into account by the Noise Figure F of [7]. In this case, the noise Pedestal becomes:

$$S_{VNQ}(f) = 2FkTR \times \frac{1}{1 + \left(\dfrac{f}{1002 f_C}\right)^2} \left[V^2/Hz\right] \quad (11)$$

Given the difficulty to handle the in-quadrature term of a signal of $f_0 \to 0$, we won't go further with this reasoning, thus leaving (11) as a good reason to find a broad *Pedestal of electrical noise at $2FkTR$ V²/Hz added to the carrier whose amplitude is kept in time by a CF that becomes synchronous with it. This Pedestal is *the collateral effect of thermal noise sampled in-quadrature by the feedback electronics* governing the ALC system of oscillators. This Pedestal shown by curve c) of **Figure 8** represents *more noise power* than the 50% noise power sampled in-quadrature because the Clamping Feedback reduces the noise it samples in-phase as shown by curve b) of **Figure 8**, *but enhances the noise it finds with phase error of* −90°, because it lacks the right phase to be negatively feedback. Updating (9) with $F > 1$ and this noise partition we have:

$$S_{VNP}(f) = \frac{2FkTR}{(1001)^2} \times \frac{1}{1 + \left(\dfrac{f}{1001 f_C}\right)^2} \left[V^2/Hz\right] \quad (12)$$

Since this mix of discrete noise, electronic feedback and noise partition can be hard to be accepted at first sight, we will give added proofs by PSPICE that can be refined at the expenses of a higher computational cost or by other simulation tools. **Figure 9(a)** shows the Lorentzian noise spectrum that appears when a discrete and pseudo-random noise current mimicking the noise model of [4] drives the resonator of $f_0 \to 0$ of **Figure 9(b)** formed by a capacitor of 10 pF whose losses are represented by 10 GΩ. To have unambiguous results, TAs displacing $q = 1.605 \times 10^{-19}$ C each in [4], have been replaced by big TAs, each displacing a *charge packet* $q_{big} = 10^{-13}$ C by a current pulse of 10^{-9} A height and 0.1 ms width, whose appearance in time is each 2.1 ms, with random sign to give a rough emulation of thermal noise in the resonator of **Figure 9(b)** where it is injected through the transconductance generator G1. Thus, we have a pulsed "noise current" of $\delta \approx 5\%$ duty cycle and

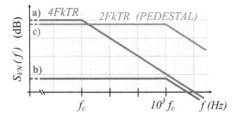

Figure 8. (a) Noise spectrum of C in TE; (b) Damped noise created by the CF from noise sampled in-phase; (c) Pedestal of noise from noise sampled in quadrature by the CF.

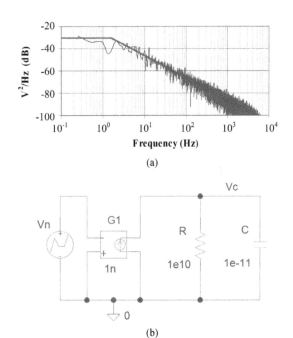

(a)

(b)

Figure 9. (a) Native noise spectrum of the circuit of Figure 9(b) driven by the charge noise described in the text. (b) Circuit of a capacitor of capacitance *C* and losses represented by *R*, driven by a charge noise (see text).

fixed rate $\lambda = 10^3/2.1 = 476$ s^{-1} (a Pseudo-Random Noise PRN) to emulate the thermal *charge noise power* of $4kT/R$ C^2/s [4] in $C = 10$ pF shunted by $R = 10$ GΩ.

This *power* or "Nyquist noise density $4kT/R$ A^2/Hz on *R*" is: 1.7×10^{-30} C^2/s (or A^2/Hz) at room *T*, whereas the power of the PRN is: $2\lambda \times \left(10^{-13}\right)^2 = 9.6 \times 10^{-24}$ C^2/s (or A^2/Hz), the factor 2 coming from the fact that each "fat TA" or fast displacement of a charge q_{big} in *C*, triggers a "fat DR" or slower displacement of charge $-q_{big}$ (an opposed displacement) to Dissipate the energy stored by the fat TA, thus doubling the charge noise

power of λ "fat TAs" per unit time taking place in *C*, as it happens with the TA-DR or Cause-Effect pairs in [4]. The higher power of the PRN respect to $4kT/R$ avoids *resolution problems* with non ideal rectifiers (see below). On the other hand, the average rate $\lambda_T = 2kT/\left(q^2 R\right)$ of true TAs in this resonator of $f_0 \to 0$ would be: $\lambda_T \approx 3.2 \times 10^7$ s^{-1} whereas the PRN has a fixed rate λ that roughly is 7×10^4 times lower than λ_T. Thus, the $\approx 10^6$ times higher charge noise power of the PRN comes from the "fat electrons" (each of charge $-q_{big}$) that it uses to emulate electrical noise in an Admittance accordingly to [4].

Figure 9(b) shows the PSPICE circuit used to inject this pulsed PRN into the *R-C* resonator in order to create the voltage noise on *C* that will emulate Johnson noise in this resonator of $f_0 \to 0$. Considering that each q_{big} shifts the voltage V_C in *C* by $\Delta V_C = q_{big}/C = 10$ mV and that the time constant of the subsequent decay is: $\tau = 0.1$ s, we can use these values and (2) multiplied by $\lambda = 476$ s^{-1} to predict the spectrum of this PRN in V_C. This way the flat region of the Lorentzian shown in **Figure 9(a)** would be: $2 \times 476 \times 10^{-6}$ V^2/Hz (e.g. –30 dB), thus agreeing well with the FFT of the V_C-time series given by PSPICE in the circuit of **Figure 9(b)**. This same value appears by converting A^2/Hz into V^2/Hz through the square of the Resistance where the Nyquist noise (in A^2/Hz) "is being applied". Multiplying 9.6×10^{-24} A^2/Hz by $R^2 = 10^{20}$ Ω^2, we have: 9.6×10^{-4} V^2/Hz, as expected. The two asymptotes drawn in **Figure 9(a)** show the cut-off frequency $f_C = 1.59$ Hz of this spectrum, as it must be for this τ of 0.1 s. This PRN is the charge noise driving continuously the resonator during the simulations to come.

Figure 10 shows the PSPICE circuit that simulates the "oscillator of $f_0 \to 0$" proposed in **Figure 4** to build a dc voltage V_0 in *C*. Its dc reference V_{Ref} leads to build a V_C voltage on *C* close to 3 V. The voltage amplifier E1 of

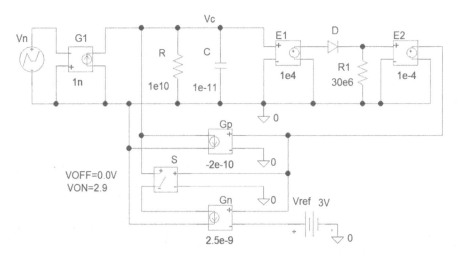

Figure 10. Positive feedback and CF loops used to build and to sustain next a voltage V_0 in the resonator of Figure 9(b).

gain 10^4 V/V driving the diode D, followed by the amplifier E2 of inverse gain 10^{-4} V/V allows to rectify small voltage signals in V_C as if the diode D (model 1N4007) had a turn-on voltage of $0.6V/E1 \approx 60$ μV, thus negligible for the voltage steps $\Delta V_C = \pm 10$ mV created in C by each charge packet q_{big} of the PRN. This way, the first positive ΔV_C on C will appear at the output of E2 with amplitude $\Delta V_{Cfirst} = 9.94$ mV due to the *precision rectifier* that form E1, D, R1 and E2. This ΔV_{Cfirst} will be positively feedback to the input through the transconductance amplifier of gain $Gp = -2 \times 10^{-10}$ A/V that is 2 times the $-1/R$ gain required to compensate resonator losses represented by its $R = 10$ GΩ. Thus, the loop starts with $T_{start} = 2$, the same value we used to describe **Figure 4**. Since any $\Delta V_C = -10$ mV is blocked by D, only positive voltage is built in C during the starting time t_{start}. When $V_C(t)$ reaches 2.9 V, switch S closes to activate the CF accomplished by the amplifier of gain $Gn = 2.5 \times 10^{-9}$ A/V, whose 25 times higher gain than Gp leads to a clamping factor: $CL = 25$ (e.g. to counterbalance the excess of PF we have in Gp driven by $\langle V_C \rangle \approx 3$ V, a signal $\langle v_\varepsilon \rangle = V_{Ref}/25 = 0.12$ V has to drive Gn in steady state). PSPICE shows that starting from $V_C = 0$, a voltage $V_C(t) = 3$ V appears in $t_{start} \approx 15$ ms and shortly after we have $\langle V_C \rangle = 3.12$ V.

We distinguish $\langle V_C \rangle$ from V_C because the 10 mV peaks due to the fat TAs of the PRN driving continuously the circuit appear onto $\langle V_C \rangle$ as PSPICE shows. To have a resolution better than 0.25 Hz, transient simulations lasting more than 4 seconds have been used while the PRN is being injected. The first 0.02 seconds corresponding to t_{start} in the V_C-time series of data given by PSPICE were not used to be in "steady state" (e.g. after t_{start}). The voltage on C in steady state mimics **Figure 5**, being formed by a dc value $\langle V_C \rangle = V_{Ref} + \langle v_\varepsilon \rangle = 3.12$ V plus the ac voltage noise due to the PRN, both governed by the CF. The error signal driving the CF is thus: $\langle v_\varepsilon \rangle + v_{ac}$ where v_{ac} represents these $\Delta V_C = \pm 10$ mV noise decays that form the noise viewed by the CF. It's worth noting that in steady state, these noise decays are feedback with gain ≈ 1 because for $\langle V_C \rangle = 3.12$ V, a dc current $\langle I_D \rangle \approx 31200/R1 \approx 1$ mA flows through diode D. With this dc bias, D converts ≈ 0.7 mW into heat and does not rectify at all the small noise decays $\Delta V_C = \pm 10$ mV that are added to $\langle V_C \rangle$. Instead, it offers a dynamical resistance $r_d = V_T/I_D \approx 25$ Ω allowing their passage to R1 with negligible attenuation (e.g. one part per million). This way, the decays of noise with amplitude ± 10 mV in C are transferred with unity gain to the output of E2 and feedback through Gp and Gn. Due to the simplicity of this circuit, R1 converts into heat 32 W in steady state, although this is irrelevant for the results.

Figure 11(a) is the spectrum of the signal that exists on C in **Figure 10**. Using $CL = 25$ in (8) and (9), the native noise spectrum of **Figure 9(a)** would be attenuated by $(25+1)^2 = 676$ (e.g. 28 dB less) whereas its cut-off frequency would be 26 times the f_C of **Figure 9(a)**. Thus, the noise on C would be a Lorentzian at -58 dB with its cut-off at $f_{Clamp} = 26 \times 1.6 \approx 42$ Hz that agrees well with the FFT of the $V_C(t)$-t series that PSPICE gives for the circuit of **Figure 10**. This is the spectrum under the dashed line drawn to guide the eye in **Figure 11(a)**.

Since this spectrum merges at high frequencies with the upper Lorentzian that repeats the asymptotic spectrum of **Figure 9(a)**, we confirm that for noise being feedback in phase, *the G × BW product is conserved*, as predicted.

Given the agreement between these simulations and our theory for the noise the CF "sees" in phase, let's try to find some proof concerning noise it sees in quadrature. The first point to consider is that for a signal like $V_C(t)$ that mostly is a dc signal of $f \to 0$, we would have to wait an infinite time to pass from phase 0° to phase $-90°$, but this is not so for its small ac components. Although we could synchronize its feedbacks with a carrier of frequency f_x. and use a signal in quadrature with f_x to build the feedback of noise in quadrature, this would modify the circuit in such a way that the results would be obscured by the extra knowledge required to handle the electronics. Thus, we will give a partial proof (only in a frequency band) about the effect we expect from a CF seeing noise in quadrature that is: a noise Pedestal of density $2FkTR$ V²/Hz. Since we need a CF working around the resonator, let's use that of **Figure 10** that clamps perfectly the amplitude to the designed value of 3.12 V. Hence, **Figure 12** is the circuit of **Figure 10** with an added path to feedback the ac voltage on C multiplied by $-j$. This feedback at $-90°$ is done by converting the ac

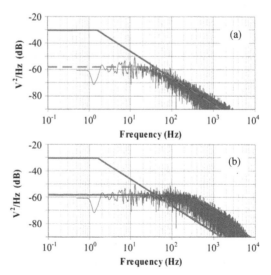

Figure 11. (a) Noise spectrum of the capacitor of Figure 9(b) under the feedbacks of Figure 10; (b) Noise spectrum of the same capacitor with the feedbacks of Figure 12 (see text).

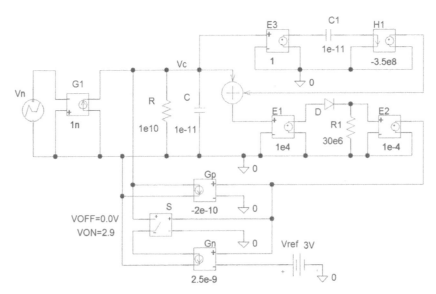

Figure 12. Electrical circuit of Figure 10 with an added path in the Negative Clamping feedback to feedback noise in quadrature as described in the text.

voltage in C into an ac current through C_1 whose Fourier components will be at +90° respect to the Fourier ones of this ac voltage because displacement currents in C_1 come from the *time derivative of each voltage component* on C_1. This current at +90° respect to voltage on C is converted into a new voltage by the transimpedance amplifier of gain H1 whose negative sign gives the –90° phase lag we are looking for.

As **Figure 12** shows, the ac voltage on C and this new voltage in-quadrature are added to drive the circuit that, being a precision rectifier during t_{start}, becomes a unity gain circuit feeding back the resonator in steady state as explained. Setting H1 = 0, the circuit of **Figure 12** becomes that of **Figure 10** and the spectrum of voltage noise that appears in C is that of **Figure 11(a)**. Since the feedback in phase of the CF has to exist continuously, (otherwise we wouldn't have a CF liable to feedback something in quadrature) and this already generates the noise spectrum of **Figure 11(a)**, this spectrum has to be viewed as the native spectrum of noise the feedback in quadrature finds when it is born by setting the gain of H1 to a non null value. Therefore, *any change in the spectrum of noise on C coming from the CF mislead by noise in quadrature, has to be referred to* **Figure** 11(*a*). For readers worried about this double feedback through the adder of **Figure 12** we will say that after t_{start} (when the E1, D, R1, E2 block becomes a *linear*, unity gain amplifier) it works perfectly because the orthogonal signals it handles do not merge, a feature used in [5] to handle the phase error in the loop gain of oscillators and its induced (Technical) phase noise. As the gain of H1 is increased, the amplitude of the noise peaks on C increases while their decay becomes faster. For H1 = –3.5 × 10^8 V/A, this amplitude roughly is five times higher than for H1 =

0 and the noise peaks decay five times faster.

Thus, this noise viewed in quadrature by the CF would be finding a capacitance $\approx C/5$ in the resonator. The FFT of the $V_C(t)$-time series PSPICE provides for the circuit of **Figure 12** gives the spectrum of **Figure 11(b)**, thus with *the same amplitude but roughly 5 times larger bandwidth* than the native noise of **Figure 11(a)**. The rather large gain we use in H1 is to compensate the low voltage-current conversion gain we have previously due to the small value of C_1. The overall value of these gains: $\beta_{Quad}(f) = 2\pi f C_1 \times H1$, depends on frequency because the +90° phase shifter we had to use is not the differentiator we have used, where the amplitude of its output signal rises with f. With a –90° phase shifter of flat response we could do a better simulation, but this would complicate more than clarify the circuit. Therefore we will say that **Figure 11(b)** *shows the trend of the CF to create a Pedestal* of electrical noise in the resonator when it is mislead by noise in quadrature. The gain $\beta_{Quad}(f)$ in the circuit of **Figure 12** that is unity around $f \approx 45$ Hz, thus near the frequency $f_{Clamp} \approx 42$ Hz of **Figure 11(a)**, means that this feedback of noise at –90° and that of noise in-phase are of similar strength around f_{Cclamp}, where the native noise spectrum had dropped 3 dB in **Figure 11(a)**. However, *the noise spectrum recovers its flat or low-f value around f_{Clamp}* as **Figure 11(b)** shows, thus meaning that this CF in quadrature tends to sustain the native noise amplitude when its magnitude is similar to that of the feedback in phase. This proves quite convincingly *the generation of a Pedestal of $2FkTR$ V^2/Hz amplitude by the CF confused by a noise density of $2FkTR$ V^2/Hz that it will find in quadrature with the carrier in oscillators with $f_0 \neq 0$.*

It is worth noting that the noise we have considered in

TE ($V_0 = 0$) and out of TE with $V_0 \neq 0$ has been the same despite the very different electrical power linked with R in TE and out of TE. We mean that the noise power Dissipated by R in TE is $kT/(RC)$ W following [4] whereas the power handled by R, $p_i(t) = V_0 \times I = V_0^2/R$ W out of TE, *can be millions of times larger*. If neither the rate λ_T of DRs nor the energy $\Delta U = q^2/(2C)$ Dissipated by each DR [4] are changed by the feedbacks, two questions that are essential to understand Phase noise in oscillators arise: 1) *what happens with the instantaneous power $p_i(t)$ that the feedback generators inject continuously to sustain $V_0 \neq 0$?*. And 2) *How does this $p_i(t)$ affect the TA-DR pairs of events* [4] *or the Fluctuation-Dissipation phenomena* [12] *that underlie electrical noise?*. Next Section considers these questions.

3. Dissipation of Energy and Conversion of Energy into Heat

The Signal power $p_i(t)$ W that enters the resonator in electrical form to sustain its V_0 uses to be considered as *power dissipated in R* that heats the resonator. Since Dissipation was linked to Fluctuation long time ago in a Quantum treatment of noise [12], we prefer to say: "*the power $p_i(t)$ that enters the resonator in electrical form is equal to the power that leaves it converted into heat*". This unbinds $p_i(t)$ from each Dissipation of electrical energy started by its previous Fluctuation in the Admittance where electrical noise appears [4]. This distinction is needed because if $p_i(t)$ was Dissipated in the same way each energy Fluctuation is, it would affect strongly the observed noise and this is not so. We refer to the noise of a resistor in TE with its R Dissipating $N = kT/(RC)$ W by kT/C V^2 driving its R and to the noise of this resistor absorbing millions of times this power under $V_0 \neq 0$, thus out of TE, that are *similar when the heating effect is low*. Using the Admittance of **Figure 1(a)** as a cogent circuit for their electrical noise [4], this noise comes from a random series of (TA-DR) pairs of events occurring in C at this average rate [4]:

$$\lambda_T = \frac{2kT}{Rq^2} \Rightarrow G = \frac{1}{R} = \lambda \frac{q}{2V_T} \qquad (13)$$

where $V_T = kT/q$ is the thermal voltage.

Conductance is thus a rate of chances in time to Dissipate electrical energy in TE, each involving the elemental charge unit q. Since C is the *direct transducer* converting kinetic or thermal energy of carriers into electrical one [4], let's find the *inverse transducer* that converts electrical energy entering the resistor into disordered energy observed as heat. Considering that the thermal noise of a resistor doesn't vary noticeably when a dc current is allowed to flow provided its heating effect is low, we can find that the *inverse transducer also is a capacitance C_f,*

quite different from C. To have some figures, let's consider a resistor of $R = 1$ MΩ shunted by $C = 0.4$ pF under open-circuit conditions. Integrating (3) from $f \rightarrow 0$ to $f \rightarrow \infty$, the mean square voltage on R at $T = 300$ K is: $\langle v_n^2 \rangle = 10^{-8}$ V^2 (e.g. 100 μV$_{rms}$ or the well known kT/C noise of C). This voltage generated in C that is driving R means that the mean noise power Dissipated by R is: $N = 10^{-8}/10^6 = 10^{-14}$ W in TE at 300 K. Injecting a dc current $I_{dc} = 1$ μA to this resistor, a dc voltage between terminals $V_{dc} = 1$ V will appear and the electrical power entering this resistor out of TE will be: $S = 1$ μW. For a macroscopic resistor with dimensions in the mm range, this Signal power S won't rise noticeably its T. Thus, the noise in TE at T with R Dissipating N watts and the noise out of TE with R "handling" $S = 10^8 N$ at $T^* \approx T$, will be quite the same as one finds measuring noise in resistors. This similarity in spite of the 100 millions factor of the power *handled* by R suggests that the Dissipations of energy in TE [4] and those converting $p_i(t)$ into the heat power that appears in the device, are different. Thus we have to look for a way to convert $p_i(t)$ into heat while keeping its electrical noise for $T^* \approx T$. Following [4], this requires to conserve λ_T with $V_0 \neq 0$, to keep the average number of electronic charges arriving at the terminals (or plates) of the resistor. Since $p_i(t)$ is $G = 1/R$ times V_0^2, a way to convert $p_i(t)$ into heat with this V_0^2 dependence is by loading each carrier arriving to a plate with an energy proportional to V_0^2 *as if each carrier giving noise had a capacitance C_f* driven by V_0. The word *loading* means that each carrier has to offer a reactive behaviour to V_0, like a *capacitive Susceptance able to store electrical energy taken from V_0*. This energy loaded onto the carrier would be released to the terminal (Collector) where the aforesaid carrier was captured.

In a device made from two plates at temperature T separated by a distance d in vacuum (an R-C cell studied in [1]), a reactive behaviour could be expected from the mass (inertia) of free electrons accelerated by the electric field V_0/d. This way, an electron emitted with kinetic energy U_i from the negative plate (cathode) would reach the anode with total energy $U_{Tot} = U_i + qV_0$ J. The displacement current that began when it left the cathode would cease at its arrival to the anode and this would store a Fluctuation of $\Delta U = q^2/(2C)$ J in C due to the charge q displaced between its plates. This is an *energy stored by the device in its susceptance between terminals*, thus able to drive the subsequent DR in TE that is what we call Dissipation in [4] to agree with the Fluctuation-Dissipation of energy studied in [12]. Without other ways to store energy between terminal, the excess of energy brought by the carrier: $U_{Conv} = U_{Tot} - \Delta U$, will be released to the Collector plate by phonons, thus as heat. Therefore the fast *Fluctuations* of energy (TAs) creating electrical noise *in a device* would be the energy packets it stores in electrical form each time an elemental charge is displaced between its two terminals and only this energy is *Dissipated* after each Fluctuation accordingly to the TA-DR or Cause-Effect dynamics of [4] and the extra energy surpassing ΔU is *Converted into heat*.

This difference between energy Dissipated and that Converted into heat is clear in this vacuum device, where the power converted into heat would be, however, proportional to V_0, not to V_0^2 (at least for $qV_0 \gg \Delta U$). This means that *kinetic energy acquired by charges* like electrons in vacuum doesn't give the reactive behaviour we are looking for, but this will be different in Solid State devices, whose *free carriers* in bulk regions between two terminals tend to bear *charge neutrality* by two opposed charges screening one to each other. The average number λ_T of electrons per second reaching the two plates or terminals of the *two-terminal device* (2TD) like a resistor or capacitor *one has to build to measure Johnson noise* is given by (13). These 2TD can be made small (e.g. differential) and repeated many times if necessary (e.g. connected in series or parallel) to study noise within a macroscopic device for example, but its 2TD character never is lost because the electrical noise "of a material" hardly will be measured. Only the noise *of a device made from this material* can be measured, but this device can produce its own noises like those of [1,2] that become puzzling when they are assigned to the material and not to the device that produces them. For a resistor made of n-type semiconductor, *free carriers* for electrical conduction are electrons in the Conduction Band (CB) whose name "free electrons" as opposed to trapped ones, does not mean "free electrons in vacuum".

An electron in a quantum state (QS) of the CB has a extended wavefunction within the device that "connects" its two terminals in the sense that one terminal can emit an electron to this QS as soon as it is left empty by the other terminal having captured the electron that was previously in this QS, being this a mechanism allowing the TAs of [4]. Since the electrical noise observed in a resistor in TE and when it conducts a dc current I_{dc} is quite the same provided heating effects are small, we have to keep λ_T while conducting I_{dc}. On the other hand, to convert electrical energy taken from the applied V_0 into heat as Joule effect requires, a starting point is *to look for a way to load each carrier* with energy proportional to V_0^2 or for a way to convert each carrier into an *electrically reactive element sensing V_0* and storing an energy proportional to V_0^2 as a Susceptance driven by V_0 would do. This leads to consider the *electrical structure* of an electron in the CB as formed by a mobile *cloud* of charge $-q$ screening its corresponding positive charge $+q$ that would be *a sort of fixed density of charge distributed in the volume* of the resistor, both depending on lattice atoms, defects, etc. as well as on the Bloch functions that

define the wavefunction of this electron within the solid matter of the device. What matters is to realize that a "free carrier" in the CB is not a charged particle like an electron in vacuum, but a neutral charge structure to keep charge neutrality in the bulk region we are considering between terminals.

For an electron emitted to the lowest energy level or QS of the CB at $t = 0$, the first "image" of its associated charge density would be one with the $-q$ cloud of charge wrapping closely its corresponding $+q$ charge array, thus with a *good screening at each spatial point* within the resistor. This picture would correspond to a carrier very "cold", not yet in TE with its surrounding universe. It's easy to realize that this carrier can store electrical energy or has a Degree of Freedom to do it *by changing the average screening* between its $-q$ charge cloud and its $+q$ charge array. Thus, it will interact thermally with its environment by energy exchanges leading it to hold an average thermal energy of $kT/2$ J in the form of *an average, non-perfect screening* between the aforesaid $+q$ and $-q$ charges densities, a screening fluctuating randomly in time due to thermal activity. Using the *quantization of the electrical charge* no matter its spatial distribution in a QS of the CB, each *free electron in the CB* reacting as a sort of capacitance C_f with opposed charges $+q$ and $-q$ on its plates, would be *an energy carrier liable to load electrical energy* from the electric field sustained by the external generator of current I_{dc} that sets $V_0 \neq 0$ between terminals. Using Equipartition for this Degree of Freedom as we did for C in [4], the *average* capacitance C_f that thermal activity will set in each free electron of the CB will be obtained by equating the energy stored by this reactive Degree of Freedom: $U_f = q^2/(2C_f)$ to the thermal energy per degree of freedom $kT/2$. This gives:

$$\frac{1}{2}kT = \frac{q^2}{2C_f} \Rightarrow C_f = \frac{q^2}{kT} = \frac{q}{V_T} \qquad (14)$$

Equation (14) that we have obtained here in TE after having presented C_f, was first obtained as a way to extract the electrical power $p_i(t)$ from the resistor body without varying its noise, thus keeping λ_T. Assuming that the λ_T electrons per second reaching the contacts of the resistor were responsible for this extraction, the energy U_f that each electron had to bring was:

$$\frac{V_0^2}{R} = \lambda_T \times U_f \Rightarrow U_f = \frac{V_0^2}{\lambda_T \times R} \Rightarrow$$

$$U_f = \frac{1}{2} \times \frac{q^2}{kT} \times V_0^2 = \frac{1}{2} \times C_f \times V_0^2 \qquad (15)$$

an equation suggesting that this extraction was accomplished by electrons of charge q reaching the contacts thermally, but previously loaded with an energy U_f taken from V_0 as if they were capacitances C_f sensing V_0. From this idea, the meaning of C_f expressed by Equation (14) was obtained and the conversion of electrical energy from the external generator into heat was separated from the Dissipations associated to Fluctuations.

Therefore, when a free carrier of the CB leaves this band to *appear as a charge* $-q$ on the contact where it is collected, it stores an *energy Fluctuation* ΔU in C (*cause*) subsequently *Dissipated* by the DR it produces (*effect*) [4]. This produces the electrical noise observed in TE and out of TE provided the heating effect is low $\left(T^{*} \approx T\right)$. Out of TE, however, any energy brought by the free carrier in excess of ΔU, like U_f in Solid-State devices or kinetic energy of electrons moving in vacuum, can't be stored in C as a Fluctuation of electrical energy, thus being converted into heat. The noise power of a resistor in TE: $N = kT/(RC)$ W *is Dissipated* accordingly to the Fluctuation-Dissipation Theorem derived from [12], but the electrical power $S = p_i(t)$ entering the device out of TE *is Converted into heat* as explained. The loading of C_f with U_f or the passage of a carrier in the bottom of the CB to a level of higher energy, involve fluctuations of energy that, not being stored by the device (e.g. in its C) are not Fluctuations of energy liable to produce Dissipations in the sense of [4,12]. This *distinction between Dissipation and Conversion is essential to understand Phase Noise* in actual oscillators.

4. Conclusions

When a voltage $v(t)$ coming from positive feedback of $v(t)$ itself is clamped to a value close to a reference V_{Ref}, a NF called Clamping Feedback driven by an error signal v_ε appears. This way, the output voltage becomes: $V_0 = V_{Ref} + v_\varepsilon$ and since $v_\varepsilon \ll V_{Ref}$, this negative feedback is very strong for v_ε and its added noise. The action of this NF on small signals like noise added to the output amplitude is thus a High Damping effect aiming to remove them quickly. Due to this effect, the Dissipation of electrical energy that each DR carries out is accelerated, thus producing attenuation and broadening of the native noise spectrum so as to conserve the Gain×Bandwidth product. This situation coming from feedbacks at 0° and 180°, no longer holds when this NF becomes phase-locked to a carrier whose amplitude it has to keep in time. In this case, this Clamping Feedback finds 50% of noise power in-phase and 50% noise power in quadrature. Whereas the noise in phase is heavily damped as explained, the noise in quadrature confuses the Clamping Feedback in such a way that creates the Pedestal of electrical noise that appears in systems like Automatic Level Control and amplitude limiters used in electronic oscillators. Con-

cerning the electrical power (Signal power) that enters a resonator where a voltage V_0 is sustained in time by any means, it is Converted into heat without affecting its noise provided its heating effect is low. This will be quite the case for High-Q resonators whose small heating effect will be accounted for easily by the effective Noise Figure F of the oscillator loop.

REFERENCES

[1] J. I. Izpura, "On the Electrical Origin of Flicker Noise in Vacuum Devices," *IEEE Transactions on Instrumentation and Measurement*, Vol. 58, No. 10, 2009, pp. 3592-3601.

[2] J. I. Izpura, "1/f Electrical Noise in Planar Resistors: The Joint Effect of a Backgating Noise and an Instrumental Disturbance," *IEEE Transactions on Instrumentation and Measurement*, Vol. 57, No. 3, 2008, pp. 509-517.

[3] H. Nyquist, "Thermal Agitation of Electric Charge in Conductors," *Physical Review*, Vol. 32, 1928, pp. 110-113.

[4] J. I. Izpura, J. Malo, "A Fluctuation-Dissipation Model for Electrical Noise," *Circuits and Systems*, Vol. 2, No. 3, 2011, pp. 112-120.

[5] J. Malo and J. I. Izpura, "Feedback-Induced Phase Noise in Microcantilever-Based Oscillators," *Sensors and Actuators A*, Vol. 155, No. 1, 2009, pp. 188-194.

[6] J. Malo and J. I. Izpura, "Feedback-Induced Phase Noise in Resonator-Based Oscillators," *Proceedings of DCIS'09 Conference*, Zaragoza, November 2009, pp. 231-236. http://www.linkpdf.com/ebook-viewer.php?url=http://dcis2009.unizar.es/FILES/CR2/p5.pdf

[7] D. B. Leeson, "A Simple Model of Feedback Oscillator Noise Spectrum," *Proceedings of IEEE*, Vol. 54, 1966, pp. 329-330.

[8] D. Ham and A. Hajimiri, "Virtual Damping and Einstein Relation in Oscillators," *IEEE Journal of Solid-State Circuits*, Vol. 38, No. 3, 2003, pp. 407-418.

[9] A. Hajimiri and T. H. Lee, "A General Theory of Phase Noise in Electrical Oscillators," *IEEE Journal of Solid-State Circuits*, Vol. 33, No. 2, 1998, pp. 179-194.

[10] T. H. Lee and A. Hajimiri, "Oscillator Phase Noise: A Tutorial," *IEEE Journal of Solid-State Circuits*, Vol. 35, No. 3, 2000, pp. 326-336.

[11] http://www.ti.com/lit/an/slod006b/slod006b.pdf

[12] H. B. Callen and T. A. Welton, "Irreversibility and Generalized Noise," *Physical Review*, Vol. 83, No. 1, 1951, pp. 34-40.

8

Thermodynamical Phase Noise in Oscillators Based on *L-C* Resonators[*]

Javier Malo, Jose-Ignacio Izpura

Group of Microsystems and Electronic Materials (GMME-CEMDATIC), Universidad Politécnica de
Madrid (UPM), Madrid, Spain

ABSTRACT

Using a new Admittance-based model for electrical noise able to handle Fluctuations and Dissipations of electrical energy, we explain the phase noise of oscillators that use feedback around *L-C* resonators. We show that Fluctuations produce the Line Broadening of their output spectrum around its mean frequency f_0 and that the Pedestal of phase noise far from f_0 comes from Dissipations modified by the feedback electronics. The charge noise power $4FkT/R$ C^2/s that disturbs the otherwise periodic fluctuation of charge these oscillators aim to sustain in their *L-C-R* resonator, is what creates their phase noise proportional to Leeson's noise figure F and to the charge noise power $4kT/R$ C^2/s of their capacitance C that today's modelling would consider as the current noise density in A^2/Hz of their resistance R. Linked with this (A^2/Hz↔C^2/s) equivalence, R becomes a random series in time of discrete chances to Dissipate energy in Thermal Equilibrium (TE) giving a similar series of discrete Conversions of electrical energy into heat when the resonator is out of TE due to the Signal power it handles. Therefore, phase noise reflects the way oscillators sense thermal exchanges of energy with their environment.

Keywords: Phase Noise; Admittance-Based Noise Model; Fluctuation; Dissipation; Conversion into Heat

1. Introduction

In a previous paper under this title [1] we have shown that when a Positive Feedback (PF) building a voltage in a capacitor is counterbalanced by a Negative Feedback (NF) we called Clamping Feedback (CF), to keep such voltage close to a reference V_{Ref}, a Pedestal of electrical noise was generated. This Pedestal of 50% the amplitude of the native noise but wider bandwidth was due to the confusing action of the 50% noise the CF samples in quadrature with the carrier whose amplitude it aims to sustain in time. This is so because the CF implicit in the Automatic Level Control (ALC) systems or limiters of actual oscillators is phase-locked to the carrier whose amplitude it has to keep in time. This subtle effect was shown in a convenient resonator of $f_0 \rightarrow 0$, which was a capacitor of capacitance C shunted by a resistance R to account for its losses. Accordingly to [2], losses due to a conductance $G = 1/R$ are a random series of discrete opportunities in time to Dissipate electrical energy in Thermal Equilibrium (TE) and to Convert it into heat out of TE [1]. This resonator was used to build an "oscillator of $f_0 \rightarrow 0$" where it was easy to show that the ampli-

tude the CF keeps at each instant is the sum of V_{Ref} plus a small amplitude offset $v_\varepsilon \ll V_{Ref}$ that is the error signal driving the CF towards its goal: to counterbalance the excess of PF used during the start of the oscillator. When this counterbalance was achieved, this oscillator of $f_0 \rightarrow 0$ sustained a voltage $V_0 = V_{Ref} + v_\varepsilon(t) \approx V_{Ref}$ where $v_\varepsilon(t)$ was a constant average value $\langle v_\varepsilon(t) \rangle$ plus electrical noise superposed to it. The reference $V_{Ref}(t_n)$ that the CF needs at instant n to clamp the output amplitude was available from the reference $V_{Ref}(t_{n-1})$ at instant $n-1$ because $V_{Ref}(t_n) = V_{Ref}(t_{n-1})$ in this "convenient oscillator". This availability of $V_{Ref}(t_n)$, which is not possible when $f_0 \neq 0$ because it would require having in advance an electrical reference of the signal the oscillator is going to create, allowed us to show the origin of the aforesaid Pedestal of electrical noise of amplitude $2FkTR$ V^2/Hz. Whereas the 50% of noise power sampled in phase by the CF was heavily damped as expected, the 50% noise power sampled in quadrature (e.g. "midway" 0° for NF and 180° for PF) was enhanced by the CF and gave the aforesaid Pedestal. As we advanced in [1], a similar reasoning for $f_0 \neq 0$ would require a sinusoidal reference $V_{Ref}(t)$ whose generation in advance (e.g. just before to be used) didn't help to explain the noise Pedestal, whence it can be seen the usefulness of the "resonator

[*]Work supported by the Spanish CICYT under the MAT2010-18933 project, by the Comunidad Autónoma de Madrid through its IV-PRICIT Program, and by the European Regional Development Fund (FEDER).

of $f_0 \rightarrow 0$ " we handled in [1] for this purpose.

Shunting the R-C parallel circuit of a capacitor with a finite inductance $L \neq 0$ one gets an L-C-R parallel resonator whose resonance frequency $f_0 \neq 0$ allows oscillators repeating phase each $T_0 = 1/f_0$ seconds. Actually, this repetition exactly each T_0 seconds is impossible, thus meaning that the spectrum of their output signal won't give a "line" or $\delta(f - f_0)$ function. Instead, it will have a non null width due to the charge noise existing in the resonator at temperature T, as we will show. This noise coming from the charge noise of the lossy resonator and from the noise added by the electronics, both collected by Leeson through an effective noise figure F [3], has a *power* $4FkT/R$ C²/s [2]. This charge noise disturbing the otherwise periodic charge fluctuation of the lossless L-C resonator, not only justifies Leeson's empirical formula, but also explains the non null width (Line Broadening) of the output spectrum of this type of oscillators [4]. This is possible because the new model [2] not only considers *Dissipations* of electrical energy, but also *Fluctuations* of electrical energy in C that precede the former ones in an electrical Admittance.

Before handling resonators with $f_0 \neq 0$, let's recall that to sustain the amplitude of their output signal $v(t)$ in time endures *to sample $v(t)$* each T_0 seconds and the ALC system or limiter will react from this set of sampled data. Due to the phase noise (jitter in time domain) of the own amplitude thus generated, this sampling won't be done *exactly* each T_0 (or each $T_0/2$ seconds by sampling positive and negative peaks), although we will consider it as fast and accurate enough to allow the ALC system to handle properly amplitude changes with spectral content up to $f_0/2$ or up to f_0 by sampling each $T_0/2$, accordingly to Nyquist sampling theorem. The high speed this sampling rate could provide to the ALC system is not used in general because amplitude changes endure energy ones in the resonator. Since the quality factor Q_0 of an L-C-R resonator at its resonance frequency is: "π times the lifetime of its output voltage $v(t)$ measured in periods T_0", amplitude changes during one period in high-Q resonators will be small. Thus, the aforesaid sampling rate will work well for quartz resonators like that of [3], where Q_0 factors over 10^4 are often found. This allows considering that the CF associated to the ALC system or limiter works as expected and since these electromechanical resonators use to be studied by highly selective L-C-R circuits, our results can be applied to them easily.

2. Dissipation and Feedback-Induced Noise in an *L-C-R* Resonator

It's well known that the sinusoidal voltage and current existing at any frequency f in an electrical Susceptance are *in-quadrature*. To work in parallel mode let's use the

Admittance function of frequency $f = \omega/2\pi$ whose real part is Conductance $G(j\omega)$ and whose imaginary part is Susceptance $B(j\omega)$: $Y(j\omega) = G(j\omega) + jB(j\omega)$, where the imaginary unit j means that currents through $G(j\omega)$ and those through $B(j\omega)$ are in-quadrature. Considering a sinusoidal voltage existing between the two terminals of $Y(j\omega)$, currents through $B(j\omega)$ allow Fluctuations of electrical energy in $Y(j\omega)$ whereas those through $G(j\omega)$ lead to Dissipations of electrical energy [2]. This is the basis of the new model for electrical noise we will use for L-C-R resonators that agreeing with [5], is thus a Quantum-compliant model leading us to consider *Fluctuations* of electrical energy in the Susceptance of these resonators together with *Dissipations* of electrical energy associated to their Conductance $G = 1/R$.

Figure 1(a) shows an L-C-R parallel resonator with losses proportional to the energy stored in C at each instant $U_E(t) = Cv^2(t)/2$ because $p_i(t) = v^2(t)/R$ is the instantaneous power lost in R. Thus, the energy stored in magnetic form does not produce losses in this resonator. Although these *losses represented by R* may be due to a resistance R_S in series with the inductance L_S of an inductor shunting C, the circuit transform leading to the circuit of **Figure 1(a)** makes them equivalent to those of a lossy capacitor shunted by the lossless inductance L.

A native L_S-C-R_S series resonator is thus replaced by its parallel equivalent circuit of **Figure 1(a)** to use directly the new model of [2] for the electrical noise of the Ad-

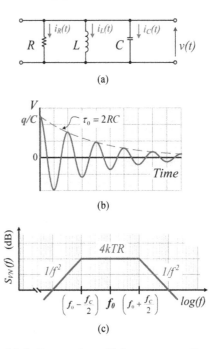

(a)

(b)

(c)

Figure 1. (a) *L-C* resonator with losses proportional to the energy stored in *C* at each instant; (b) Impulse response of this *L-C* resonator to a charge Fluctuation of one electron; (c) Unilateral spectrum of $v(t)$ (see text).

mittance formed by C and R in parallel. This noise comes from a random series of Thermal Actions (TA) that occur in C at an average rate λ_T (TAs per second), given by [2]:

$$\lambda_T = \frac{2kT}{Rq^2} \Rightarrow G = \frac{1}{R} = \lambda_T \frac{q}{2V_T} \qquad (1)$$

where q is the electronic charge and $V_T = kT/q$ is the thermal voltage at Temperature T.

Each TA triggers a Device Reaction (DR) aiming to remove the previous Fluctuation of energy in C due to the TA. The use of the parallel circuit of **Figure 1(a)**, whose noise will come from *Fluctuations of electrical energy*, has to do with the Cause-Effect or TA-DR pairs producing electrical noise in resistors and capacitors [2], where each TA is a charge noise of one electron. This TA or impulsive displacement current of weight q in C creates a voltage step $\Delta v = q/C$ V in C and thus in $v(t)$. **Figure 1(b)** shows the time evolution of $\Delta v(t)$ after a TA on C discharged previously, thus showing the DR of this lossy L-C resonator. This DR is a damped oscillation of angular frequency $\omega_0 = (LC)^{-1/2}$ rad/s and initial amplitude q/C V that can be built from the product of the exponential decay of **Figure 1(b)** of [1] with amplitude $V_0 = q/C$, by a cosine carrier of frequency f_0. Since these random DRs occur in time at the average rate λ_T of (1), the spectral content of the noise they will give will be like that of Figure 8(a) of [1], but around f_0 and with half its bandwidth due to the two times larger time constant ($2RC$) of **Figure 1(b)**. This is the noise spectrum of the L-C-R resonator without feedback shown in **Figure 1(c)**, that will differ from the noise spectrum under the action of the Positive (PF) and Negative (NF) Feedbacks we need to start these oscillators from noise and to keep them oscillating with constant amplitude in time, two tasks that we did in [1] by the counterbalance of an excess of PF by a CF in a convenient oscillator of $f_0 \to 0$.

With an output carrier of non null frequency $f_0 \neq 0$ (not the "dc carrier" used to show basic ideas on a CF in [1]) we can speak properly about noise that the CF finds in-phase with the carrier whose amplitude it keeps in time and about noise it finds in-quadrature with it. Added to this, a baseband noise of some kHz bandwidth only occupies a relative narrow band around a carrier with f_0 in the tens of MHz for example. This allows using a narrow-band approach around f_0 to speed calculations (e.g. the factor Q_0 of the L-C-R of **Figure 1(a)** is defined at f_0, but for $Q(f_0) = Q_0 = 100$, its value and meaning remains for a sideband frequency $1.001f_0$). From the above it isn't difficult to realize that a narrow-band CF *working synchronously with the carrier* at frequency $f_0 \neq 0$ will damp well the noise $2FkTR$ V^2/Hz it sees in phase, whereas the noise $2FkTR$ V^2/Hz it sees with phase error of $-90°$ will mislead it so as to create the Pedestal of $2FkTR$ V^2/Hz

around f_0 shown in [1]. We have to say that this Pedestal of noise that will lead to a *feedback-induced Pedestal of phase noise* was not considered in [6] because it is not the random modulation of f_0 that we called *Technical phase noise* in [1].

It is worth noting that the oscillating voltage of **Figure 1(b)** decays with $\tau_0 = 2RC$, not with $\tau_E = RC$ as one might expect from the R-C circuit used in [1]. The reason is that the energy stored in this L-C resonator not always gives voltage liable to Convert electrical energy into heat as it gave in the R-C circuit of [1]. Due to the (electric $\leftrightarrow$magnetic) exchange of energy existing in this resonator of $f_0 \to 0$, *the energy it contains only is in electrical form half the time on average*, as it is shown in **Figure 2** for a lossless L-C resonator. This is why the energy present in an L-C-R resonator with $f_0 \neq 0$ has two times larger lifetime ($\tau_U = RC$) than that of the energy present in the resonator with $f_0 \to 0$ studied in [1] that was $\tau_U = RC/2$. Hence, the noise spectrum of DRs taking place in the resonator of **Figure 1(a)** will have half the bandwidth (e.g. $f_c/2$ around f_0, see **Figure 3(b)**) of the bandwidth found in [1] for the baseband noise of the L-C-R parallel resonator with $L \to \infty$ that was $f_C = 1/(2\pi\tau)$ Hz around $f_0 \to 0$ (see **Figure 3(a)**).

Since the noise power Dissipated by R does not depend on the L shunting C because Equipartition sets the mean square voltage noise in C [2], the two spectra of **Figure 3** must have the same $4kTR$ V^2/Hz amplitude for $f_0 \gg f_C$ as it will happen in high-Q_0 resonators where $f_C \ll f_0$. This reasoning becomes less straightforward in low-Q_0 resonators where $f_C \approx f_0$ and they won't be considered for simplicity. The case with $f_0 \to 0$ of [1] can help in this case to sketch the aimed noise spectrum.

This reasoning giving directly the spectrum of thermal noise in L-C-R resonators considers that the energy each DR dissipates is no other than the Fluctuation of energy $\Delta U = q^2/(2C)$ stored by its preceding TA [2] and that the rate λ_T of TA-DR pairs only depends on R since λ_T defines G by (1). It's worth noting that $f_C/2 = f_0/(2Q_0)$

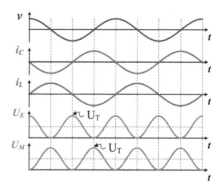

Figure 2. Voltage, currents and periodic Fluctuation at $2f_0$ of the electrical (U_E) and magnetic (U_M) energies when the resonator of Figure 1(a) has no losses (e.g. $R \to \infty$).

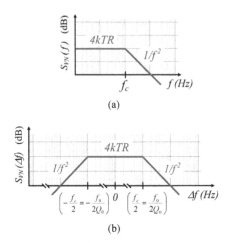

(a)

(b)

Figure 3. (a) Noise spectrum of the *L-C* resonator of Figure 1(a) when its $L \to \infty$; (b) Noise spectrum of the *L-C* resonator of Figure 1(a) when its $L > 0$ is finite.

in **Figure 3(b)** is the offset Δf from the carrier frequency f_0 where the Pedestal of Phase Noise [3,7,8] meets the Lorentzian line proposed in [4].

Mimicking what we did in [1] to sustain a dc voltage $v(t) = V_{Ref} + v_\varepsilon = V_0$ in C by a CF counterbalancing at each instant the excess of PF that had built $v(t)$ previously, let's use again those feedbacks to build a sinusoidal voltage $v(t)$ of amplitude V_0 in C from its own thermal noise and to sustain it in time once it has reached an amplitude close to a reference $V_{Ref}(t)$. Knowing that the ideal *L-C* resonator for which **Figure 2** applies would sustain a sinusoidal Fluctuation of electrical *energy* at $2f_0$ where $2\pi f_0 = (LC)^{-1/2}$, **Figure 4** shows the PF used to shunt an *L-C-R* resonator by a resistance $-R_{FB}$ to overcompensate its losses represented by R. This is done by feeding-back a current $iFB(t) = v(t)/R_{FB}$ by the network of transconductance $\beta_Y = -1/R_{FB}$ V/A, the same type of feedback used in Figure 4 of [1]. For $R_{FB} = R$, this PF would compensate exactly the power lost at each instant in R, thus the power lost in R at any f. Although this exact compensation will fail at high f because the finite bandwidth BW_{FB} of the feedback of **Figure 4**, it will work well at typical oscillation frequencies f_0, provided a fast enough electronics is used. Given that the effects of any phase error in the loop due to the finite BW_{FB} and its associated phase noise were shown in [6], we will consider this PF as perfectly in-phase at f_0.

To start the oscillator from thermal noise of C, the PF of **Figure 4** has to create a Gain > Losses condition in the loop (e.g. $1/R_{FB} > 1/R$). Comparing this **Figure 4** with **Figure 4** of [1] with a similar PF, we can see that the rectifier D_1 of [1] disappears due to the irrelevance of the sign of the first step $\pm q/C$ V of noise that, amplified by the PF during t_{start}, will build the oscillating $v(t)$ whose amplitude will drive the CF of the ALC system or limiter. Mimicking [1], a NF counterbalances the excess

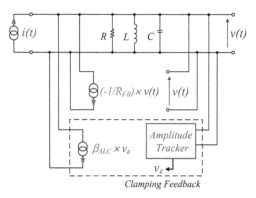

Figure 4. Feedback scheme of an oscillating loop around the *L-C* resonator of Figure 1(a) that uses PF to provide loop gain and NF to clamp the output amplitude (see text).

of PF once the aimed amplitude is reached. This is a CF whose implementation was discussed in [1] and that we will simplify by considering that an "amplitude tracker" gives the small error signal $v_\varepsilon = V_0 - V_{Ref}$ required to drive this CF. Without electrical noise, $v_\varepsilon(t)$ would be the difference between the sinusoidal signal $v(t)$ of amplitude V_0 and a reference signal of the same frequency and phase, but slightly lower amplitude V_{Ref} to generate this error signal. Thus, $v_\varepsilon(t)$ would be a sinusoidal signal synchronous with $v(t)$, with amplitude $v_\varepsilon \gg V_{Ref}$ The NF of $v_\varepsilon(t)$ through the transconductance β_{ALC} would counterbalance at each instant the excess of transconductance $\Delta\beta_Y$ used during t_{start}. Using the Clamping Factor of [1] given by $CL = V_{Ref}/v_\varepsilon \gg 1$ and considering that $\Delta\beta_Y$ is driven by $v(t)$, which is $(CL+1)$ times larger than the $v_\varepsilon(t)$ signal driving the CF (see Equation (8) in [1]), the aforesaid counterbalance requires:

$$(CL+1)\Delta\beta_Y = \beta_{ALC} \Rightarrow \beta_{ALC} = (CL+1) \times \frac{R - R_{FB}}{(R \times R_{FB})} \quad (2)$$

Thus, the transconductance β_{ALC} that feeds back negatively the resonator with the error signal $v_\varepsilon(t)$ will be much higher than the transconductance $\beta_Y = 1/R_{FB}$ that allows the reliable start of the oscillator (e.g. by a loop gain $T_{start} = 2$ as we used in [1]).

Accepting a 0.1% amplitude error and $T_{start} = 2$ (e.g. $R_{FB} = R/2$) like those values used in [1] we have: $CL = 10^3$. Using these values in (2) we find that the NF counterbalancing the excess of PF to clamp the output amplitude at $1.001 V_{Ref}$ will be shunting the resonator by a resistance $R_{DIF} = R/1001$. This will be so for any signal affecting $v_\varepsilon(t)$ as the random series of DRs that form the noise of C. Because DRs appear randomly in time, they endure 50% noise in-phase with $v_\varepsilon(t)$ or with the carrier to which the CF is phase-locked, and 50% noise in-quadrature with $v_\varepsilon(t)$ (recall **Figure 7** of [1]). Therefore, the 50% noise power born in-phase with the carrier will be highly damped by the CF (recall **Figure 8** of [1]) whereas the other 50%, (a Lorentzian or band-pass noise spectrum of density $2kTR$ V^2/Hz around f_0 with bandwidth f_c) will be enhanced by the broadening of its spectrum away from $\pm f_c/2$ [1] as shown in **Figure 5**. This is the Pedestal of electrical noise that will exist for separations from the carrier (Δf) higher than $f_C/2 = f_0/(2Q_0)$.

As we discuss in [1] the width of this Pedestal will depend on the factor Q_0 of the resonator and on the loop gain T_{start} and Clamping Factor CL used in the design of the oscillator. Added to this, the CL of a limiter would have to be taken in an average form, because as the output amplitude approaches its limit, the clamping action becomes harder. This means that the bandwidth of the Pedestal shown in **Figure 5** is design-dependent and that is why it has not been specified.

3. Fluctuation-Induced Noise in L-C Resonators: Thermal FSK or PSK Modulations

In the model for electrical noise of [2], the voltage noise coming from the DRs taking place in the resonator is the *Effect* whose *Cause* is the series of TAs appearing randomly at the average rate λ_T s^{-1} of (1). Since each DR comes from the *integration in time* of the impulsive current of each preceding TA, a possible Phase Modulation (PM) of the carrier by DRs will be equivalent to its Frequency Modulation (FM) by TAs. This way, the PM approach to Phase Noise of [4] and the FM one of [9] are well understood by the equivalence between FM due to a modulating signal $x_m(t)$ and PM due to the time integral of $x_m(t)$. Concerning noise, it's worth mentioning that when the *L-C-R* resonator is in Thermal Equilibrium (TE), its noise spectrum is that of **Figure 3(b)**. No noise figure F exists in this case because there is neither feedback electronics nor heating effects that could increase resonator's temperature $(T^* > T)$ as we discuss in [1]. When the PF and CF of the loop balance mutually to sustain the output amplitude V_0, the noise increases by F and also split into the damped noise and Pedestal of **Figure 5**, which shows *noise with reference to TE* (a native spectrum of density $4kTR$ V^2/Hz increased by the noise of the electronics and by any small heating effect $T^* > T$, both included in F) *together with two noises that only exist out of TE* when the resonator stores the energy

U_E corresponding to the amplitude V_0 of $v(t)$.

Since $v(t)$ is quite a sinusoid let's have some figures by using $v(t) = V_0 \times \sin(2\pi f_0 t)$. Therefore, the energy stored in the resonator is: $U_E = CV_0^2/2$ J and the average power converted into heat by R (e.g. the mean power leaving the resonator as heat) is: $P_0 = V_0^2/(2R)$. This leakage of energy per unit time is the price we pay to store U_E in this resonator out of TE. Another price we pay concerns the purity of the voltage $v(t)$ on C because the aimed *exchange of energy at $2f_0$* shown in **Figure 2** will be disturbed by the thermal interaction between the resonator and its environment. This exchange of energy represented by R is carried out by a *charge noise* [2] disturbing the otherwise periodic exchange of charge between L and C that would give the sinusoid of V_0 volts peak (or CV_0 Coulombs peak) we aim to have in C. Considering the distinction made in [1] between power *Converted* into heat and power *Dissipated* by DRs we can leave aside the power $P_0 = V_0^2/(2R)$ assuming that the small heating of the resonator it will produce $(T^* > T)$ will be included in F. Having considered the *effects due to Dissipations of energy in the electrical noise* of the loop, we have to consider now the *effects due to each Fluctuation of electrical* energy preceding each Dissipation because both processes endure a charge noise associated with Displacement Currents (DiC) in C that disturb its otherwise periodic Fluctuation of charge coming from the energy exchange between magnetic and electric susceptances in an *L-C* resonator. The factor 2 we had to use in [1] to obtain the charge noise power of a series of current pulses mimicking fat TAs, reflected these two charge noises. To say it bluntly, each fast DiC of weight q in C due to a TA is followed by an opposed and slower DiC of equal weight q and opposed sense linked with its DR. This is why phase noise is a nice scenario to test the validity of the Quantum-compliant model of [2], which was able to explain $1/f$ excess noise [10] and flicker noise [11] as consequences of thermal noise.

Considering that the damping of a DR during a period of $v(t)$ is small, **Figure 6** shows the Phase and Amplitude changes that a TA produces in the otherwise sinusoidal signal $v(t)$ when it occurs at instant $t = \alpha$ within one period T_0. It's worth realizing that a null damping of this DR triggered by a TA would mean that this resonator has no losses, but having suffered a TA it must be lossy [2]. This contradiction, however, is solved by considering that the damping of a DR in a resonator with only one TA per period (e.g. $\lambda_T/f_0 \approx 1$) would be vanishingly small: Using (1) at room T, a $Q_0 \approx 0.3$ C/q would appear. Thus, **Figure 6** is undistinguishable from the true one for typical *L-C-R* resonators with $Q_0 > 50$ for example. Since each TA is a charge noise of one electron in C, it always gives the same voltage shift $\pm q/C$ V no matter the instant α it takes place. However, the *Amplitude Modulation*

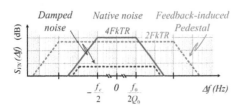

Figure 5. Noise spectra of the *L-C* resonator of Figure 4 (dotted lines) together with the noise it had in Thermal Equilibrium (solid line) without feedbacks (see text).

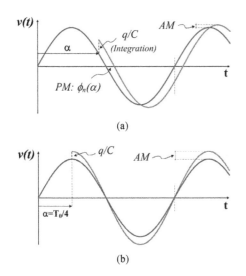

Figure 6. Effects of a Thermal Action in the capacitance of the *L-C* oscillator of Figure 4 when the damping of this Fluctuation of energy is small during one period (see text).

(AM) it produces depends on α [7,8], reaching its maximum for $\alpha = T_0/4$ or $\alpha = 3T_0/4$, when the charge in C has its peak value $Q_p = CV_0$ C. From typical circuit values we can say that this non null AM is negligible however, because in an *L-C* tank with $C = 16$ pF and $V_0 = 10$ V, the peak charge appearing in one of the plates of C is: $Q_p = 1.6 \times 10^{-10}$ C, thus $N \approx 10^9$ electrons. The change of ± 1 electron in N at $\alpha = T_0/4$ by a TA would be an AM of 0.001 parts per million (-180 dB) that would be lower for AM due to TAs taking place at other instants. Thus, we won't consider this AM in this introductory paper on phase noise, although it can play a role in high-frequency, low-power oscillators.

The spectrum of the output signal will contain both the Damped and the Feedback-induced Pedestal of noise shown in **Figure 5**, although the former will be buried by the Pedestal. Added to them there will be a high line *at f_0* due to the "carrier" whose amplitude is kept by the CF or better said: *a broadened line around f_0*, because **Figure 6** shows an undeniable *Phase Modulation* (PM) for each TA, except for two among millions that could take place *exactly* at $\alpha = T_0/4$ or $\alpha = 3T_0/4$. Since each TA displaces one electron in C, it shifts its voltage by $\Delta v = \pm q/C$ V depending on its sign and the oscillation continues with new amplitude A and phase $(\omega_0 t + \phi \Delta)$. Thus we have:

$$A\sin\left(\omega_0 t + \Delta\phi\right) = V_0 \sin\left(\omega_0 t\right) \pm \frac{q}{C} \quad (3)$$

Since each TA is an impulsive current unable to change the magnetic energy stored in the resonator (this requires some elapsed time), it only will modify the instantaneous energy of C to pass its charge $Q(t)$ to $Q(t) \pm q$ C. The associated energy change is therefore:

$$\Delta U_{TA} = \frac{\left(Q(t)\pm q\right)^2}{2C} - \frac{\left(Q(t)\right)^2}{2C}$$

$$= \frac{q^2}{2C} \pm \frac{2qQ(t)}{2C} = \frac{q^2}{2C} \pm qV_0 \sin\left(\omega_0 t\right) \quad (4)$$

thus equal to the Fluctuation $\Delta U = q^2/(2C)$ J needed to displace one electron between plates of C (or to break charge neutrality separating $+q$ and $-q$ charges in C) plus the energy required to move a charge q in a region where charge neutrality already was broken by opposed charges like the dipolar charge of C that is the source of its voltage $V_0 \sin\left(\omega_0 t\right)$ between terminals.

The very different scale for ΔU and qV_0 in actual circuits appears by considering their ratio $qV_0/\Delta U = 2N$, for N being the peak number of electrons in one of the plates of C. For $C = 16$ pF and $V_0 = 5$ V we have: $qV_0/\Delta U = 10^9$, thus meaning that the addition of one electron to the negative plate of this circuit needs a 10^9 times higher energy than the Fluctuation of energy ΔU required to displace one electron between the plates of C with $V_0 = 0$. This huge value raises this question: *Where comes from this huge energy when a TA makes an electron to appear as a charge $-q$ on the negative plate of C?* A likely source is $U_f = C_f V_0^2/2$ [1], a big energy the free electron had in the Conduction Band (CB) just before being captured or collected by the negative plate. The ratio $U_f/qV_0 = V_0/(2V_T) \approx 100$ at room T suggests that to appear as a charge $-q$ at the negative plate of C with $V_0 = 5$ V, the electron borrows a small fraction (1%) of the energy U_f it had as a free carrier in the CB, thus releasing only $0.99 U_f$ J as heat in the negative plate that collects it. For a TA of opposed sign in which the electron appeared as a charge $-q$ at the positive plate of C with $V_0 = 5$ V, an energy $1.01 U_f$ J would be released as heat on the positive plate on its arrival (e.g. the energy U_f it had as a free carrier in the CB plus the energy acquired from the electric field in C by an electron passing from its negative plate to its positive one).

Due to the equal probability for positive and negative TAs, the average energy Converted into heat by each TA is U_f and this account well for Joule effect accordingly to [1]. Continuing our reasoning from (4), the new amplitude A of the oscillation after a TA will come from this energy balance:

$$\frac{1}{2}CA^2 = \frac{1}{2}CV_0^2 + \frac{q^2}{2C} \pm qV_0 \sin\left(\omega_0 t\right) \quad (5)$$

From (4) and (5), the phase shift $\Delta\phi$ produced by a TA occurring at time t within the period is [12]:

$$\Delta\phi = \arcsin\left(\frac{V_0 \sin\left(\omega_0 t\right) \pm \dfrac{q}{C}}{A = \sqrt{V_0^2 + \dfrac{q^2}{C^2} \pm \dfrac{2q}{C}V_0 \sin\left(\omega_0 t\right)}}\right) - \left(\omega_0 t\right) \quad (6)$$

Using N, the peak number of electrons accumulated in the negative plate of C without TAs, (6) becomes:

$$\Delta\phi = \arcsin\left(\frac{N\sin(\omega_0 t)\pm 1}{A = \sqrt{N^2 + 1 \pm 2N\sin(\omega_0 t)}}\right) - (\omega_0 t) \quad (7)$$

Because TAs have the same probability to increase N than to decrease it, the average phase shift resulting from (7) for the λ_T TAs per second given by (1) is null, but this is not so for *the mean square phase shift* due to the huge amount of TAs taking place within a period $T_0 = 1/f_0$ of the output signal. Although it's easy to show that for N values like those found in actual oscillators (e.g. $N > 10^6$) an increment or decrement of one electron gives a similar $\Delta\phi$ shift with opposed sign, we prefer to use the equal number of positive and negative TAs on average to add the square of (7) for a positive TA (e.g. with its $\pm$ signs replaced by $+$ signs) to the square of (7) with its $\pm$ signs replaced by $-$ ones, thus obtaining *twice the mean square phase shift* of a TA taking place at time t in C. Representing half this sum in the first quarter of period ($0 \le \omega_0 t \le \pi/2$) we obtain the *s-curve* shown in **Figure 7** by a solid line that represents the *square phase shift due to a TA occurring at time $t = \alpha$* within the first quarter of period of the output signal.

For $N > 20$, this averaging of positive and negative TAs is numerically irrelevant and one can take directly the *s-curve* of **Figure 7** from *the square* of (7) for any sign of TAs. The dashed line of **Figure 7** is the linear approximation to the *s-curve* that shows quickly that its mean value in this quarter of period is half its maximum value for $\omega_0 t = 0$, thus $1/2N^2$. Since this *s-curve* and $\Delta\phi(\omega_0 t) = \left[1 + \cos(2\omega_0 t)\right]/(2N^2)$ fit very well, we can integrate directly $\Delta\phi(\omega_0 t)$ to obtain the same mean value. Therefore, the *mean square phase modulation* (PM) of each TA is:

$$\left\langle(\Delta\phi)^2\right\rangle = \frac{1}{2}\times\left(\frac{q}{C\times V_0}\right)^2 = \frac{q^2}{2\times V_0^2 \times C^2} = \frac{1}{2N^2} \quad (8)$$

Although (8) is the mean square PM expected for TAs

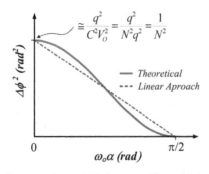

Figure 7. Square phase-shift due to a Thermal Action as a function of the instant α where it takes place (solid line) and its linear fitting giving its mean square phase shift $1/(2N^2)$.

occurring in the first quarter of the period, the mean square PM expected for TAs occurring in other quarters is the same because the s-curve for $\pi/2 \le \omega_0 t \le \pi$ is the mirror image of **Figure 7** around $\pi/2$, thus an s-curve increasing from zero to $1/N^2$. Since (1) is the rate of TAs giving the *charge noise power* $4kT/R$ C^2/s of the capacitance C [2] (usually taken as the noise density $4kT/R$ A^2/Hz *of the resistance R*) the extra noise added by the feedback electronics, collected by the effective Noise Figure F used in [3], leads to multiply (1) by F to collect all the TAs disturbing the resonator per unit time. Thus, the mean square Phase Modulation accumulated during one period T_0 by $F\lambda_T$ TAs per second disturbing the otherwise sinusoidal carrier of amplitude V_0, will be:

$$F\times\lambda_T\times T_0\times<(\Delta\phi)^2> = F\times\frac{2\pi}{Q_0}\times\frac{kT/2}{U_E} \quad (9)$$

when a period finishes, a new one starts and the phase modulation accumulated in the finished period is lost. Thus the way the phase of $v(t)$ is degraded by TAs *as time passes within each period* will be:

$$\left\langle\phi_n^2(t)\right\rangle = F\lambda_T\left\langle(\Delta\varphi)^2\right\rangle t = F\times\frac{kT}{C}\times\frac{1}{V_0^2\times RC}\times t \quad (10)$$

This linear dependence with time comes from the cuasi-linear, cuasi-continuous accumulation of TAs as time passes due to its huge rate $F\lambda_T$. Considering now the Phase Noise model of [4], *where the Phase in an ensemble of many identical oscillators subjected to white noise diffuses in time*, we can consider that this diffusion is a Wiener process whose mean square is given by Equation (3) of [4], which is:

$$\left\langle\phi_n^2(t)\right\rangle = 2\times D\times t \quad (11)$$

Thus, this nice model for an ensemble of M identical L-C oscillators subjected to white noise is formally equal to our single L-C-based oscillator subjected to the white charge noise of [2]. Identifying terms in (10) and (11) we have:

$$D^* = F\times\frac{kT}{C}\times\frac{1}{V_0^2\times 2RC}$$
$$= \frac{F}{2}\times\frac{kT}{C}\times\frac{1}{V_0^2}\times\frac{\omega_0}{Q_0} = \frac{F}{2}\times D \quad (12)$$

that gives the phase diffusion constant D found in Equation (21) of [4], but multiplied by $F/2$. This discrepancy concerning F comes from the fact that oscillators used in the theoretical ensemble of [4] have perfect electronics ($F = 1$), but the discrepancy concerning the factor $1/2$ is more subtle because it is the factor $1/2$ that appears for *the average efficiency of TAs to modulate the Phase of the carrier depending on the instant* α *where they take place* (see **Figure 7**). Therefore, let's replace the *phase* *diffusion constant D* handled in [4] by our *phase degradation constant* D^* given by (12) that is $F/2$ times higher (although its physical meaning is similar) in order to use Equation (3) of [4] for the Lorentzian line that gives the spectral content of the output signal $v(t)$ of our oscillator. Doing it and for D^* given in rad/s, we obtain:

$$S_V(\Delta\omega) = V_0^2 \times \frac{D^*}{(\Delta\omega)^2 + (D^*)^2} = \frac{V_0^2}{D^*} \times \frac{1}{1 + \left(\frac{\Delta\omega}{D^*}\right)^2} \quad (13)$$

where $\Delta\omega$ is 2π times the frequency offset $\Delta f = f - f_0$ from the central frequency f_0 taken as carrier frequency (see below (3) of [4] for example), although the spectrum of $v(t)$ is not monochromatic, but a Lorentzian line having a -3 dB bandwidth $BW_C = D^*/\pi$ Hz around f_0 as (13) shows. Moreover, given the *integration in time* done by C of each impulsive displacement current or TA to give a voltage step $\Delta v = q/C$ *modulating in phase* the "carrier" of static frequency f_0, what we have described is the *Frequency Modulation* (FM) of this carrier at f_0 by the impulsive current noise of the TAs. To say it bluntly: the displacement currents generating electrical noise [2] modulate in frequency the aimed carrier of static frequency f_0 and this shows vividly that $v(t)$ is not a pure sinusoidal carrier giving a spectral line at f_0, but a FM carrier whose frequency $f(t)$ wanders randomly with time around f_0, tracking the random wandering around zero of the noise current of spectral density $4FkT/R$ A²/Hz that reflects the thermal noise of C. This noise includes the Nyquist noise traditionally assigned to R, the noise coming from the feedback electronics and the extra noise coming from the unavoidable heating of the resonator Converting into heat a power $P_0 = V_0^2/(2R)$ W on average when it stores the energy U_E fluctuating at $2f_0$.

Equation (13) gives the spectral dispersion $S_V(\Delta\omega)$ of the mean-square carrier voltage $V_0^2/2$ of $v(t)$ due to the effect of TAs (*Fluctuations*) creating electrical noise in C [2]. Therefore, $S_V(\Delta\omega)$ is a spectral density with the same units V²/Hz of the noise density $S_{NV}(\Delta\omega)$ coming from energy *Dissipations* shown in **Figure 5**. Integrating (13) from $\Delta\omega \to -\infty$ to $\Delta\omega \to +\infty$ we obtain: $V_0^2/2$, thus indicating that the mean Signal power $P_0 = V_0^2/(2R)$ converted into heat by R that we have calculated considering $v(t)$ as perfectly sinusoidal, is scattered in a line of non null width around f_0. It is worth noting that (13) nothing says about the small, but not null AM of $v(t)$ already discussed concerning **Figure 6**. A possible reason is that an AM lower than one electron in $N \approx 10^8 - 10^9$ is a residual AM lying below -180 dB from V_0 itself taken as 0 dB reference, although perhaps the reason is a deeper one because this residual AM disappears when the quantization of charge for each TA is neglected, as it would do a noise model unaware about the discrete nature of the electrical charge. In any case,

the power density $S_V(\Delta\omega)$ near f_0 is so high, that the noise sidebands due to this residual AM will be overridden by it in the same way the feedback-induced Pedestal overrides the damped noise in **Figure 5**.

The random noise added by the TA-DR pairs to the sinusoidal $v(t)$ of **Figure 6** also can be handled by a small, randomly-oriented, noise vector A_N, added to a big phasor of amplitude V_0 rotating uniformly in time at f_0 times per second to represent a "carrier" of static frequency f_0. This noise vector can be decomposed into a small noise vector A_{AM} *along* the phasor that represents a random AM of the carrier, and a small noise vector A_{PM} *orthogonal* to the phasor that represents random PM of the carrier. Due to the random orientation of A_N, there is equal probability for A_{AM} and A_{PM} at each instant, thus meaning that the native noise density $4FkTR$ V²/Hz of **Figure 5** (e.g. that of the resonator without feedback), would contain a 50% Amplitude noise and 50% Phase noise added to the carrier. Whereas the ALC system or amplitude limiter would reduce (by design) the 50% AM noise quite effectively, the remaining 50% Phase noise would mislead this system it in such a way that its $2FkTR$ V²/Hz density would be extended up to frequencies well above $f_0/(2Q_0)$, being this the Pedestal of electrical noise shown in **Figure 5**. We could say that the Pedestal of noise of **Figure 5** only is *Phase noise of the resonator amplified by the ALC system* or limiter designed to reduce amplitude noise because electrical noise contains both Amplitude as well as Phase noise when the ALC system is phased locked to a frequency $f_0 \neq 0$.

The Pedestal of $2FkTR$ V²/Hz shown in **Figure 5** leads to the Pedestal of Phase noise shown in **Figure 8**, where it appears together with $S_V(\Delta\omega)$ given by (13), *both normalized by the mean-square carrier voltage $V_0^2/2$* in order to have the familiar single-sideband spectral density of Phase Noise $L\{\Delta\omega\}$ found in Equation (12) of [7] for example. Using (12) in (13) to find the frequency offset Δf_{F-D} where $S_V(\Delta\omega)$ drops down to $2FkTR$ V²/Hz or where the phase noise due to Fluctuations of energy in C and the phase noise due to Dissipations of energy in R modified by the feedback are equal, we obtain:

$\Delta f_{F-D} = f_0/(2Q_0)$ as shown in **Figure 8**. This result harmonizes the Line Broadening proposed in [4] with Lesson's formula concerning the transition from a region where phase noise varies as $1/(\Delta\omega)^2$ to a Pedestal of Phase Noise far from f_0 [3]. Added to the above, Leeson also gave a region where Phase Noise passed to vary as $1/(\Delta\omega)^3$ as we approach more f_0 [3], a region that does not appear in **Figure 8**. This is so because we haven't considered yet "coloured noises" like those coming from the resistance noise known as excess noise in Solid-State devices [10] or from the flux noise known as flicker noise in vacuum devices [11] that we are going to consider next.

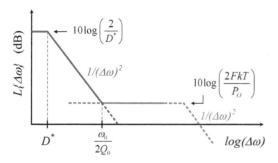

Figure 8. Lorentzian line of phase noise ("carrier" line) due to Thermal Actions in C, together with the phase noise pedestal generated by the clamping feedback (see text).

Recalling what we wrote about (13): that its Lorentzian Line reflects a FM of the carrier of frequency f_0 by a noise of flat spectrum that is F times the Nyquist noise current usually assigned to R, we can explain easily the region of Phase Noise varying as $1/(\Delta\omega)^3$ that appears in oscillators, especially in those using resonators of high Q_0 (thus $D^* \to 0$) and with electronics bearing $1/f$-like noise below some frequency f_{CN}, no matter if it is excess noise (resistance noise in Solid-State devices [10]) or flicker noise (flux noise in vacuum ones [11]). As we wrote under (13), the output power of the oscillator appears within a –3 dB bandwidth $BW_C = D^*/\pi$ Hz around f_0. From (12), the constant D^* for resonators with high Q_0 values is correspondingly low. This is why the phase noise found in these oscillators uses to be the region of (13) where it is proportional to $1/(\Delta\omega)^2$, a "skirt" of Phase Noise that drops down to the Pedestal as $\Delta\omega$ increases for $\Delta\omega \gg D^*$. Let's consider the Phase Noise of these oscillators that use high Q_0 resonators when the flat spectrum of noise that modulates in Frequency the carrier is filtered previously by a *low-pass filter* with cut-off frequency $f_{col} = \omega_{col}/(2\pi) < f_0/(2Q_0)$.

Figure 9(a) shows the spectrum of this filtered noise modulating the carrier of static frequency f_0 and **Figure 9(b)** shows the Phase Noise spectrum it produces. The Phase Noise roll-off changes from $1/(\Delta\omega)^2$ for $\Delta\omega < \omega_{col}$ to $1/(\Delta\omega)^4$ for $\Delta\omega > \omega_{col}$, an effect due to the integration of the modulating signal that precedes the Phase Modulation in a Frequency Modulator. This integration in t leads to a term inversely proportional to the modulating frequency f_m, whose effect in the phase noise spectrum appears at $\Delta\omega = \omega_m$. Hence, the flat spectrum of the modulating signal gives phase noise proportional to $1/(\Delta\omega)^2$ whereas the region whose power density drops as $1/(\omega_m)^2$ gives phase noise proportional to $1/(\Delta\omega)^4$. From this fact, it is easy to understand that a sum of the above low-pass filtered signals will give a sum of Phase Noise spectra like that of **Figure 9(b)**, because the FM modulator we are handling is *linear and time-invariant*. With our new noise model [2] we don't need to abandon time-invariance as it is done in [7,8].

Thus, a sum of low-pass filtered noise spectra like those of **Figure 10(a)** that synthesize a region of $1/f$ noise, will give the Phase Noise spectrum of **Figure 10(b)** with a region of Phase Noise proportional to $1/(\Delta f)^3$, as the empirical one reported by Leeson [3].

Considering that the $1/f$ noise of Solid-State devices is synthesized in the way shown in **Figure 10(a)** [10] and that the flicker noise of vacuum tubes with $1/f^\xi$ with $\xi \approx 1$ also comes from a similar synthesis process [11],

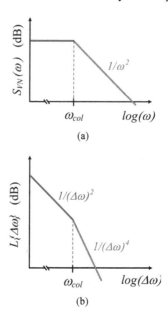

Figure 9. (a) Low-pass filtered white noise modulating in frequency (FM) a carrier of static frequency f_0; (b) Energy spectrum of the FM carrier thus obtained represented as Phase Noise around f_0 (see text).

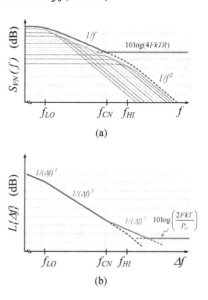

Figure 10. (a) White noise together with $1/f$ excess noise that modulate in frequency (FM) a carrier of static frequency f_0; (b) Energy spectrum of the modulated carrier represented as Phase Noise around f_0 (see text).

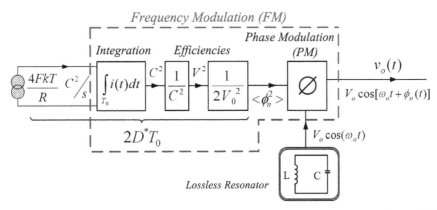

Figure 11. Embedded FM modulator existing in oscillators based on L-C resonators due to the Thermal Actions that the new model for electrical noise identifies with the charge noise power $4FkT/R$ C^2/s existing in C at temperature T due to its losses represented by R and to its noise figure F.

we have shown the origin of Phase Noise varying as $1/(\Delta f)^3$. As a way to show the mechanism giving the Line Broadening of the output spectrum of oscillators based in L-C resonators, **Figure 11** summarizes the Charge Controlled Oscillator (CCO) we have when we use an L-C resonator and feedback electronics aiming to sustain a periodic Charge Fluctuation at f_0 in this resonator at temperature T. This CCO models the Line Broadening around f_0 of these oscillators that will be a Lorentzian line for white current noise and that will have another shape if the current noise modulating the carrier is "coloured" noise. This Phase Noise around f_0 is the random Phase Modulation of the carrier by DRs (or its random FM by TAs) that one obtains neglecting the decay of each DR within one period of $v(t)$, thus being valid for resonators with negligible Dissipation (e.g. $Q_0 > 50$). Since each DR really decays as it dissipates the electrical energy stored in C by its preceding Fluctuation or TA, these random decays also generate electrical noise of bandwidth $\pm f_C/2$ around f_0 whose power in-quadrature with the output signal mislead the CF designed to reduce amplitude noise, thus producing the Pedestal of phase noise $2FkT/P_0$ that accompanies their carrier Line Broadening and that the FM modulator of **Figure 11** does not take into account.

4. Conclusions

Using a new model for electrical noise based on Fluctuation-Dissipation of electrical energy in an Admittance, the Phase Noise of resonator-based oscillators is explained as a simple consequence of thermal noise. The discrete Fluctuations of energy involving single electrons produce the observed Line Broadening whereas the noise associated to subsequent Dissipations modified by the feedback electronics, lead to the Phase Noise Pedestal far from the "carrier". Therefore, a monochromatic carrier of static frequency f_0 never is obtained and the oscillator's

output corresponds to a Frequency Modulated carrier of central frequency f_0 whose instantaneous frequency $f(t)$ wanders randomly with time around f_0, tracking the random wandering of the noise current of density $4FkT/R$ A^2/Hz that collects the noise of the resonator, its electronics and the extra noise due to any heating effect due to the Signal power converted into heat in the resonator. In summary: Phase Noise shows the way the oscillator senses the charge noise power $4FkT/R$ C^2/s that exists in its L-C resonator while it stores the energy corresponding to the output signal it sustains in time because these oscillators always are CCOs driven by the charge noise of their capacitance.

REFERENCES

[1]   J. I. Izpura and J. Malo, "Thermodynamical Phase Noise in Oscillators Based on L-C Resonators (Foundations)," *Circuits and Systems*, 2011, Article in Press.

[2]   J. I. Izpura and J. Malo, "A Fluctuation-Dissipation Model for Electrical Noise," *Circuits and Systems*, Vol. 2, No. 3, 2011, pp. 112-120.

[3]   D. B. Leeson, "A Simple Model of Feedback Oscillator Noise Spectrum," *Proceedings of IEEE*, Vol. 54, 1966, pp. 329-330.

[4]   D. Ham and A. Hajimiri, "Virtual Damping and Einstein Relation in Oscillators," *IEEE Journal of Solid-State Circuits*, Vol. 38, No. 3, 2003, pp. 407-418.

[5]   H. B. Callen and T. A. Welton, "Irreversibility and Generalized Noise," *Physical Review*, Vol. 83, No. 1, 1951, pp. 34-40.

[6]   J. Malo and J. I. Izpura, "Feedback-Induced Phase Noise in Microcantilever-Based Oscillators," *Sensors and Actuators A*, Vol. 155, No. 1, 2009, pp. 188-194.

[7]   T. H. Lee and A. Hajimiri, "Oscillator Phase Noise: A Tutorial," *IEEE Journal of Solid-State Circuits*, Vol. 35, No. 3, 2000, pp. 326-336.

[8]   A. Hajimiri and T. H. Lee, "A General Theory of Phase Noise in Electrical Oscillators," *IEEE Journal of Solid-State Circuits*, Vol. 33, No. 2, 1998, pp. 179-194.

[9]   E. Hegazi, J. Rael and A. Abidi, "The Design Guide to High Purity Oscillators," Kluwer Academic, New York, 2005.

[10] J. I. Izpura, "1/f Electrical Noise in Planar Resistors: The Joint Effect of a Backgating Noise and an Instrumental Disturbance," *IEEE Transactions on Instrumentation and Measurement*, Vol. 57, No. 3, 2008, pp. 509-517.

[11] J. I. Izpura, "On the Electrical Origin of Flicker Noise in Vacuum Devices," *IEEE Transactions on Instrumentation and Measurement*, Vol. 58, No. 10, 2009, pp. 3592-3601.

[12] J. Malo, "Contribución al diseño de lazos de reali- mentación Electrónica para sistemas electromecánicos (MEMS) resonantes: ruido de fase generado en lazos osciladores por sus realimentaciones," PhD. Thesis, Chapter III (in Spanish) Universidad Politécnica de Madrid, Madrid, Article in Press, 2012, pp. 70-145.

9

Floquet Eigenvectors Theory of Pulsed Bias Phase and Quadrature Harmonic Oscillators

Fabrizio Palma, Stefano Perticaroli
Department of Information Engineering, Electronics and Telecommunications, Sapienza Università di Roma, Rome, Italy

ABSTRACT

The paper presents an analytical derivation of Floquet eigenvalues and eigenvectors for a class of harmonic phase and quadrature oscillators. The derivation refers in particular to systems modeled by two parallel RLC resonators with pulsed energy restoring. Pulsed energy restoring is obtained through parallel current generators with an impulsive characteristic triggered by the resonators voltages. In performing calculation the initial hypothesis of the existence of stable oscillation is only made, then it is verified when both oscillation amplitude and eigenvalues/eigenvectors are deduced from symmetry conditions on oscillator space state. A detailed determination of the first eigenvector is obtained. Remaining eigenvectors are hence calculated with realistic approximations. Since Floquet eigenvectors are acknowledged to give the correct decomposition of noise perturbations superimposed to the oscillator space state along its limit cycle, an analytical and compact model of their behavior highlights the unique phase noise properties of this class of oscillators.

Keywords: Floquet Eigenvectors Noise Decomposition; Phase and Quadrature Oscillators; Pulsed Bias Oscillator; Oscillator Phase Noise

1. Introduction

Quadrature oscillators may represent important components of integrated digital modulations transceivers. The huge demand for wireless communications has indeed led to develop compact and low power circuits in order to reduce both implementation costs and devices consumptions. The need of precise quadrature signals can be found for example in low-IF or direct conversion mo-demodulator architectures. A quadrature oscillator can easily fit such request avoiding the use of a dedicated circuitry in conjunction with a single standard oscillator. However there are still many issues with quadrature oscillators concerning in particular the relation between phase noise and quadrature error [1]. In authors opinion, quadrature oscillators should be regarded a coupled system in the whole and this aspect increment the difficult of a theoretical noise treatment.

In this paper we propose to achieve a full analysis of a new phase-quadrature architecture based on pulsed bias we recently presented in [2]. This aim matches with the general effort toward the reduction of phase noise in oscillators. Stimulated from the idea of Hajimiri-Lee [3] and even dating back from the Colpitts oscillator, pulsed bias in oscillators represents a new attractive solution attempting to concentrate the necessary energy refill in

the portion of the oscillator limit cycle where noise projection on the first Floquet eigenvector (thus the contribution to the phase noise close to the fundamental) is minimum.

The main properties of this class of harmonic oscillators architecture are derived through an analytical treatment based on Floquet eigenvectors noise decomposition. Floquet eigenvectors approach is indeed acknowledged as a correct analytical methodology for the description of noise perturbations [4].

In addition Coram [5] remarked that the correct noise decomposition is obtained following eigenvectors relative orientation. Floquet eigenvectors determination is then necessary in order to produce a consistent noise analysis. We notice that, since in a pulsed bias architecture the pulse itself modifies eigenvectors, even the choice of an eventual optimal position of the bias pulse is not simply determinable [6]. Hence the calculation we present must take into account the mutual dependence of bias pulse and eigenvectors. Following this approach we derive an analytical formulation which allows to point out some important properties of this class of oscillators:

1) the orthogonal dynamic of coupled oscillators;

2) the minimization of noise introduced by the bias pulse due to minimum projection on first eigenvector;

3) the intrinsic orthogonality of eigenvectors which

ensures minimization of noise contribution from parasitic resistances in resonators.

2. Oscillator Model

The simplified model we refer to is reported in **Figure 1**. It presents only four state variables corresponding to capacitors voltages and inductors currents of two identical RLC resonators and referred respectively as OSC_I and OSC_Q. The resulting state vector is $\underline{X}(t) = \begin{bmatrix} V_I(t) & I_I(t) & V_Q(t) & I_Q(t) \end{bmatrix}^T \in \mathbb{R}$. Here and in the following all vectors and parameters quantities are in real numbers field if not differently specified. Coupling between resonators in a positive feedback configuration is accomplished by pulsed current generators emulating active devices. This model can be seen as a rather drastic simplification of a real oscillator, however if we assume the parasitic introduced by transconductors to be much smaller than those in resonators they can be merged in resonators themselves, thus avoiding to increment the effective space state dimension.

The model assumes a current pulse of fixed duration injected in the driven resonator and triggered by crossing 0V common mode level of the capacitance voltage of the driving oscillator. The impulsive characteristic of the generators is described by the piecewise linear expressions in (1) where I_{max} and T_P represent respectively the limiting current and the pulse width. The t_{th_Y} represents time instant of threshold crossing of the driver oscillator. $Y = I, Q$ and $\overline{Y} = Q, I$ indicate respectively the driver and the driven oscillator. There are two pulses in each period with alternated sign depending on the sign of driver voltage derivative.

$$I_{p\_\overline{Y}}(t) = \begin{cases} 0 & t < t_{th\_Y} \\ \pm I_{max} \cdot \dfrac{\dot{V}_{CY}(t_{th\_Y})}{\left| \dot{V}_{CY}(t_{th\_Y}) \right|} & t_{th\_Y} \leq t \leq t_{th\_Y} + T_P \quad (1) \\ 0 & t_{th\_Y} + T_P < t \end{cases}$$

Furthermore the "±" takes into account the possible degree of freedom in determination of $\pm\pi/2$ reciprocal phase. Sign choice determines indeed the quadrature relationship between the oscillators. In order to roughly depict the role of the sign one can notice that, assuming in (1) the sign "-" for current pulse in OSC_Q at the zero crossing of OSC_I with positive derivative, a negative

pulse is applied to OSC_Q. Such pulse corresponds to a negative half-wave for driven oscillator OSC_Q that becomes delayed of $-\pi/2$ with respect to driver oscillator OSC_I. In the following calculations we shall always assume the sign "-" for current pulse in OSC_Q.

3. Proof of Quadrature Mode Stability

Since the pulses arise at the crossing of a threshold equal to the common mode voltage of the oscillators, subsequent pulses can be assumed to impinge in two different semi-periods of the oscillation with opposite sign. It can be shown that, in a stable condition, the symmetric scheduling of the pulses leads to the symmetry of the two semi-periods of oscillation. Nevertheless, in order to concentrate our effort on the eigenvector extraction, we propose to adopt semi-periods symmetry as a preliminary assumption. Once the first eigenvector and thus the large signal dynamic will be calculated also the preliminary assumption will be proved. In the following analytical derivations semi-periods symmetry will be formalized as the *reflection conditions* on the eigenvectors space state.

3.1. First Eigenvector Extraction

As can be easily derived form the adopted model, the evolution of any state variation is a sinusoidal damped function of pulsation ω_n In time intervals when the pulse generators are not active, following RLC system equations, eigenvectors can be described by

$$\underline{u}_J(t) = \begin{bmatrix} u_{J\_CI}(t) \\ u_{J\_LI}(t) \\ u_{J\_CQ}(t) \\ u_{J\_LQ}(t) \end{bmatrix}$$

$$= \begin{bmatrix} h_{J\_I} e^{-\mu t} \cos\left(\omega_n t - \varphi - \chi_{J\_I}\right) \\ \dfrac{h_{J\_I}}{F} e^{-\mu t} \sin\left(\omega_n t - \chi_{J\_I}\right) \\ h_{J\_Q} e^{-\mu\left(t + \frac{\pi - \chi_{J\_Q}}{\omega_n}\right)} \cos\left(\omega_n t - \varphi - \chi_{J\_Q}\right) \\ \dfrac{h_{J\_Q}}{F} e^{-\mu\left(t + \frac{\pi - \chi_{J\_Q}}{\omega_n}\right)} \sin\left(\omega_n t - \chi_{J\_Q}\right) \end{bmatrix} \quad (2)$$

where subscripts $J = 1, 2, 3, 4$ refer to the relative eigenvector number. h_{J_I} and h_{J_Q} are unknown eigenvector amplitudes, χ_{J_I} and χ_{J_Q} are the unknown phase displacements between eigenvector components in the two resonators. The $F \in \mathbb{R} > 0$ factor accounts for the ratio between currents and voltages whereas $\varphi \in [0 : \pi/2]$ factor accounts for relative phase between currents and voltages in a resonator and are given respectively by

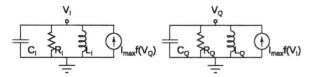

Figure 1. Simplified adopted model for pulsed bias phase and quadrature harmonic oscillator.

$$F = \sqrt{\frac{L}{C}} \cdot \sqrt{1 - \frac{1}{(2Q)^2}}$$

$$\varphi = arctg\left(-\frac{1}{2Q}\right)$$
(3)

For the sake of calculation simplicity in (2) we define h_{J_Q} as the amplitude of components related to OSC_Q at $t = -(\pi - \chi_{J\_Q})/\omega_n$ rather than at $t = 0$. We recall that in a stable oscillator always exists a "first" eigenvector with unitary eigenvalue and with components tangent to the space state orbit. This property makes first eigenvector behavior directly related to the oscillator state. E.g. the threshold crossing which triggers the bias current pulse can be indicated either in term of eigenvector components or of oscillator state. In the two oscillators the threshold is indeed crossed as the capacitance voltage zeroes, i.e. when current component of eigenvector is null

$$V_{CY}\left(t_{th\_Y}\right) = L_Y \frac{dI_{LY}\left(t_{th\_Y}\right)}{dt} = u_{1\_LY}\left(t_{th\_Y}\right) = 0. \quad (4)$$

We assume for the first eigenvector $J = 1$. Since eigenvectors components can always be defined by a proportionality constant, we choose to fix $h_{1\_I} = 1$ with no loss of generality. Similarly we assume the threshold of OSC_I is crossed at $t_{th\_I} = 0$ and for $\chi_{1\_I} = 0$. We recall once more that the value of the eigenvalue of first eigenvector must be one. This aspect brings to *four* the number of independent conditions on eigenvector components. We notice that Equations (2) contain only two unknowns in front of four conditions. The two exceeding conditions indeed will lead to determination of both oscillation period and amplitude.

At this point we must introduce the basic assumption that if T_P is short enough compared to actual oscillation period T, the overall effect of the current pulse can be approximated with a drop in current components of eigenvectors. In [6] we showed that current drop has the general form

$$\Delta I_{J\_\bar{Y}} = \pm \frac{I_{max}}{CF} \frac{u_{J\_CY}\left(t_{th\_Y}\right)}{\dot{V}_{CY}\left(t_{th\_Y}\right)} \omega_n T_P. \quad (5)$$

The sign of current drops depends upon the sign of capacitor voltage derivative and eigenvector amplitude of the driven oscillator at threshold crossing and on the quadrature sign chosen in Equation (1). Resulting current drops are sketched in **Figure 2** by thick arrows for a semi-period. Due to circuit loss $(\varphi \neq 0)$ currents and voltages components in resonators are not exactly in quadrature, then current drops may produce both amplitude variations and phase shifts of the orbit. In **Figure 2** phase shifts are respectively indicated as $\Delta\varphi_{1\_I}$ and $\Delta\varphi_{1\_Q}$ for the two oscillators.

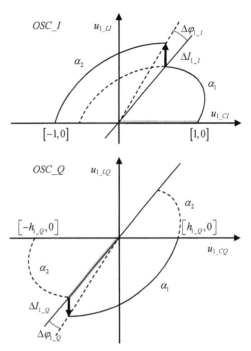

Figure 2. Sketch of evolution of first eigenvector subdivided into OSC_I and OSC_Q plane components. Thick gray line indicates the eigenvector at *t* = 0.

As previously indicated, under semi-periods symmetry we impose the *reflection conditions*: after a semi-period each component of the first eigenvector must return to the initial value changed in sign. For the other eigenvectors the conditions will impose each component to reach the initial value times the square root of the eigenvalue changed in sign. Using expressions (2) the *reflection conditions* can be written as in Equations (6). Before we develop such conditions the evolution along a

$$\begin{bmatrix} \cos(-\varphi) \\ 0 \\ h_{1\_Q} e^{-\mu\frac{\gamma_1}{\omega_n}} \cos(-\varphi + \gamma_1) \\ \frac{h_{1\_Q}}{F} e^{-\mu\frac{\gamma_1}{\omega_n}} \sin(\gamma_1) \end{bmatrix} = - \begin{bmatrix} u_{1\_CI}\left(\frac{T}{2}\right) \\ u_{1\_LI}\left(\frac{T}{2}\right) \\ u_{1\_CQ}\left(\frac{T}{2}\right) \\ u_{1\_LQ}\left(\frac{T}{2}\right) \end{bmatrix}. \quad (6)$$

semi-period must be analytically expressed including the drops induced by pulses. This result can be achieved combining damped evolutions (following RLC system equations) and amplitude and phase shifts due to bias pulses.

We define as α_1 the phase evolution in (2) between application of the bias pulse to OSC_Q resonator and the time instant when its current component, u_{1_LQ}, zeroes (0 V threshold crossing by OSC_Q voltage component). We define as α_2 the phase change between the application of the bias pulse to OSC_I resonator and the instant when its current component, u_{1_LI}, zeroes (0V threshold crossing by OSC_I voltage component).

In [6] the effect of the current pulse is represented as the drop to an equivalent damped sinusoidal evolution always with origin in $t = 0$ but with a different amplitude and an additional phase shift.

First pulse is applied at $t = 0$ to OSC_Q resonator giving rise to phase shift

$$\Delta\varphi_{1\_Q} = \frac{\dfrac{\Delta I_{1\_Q} F}{u_{1\_LQ}\left(t_{th\_I}\right)}\cos\left(-\varphi - \chi_{1\_Q}\right)}{\cos\left(-\varphi\right)}. \tag{7}$$

After a damped evolution by a $\alpha_1 = \chi_{1\_Q} - \Delta\varphi_{1\_Q}$ phase, $u_{1\_LQ}\left(t_{th\_Q}\right) = 0$ (the OSC_Q threshold) is crossed and a second current pulse is applied this time to OSC_I. The second induced phase shift $\Delta\varphi_{1\_I}$ *retains memory* of former phase shift $\Delta\varphi_{1\_Q}$ resulting in

$$\Delta\varphi_{1\_I} = \frac{\dfrac{\Delta I_{1\_I} F}{u_{1\_LI}\left(t_{th\_Q}\right)}\cos\left(-\varphi + \chi_{1\_Q} - \Delta\varphi_{1\_Q}\right)}{\cos\left(-\varphi\right)}. \tag{8}$$

A further phase evolution of α_2 closes the semi-period. Since damped evolution of the two oscillators is identical in both semi-period, total phase evolution must equalize. We may thus write the *reflection condition* as

$$\alpha_1 + \Delta\varphi_{1\_Q} + \alpha_2 = \alpha_1 + \Delta\varphi_{1\_I} + \alpha_2 = \pi$$
$$\downarrow \tag{9}$$
$$\Delta\varphi_{1\_Q} = \Delta\varphi_{1\_I} = \Delta\varphi_1$$

i.e. the two phase shifts must be equal.

Drop ΔI_{1_I} is dependent on the amplitude $h_{1\_Q}\left(t_{th\_Q}\right)$ which is still an unknown. In order not to run through an intricate calculation we now attempt a *by inspection solution* (requiring a later verification). Basing again on symmetry we assume

$$\frac{\Delta I_{1\_I}}{u_{1\_LI}\left(t_{th\_Q}\right)} = -\frac{\Delta I_{1\_Q}}{u_{1\_LQ}\left(t_{th\_I}\right)}. \tag{10}$$

With this assumption and inserting (7)-(8) into condition (9) the expression can be solved equating the arguments of cosine functions

$$\chi_{1\_Q} = \frac{\pi + \Delta\varphi_1}{2}. \tag{11}$$

Using (11) in (6) an implicit form for $\Delta\varphi_1$ phase shift is obtained

$$\Delta\varphi_1 \cos\left(\varphi\right) = \frac{\Delta I_{1\_I} F}{u_{1\_LI}\left(t_{th\_Q}\right)}\sin\left(\frac{\Delta\varphi_1}{2} + \varphi\right) \tag{12}$$

which needs to be solved for $\pi/2 < \Delta\varphi_1 < \pi/2$.

We notice that $\varphi \approx 0$ is well approximated with resonator quality factor just greater then few unities. In the simplified case of $\varphi = 0$ expression (11) is verified only for $\Delta\varphi_1 = 0$. This assumption implies $T = T_n = 2\pi/\omega_n$, *i.e.* the oscillation period is equal to the natural period of damped RLC resonator. The assumption would also lead to state that $\chi_{1\_Q} = \pi/2$. In sections 3.2 and 3.3 we are going to perform further calculations on remaining eigenvectors under this particular assumption. Then in section 5 this approximation will be verified through comparison with a dedicated Matlab simulator.

If $\varphi \approx 0$ we may assume $\chi_{1\_Q} = \pi/2$ in (2) and this ensures that OSC_Q is delayed with respect to OSC_I, thus confirming the effect of signs choice in (1).

Beside these approximations we further use (10) and the reflection conditions to obtain

$$\alpha_1 = \gamma_1 - \Delta\varphi_{1\_Q} = \frac{\pi}{2} - \frac{\Delta\varphi_1}{2}$$
$$\alpha_2 = \pi - \gamma_1 = \frac{\pi}{2} - \frac{\Delta\varphi_1}{2} = \alpha_1 \tag{13}$$

From (13) we may infer that the two oscillators are intrinsically in quadrature, since the bias pulse generated at the 0V crossing of one of the two resonators is applied at the center of two identical time evolutions between the two bias pulses applied to the other resonator. This property is independent from resonators losses. The oscillation period can indeed be written as

$$T = \frac{4\alpha_1}{\omega_n} = T_n - \frac{2\Delta\varphi_1}{\omega_n}. \tag{14}$$

It is possible now to express the reflection conditions (6) in a compact form. Being ensured the parallelism of the eigenvector at $t = T/2$ by (9), we may impose the condition only to one component of eigenvector. If we consider $u_{1\_LQ}\left(T/2\right) = 0$ its value must be equal to current state component at time origin changed in sign

$$\left(\frac{h_{1\_Q}}{F}e^{-\mu\frac{T}{4}} + \frac{I_{max}}{C\dot{V}_{CI}\big|_{t=0}F}\omega_n T_p\right)e^{-\mu\frac{T}{2}} = -\frac{h_{1\_Q}}{F}e^{-\mu\frac{T}{4}}. \tag{15}$$

Equation (15) can be solved for h_{1_Q} obtaining

$$h_{1\_Q} = \frac{1}{\left(e^{+\mu\frac{T}{4}} - e^{-\mu\frac{T}{4}}\right)}\frac{I_{max}}{C\dot{V}_{CI}\big|_{t=0}}\omega_n T_p$$
$$= \frac{1}{\sinh\left(\mu\frac{T}{4}\right)}\frac{I_{max}}{C\dot{V}_{CI}\big|_{t=0}}\omega_n T_p. \tag{16}$$

Since expression (16) has still two unknowns ($h_{1\_1} = 1$ and $\dot{V}_{CI}$) it must be solved in conjunction with evolution of OSC_I components. We may calculate the evolution of $u_{1\_LI}(t)$ at $t = T/4^+$ just after the current drop is added by the bias pulse (superscript '+' indicates in the limit from the right). In particular ΔI_{1_I} can be expressed through (5) at a time instant $t = -T/4$ when the OSC_Q component can be easily calculated using reflection condition as $\begin{bmatrix} h_{\_Q} & 0 \end{bmatrix}^T$. We hence obtain

$$u_{1\_LI}\left(\frac{T^+}{4}\right) = \frac{1}{F}\left[e^{-\mu\frac{T}{4}} - \frac{I_{max}}{C\dot{V}_{CQ}\big|_{t=\frac{T}{4}}}\omega_n T_p h_{\_Q}\right]. \quad (17)$$

After a further evolution of $T/4$ the u_{1_LI} zeroes. Reflection conditions can now be imposed on the voltage component u_{1_CI}

$$u_{1\_CI}\left(\frac{T}{2}\right) = e^{-\mu\frac{T}{4}}\left[e^{-\mu\frac{T}{4}} - \frac{I_{max}}{C\dot{V}_{CQ}\big|_{t=\frac{T}{4}}}\omega_n T_p h_{\_Q}\right] = -1 \quad (18)$$

to solve again for

$$h_{\_Q} = \sinh\left(\mu\frac{T}{4}\right)\frac{C\dot{V}_{CQ}\big|_{t=\frac{T}{4}}}{I_{max}\,\omega_n T_p}. \quad (19)$$

We immediately point out that Equations (16) and (19) can be verified simultaneously only if $h_{\_Q} = 1/h_{\_Q} = 1$. A straightforward consequence is

$$\dot{V}_{CQ}\big|_{t=\frac{T}{4}} = \dot{V}_{CI}\big|_{t=0} = \dot{V}_C \quad (20)$$

Equal oscillation amplitudes for both resonators verify the assumption (10) of equal amplitudes for current drops. This ensures the correctness of the entire calculation. From this statement and considering that also the amplitude of oscillation is a damped sinusoidal function its amplitude can be derived as

$$V_C = \frac{T_p}{\sinh\left(\mu\frac{T}{4}\right)}\frac{I_{max}}{C}. \quad (21)$$

As anticipated at the beginning of this section the conditions on the first eigenvector lead to the determination of oscillation amplitude and oscillation period. The existence of a fixed oscillation amplitude ensures also stability of system.

3.2. Extraction of Second and Third Eigenvectors

The second eigenvector can be expressed through (2) with $J = 2$. Again h_{2_I} and h_{2_Q} are unknown eigenvectors amplitudes, χ_{2_I} and χ_{2_Q} are the unknown phase displacements between eigenvector components in the two resonators.

We perform a normalization on amplitudes assuming $h_{2\_I} = 1$. Since second eigenvector cannot be related to

the oscillator state evolution, the only additional condition we may impose is the independence from the first one. We recall we are going again to perform the calculation under the particular assumption that $\varphi = 0$ (which corresponds to assume $T = T_n$), i.e. a damped sinusoidal evolution must cover a phase of π in a semi-period.

We combine the extractions of second and third eigenvectors since we may demonstrate that both eigenvectors are related to a unique Floquet eigenvalue with algebraic multiplicity equal to two.

Pulses positions are fixed by the oscillator state. We individuated at $t = 0$ a first current pulse is applied to OSC_Q whereas at $t = T_n/4$ the second current pulse (in first half of period) is applied to OSC_I.

With the adopted assumptions we obtained $\chi_{1\_Q} = \pi/2$, thus at $t = 0$ the first eigenvector has the OSC_Q components in the {I} current axis direction and the OSC_I in the {V} voltage axis direction.

In order to preserve geometric multiplicity equal to two, second and third eigenvector must be independent and this requires them to have at $t = 0$ for OSC_Q at least a finite component in the {V} direction and for OSC_I a finite component in the {I} direction.

In addition we must notice that, as in first eigenvector, the phase steps due to bias current pulses must be null to ensure that in $T_n/2$ a total phase evolution π is achieved. Damped sinusoidal evolution (which is equal in all the eigenvectors) is already π and no additional phase can be added.

Referring again to **Figure 1**, a null phase step can be achieved only for two conditions:

1) if the eigenvector is in the {I} current direction at instant of application of the pulse, but this is not possible for the independence condition;

2) if the current drops discontinuities induced by the bias pulses are null.

As demonstrated in [6] this can be achieved only if the OSC_I voltage components of eigenvectors is null at $t = 0$ and if the OSC_Q voltage components is null at $t = T_n/4$.

Imposing these two conditions in (2) we immediately obtain

$$u_{2\_CI}(0) = \cos\left(-\chi_{2\_I}\right) = 0$$
$$u_{2\_CQ}\left(\frac{T_0}{4}\right) = h_{2\_Q}e^{-\mu\left(\frac{T_0}{4} + \frac{\chi_{2\_Q}}{\omega_n}\right)}\cos\left(\frac{\pi}{2} - \chi_{2\_Q}\right) = 0. \quad (22)$$

Hence it must be verified that $\chi_{2\_I} = \pi/2$ and $\chi_{2\_Q} = 0$.

Without any current drop the eigenvector amplitude exponentially decreases with the natural $\mu = (2RC)^{-1}$ damping of the system. There is no further condition to be applied in order to calculate the unknown amplitude

h_{2_Q}. This means that *reflection conditions* on second and third eigenvectors are satisfied for any vectors laying in the plane $\begin{bmatrix} 0 & a & b & 0 \end{bmatrix}^T$ where $a, b \in \mathbb{R}$, *i.e.* that there are two independent eigenvectors with the same eigenvalue:

$$\lambda_{2,3} = e^{-\mu T_n} . \tag{23}$$

With no loss of generality we may thus assume $\underline{u}_2(0) = \begin{bmatrix} 0 & 1 & 0 & 0 \end{bmatrix}^T$ and $\underline{u}_3(0) = \begin{bmatrix} 0 & 0 & 1 & 0 \end{bmatrix}^T$.

3.3. Extraction of Fourth Eigenvector

The fourth eigenvector can be expressed through (2) with $J = 4$. Again h_{4_I} and h_{4_Q} are unknown eigenvectors amplitudes, χ_{4_I} and χ_{4_Q} are the unknown phase displacements between eigenvector components in the two resonators.

Fourth eigenvector must be independent from all the formerly calculated $\underline{u}_1$, $\underline{u}_2$, and $\underline{u}_3$.

We recall that with approximation $\varphi = 0$ the phase propagation of both OSC_I and OSC_Q amounts in total to π. Thus also $\underline{u}_4$ must have null values of phase steps. This condition occurs if one of the following two conditions is satisfied:

1) $\chi_{4\_I} = \pi/4$ and $\chi_{4\_Q} = 0$. Null values of voltage displacement components at threshold crossing corresponding to null current drops, but this condition is completely dependent on eigenvectors $\underline{u}_2$ and $\underline{u}_3$;

2) $\chi_{4\_I} = 0$ and $\chi_{4\_Q} = \pm\pi/4$. Eigenvector is parallel to current drops at the time of thresholds crossings thus giving rise to null phase steps. The condition with sign "+" is that of $\underline{u}_1$.

This means we must choose the condition b) with sign "-". With no loss of generality we fix $h_{4\_I} = 1$ then we write at $t = 0$ the independence condition among the four eigenvectors

$$\begin{vmatrix} 1 & 0 & 0 & \dfrac{1}{F} \\[2mm] 0 & 1 & 0 & 0 \\[2mm] 0 & 0 & 1 & 0 \\[2mm] \cos(\chi_{4\_I}) & \dfrac{\sin(\chi_{4\_I})}{F} & h_{4\_Q}\cos(\chi_{4\_Q}) & \dfrac{h_{4\_Q}\sin(\chi_{4\_Q})}{F} \end{vmatrix} \neq 0 . \tag{24}$$

For $\chi_{4\_I} = 0$ and $\chi_{4\_Q} = -\pi/2$ we obtain

$$1 + h_{4\_Q} \neq 0 \tag{25}$$

which is satisfied for any positive value of h_{4_Q} The fourth eigenvector evolution is reported in **Figure 3** Reported current drops follow the sign imposed by condition (5) as chosen in (1). This make fourth eigenvector components in OSC_Q to be in advance. Change of the eigenvector components sign determines change of sign of current drops contributions to OSC_I. A decrease of eigenvector amplitude is then found in both resonators components.

Being ensured the parallelism of the eigenvector at $t = T_n/2$ and $t = 0$ for (9) we may impose the *reflection conditions* only to one component: after a semi-period evolution any eigenvector component must reach a value which is the square root of λ_4 times its values at $t = 0$ changed in sign. We follow the calculation performed for the first eigenvector. For OSC_Q at $t = T_n/4$ we have

$$u_{4\_LQ}\left(\frac{T_n}{4}\right) = -\sqrt{\lambda_4}\ u_{4\_LQ}\left(-\frac{T_n}{4}\right)$$

$$\downarrow \tag{26}$$

$$\left(h_{4\_Q}\sqrt{\frac{C}{L}}e^{-\mu\frac{T_n}{4}} - \frac{I_{\max}}{C\dot{V}_{CI}\big|_{t=0}}F\right)\sqrt{\frac{L}{C}}e^{-\mu\frac{T_n}{4}} = \sqrt{\lambda_4}\,h_{4\_Q}$$

Equation (26) can be solved for h_{4_Q} obtaining

$$h_{4\_Q} = \frac{1}{\left(e^{-\mu\frac{T_n}{4}} - \sqrt{\lambda_4}e^{+\mu\frac{T_n}{4}}\right)}\frac{I_{\max}}{C\dot{V}_{CI}\big|_{t=0}}\omega_n T_p . \tag{27}$$

For OSC_I we must first consider the evolution of

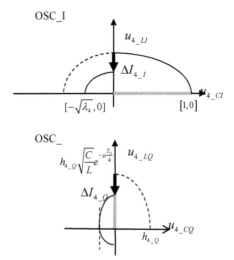

Figure 3. Sketch of evolution of fourth eigenvector subdivided into OSC_I and OSC_Q plane components. The approximation $\varphi = 0$ is assumed. Thick gray line indicate the eigenvector at $t = 0$.

$u_{4\_LI}(t)$ at $t = T_n/4$ where the current drop is added due to the bias pulse. ΔI_{1_I} can be expressed through (5). Pulse on OSC_I depends on the amplitude h_{4_Q} The reflection condition on OSC_I is written as

$$u_{4\_CI}\left(\frac{T_n}{2}\right) = e^{-\mu\frac{T_n}{4}}\left[e^{-\mu\frac{T_n}{4}} - \frac{I_{max}}{C\dot{V}_{CQ}\big|_{t=-\frac{T_n}{4}}}\omega_n T_p h_{4\_Q}\right]$$

$$= \sqrt{\lambda_4} \qquad (28)$$

Equation (28) needs to be solved again for h_{4_Q}

$$h_{4\_Q} = \left(e^{-\mu\frac{T_n}{4}} - \sqrt{\lambda_4}e^{+\mu\frac{T_n}{4}}\right)\frac{C\dot{V}_{CQ}\big|_{t=\frac{T_n}{4}}}{I_{max}\,\omega_n T_p}. \qquad (29)$$

We immediately point out that Equations (27) and (29) can be verified simultaneously only if $h_{4\_Q} = 1/h_{4\_Q} = 1$ $h_{4\_Q} = 1/h_{4\_Q} = 1$.

It remains the calculation of λ_4. Recalling that the reflection condition can be written as

$$\left(e^{-\mu\frac{T_n}{4}} - \sqrt{\lambda_4}e^{+\mu\frac{T_n}{4}}\right) = \frac{I_{max}\,\omega_n T_p}{C\dot{V}_{CI}\big|_{t=0}} \qquad (30)$$

and that from the first eigenvector assuming $\varphi = 0$ we know that

$$\left(e^{+\mu\frac{T_n}{4}} - e^{-\mu\frac{T_n}{4}}\right) = \frac{I_{max}\,\omega_n T_p}{C\dot{V}_{CI}\big|_{t=0}}, \qquad (31)$$

we finally obtain

$$\lambda_4 = \left(\frac{2e^{-\mu\frac{T_n}{4}} - e^{+\mu\frac{T_n}{4}}}{e^{+\mu\frac{T_n}{4}}}\right)^2. \qquad (32)$$

4. Noise Projections and Zero Projection Times

Noise introduced by the bias pulse generators and from parasitic resistances projects onto the eigenvectors and evolves following the eigenvalues damping in time. The relationship between these projections and the overall phase noise has been extensively described elsewhere [7-10]. We can briefly state that the lower is the integral along the period of the variance of the projection of noise contributions onto the first eigenvector, the lower is the $1/f^2$ component of phase noise close to the fundamental. We can thus try to evaluate the contribution of projection of the two cited main noise sources.

We define as Zero Projection Times (ZPT) the instants of the limit cycle when noise introduced by a generic source does not project onto the first eigenvector. This is particularly important for the bias current generators which should be switched on preferably around a ZPT.

As we have seen along the calculation, eigenvectors evolution is strictly related to the pulse position. Then eigenvectors and pulses cannot be defined independently. Actually we may show that in the presented architecture ZPTs in the optimal position correspond to the time of application of the bias pulses.

We recall at $t = 0$ and $t = T_n/2$ current pulses are found on OSC_Q. We model a normalized white Gaussian process as two additional parallel and independent current sources (one source per resonator). Such noisy process generates a state variation in the direction $[0\ 0\ 1\ 0]^T$ for OSC_Q. This variation is in the plane of eigenvectors $\underline{u}_2$ and $\underline{u}_3$ and orthogonal to $\underline{u}_1$. Thus it implies a null projection onto the first eigenvector.

At $t = -T_n/4$ and $t = T_n/4$ the pulse is in OSC_I. In this case the process generates a state variation in the direction $[1\ 0\ 0\ 0]^T$. Eigenvectors $\underline{u}_2$ and $\underline{u}_3$ after a phase evolution of $\pm\pi/2$ still span a plane which contains this vector and thus remains orthogonal to $\underline{u}_1$. This implies again a null projection onto the first eigenvector.

Hence we state that ZPTs correspond exactly to the bias pulses application instants. This aspect represents the main property of the presented architecture, since it ensures that noise introduced by the bias does not project onto the phase noise close to the fundamental. In section 5 simulation will confirm this peculiar behavior.

A second relevant property can be inferred form the eigenvectors description. Further relevant noise sources come from parasitic resistances of the resonators. These noise contributions exist all along the period (stationary source) and are not time limited as the bias noise (ciclostationary source). In this case it is essential that the projections occur onto orthogonal eigenvectors. Indeed non orthogonal orientation of the eigenvectors would give rise to an enlargement of the stationary noise source projections. Since any projection on $\underline{u}_1$ is not decreased by the exponential damping due to the eigenvalue $\lambda_1 = 1$, non orthogonal eigenvectors reflect unavoidably in a phase noise enhancement.

We showed in [6] minimization of the integral of a stationary variance projected onto the first eigenvector occurs under the condition of orthogonal eigenvectors. We may adapt this result to the case of noise vector $\underline{n}$ generated by the parasitic resistance in one of the two resonant circuit and verify the condition of minimum projection in a period. We extract in (33) the left eigenvectors $\mathbf{v}$ at $t = 0$ inverting the right eigenvectors matrix $\mathbf{u}$ derived from former results. The components of first eigenvector are normalized to one in order to make more explicit the result of projection even if a normalization is not necessary. Being uncorrelated, noise contributions from the two resonators can be considered independently. Noise has a fixed direction while each component of the eigenvectors rotates with pulsation ω_n as given in Equation (2). For the sake of simplicity we may change the reference assuming new axes solid with the eigenvectors, so that noise components appear as a rotating $\underline{n}(t)$ vector. At every time instant the total energy from the two noise components is maintained constant.

$$
\mathbf{v} = \mathbf{u}^{-1} = \begin{bmatrix} 1 & 0 & 0 & 1 \\ 0 & 1 & 0 & 0 \\ 0 & 0 & 1 & 0 \\ -e^{-\mu\frac{T_n}{4}} & 0 & 0 & e^{-\mu\frac{T_n}{4}} \end{bmatrix}^{-1}
$$

$$
= \frac{1}{2} \begin{bmatrix} 1 & 0 & 0 & -\dfrac{1}{e^{-\mu\frac{T_n}{4}}} \\ 0 & 2 & 0 & 0 \\ 0 & 0 & 2 & 0 \\ 1 & 0 & 0 & \dfrac{1}{e^{-\mu\frac{T_n}{4}}} \end{bmatrix}. \tag{33}
$$

It can be easily verified from (34) that each noise generator arising from one single resonant circuit always results projected only along two state components and that the two directions are orthogonal. E.g noise from OSC_I is projected along $\begin{bmatrix} 1 & 0 & 0 & 0 \end{bmatrix}^T$ and $\begin{bmatrix} 0 & 0 & 1 & 0 \end{bmatrix}^T$. It is worth to notice that the projections onto first and fourth eigenvectors are identical with coefficient $1/2$ while there is a projection on eigenvector $\underline{u}_3$ with coefficient 1.

$$
\mathbf{v}\underline{n}(t) = \frac{1}{2} \begin{bmatrix} 1 & 0 & 0 & -\dfrac{1}{e^{-\mu\frac{T_n}{4}}} \\ 0 & 2 & 0 & 0 \\ 0 & 0 & 2 & 0 \\ 1 & 0 & 0 & \dfrac{1}{e^{-\mu\frac{T_n}{4}}} \end{bmatrix} \begin{bmatrix} \cos(-\omega_n t) \\ \dfrac{\sin(-\omega_n t)}{F} \\ 0 \\ 0 \end{bmatrix}. \tag{34}
$$

Vice versa contribution from noise in OSC_Q results projected along two constant orthogonal directions $\begin{bmatrix} 0 & 0 & 1 & 0 \end{bmatrix}^T$ and $\begin{bmatrix} 0 & 0 & 0 & 1 \end{bmatrix}^T$. Projections onto the first and fourth eigenvectors are again identical with coefficient $1/2$ while this time we have projection on eigenvector $\underline{u}_2$ with coefficient 1.

Having assumed noise generators independent in the two resonators, the variances of projections onto first and fourth eigenvectors can be summed. Hence due to the coefficient on the amplitudes, the total variance of the projection on first eigenvector results to be $1/2$ of the value obtainable in a single resonator. In other words and to our knowledge, we obtained the first analytical demonstration of effective reduction of noise projection onto the first eigenvector due to phase and quadrature cou-

pling of oscillators.

5. Simulation Results and Discussion

The approximation introduced in the former calculation requires a numerical verification. This is done in the present section by the use of a piece-wise linear integration method that gives an exact evaluation of the system reported in **Figure 1**.

The simulation method adopts in particular Interface Matrices for the description of the state variation at the current pulse discontinuities [11]. This method allows to extract eigenvectors and eigenvalues with high accuracy. For the simulation we choose two given values for capacitances and inductances respectively $C = 1.05\,pF$ and $L = 0.912\,nH$ producing ideal resonance at $F_0 = 5.14313\,\text{GHz}$ even if the developed theory is not frequency dependent. We fix also the total charge of a single current pulse in $0.66e-12\,As$. In **Figure 4**. the eigenvalues for the pulsed bias phase and quadrature oscillator are reported in both calculated (continuous traces) and simulated (dotted traces) cases as a function of resonators quality factor. It can be observed a very good match between calculated and simulated $\lambda_{2,3}$ (error always $<1\%$) whereas calculated λ_4 is underestimated with respect to the simulated one (error $<5\%$ for $Q > 10$). Underestimation is due to $\varphi = 0$ assumption which leads to higher error in determination of expression (32).

In **Figure 5**. we report the simulated projections of $\begin{bmatrix} 1 & 0 & 0 & 0 \end{bmatrix}^T$ and $\begin{bmatrix} 0 & 0 & 1 & 0 \end{bmatrix}^T$ noise perturbation vectors onto the first eigenvector in case $Q = 10$. Such noise vectors describe both the effect of bias current generator and parasitic resistance noise respectively of

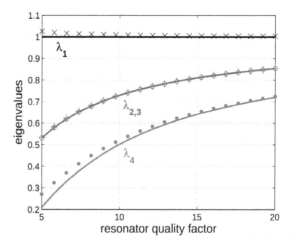

Figure 4. Eigenvalues of proposed oscillator as a function of resonator quality factor. In continue traces (black line is λ_1, red line are $\lambda_{2,3}$ and green line is λ_4) the analytical expressions are plotted whereas in dotted traces (black "x" is λ_1, red "+" and blue "o" are respectively λ_2 and λ_3 and green solid "o" is λ_4) the results of simulator are reported.

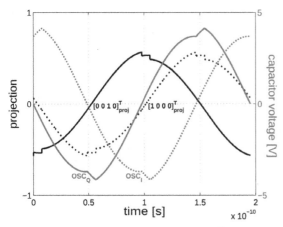

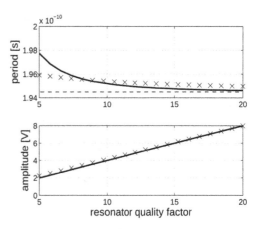

Figure 5. Simulated projections of $[1\ 0\ 0\ 0]^T$ (black dotted trace) and of $[0\ 0\ 1\ 0]^T$ (black continuous trace) onto first eigenvector $\underline{u}_1$ and related capacitors voltages (OSC_I in red dotted trace, OSC_Q in red continuous trace) of resonators in time of proposed oscillator for Q = 10.

Figure 6. Period and amplitude of oscillation of proposed oscillator as a function of resonator quality factor. In continue traces the analytical expressions are plotted whereas in dotted "x" traces the results of simulator are reported. The dashed line in top subfigure represents period of resonator with no loss.

the two resonators. The phase and quadrature oscillation of capacitances voltages is also reported in the figure. The evident presence of discontinuities on voltage waveforms induced by bias pulsed currents allows to verify that null projections correspond exactly to the pulses injected in relative resonators. We remark that maximum projection is 1/2 corresponding to the normalized noise charge injected onto the $1.05\ pF$ capacitor. Absence of any increase above value 1/2 of projection is the effect of the eigenvectors orthogonality.

Finally in **Figure 6**, we report the value of the oscillation period and amplitude in calculated (continuous traces) and simulated (dotted traces) as a function of the resonators quality factor. In this evaluation the calculated expressions present a maximum of 1.8% error for period and of 11.8% error for amplitude at low quality factor value compared to simulated results. Both errors become *<1%* as Q increases above 10.

6. Concluding Remarks

We presented the full analytical description of a new class of pulsed bias phase-quadrature oscillators. Introducing a new methodology entirely based on system state Floquet eigenvectors we proved existence and stability of the quadrature mode and derived a consistent noise analysis. We pointed out a direct relationship between circuit parameters and the exclusive noise performances of the architecture. In particular we highlighted the intrinsic orthogonal behavior of the coupled oscillators, the possibility to obtain a minimum projection of noise introduced by the bias pulse on first eigenvector and finally the intrinsic orthogonality of the eigenvectors. We furthermore demonstrated that such properties ensure minimization of phase noise contributions from both the

parasitic resistances and the eventual active devices performing the pulsed energy restore. Exploited properties should be common to the entire class of phase-quadrature oscillators with fixed duration current bias pulses. Nevertheless the analysis of a practical electronic realization of the architecture and its evaluation requires and deserves a dedicated work.

REFERENCES

[1]   P. Andreani and X. Wang, "On the Phase-Noise and Phase-Error Performances of Multiphase LC CMOS VCOs," *IEEE Journal of Solid State Circuits*, Vol. 39, No. 11, 2004, pp. 1883-1893.

[2]   S. Perticaroli and F. Palma, "Phase and Quadrature Pulsed Bias LC-CMOS VCO," *SCIRP Circuit and Systems*, Vol. 2, No. 1, 2011, pp. 18-24.

[3]   T. H. Lee and A. Hajimiri, "Oscillator Phase Noise: A Tutorial," *IEEE Journal of Solid-State Circuits*, Vol. 35, No. 6, 2000, pp. 326-336.

[4]   A. Demir, "Floquet Theory and Non-Linear Perturbation Analysis for Oscillators with Differential-Algebraic Equations," *International Journal of Circuit and Theory Applications*, Vol. 28, No. 2, 2000, pp. 163-185.

[5]   G. J. Coram, "A Simple 2-D Oscillator to Determine the Correct Decomposition of Perturbations into Amplitude and Phase Noise," *IEEE Transactions on Circuits and Systems—I: Fundamental Theory and Applications*, Vol. 48, No. 7, 2001, pp. 896-898.

[6]   S. Perticaroli and F. Palma, "Design Criteria Based on Floquet Eigenvectors for the Class of LC-CMOS Pulsed Bias Oscillators," *Microelectronics Journal*, 2011, Article in Press.

[7]   F. X. Kaertner, "Analysis of White and f^α Noise in Os-

cillators," *International Journal of Circuit and Theory Applications*, Vol. 18, No. 5, 1990, pp. 485-519.

[8] A. Demir, A. Mehrotra and J. S. Roychowdhury, "Phase Noise in Oscillators: A Unifying Theory and Numerical Methods for Characterization," *IEEE Transactions on Circuits and Systems—I: Fundamental Theory and Applications*, Vol. 47, No. 5, 2000, pp. 655-674.

[9] A. Carbone, A. Brambilla and F. Palma, "Using Floquet Eigenvectors in the Design of Electronic Oscillators," *Emerging Technologies*: *Circuits and Systems for 4G

Mobile Wireless Communications*, 2005. *ETW'05*. 2005 *IEEE 7th CAS Symposium*, 23-24 June 2005, pp. 100-103.

[10] A. Carbone and F. Palma, "Considering Orbital Deviations on the Evaluation of Power Density Spectrum of Oscillators," *IEEE Transactions on Circuits and Systems —II: Express Briefs*, Vol. 53, No. 6, 2006, pp. 438-442.

[11] A. Carbone and F. Palma, "Discontinuity Correction in Piecewise-Linear Models of Oscillators for Phase Noise Characterization," *International Journal of Circuit Theory and Applications*, Vol. 35, No. 1, 2007, pp. 93-104.

10

Design of Robust Power System Stabilizer Based on Particle Swarm Optimization

Magdi S. Mahmoud[1], Hisham M. Soliman[2]

[1]Systems Engineering Department, King Fahd University of Petroleum and Minerals (KFUPM), Dhahran, Saudi Arabia

[2]Electrical Engineering Department, Cairo University, Giza, Egypt

ABSTRACT

In this paper, we examine the problem of designing power system stabilizer (PSS). A new technique is developed using particle swarm optimization (PSO) combined with linear matrix inequality (LMI). The main feature of PSO, not sticking into a local minimum, is used to eliminate the conservativeness of designing a static output feedback (SOF) stabilizer within an iterative solution of LMIs. The technique is further extended to guarantee robustness against uncertainties wherein power systems operation is changing continuously due to load changes. Numerical simulation ahs illustrated the utility of the developed technique.

Keywords: Dynamic Stability; Power System Stabilizer; Static Output Feedback; Particle Swarm Optimization; Linear Matrix Inequality

1. Introduction

Dynamic system stability is a fundamental property of power systems that describes its ability to remain in a state of equilibrium under normal operating conditions and to regain an acceptable state of equilibrium in face of an external disturbance. It is generally observed that power system stability margins generally decrease, mainly due to Kundur [1]:

1) The restructuring of the electric power industry. Such a process decreases the stability margins due to the fact that power systems are not operated in a cooperative way anymore.

2) The inhibition of further transmission or generation constructions by economical and environmental restrictions. Consequently, power systems must be operated with smaller security margins.

3) The multiplication of pathological characteristics when power system complexity increases. These include: large scale oscillations originating from nonlinear phenomena, frequency differences between weakly tied power system areas, interactions with saturated devices, and interactions among power system controls.

Beyond a certain level, the decrease of power system stability margins can lead to unacceptable operating conditions and/or to frequent power system instability. One way to avoid this phenomenon and to increase power system stability margins is to control power systems more efficiently.

Synchronous generators are normally equipped with power system stabilizers (PSS) which provide supplementary feedback stabilizing signals through the excitation system. The stability limit of power systems can be extended by PSS, which enhances system damping at low frequency oscillations associated with electromechanical modes [2,3]. The problem of PSS design has been addressed in the literature using many techniques including, but not limited to, root locus and sensitivity analysis, adaptive control, robust control, pole placement, H_∞ design, and variable structure control [4-8]. The powerful optimization tool of linear matrix inequalities is also used to enhance PSS robustness through state and output feedback [9-11]. The availability of phasor measurement units was recently exploited in [12] for the design of an improved stabilizing control based on decentralized and/or hierarchical approach. Furthermore, the application of multi-agent systems to the development of a new defense system which enabled assessing power system vulnerability, monitoring hidden failures of protection devices, and providing adaptive control actions to prevent catastrophic failures and cascading sequences of events, was proposed in [13]. Attempts to enhance power system stabilization in case of controllers' failure are given in [14-16].

The conventional PSS commonly used in practice is a dynamic output feedback, a lead controller type, with a single or double stage and uses the speed deviation $\Delta\omega$ as a feedback signal. In the present work, we propose a static output feedback (SOF) controller that uses two feedback signals $\Delta\delta$, and $\Delta\omega$. The problem of SOF is treated in [17], where a quadratic matrix inequality (QMI) necessary and sufficient condition is provided. This condition is later transformed into a linear matrix inequality (LMI) sufficient condition that can be solved in an iterative fashion using an additional variable. It turns out that the results are generally conservativeness. Improvements to [17] can be found in [18].

Based thereon, this paper builds upon [17,18] and extends them further. It combines the particle swarm optimization (PSO) with LMI to solve the necessary and sufficient condition in a direct way without any additional variable, thus eliminating the conservativeness. Essentially PSO, as a powerful probabilistic search technique [19,20] is used to minimize a design variable at the upper level, whereas the LMIs resulting from the constraints of output feedback structure are solved via optimization routines provided with MATLAB's LMI control toolbox [21]. The coordination between PSO and LMI, developed in this paper, is needed because the formulated control design is in terms of non-convex optimization problem cannot be solved by using LMI techniques alone.

The manuscript is organized as follows: Section 2 describes the problem addressed in this paper. A dynamic model of a single machine infinite bus is presented in Section 3. Next, the technical background including robust control design by LMI approach and PSO is given in Section 4. Afterwards, result validation is given in Section 5. Finally the paper is concluded in Section 6.

Notation and Facts

In this paper, W', W^{-1}, and $\|W\|$ will denote respectively the transpose, the inverse, and the induced norm of any square matrix W. $W > 0$ ($W < 0$) will denote a symmetric positive (negative)-definite matrix W, and I will denote the identity matrix of appropriate dimension. The symbol • is as an ellipsis for terms in matrix expressions that are induced by symmetry,

Fact 1: Any congruence transformation $z'Wz$ does not change the definiteness of W.

Fact 2: [22]: For any real matrices W_1, W_2 and $\Delta(t)$ with appropriate dimensions and $\Delta'\Delta \leq I$, $\leftrightarrow \|\Delta\| \leq 1$, it follows that $W_1\Delta W_2 + W_2'\Delta'W_1' \leq \varepsilon^{-1}W_1W_1' + \varepsilon W_2'W_2$, $\varepsilon > 0$ where $\Delta(t)$ represents system bounded norm uncertainty.

2. Power System Model

The system under study consists of a single machine connected to an infinite bus through a tie-line as shown in the block diagram of **Figure 1**. It should be empha-

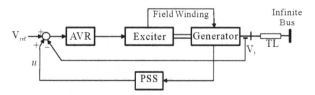

Figure 1. Power system model.

sized that the infinite bus could be representing the Thévenin equivalent of a large interconnected power system. The machine is equipped with a static exciter. The nonlinear model of the system is given through the following differential equations [1]:

$$\dot{\delta} = \omega_o\left(\omega - 1\right)$$

$$\dot{\omega} = \frac{\left(T_m - T_e\right)}{M}$$

$$\dot{E}_q' = \frac{1}{T_{d0}'}\left[E_{fd} - E_q' - \left(x_d - x_d'\right)i_d\right]$$

$$\dot{E}_{fd} = \frac{1}{T_E}\left[K_E\left(V_{ref} - V_t + u\right) - E_{fd}\right]$$

$$T_e \cong P_e \cong \frac{E_q'V\sin\delta}{x_d' + x_e},$$

$$i_d = \left(E_q' - V\cos\delta\right)/\left(x_d' + x_e\right),$$

$$i_q = V\sin\delta/\left(x_q + x_e\right)$$

$$V_t = \sqrt{\left(i_qx_q\right)^2 + \left(E_q' - i_dx_d'\right)^2}$$

Typical data for the system under consideration, which are used in the present work, are given as follows:
- Synchronous machine parameters:

$$x_d = 1.6, x_d' = 0.32, \ x_q = 1.55, \ \text{M} = 10\text{sec},$$

$$\omega_0 = 2\pi \times 50 \ rad/\text{sec}, \ T_{d0}' = 6 \text{ sec}.$$

- Exciter amplifier parameters:

$$K_E = 50, T_E = 0.05\text{sec}$$

- Transmission line reactance:

$$x_e = 0.4\,pu \,.$$

For PSS design purposes, the linearized forth order state space model around an equilibrium point is usually employed [1]. The parameters of the model have to be computed at each operating point since they are load dependent. Analytical expressions for the parameters (k_1 through k_6) are listed in the Appendix 1 as derived in [14-16]. The parameters are functions of the loading condition, real and reactive powers, P and Q respectively. The operating points considered vary over the intervals (0.4, 1.0), and (0.1, 0.5), respectively.

The n-dimensional linear state equation of the system

under study is given by,

$$\dot{x} = Ax + Bu, \qquad y = Cx \qquad (2)$$

where

$$x = \begin{bmatrix} \Delta\delta & \Delta\omega & \Delta E_q' & \Delta E_{fd} \end{bmatrix},$$

$$A = \begin{bmatrix} 0 & \omega_0 & 0 & 0 \\ \dfrac{-k_1}{M} & 0 & -\dfrac{k_2}{M} & 0 \\ -\dfrac{k_4}{T_{do}'} & 0 & -\dfrac{1}{T} & -\dfrac{1}{T_{do}'} \\ -\dfrac{k_5 k_E}{T_E} & 0 & -\dfrac{k_6 k_E}{T_E} & -\dfrac{1}{T_E} \end{bmatrix}, \qquad (3)$$

$$B = \begin{bmatrix} 0 & 0 & 0 & \dfrac{k_E}{T_E} \end{bmatrix}', C = \begin{bmatrix} 1 & 0 & 0 & 0 \\ 0 & 1 & 0 & 0 \end{bmatrix},$$

$$T = k_3 T_{do}'$$

In the above equation the C matrix is so selected because $\Delta\delta$, $\Delta\omega$, can be easily calculated/measured.

System model (2) is assumed to be stabilizable via static output feedback. The static output feedback stabilization problem is to find a static output feedback $u = Fy$, such that the closed-loop system given by

$$\dot{x} = (A + BFC)x \qquad (4)$$

is stable, that is, with poles in the open left-half-plane.

As we all know, the closed-loop system (3) is stable if and only if there exists a $P = P' > 0$ such that

$$P(A + BFC) + (A + BFC)' P < 0 \qquad (5)$$

Condition (5) is a bilinear matrix inequality (BMI) which is not a convex optimal problem. An ILMI method was proposed in [17], where a new variable X was introduced such that the stability condition becomes a sufficient one when $X \neq P$. The algorithm presented in [17], tried to find some X close to P by using an iterative method and the iterative procedure carries between P and X.

As mentioned in [17], if

$$P(A + BFC) + (A + BFC)' P - \alpha P < 0 \qquad (6)$$

holds, the closed-loop system matrix $A + BFC$ has its eigenvalues in the strict left-hand side of the line $\alpha/2$ in the complex s-plane. If an $\alpha < 0$ satisfying (5) can be found, the SOF stabilization problem is solved.

Note that (6) a nonlinear matrix inequality, difficult to solve being non convex. In [17], Inequality (6) is simplified into LMIs using an additional variable, and α is minimized iteratively till it becomes negative. Note that all eigenvalues of the closed loop matrix $A + BFC$ are shifted progressively towards the left-half-plane through the reduction of α. A feasible solution, feedback matrix F,

is thus obtained. However; it results in an only sufficient condition, causing conservativeness.

Now to represent system dynamics at different loads, system (2) can be cast in the following norm-bounded form

$$\dot{x} = (A_o + \Delta A)x + Bu \qquad (7)$$

where A_o is the state matrix at the nominal load , the uncertainty in A is

$$\Delta A = M \, \Delta(t) N \qquad (8)$$

The matrices M and N being known constant real matrices, and $\Delta(t)$ the uncertain parameter matrix. The matrix ΔA has bounded nom given by $\|\Delta\| \leq 1$, Appendix 2. It is worth mentioning that $\Delta(t)$ can represent power system uncertainties, unmodelled dynamics, and/or nonlinearities.

Table 1 gives the extreme operating range of interest, heavy and light loads, as well as the nominal load. The corresponding system matrices are given in Appendix B.

Our objective now is to study two main problems:

How to eliminate the conservativeness of [17]?

How to robustify F in face of system uncertainties due to load variations?

3. Problem Solution

This section gives a brief overview of control design when formulated in terms of PSO and LMI.

3.1. Particle Swarm Optimization (PSO)

For unconstrained nonlinear optimization, we have the following problem

$$\text{Minimize}_z \quad J = f(z) \qquad (9)$$

The existence of a solution is verified numerically by minimizing J. Such problem is solved using particle swarm optimization (PSO). Like any other optimizer, the PSO converges to a solution, if exists. Most of the traditional deterministic optimization methods have the calculation burden of gradients or Hessians. In other words, they are based on the unrealistic assumptions, e.g., unimodal, differentiable, and continuous objective function. In non-gradient conventional optimization techniques, the gradient is numerically estimated. Deterministic me-

Table 1. Loading conditions.

Loading	P (p.u)	Q (p.u)
Heavy	1	0.5
Nominal	0.7	0.3
Light	0.4	0.1

thods can potentially converge to a local minimum instead

of the global minimum. There is no criterion to decide whether a local solution is also the global solution.

Therefore, the conventional optimization methods are, in general, not able to locate or identify the global optimum. Recently, many researchers are investigating probabilistic (stochastic) global optimizers, which seem to be a promising alternative to the traditional gradient- based approaches. Several stochastic search techniques have appeared, most notably, simulated annealing, tabu search, and evolutionary routines. Upon comparing evolutionary methods, the genetic algorithm (GA) has a big computational complexity unlike PSO, which is another stochastic global optimization technique. PSO has been found robust in solving continuous nonlinear optimization problems. In addition, PSO can generate a high-quality solution with less calculation time and more stable convergence characteristic than other stochastic methods. Due to its distinct advantages as a global optimizer, PSO has been selected to tune the reliable controllers presented in this paper.

Particle swarm optimization is an evolutionary optimization technique. Such approach is biologically inspired by the natural evolution of populations to Darwin's principle of natural selection "Survival of the fittest". The promising optimization algorithm of PSO, Parsopoulos and Vrahatis (2004), is a multi agent search technique that traces its evaluation to the emergent motion of a flock of birds searching for food. Each bird traverses to the search space looking for the global minimum (or maximum). PSO is a computationally sim- ple technique since it does not involve gradient calcula- tions. Moreover, the function to be optimized does not have to be convex. PSO is a stochastic optimization technique with large number of agents having the advan- tage of being unlikely trapped at local minima.

While the agents in the PSO algorithm are searching the space, each agent remembers two positions. The first is the position of the best point the agent has found (self-best), while the second is the position of the best point found among all agents (group-best). The motion of each agent is governed through the following equation:

$$S_{new} = \left[S + v \right]_{old}$$
$$v\big|_{new} = \Big[\omega v + ar(0,1)\big(S_{self-best} - S\big)$$
$$\qquad + br(0,1)\big(S_{group-best} - S\big)\Big]_{old} \qquad (10)$$

where (S) is a position vector of a single particle,
  (v) is the velocity of this particle,
  (a,b) are two scalar parameters of the algorithm,
  (ω) is an inertia weight,
  $r(0, 1)$ is a uniform random number between 0 and 1,

It should be noted that group-best is the best solution of all particles and self-best is the best solution observed by the current particle. A maximum velocity (v_{max}) that cannot be exceeded may also be imposed.

3.2. Control Design

System (2) is stabilizable if and only if there is a solution, $P > 0$, F, $\alpha < 0$, for the following nonlinear matrix Inequality (6).

If P is given, Inequality (6) becomes linear in F, and the minimized $\alpha = \alpha^*$ can be easily solved by LMI control toolbox.

The idea proposed in this manuscript is to minimize α^* by P generated by PSO in an outer loop of iteration as shown below.

3.3. PSO-Based Static Output Feedback Design

Step 0: Initialize the PSO by selecting randomly a vector $z \in R^{2n}$.

Step 1: Cast z into its matrix equivalent Z. Form $P = ZZ'$. In this way $P = P' > 0$ is generated. Set $i = 1$ and $P_i = P$

Step 2: Solve the following optimization problem for F and α_i.

Minimize α_i subject to the following LMI constraints

$$P_i\big(A + BFC\big) + \big(A + BFC\big)' P_i - \alpha_i P_i < 0 \qquad (11)$$

Denote α_i^* as the minimized value of α_i.

Step 3: If $\alpha_i^* < 0$, F is a stabilizing static output feedback gain. Stop.

If no $\alpha_i^* < 0$ is found, the system cannot be stabilized by a SOF.

Step 4: Use PSO to solve the following optimization problem

$$\text{Minimize}_z \quad J = \alpha_i^*(z) \qquad (12)$$

Set $i > i + 1$, then go to *Step* 1.

The above algorithm is applied to example 1 of [17]. The proposed algorithm is better than that of [18] as it stabilizes the system with less control gain, see Appendix C. This is expected as the proposed algorithm solves a necessary and sufficient condition, rather than an only sufficient of [17].

3.4. Robust Design

Since power systems undergo load changes that result in uncertainty in the state model, the SOF that robustly stabilizes the system is given by the following sufficient condition:

Theorem 1: *The uncertain system (7) can be robustly stabilized if there exist $P = P' > 0$, F, $\alpha < 0$ such that the following nonlinear matrix inequality*

$$\begin{bmatrix} \left(PA_o + PBFC + A^t_{\,o}P + \ C^tF^tB^tP \right) & PM \\ -\alpha P + \varepsilon N'N & \\ \bullet & -\varepsilon I \end{bmatrix} < 0 \qquad (13)$$

has a feasible solution.

Proof: By replacing A by $A_o + \Delta A$ in (6), it yields

$$\left(PA_o + PBFC + A^t_{\,o}P + C^t F^t B^t P \right) \\ -\alpha P + \left(P\Delta A + \Delta A^t P \right) < 0 \qquad (14)$$

Using **Fact 2**, Inequality (14) is satisfied if the following equation is satisfied

$$\left(PA_o + PBFC + A^t_{\,o}P + C^t F^t B^t P \right) \\ -\alpha P + \varepsilon^{-1} PM \left(PM \right)' + \varepsilon N'N < 0 \qquad (15)$$

By the Schur complements [22], we can put (15) in the form (13) as desired. This completes the proof.

An algorithm for robust SOF design can be constructed similar to the previous algorithm with replacing (11) by (13).

4. Design Validation Based on Nonlinear Model

4.1. SOF-PSS

Applying the proposed algorithm, Sec 3.3, to the linearized power system model at heavy load, Appendix B, and the results are summarized as:

- Controller matrix $F = [-0.2013 - 4.3512]$
- $\alpha^* = -0.2689$
- Closed-loop eigenvalues = $\{-0.42814 \pm i\,6.2841,$
- $-13.019, -6.5878\}$

The minimization of α^* via PSO is shown in **Figure 2**. Since power system operators generally welcome the damping of transient oscillations following small distur-

bances within a settling time of 10 - 15 sec [23], or equivalently the closed loop eigenvalues should lie to the left of the vertical line –0.3; the proposed algorithm is run till this objective is satisfied.

The proposed controller tested is on the nonlinear model (1), at the heavy load. It is assumed that the mechanical torque input undergoes a step change increase of 0.1 pu. The system is subject to a large disturbance at $t = 3$ s, a three-phase to ground fault occurs for 100 ms. The system without a PSS is unstable at this point, see **Figure 3(a)**. On the other hand, the proposed stabilizer successfully suppresses and damps the oscillations in almost 7 s, see **Figure 3(b)**.

The success of the proposed PSS, which is designed based on a linearized model, to stabilize the original nonlinear system follows from the Lyapunov indirect theorem. According to that theorem, the behavior of the origiinal nonlinear system is similar to its linearized approxi-

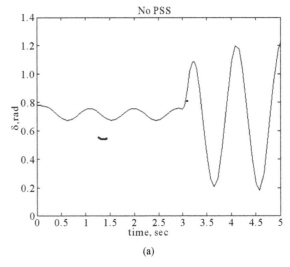

(a)

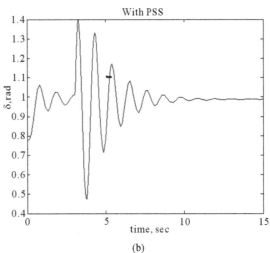

(b)

Figure 3. Time response of the nonlinear model of SMIB with and without PSS. (a) Without PSS; (b) With PSS.

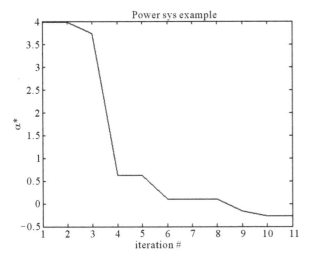

Figure 2. α^* vs. iterations.

mation provided that none of the eigenvalues lies on the imaginary axis.

4.2. Robust SOF-PSS

The algorithm described in Subsection 3.3 is applied find a robust SOF_PSS against the variation of power system operation; $p \in [0.4,1]$, and $Q \in [0.1, 0.5]$ respectively. The results are: $F = [-0.1797 \ -6.1133]$, and $\alpha^* = -0.4231$. The minimization of α^* vs. iterations are shown in **Figure 4**.

Out of the aforementioned power system operating range, the point $P = 0.8$ p.u, and $Q = 0.3$ p.u is selected to show the effectiveness of the proposed design. For 0.1 p.u. step increase in mechanical power, simulation results of a large disturbance are shown in **Figure 5**. At $t = 3$ s, a three-phase to ground fault occurs for 100ms. The proposed stabilizer succeeds to damp the disturbance within 5 sec.

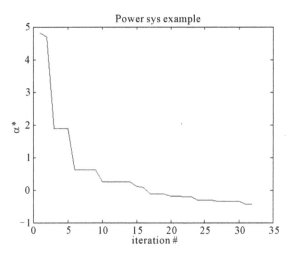

Figure 4. α^* vs. iterations, robust SOF-PSS.

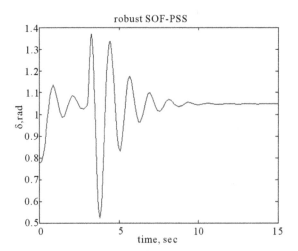

Figure 5. Performance of proposed robust stabilizer for 0.1 step increase in mech. power and the system undergoes a 3-phase to ground fault at infinite bus for 100 ms.

5. Conclusion

In this paper, a new algorithm is presented to solve a necessary and sufficient condition to stabilize linear time-invariant systems via static output feedback. The iterative algorithm combines the PSO and LMI. The algorithm is effective and convergent. The numerical procedure may be useful to solve this kind of bilinear matrix inequality problem. In this respect, the crucial part is to obtain an iterative condition. The proposed PSO-ILMI algorithm has low dimension because no additional variable is imposed. The algorithm can be applied to PID, decentralized stabilizers as well. A numerical example shows that the proposed algorithm produces better result than the existing one. A sufficient condition for the design of robust static output feedback using PSO with iterative LMI has been proposed. The method obtains the PSS for the linearized model of a single machine infinite bus system. Simulation results based on a nonlinear model of the power system confirm the ability of the proposed compensator to stabiles the system over a wide range of operating points.

6. Acknowledgements

This work is supported by the deanship of scientific research (DSR) at KFUPM through research group project RG1105-1.

REFERENCES

[1] P. Kundur, "Power System Stability and Control," McGraw Hill, New York, 1994.

[2] G. Guo, Y. Wang and D. Hill, "Nonlinear Output Stabilization Control for Multi-Machine Power Systems," *IEEE Transactions on Circuits and Systems*, Vol. 47, No. 1, 2000, pp. 46-53.

[3] Z. Qu, J. Dorsey, J. Bond and J. McCalley, "Application of Robust Control to Sustained Oscillations in Power Systems," *IEEE Transactions on Circuits and Systems*, Vol. 39, No. 2, 1992, pp. 470-476.

[4] R. You, H. J. Eghbali and M. H. Nehrir, "An Online Adaptive Neuro-Fuzzy Power System Stabilizer for Multimachine Systems," *IEEE Transactions Energy Conversion*, Vol. 18, No. 1, 2003, pp. 117-125.

[5] H. M. Soliman, A. Elshafei, A. Shaltout and M. Morsi, "Robust Power System Stabilizer," *IEE Proceeding Generation, Transmission, and Distribution*, Vol. 147, No. 2, 2000, pp. 285-291.

[6] B. Pai and B. Chaudhuri, "Robust Control in Power Systems," Springer, New York, 2005.

[7] C. J. Zhu, M. Khammash, V. Vittal and W. Qiu, "Robust Power System Stabilizer Design using H_∞ Loop Shaping Approach," *IEEE Transactions on Power Systems*, Vol. 18, No. 2, 2003, pp. 810-818.

[8] V. Bandal, B. Bandyopadhyay and A. M. Kulkarni, "De-

centralized Sliding Mode Control Technique Based Power System Stabilizer (PSS) for Multimachine Power System," *Proceedings Control Applications*, Toronto, 28-31 August 2005, pp. 55-60.

[9] A. I. Zecevic and D. D. Šiljak, "Control of Complex Systems: Structural Constraints and Uncertainty," Springer, London, 2009.

[10] R. Gupta, B. Bandyopadhyay and A. Kulkarni, "Robust Decentralized Fast-Output Sampling Technique based Power System Stabilizer for a Multi Machine Power System," *International Journal of Systems Sciences*, Vol. 36, No. 5, 2005, pp. 297-314.

[11] S. Rao and I. Sen, "Robust Pole Placement Stabilizer Design using Linear Matrix Inequalities," *IEEE Transactions Power Systems*, Vol. 15, No. 1, 2003, pp. 313-319.

[12] I. Kamwa, R. Grondin and Y. Hebert, "Wide-Area Measurement Based Stabilizing Control of Large Power Systems—A Decentralized/Hierarchical Approach," *IEEE Transactions Power Systems*, Vol. 16, No. 1, 2001, pp. 136-153.

[13] C. Liu, J. Jung, G. T. Heydt and V. Vittal, "The Strategic Power Infrastructure Defense (SPID) System," *IEEE Control System Magazine*, Vol. 20, No. 1, 2000, pp. 40-52.

[14] H. M. Soliman, M. Morsi, M. F. Hassan and M. Awadallah, "Power system reliable stabilization with actuator failure," *Electric Power Components and Systems*, Vol. 37, No. 1, 2009, pp. 61-77.

[15] H. M. Soliman, H. E. Ehab, E. H. E. Bayoumi and M. A. Awadallah, "Reconfigurable Fault-Tolerant PSS and FACTS Controllers," *Electric Power Components and*

Systems, Vol. 38, No. 10, 2010, pp. 1446-1468.

[16] H. M. Soliman, A. Dabroum, M. S. Mahmoud and M. Soliman, "Guaranteed-Cost Reliable Control with Regional Pole Placement of a Power System," *Journal of the Franklin Institute*, Vol. 348, No. 4, 2011, pp. 884-898.

[17] Y. Y. Cao, J. Lam and Y. X. Sun, "Static Output Feedback Stabilization: An ILMI Approach," *Automatica*, Vol. 34, No. 12, 1998, pp. 1641-1645.

[18] Y. He and Q. G. Wang, "An Improved ILMI Method for Static Output Feedback Control with Application to Multivariable PID Control," *IEEE Transactions Automatic Control*, Vol. 51, No. 10, 2006, pp. 2356-2361.

[19] K. E. Parsopoulos and M. N. Vrahatis, "On the Computation of All Global Minimizes Through Particle Swarm Optimization," *IEEE Transactions Evolutionary Computation*, Vol. 8, No. 3, 2004, pp. 211-220.

[20] R. Mendes, J. Kennedy and J. Neves, "The Fully Informed Particle Swarm: Simpler, Maybe Better," *IEEE Transactions. Evolutionary Computation*, Vol. 8, No. 3, 2004, pp. 345-360.

[21] P. Gahinet, A. Nemirovski, A. J. Laub and M. Chilali "LMI Control Toolbox," The Math Works Inc., Natick, 1995.

[22] M. S. Mahmoud, "Decentralized Control and Filtering in Interconnected Dynamic Systems," CRC Press, New York, 2010.

[23] J. Passerby, "Analysis and Control of Power System oscillations," *Technical Brochure* 111, CIGRE, 1996.

Appendix

A. Model Parameters

$$k_1 = C_3 \frac{P^2}{P^2 + (Q + C_1)^2} + Q + C_1,$$

$$k_2 = C_4 \frac{P}{\sqrt{P^2 + (Q + C_1)^2}},$$

$$k_3 = \frac{x_d' + x_e}{x_d + x_e},$$

$$k_4 = C_5 \frac{P}{\sqrt{P^2 + (Q + C_1)^2}},$$

$$k_5 = C_4 x_e \frac{P}{V^2 + Q x_e} \left[C_6 \frac{C_1 + Q}{P^2 + (C_1 + Q)^2} - x_d' \right],$$

$$k_6 = C_7 \frac{\sqrt{P^2 + (C_1 + Q)^2}}{V^2 + Q x_e} \left[x_e + \frac{C_1 x_q (C_1 + Q)}{P^2 + (C_1 + Q)^2} \right].$$

$$C_1 = \frac{V^2}{x_e + x_q},$$

$$C_2 = k_3$$

$$C_3 = C_1 \frac{x_q - x_d'}{x_e + x_d'},$$

$$C_4 = \frac{V}{x_e + x_d'}$$

$$C_5 = \frac{x_d - x_d'}{x_e + x_d'},$$

$$C_6 = C_1 \frac{x_q (x_q - x_d')}{x_e + x_q}$$

$$C_7 = \frac{x_e}{x_e + x_d'}$$

B. State Model

	Algorithm of [17]	Proposed algorithm
α	−0.0377	−0.0021
F	−0.7369	−0.0747

The numerical values of state space model for the three operating conditions are given as follows:

Nominal load:

$$A_o = \begin{bmatrix} 0 & 314 & 0 & 0 \\ -0.1186 & 0 & -0.0906 & 0 \\ -0.1934 & 0 & -0.4633 & 0.1667 \\ -11.864 & 0 & -511.6 & -20 \end{bmatrix}$$

Heavy load:

$$A = \begin{bmatrix} 0 & 314 & 0 & 0 \\ -0.1445 & 0 & -0.0976 & 0 \\ -0.2082 & 0 & -0.4633 & 0.1667 \\ 32.097 & 0 & -525.44 & -20 \end{bmatrix}$$

Light load:

$$A = \begin{bmatrix} 0 & 314 & 0 & 0 \\ -0.0875 & 0 & -0.0759 & 0 \\ -0.162 & 0 & -0.4633 & 0.1667 \\ -54.214 & 0 & -511.94 & -20 \end{bmatrix}$$

$$B = \begin{bmatrix} 0 & 0 & 0 & 1000 \end{bmatrix}'$$

Neglecting small deviations in A, the uncertainty in A over the different loads can be approximated by a norm-bound structure $M\Delta(t)N$, $M = [0, 0, 0, 6.63]'$, $N = [6.63, 0, -2.08, 0]$.

C. Comparison

Example 1 of [17] gives

$$A = \begin{bmatrix} 0 & 1 \\ 1 & 0 \end{bmatrix}, B = \begin{bmatrix} 1 \\ 0 \end{bmatrix}, C = \begin{bmatrix} 1 & 15 \end{bmatrix}$$

Applying the proposed algorithm, the reduction in α^* vs. iteration is shown in **Figure 4** and the comparison between the results of [17] and the proposed algorithm is shown below.

It is clear the superiority of the proposed algorithm over that of [17] as it stabilizes the system with less controller gain.

11

Switching Optimization for Class-G Audio Amplifiers with Two Power Supplies

Patrice Russo[1,2], Firas Yengui[1], Gael Pillonnet[1,2], Sophie Taupin[2], Nacer Abouchi[1]
[1]Lyon Institute of Nanotechnology (INL-UMR5270), University of Lyon, Lyon, France
[2]ST Microelectronics, Grenoble, France

ABSTRACT

This paper presents a system-level method to decrease the power consumption of integrated audio Class-G amplifiers for mobile phones by using the same implementation of the level detector, but by changing the parameters of the switching algorithm. This method uses an optimization based on a simplified model simulation to quickly find the best power supply switching strategy in order to decrease the losses of the internal Class-AB amplifier. Using a few relevant equations of Class-G on the electrical level and by reducing the number of calculation points, this model can dramatically reduce the calculation time to allow power consumption evaluation in realistic case conditions compared to the currently available tools. This simplified model also evaluates the audio quality reproduction thanks to a psycho-acoustic method. The model has been validated by comparing model results and practical measurements on two industrial circuits. This proposed model is used by an optimizer based on a genetic algorithm associated with a pattern search algorithm to find the best power supply switching strategy for the internal Class-AB amplifier. The optimization results improve life-time performance by saving at least 25% in power consumption for typical use-case (1 mW) compared to the industrial circuit studied and without losses in audio quality.

Keywords: Audio Amplifier; Class-G; Hybrid Optimization

1. Introduction

The battery-powered systems, such as mobile phone, PDA and MP3, integrate more and more complex and power-consuming functions: large screen, GPS and audio applications, etc. The IC designers are faced with two main challenges: higher integration and lower power consumption to reduce PCB area and increase battery life. In this work, we focus on a headphone application for cell phones. Indeed, this application uses a large part of the total power consumption of the mobile phone when the consumer is listening the music (when the screen doesn't work and no other application is running). In the first generation of headphone amplifiers, Class-AB topology was preferred because of its low relative complexity and good audio performance compared to other topologies. However this solution suffers from a limited efficiency given by:

$$\eta_{AB} = \frac{\pi}{4} \times \frac{V_{OUT}}{V_{DD}} \qquad (1)$$

where, V_{DD} is the power supply of the Class-AB amplifier and V_{OUT} the RMS audio output voltage. In (1), the quiescent current is considered as negligible. Due to the low RMS voltages of a standard audio signal and the low RMS voltages of a standard audio signal and the power required by the headphone, the efficiency is only a few percent because of the low ratio between the output signal level and the power supply (V_{OUT}/V_{DD}), and also the quiescent current.

Other solutions could be used for headphone applications, such as switching (Class-D) or hybrid (Class-G, H and K) amplifiers. Recent work proposed Class-D amplifiers for headphone applications [1,2] but they suffer from a higher static current consumption with a DC coupling capacitor and unpredictable electromagnetic interference. The Class-K amplifier also suffers from high consumption [3]. Class-G topology has been proposed to reduce the V_{OUT}/V_{DD} ratio, see (1), by powering the linear amplifier with a dynamic power supply. Reducing the current consumption by a factor of 3 (at average output power) compared to the Class-AB, means there are now alternative solutions in headphone applications [4-8]. **Figure 1** shows a Class-G block diagram and an example of power supply variation with a real audio signal. An integrated Class-G amplifier is therefore composed of a dynamic power supply converter associated with a switching power supply algorithm and a linear amplifier.

Present Class-G amplifiers [6-8] use two different power supply rails to decrease the conducted power

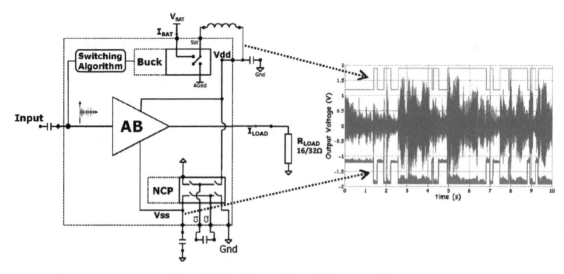

Figure 1. Class-G amplifier with two supplies.

losses $(V_{DD} - V_{OUT})/I_{LOAD}$ in the linear amplifier, and only a few papers introduce hybrid amplifiers with more than two power supplies [9-11]. Class-G exhibits higher efficiency at low output power where the audio amplifier is widely used. Indeed, average listening power is ten times less than the maximal output power. In addition to their improved efficiency, Class-G amplifiers exhibit a comparable audio quality to classic Class-AB solution [6-8].

Due to the complexity of multi-level Class-G electrical implementation, which could increase the global power consumption, the multi-levels (also called Class-H) are not yet used in industrial applications.

To find the optimal algorithm of power switching, a thorough analysis of amplifier efficiency for many different cases has to be undertaken. Indeed, [10] and [12] present an optimization made by experts in this domain and suggest optimal parameters for the switching algorithm in amplifiers with two or three power supplies. [4], [5] and [13] focus more on optimizing the electrical implementation by proposing solutions on the improvement of consumption and harmonic distortion (*i.e.* one component of the audio quality).

The objective of this work is therefore to optimize the power consumption that could be achieved with a Class-G with two power supplies for headphone applications by finding the optimal value of several parameters of the level detector. Section 2 is devoted to the modeling of the amplifier. Then, the optimization issues are described in Section 3. The last section discusses model validation and optimization results based on an existing Class-G amplifier.

2. Modelization

2.1. Objectives

Present Class-G amplifiers contain more than a few

thousand transistors and therefore require several weeks of simulation with a sinusoidal signal of a few milliseconds. In order to reduce this calculation time and enable the simulation of longer test signals such as music, a fast and accurate model is suggested. As the simulation time is strictly linked to the level of abstraction, as indicated on **Figure 2**, behavioral modeling enables a good compromise between time and precision of the simulations.

This model must allow post-processing on audio signals (interpolation, and cutting up of sound tracks, etc.), and enable us to evaluate the sound reproduction quality of the audio signal (notably using the PEAQ method, explained in Subsection 2.5). The parameters of our model must also be optimized via different search algorithms (cf. Section 3). We therefore chose a Matlab model using the version R2007a, rendering all these actions possible within the same interface.

2.2. Power Supply Switching Algorithm

The synoptic diagram of the power supply switching algorithm for a class G2 amplifier is presented in **Figure 3** and was implemented in our Matlab model.

Depending on the input voltage, the buck converter provides two different power supplies as shown in **Figure 1**. If the output voltage exceeds the upper threshold $\alpha \times |V_{ss}|$, then the higher supply is applied with a given rise time (**Figure 4**). Then, when the input audio signal falls under the lower threshold $\beta \times |V_{ss}|$, the lower supply is selected after a time, called the decay time. A parameter called the attack time was included in the model. This parameter is a delay between the time when the music is above to $\alpha \times |V_{ss}|$, and the time when the lower supply starts to move to the upper supply. The fall time depends on the discharge of the capacitor of the Negative Charge Pump (NCP) and the buck converter. All these

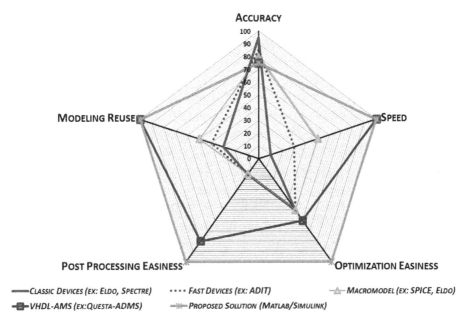

Figure 2. Modeling comparison.

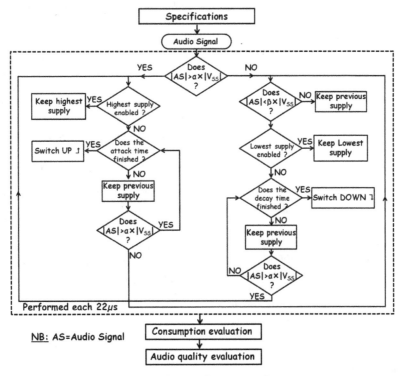

Figure 3. Algorithm synoptic.

2.3. Modeling of the Power Converters and the Linear Amplifier

In order to only study the leverage of the switching algorithm, only the transient parameters that influence the consumption and the audio quality are finely modeled.

parameters are taken into account in our proposed model.

Therefore, the linear amplifier is modeled as having a fixed gain, and its linearity, its noise and immunity to the power supply are considered ideal. Regarding the power converters, the buck is modeled with an ideal line and load transient, but its efficiency is 80% (like the current available buck) [6]. The NCP is also considered ideal (no losses R_{ON} in MOS switches) but its equivalent resistor ($R_{EQ} = 5\ \Omega$) is modeled since it's a contributor to the

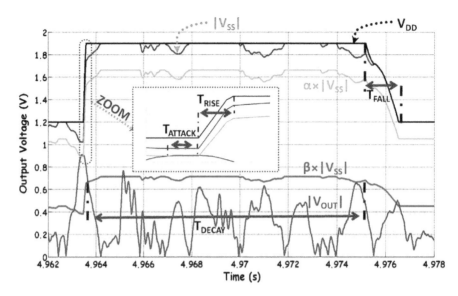

Figure 4. Switching algorithm.

clipping of the signal in transient analysis.

The buck converter and the NCP can be linearized and modeled by simplified equations while keeping a good accuracy to predict the total current consumption. The equation of the consumption, in a two mono-channel configuration can be expressed by:

$$I_{BAT} = \frac{V_{DD}}{\eta_{BUCK} \times V_{BAT}} \left(I_{Q\_BUCK} + 2I_{LOAD} \right) + I_{Q\_BAT} \quad (2)$$

$$I_{LOAD} = \frac{V_{OUT}}{R_{LOAD}} \quad (3)$$

where, I_{BAT} is the supply current, I_{LOAD} the load current, I_{Q_BUCK} the quiescent current of the buck converter, η_{BUCK} the buck converter efficiency, and I_{Q_BAT} the quiescent current on the battery.

The effects of the switch on the DC/DC converter (f_{SW} = 750 kHz) are negligible for the prediction of the consumption of the amplifier. This averaged behavior implies a reduction in the number of calculation points. In our model, the time step is 22 μs which corresponds to the inverse of the sampling rate of our audio test signal (44.1 kHz), instead of a few ns in electrical simulators.

2.4. Choice of Input Signals

Using a realistic audio test signal instead of a pure sine wave is essential because the behavior of Class-G amplifiers is quite different. Indeed, for a sine wave at 1 kHz with a crest factor of 3 dB (the ratio between V_{PEAK} and V_{RMS}), there is no switch down for a decay time greater than 100 μs (when the output power leads the power supply to switch). However, the audio signal leads the amplifier to switch up and down (**Figure 3**). The behavior of our model is thus working in realistic conditions, con-

trary to a simulator at transistor level which would require too long a calculation time if a real audio wave was used. The study takes into account that the consumer can listen to several kinds of music (jazz, rap and techno, etc.), which have a typical crest factor between 5 and 20 [14]. Based on this principle, three signals with different crest factors were chosen. Choosing three test signals allow a faster simulation and a best convergence in optimization, while providing a representative sample of the main cases in order to optimize our model. In addition to these test signals (n°1, 2 and 3), two other test signals are used in section 4 to prove the robustness of the optimization (n°4 and 5). **Table 1** summarizes the input signals used in this paper.

Figure 5 shows the current consumption for the previous test signals, and then shows the actual amplifier switch for an output power above 3 mW for a crest factor under 10 dB. Typical uses of the audio amplifier for headphone required low output power (until 100 μW and 1 mW) which means that the current amplifier is oversized. This figure also highlights the fact that the switch-

Table 1. Signal used for test.

Signal	Type	CF (dB)	Artist/Title	Length (s)
N°1	Sine Wave (f = 1 KHz)	3	-	0.05
N°2	Audio Track	14	Janis Joplin/Me and Bobby Mc Gee	10
N°3	Audio Track	7	David Guetta	10
N°4	Audio Track	17	Red Hot Chili Peppers/Under the Bridge	10
N°5	Audio Track	13	Diana Krall/Bye Bye Blackbird	10

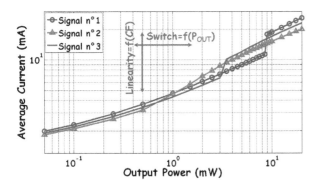

Figure 5. Current consumption for different test signals.

ing of the power supply of Class-G amplifier is dependent on the crest factor.

2.5. Evaluation of Audio Quality

Audio quality is as important as the reduction in power consumption. The model makes it possible to use the objective method to evaluate the audio quality, because Total Harmonic Distortion (THD) could only be used with a pure sine wave. For an objective method, the Perceptual Evaluation of Audio Quality (PEAQ) was chosen. This standard uses a number of psycho-acoustic measurements which are combined to give a measure of the quality difference between the reference and post-processing signal [15]. The method then returns to an ODG (Objective Difference Grade) value between 0 and –4 which reflects the impairment heard by human ears. The value 0 means than the difference is imperceptible and value –4 means than the difference is very annoying for the listener. To complete this method, listening tests (subjective method) were performed.

3. Optimization Approach

The aim of this section is to present our optimization approach to find the best strategy to switch the two power supplies of the Class-G audio amplifier. This is done in order to reach an optimal current consumption without losing audio quality, and at the same time independent of the input signals. This approach consisted in solving, numerically, design problems while respecting the limitation due to circuit constraints and specifications. Two factors require special attention when such a problem is analyzed, namely, the problem formulation and the search algorithm.

3.1. Problem Formulation

3.1.1. Design Variable

Ten parameters are defined: battery voltage, load, two power supply voltages, and six switching parameters (rise, fall, attack and decay times, α and β). We will op-timize five design variables (degrees of freedom): V_{DD_LOW}, decay time, attack time, α and β. Moreover the range of V_{DD_LOW} is limited by the IC design constraint topology and the output power selected is 1mW, even if other output power is considered.

3.1.2. Objective Function

The problem consists in minimizing supply current consumption for all three selected audio input signals. Despite the multi-objective approach, we study as a mono-objective problem using the aggregation approach [16]. It is one of the most often used methods for generation of Pareto optimal solutions. Our optimization algorithms allow us to minimize the objective function expressed as:

$$f = \sum_{i=1}^{3} wi \times Ii \text{ with } wi > 0 \text{ and } \sum_{i=1}^{3} wi = 1 \qquad (4)$$

where, Ii represents the supply current consumption for each input signal, $i \in [1, 3]$ the number of the objective and wi the weighting coefficient. In our case, $wi = 1$ because no preference between each objective is made.

3.1.3. Constraints

Constraints are conditions that must be satisfied in order to find a feasible design. Inequality constraints are used: each of the three ODGs has to be above -0.5 with the three input signals.

3.2. Optimization Algorithm

Once the problem has been formulated, we must choose the best optimization algorithm that allows us to minimize the objective function under the constraints. The Genetic Algorithm (GA) is one of the most popular and robust algorithms. It is based on natural genetic and natural selection mechanisms and some fundamental ideas are borrowed from genetics in order to artificially construct an optimization procedure. The GA acts over a population of potential solutions, applying intensification (crossover) and diversification (mutation) operators to explore the problem space. The fittest individuals are selected and give birth to a new population in the hope of improving the solution quality. More details on the mechanism of GAs can be found in [17]. GA is useful for a global search solution. However it is very slow and poor in a localized search. The direct search algorithm, Pattern Search (PS), on the contrary, is often able to find local optima for constrained optimization problems, but it cannot guarantee that the solution is the global optimum of the problem. It ensures computational robustness when it starts from a feasible initial solution [18]. By combining GA with PS, an algorithm referred to as the GA-PS hybrid algorithm is formulated in this paper. In other words, the GA looks at the whole solution space to obtain a quasi-optimal solution. Then, the PS is used to increase the quality and speed of convergence to the optimal solution.

3.3. Cascade Simulation-Based Optimization

To optimize the Class-G amplifiers for different types of input signal simultaneously, we use a multiple simulation-based optimization to find the optimal solution with respect to the three audio signals. **Figure 6** presents the concept of our approach.

For each iteration of the optimization loop, a simulation of our model, presented in Section 2, was performed for each audio input signal to find the performance such as current consumption I_{BAT} and the quality factor ODG.

4. Results

4.1. Model Validation

An existing circuit [6] was modeled with our proposed method (Section 2). Several measurements on [6] have been done to find the input parameters of the simplified electrical equations given in Equation (3) and to find the switching algorithm (α, β, etc).

In **Figure 7**, the measurement test bench is presented and allows us to compare the current found by the measurement of [6] and our proposed model. The setup configuration is a 47 Ω load, 3.6 V power supply and signal n°2. The error is less than 5% over all the output power range. Other input signals gave the same results. The comparison was also made with other existing Class-G [6] and it showed that the error is less than 10% with the same conditions. These results confirm that the Class-G amplifier model gives a reliable current consumption and can be used by the optimizer.

4.2. Optimizer Algorithm Comparison

For our application, we compared three algorithm optimizations to show the effectiveness of the proposed hybrid GA-PS algorithm. GA-PS is compared to GA and another hybrid algorithm GA-SQP, which is based on a GA coupled with the local search algorithm: Sequential Quadratic Programming (SQP). The optimization algorithms used in this study are part of the MATLAB optimization toolbox. In **Table 2**, we compared the output power of 1mW with signal 1, 2 and 3. The objective function is the mean of the consumption for these three input signals. The best result is obtained using a GA-PS optimization, in terms of minimizing the objective function while keeping an acceptable time of optimization. We therefore used this solution in order to reduce the consumption of our amplifier.

Indeed, over 100 000 simulations would be necessary with an exhaustive search. Moreover, extrapolating the results of a GA-PS optimization with a model using a transistor and macro-model would require 134 years to

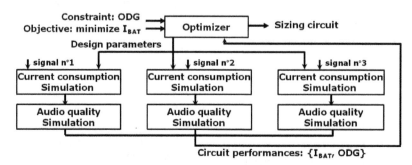

Figure 6. Cascade simulation-based optimization.

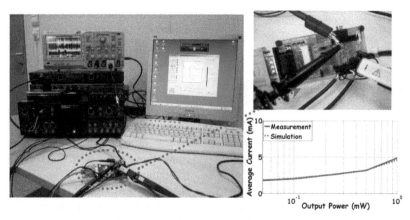

Figure 7. Comparison between [6] and our model.

Table 2. Algorithm comparison.

	Hybrid GA-SQP	Hybrid GA-PS
Number of Iterations	576	554
Objective function (mA)	2.6	2.41
Simulation Time (min)	47	45
Results	☺	☺

find an optimal solution, since a single simulation with an audio signal during ten seconds takes three months.

4.3. Optimization Results

At the moment, the minimum supply voltage of a Class-G amplifier is 1.2 V [6]. However, because of the real power needed in general, we made an optimization allowing the constraint V_{DD_LOW} to be above 700 mV (which is the actual limit for the power amplifier) in order to see the leverage of optimization by tuning V_{DD_LOW} while keeping the other constraints as before. The test signal used is signal 4. It is used to perform the optimization in order to prove the robustness of the proposed optimization. The results shown in **Figure 8** presents the gain obtained compared to [6] from 20 μW until 20 mW and highlight the need to lower the supply voltage of the power amplifier, since this reduction reduces the consumption for low power without degrading the consumption at high power. Moreover, the algorithm used in this optimization always respects the condition for the audio quality. **Figure 7** also shows that the gains in consumption start to reduce after 2 mW for V_{DD_LOW} > 1.2 V and 5 mW for V_{DD_LOW} > 0.7 V. This result is explained by the facts that highest is the output power, lower are the switches of the amplifiers until the blocking of the upper supply.

We can note that for a Class-G amplifier with two power supplies, the reduction of V_{DD_LOW} under 700 mV is not justified. Indeed, the optimization performed did not show a reduction in consumption.

This conclusion leads us to perform the optimization with constraints V_{DD_LOW} above 700 mV, as shown in

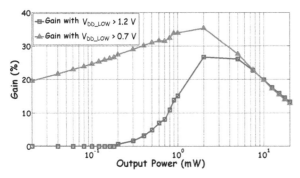

Figure 8. Current consumption vs. V_{DD_LOW} for signal n°4.

Table 3. Here, we present the results for one music used for the optimization (signal n°2) and two signals not used for the optimization (signal n°4 and 5), to prove the robustness of the proposed optimization.

It can be noted that the results presented in **Table 3** do not reduce the audio quality compared to the initial configuration of [6], which means that the ODG is always above –0.5. The results found by the optimizer are summarized in **Table 4** and compared to two industrial circuits [6,7]. These parameters are not directly found in the datasheet but are obtained using reverse engineering on their test board. This table shows that the parameters of current industrial circuits are oversized. The threshold voltage can be placed closer to the supply voltage, the decay time has to be reduced and the lowest power supply should be minimized even if the highest power supply is at 1.9 V. However, like the industrial circuits [6,7], the attack time is not reliable to gain in consumption without deteriorate the audio quality. But this parameter has to be tried for Class-G with more than two power supplies in order to see if the results could be better. Indeed, all the parameters present in **Table 4** can't be applied for Class-G with more than two power supplies.

Figure 9 shows the gain in the current consumption from 20 μW to 5mW between the initial configuration from [6] and the optimization. 18% at 100 μW and at least 25% at 1 mW are saved with an optimal configuration of the switching power supply algorithm. Even the two signals not used for the optimization give a gain in con-

Table 3. Comparison for different class-G amplifiers.

Input Signals	Results for	Current Consumption (mA)		
		0.1 mW	0.5 mW	1 mW
Signal n°2	Previous Work [6]	2.1	3.2	4.61
	This Work	1.6	2.35	3.28
Signal n°4	Previous Work [6]	2.11	3.41	4.84
	This Work	1.62	2.37	3.21
Signal n°5	Previous Work [6]	2.11	3.22	4.68
	This Work	1.61	2.36	3.24

Table 4. Value of the optimized parameters.

Parameters	[6]	[7]	This Work
V_{DD_LOW}(V)	1.2	1.3	0.7
α	$7/8 \times |V_{ss}|$	$5/8 \times |V_{ss}|$	$7.2/8 \times |V_{ss}|$
β	$3/8 \times |V_{ss}|$	$3/8 \times |V_{ss}|$	$6.5/8 \times |V_{ss}|$
Decay Time (ms)	130	4.5	0.1
Attack Time (s)	0	0	0

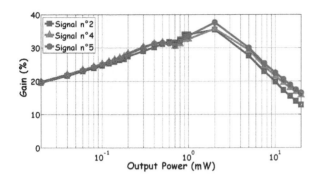

Figure 9. Gain in current consumption because of optimization.

sumption at low and nominal power. Like previously, for high power, they are few switch of the amplifier and the gain start to decrease after 2 mW. It is well to remember that the same level detector than [6] is used (based on logic gates and comparator which are few consuming).

5. Conclusion

In this paper, an original equation-based model has been introduced and associated with a hybrid optimization algorithm in order to reduce the current consumption of audio Class-G amplifiers by choosing the best parameters of the power supply switching algorithm. The proposed model has been validated. It also saves simulation time to predict the power consumption and keeps audio quality with various input signals. The optimizer coupled to this model allows us to find the best power supply switching strategy for a Class-G amplifier with two supplies by giving the optimal value of the parameters (V_{DD_LOW}, α, β, decay time and attack time). At least 25% of power consumption can be saved by optimizing the switching algorithm compared to an existing Class-G circuit with the same electrical implementation. In addition, the model is robust for operating conditions since the optimization was done for multiple input signals without loss of audio quality thanks to the PEAQ method. In future work, this approach will be used with Class-G amplifiers with more than two-power supplies, in order to optimize on all the range of power.

6. Acknowledgements

The authors gratefully acknowledge the standard linear division of ST Microelectronics for their valuable technical help.

REFERENCES

[1] K. Kang, J. Roh, Y. Choi, H. Roh, H. Nam and S. Lee, "Class-D Audio Amplifier Using 1-bit Fourth-Order Delta-Sigma Modulation," *IEEE Transaction on Circuits and Systems II*, Vol. 55, No. 8, 2008, pp. 728-732.

[2] G. Pillonnet, N. Abouchi, R. Cellier and A. Nagari, "A 0.01% THD, 70 dB PSRR Single Ended Class D Using Variable Hysteresis Control For Headphone Amplifiers," *IEEE International Symposium on Circuits and Systems*, Taipei, 24-27 May 2009, pp. 1181-1184.

[3] E. Sturtzer, G. Pillonnet, A. Huffenus, N. Abouchi, F. Goutti and V. Rabary, "Improved Class-K Amplifier for Headset Applications," *8th IEEE International NEWCAS Conference*, Montreal, 20-23 June 2010, pp. 185-188.

[4] A. Lollio, G. Bollati and R. Castello, "A Class-G Headphone Amplifier in 65 nm CMOS Technology," *IEEE Journal of Solid State Circuits*, Vol. 45, No. 12, 2010, pp. 2530-2542.

[5] A. Downey and G. Wierzba, "A Class-G/FB Audio Amplifier," *IEEE Transactions on Consumer Electronics*, Vol. 53, No. 4, 2007, pp. 1537-1545.

[6] Datasheet ST-M TS4621. http://www.st.com

[7] Datasheet TI TPA6140. http://www.ti.com

[8] Datasheet NS LM48824. http://www.national.com

[9] R. Bortoni, S. N. Filho and R. Seara, "Analysis, Design and Assessment of Class A, B, AB, G and H Audio Power Amplifier Output Stage Based on Matlab® Software," *110th Audio Engineering Society Conferences*, Amsterdam, 12-15 May 2001

[10] F. H. Raab, "Average Efficiency of Class-G Power Amplifier," *IEEE transaction on Consumer Electronics*, Vol. 32, No. 2, 1986, pp. 145-150.

[11] E. Mendenhall, "Computer Aided Design and Analysis of Class B and Class H Power Amplifier Output Stage," *Audio Engineering Society 101st Convention*, 1996.

[12] T. Sampei, S. Ohashi, Y. Ohta and S. Inoue, "Highest Efficiency and Super Quality Audio Amplifier Using MOS Power FETS in Class G Operation," *IEEE Transaction on Consumer Electronics*, Vol. CE-24, No. 3, 1978, pp. 300-307.

[13] J. Gubelmann, P. A. Dal Fabro, M. Pastre and M. Kayal, "High-Efficiency Dynamic Supply CMOS Audio Power Amplifier for Low-Power Applications," *Journal of Microelectronics*, Vol. 40, No. 8, 2009, pp. 1175-1183.

[14] M. Mijic, D. Masovic, D. Sumarac Pavlovic and M. Petrovic, "Statistical Properties of Music Signals," *Audio Engineering Society 126th Convention*, 2009.

[15] T. Thiede, *et al.*, "PEAQ the ITU Standard for Objective Measurement of Perceived Audio Quality," *Journal of Audio Engineering Society*, Vol. 48, No. 1, 2000, pp. 3-29.

[16] N. Srinivas and K. Deb, "Multiobjective Optimization Using Nondominated Sorting in Genetic Algorithms," *Journal of Evolutionary Computation*, Vol. 2, No. 3, 1994, pp. 221-248.

[17] T. El-Ghazali, "Metaheuristics: From Design to Imple-

mentation," Jonh Wiley and Sons Inc., Chichester, 2009.

[18] R. M. Lewis and V. Torczon, "Pattern Search Algorithms for Bound Constrained Minimization," *Journal SIAM on Optimization*, Vol. 9, No. 4, 1999, pp. 1082-1099.

12

Design and Analysis of a Power Efficient Linearly Tunable Cross-Coupled Transconductor Having Separate Bias Control

Vijaya Bhadauria[1*], Krishna Kant[2], Swapna Banerjee[3]

[1]Electronics and Communication Engineering Department, Motilal Nehru National Institute of Technology, Allahabad, India
[2]Department of Computer Engineering and Application, GLA University, Mathura, India
[3]Electronics and Electrical Communication Engineering Department, Indian Institute of Technology, Kharagpur, India

ABSTRACT

A common current source, generally used to bias cross-coupled differential amplifiers in a transconductor, controls third harmonic distortion (HD_3) poorly. Separate current sources are shown to provide better control on HD_3. In this paper, a detailed design and analysis is presented for a transconductor made using this biasing technique. The transconductor, in addition, is made to offer high G_m, low power dissipation and is designed for linearly tunable G_m with current mode load as one of the applications. The circuit exhibits HD_3 of less than –43.7 dB, high current efficiency of 1.18 V^{-1} and G_m of 390 µS at 1 V_{p-p} @ 50 MHz. UMC 0.18 µm CMOS process technology is used for simulation at supply voltage of 1.8 V.

Keywords: Analog Electronics; Low Power Analog CMOS Circuit; Operational Transconductance Amplifier (OTA); Multiple-Output OTA (MOTA); MOS Transconductors; Linearly Tunable G_m; Current Efficiency; Linearization Techniques; Harmonic Distortion Analysis

1. Introduction

Transconductors interface a current mode circuit to a voltage signal, making it a fundamental element of analog circuits [1-4]. Performance of a transconductor deteriorates due to higher total harmonic distortion (THD), more so at high signal level. Several techniques are devoted to improve THD of transconductors [5-20]. Sánchez-Sinencio and J. Silva-Martínez [4] have classified these as input signal attenuation [5-7], cancellation of nonlinear terms [7-12], and source degeneration [7, 11-19]. Besides these, adaptive biasing [16,19] and mobility compensation [20] techniques are also reported to improve THD.

One of the important building blocks in many analog circuits is a tunable linear transconductor [9,13,15,17, 21-25], which may be used for tuning center frequency and Q-factor of filters. Moreover it helps to compensate fabrication tolerances and environment parameters, especially temperature.

A method of tuning transconductance, G_m is to control the bias current (I_{Bias}) applied to the differential amplifier. But G_m is proportional to the square root of I_{Bias} due to

which the allowable input signal swing is limited to small value [1]. In [17], the allowable input swing for a constant value of I_{Bias} is made independent of variation in G_m by using current mirrors with source degeneration.

Another tuning method uses source degeneration resistance (R). In this method due to degeneration, THD improves but at the cost of transconductance. Further, the condition of improvement, ($1/G_m$ < R) [1] occupies large area and add noise if passive resistance is used. In [13], tunability has been achieved using active resistance. But G_m adjustment in this tuning method affects the bandwidth, which has been compensated in [15] by employing a separate source follower biased with constant current source.

Linearly adjustable G_m is realized using control voltage at inputs of one of the cross-coupled differential amplifier [8,9]. In both the papers authors have used identical transistors in the cross-coupled amplifiers to obtain linear tuning of G_m at supply voltage 5 V or higher. Different bias strategies are given in [25] to achieve tunability for ultra low range transconductance.

A low voltage transconductor on 0.18 µm technology is given by us in [23] in which bias currents of cross-coupled differential amplifiers and aspect ratio of their

---

*Corresponding author.

transistors are adjusted to cancel third harmonic distortion. Shift level biasing is used in the cross-coupled differential amplifier to obtain tunability. The circuit is designed for resistive load, not suitable for current mode signal processing.

The topology cited in [23] is analyzed in detail in this paper. In addition diode mode MOSFETs are used as load for current mode signal processing in place of active resistance. A triode mode tail transistor is used in MA for better linear tuning instead of constant current source. Design steps in detail with algorithm are given for low HD$_3$, high linearly tunable G_m and high frequency of operation at low voltage. Efforts have also been made to maintain low power operation and high current efficiency. The circuit is developed for 1 V$_{p-p}$ input signal for frequency range upto 50 MHz.

The paper is organized as follows. In Section 2, block diagram, circuit design alongwith its algorithm and analysis of the proposed circuit are given. In Section 3, simulation results are discussed and finally conclusions are drawn in Section 4.

2. Design and Analysis of Tunable Transconductor

2.1. Block Diagram of Tunable Transconductor

The proposed transconductor is designed using main differential amplifier (MA) biased using tail transistors in triode mode, compensatory differential amplifier (CA) biased using separate constant current source for minimizing HD$_3$ and level shifters (LS) are used for tunability. Separate controls of the two bias currents of MA and CA provide flexibility, improvement in HD$_3$ and better tuning in comparison to others [8,9]. Block diagram of the proposed transconductor is shown in **Figure 1** and the complete circuit diagram is furnished in **Figure 2**.

The square law model of MOSFETs is used in this work for design and analysis. Design steps are given below:

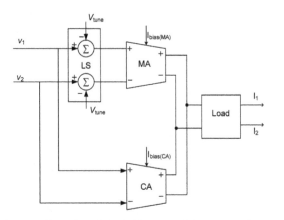

Figure 1. Functional block diagram of the trnsconductor.

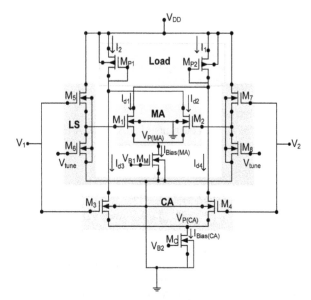

Figure 2. Circuit diagram of the transconductor.

2.1.1. Design of MA

Upper limit and lower limit of biasing current ($I_{Bias(MA)}$) for MA are given as follows [3]:

$$I_{Bias(MA)_{(max)}} \ll P_{Diss}/V_{DD} \tag{1}$$

$$I_{Bias(MA)_{(min)}} \geq \left(2 * \omega_{3dB} * C_l\right)/\left(\lambda_n + \lambda_p\right) \tag{2}$$

where P_{Diss} is the specified total power consumption, C_l is the load capacitor, ω_{3dB} is the 3 dB frequency, λ_n and λ_p are the channel length coefficients of NMOS and PMOS transistors respectively. MA is designed using NMOS transistors and load using PMOS transistors.

Transconductance, $G_{m(MA)}$ of MA and input swing, V_{swing} are given in [1,3] and are reproduced in Equation (3) and Equation (4).

$$G_{m(MA)} = \sqrt{\mu_n C_{ox} \left(W/L\right)_{MA} I_{Bias(MA)}} \tag{3}$$

$$V_{swing} = \sqrt{\left(2I_{Bias(MA)}\right)/\left\{\mu_n C_{ox} \left(W/L\right)_{MA}\right\}} \tag{4}$$

From Equation (3) $G_{m(MA)}$ is the function of $I_{Bias(MA)}$ and $\left(W/L\right)_{MA}$. To keep high $G_{m(MA)}$, higher values of $I_{Bias(MA)}$ are not used as it would lead to loss of power. The second option is to increase the aspect ratio but that may deteriorate HD$_3$ for specified input swing {Equation (4)}.

The second option is preferred wherein, for better HD_3, the method of non-linear terms cancellation with the help of compensatory amplifier is used but at the cost of area occupied by it. However, the use of CA (**Figure 2**) reduces overall transconductance. To maintain transconductance G_m of the OTA at the desired level, $G_{m(MA)}$ is adjusted {Equation (7)}. For high current efficiency ($i.e.\ G_m/I_{DD}$), $I_{Bias(MA)}$ is selected slightly greater than

$I_{Bias(MA)_{min}}$ and aspect ratio $(W/L)_{MA}$ is determined from Equation (3) for the modified value of $G_{m(MA)}$. In addition, $I_{Bias(MA)}$ is allowed to vary independently of CA as a function of tuning voltage by operating tail transistor of MA in triode mode.

2.1.2. Design of CA

The ratio "p" of bias currents of MA and CA are adjusted [11,12] in accordance with Equation (5):

$$p = q^3 \qquad (5)$$

where $p = I_{Bias(MA)}/I_{Bias(CA)}$ and $q = (W_{MA}/L_{MA})/(W_{CA}/L_{CA})$. A lower value of "$q$" not only increases power dissipation (due to high bias current of CA), but also lowers the overall transconductance, thereby, decreasing the current efficiency. On the other hand, due to higher values of "q" the harmonics will not be suppressed effectively. Moreover, it is difficult to bias the CA transistor in saturation region in the specified low voltage operation due to skewed overdrive voltages of the MA and CA. In the proposed circuit choosing a moderate "q" as 2 and equal channel length of MA and CA gives:

$$W_{MA}/W_{CA} = 2 \qquad (6)$$

and $I_{Bias(MA)}/I_{Bias(CA)} = 8$. This ratio of bias currents is adjusted for the centre value of the tuning voltage range at which specified G_m is expected to occur.

Overall transconductance G_m due to cross-coupling of MA and CA is the difference of $G_{m(MA)}$ and $G_{m(CA)}$, hence $G_{m(MA)}$ is selected to get the specified G_m in accordance of Equation (7).

$$G_{m(MA)} = \left\{ q^2 / \left(q^2 - 1 \right) \right\} G_m \qquad (7)$$

2.1.3. Design of Load

The PMOS transistors, M_{p1} and M_{p2} are selected in diode mode as load. It is possible to easily convert the proposed transconductor to Multiple-output OTA suitable for current mode signal processing by incorporating three current mirrors. The aspect ratio of load transistors is computed using the Equation (8), where in Equation (8) $V_{CM_{max}}$ is the maximum common mode input voltage at MA, V_{thn} and V_{thp} are the threshold voltages of NMOS and PMOS transistors respectively.

$$(W/L)_{load} = \frac{\left(I_{Bias(MA)} + I_{Bias(CA)} \right)}{\left\{ \mu_p C_{ox} * \left(V_{DD} - V_{CM_{max}} - V_{thn} - V_{thp} \right)^2 \right\}} \qquad (8)$$

2.1.4. Design of LS

Linearly tunable G_m is obtained by modulating common mode voltage with V_{tune} in two level shifters. The transistors (M_5 and M_6) of a level shifter of LS are selected to

have same aspect ratio to maintain same V_{tune} across gate to source in both the transistors. They are biased in saturation region by following the conditions given in Equation (9) and Equation (10).

$$V_1 (or \ V_2) < V_{DD} + V_{thn} \qquad (9)$$

$$V_{thn} < V_{tune} < \left\{ V_1 (or \ V_2) + V_{thn} \right\}/2 \qquad (10)$$

where $V_1 = \left(V_{DC} + \dfrac{v_{id}}{2} \right)$ and $V_2 = \left(V_{DC} - \dfrac{v_{id}}{2} \right)$ are the signal inputs applied at the gates of M_5 and M_7 of level shifters, respectively. Same input V_1 and V_2 are applied to the gate of M_3 and M_4 of CA. As per the Equation (10) higher values of V_1 (or V_2) give better tuning range, accordingly, V_{DC} is selected slightly less than to V_{DD}. Further, MA remains in saturation if and only if condition given in Equation (11) is satisfied.

$$V_{tune} \le V_1 (or \ V_2) - V_{thn} - V_{P_{(MA)}} \qquad (11)$$

where $V_{P_{(MA)}}$ is the drain to source voltage of tail transistor of MA Thus, the limits on V_{tune} are obtained as in Equation (12). Transistors of other level shifter of LS are also made identical on the same ground.

$$V_{thn} < V_{tune} \le \min\left[\left\{ V_1 (or \ V_2) + V_{thn} \right\}/2, \right.$$
$$\left. V_1 (or \ V_2) - V_{thn} - V_{P_{(MA)}} \right] \qquad (12)$$

2.1.5. Design of Tail Transistor of MA

As the bias current supplied to MA by its tail transistor is a function of tuning voltage, it is operated in triode mode. It needs $V_B > V_{P_{(MA)}} + V_{thn}$, where V_{B1} is gate voltage of tail transistor of MA. The aspect ratio of tail transistor of MA is derived for the mentioned operating mode and is given in Equation (13):

$$(W/L)_{T_{(MA)}} = I_{Bias(MA)} / \left\{ \left(\mu_n C_{ox} \right) \left(V_{B1} - V_{thn} \right) V_{P_{(MA)}} \right\} \qquad (13)$$

2.1.6. Design of Tail Transistor of CA

Tail transistor of CA is chosen as constant current source independent of $I_{Bias(MA)}$ by biasing the transistor in saturation. The aspect ratio of it is given in Equation (14):

$$(W/L)_{T_{(CA)}} = \frac{2 I_{Bias(CA)}}{\left(\mu_n C_{ox} \right) \left(V_{B2} - V_{thn} \right)^2} \qquad (14)$$

where V_{B2} is gate voltage of tail transistor of CA.

2.2. Algorithm for Designing the Proposed Transconductor

The algorithm to design proposed transconductor is summarized as below:

Step 1	Compute $I_{Bias(MA)_{(max)}}$	/* from specified P_{Diss}; refer Equation (1)*/
Step 2	Compute $I_{Bias(MA)_{(max)}}$	/* from specified ω_{3dB}; refer Equation (2)*/
Step 3	Select $I_{Bias(MA)} \geq I_{Bias(MA)_{(max)}}$	/* to increase current efficiency*/
Step 4	Compute $G_{m(MA)}$	/* for specified G_m; refer Equation (7)*/
Step 5	Compute $(W/L)_{MA}$	/* using Equation (3)*/
Step 6	Calculate $(W/L)_{CA}$	/* using Equation (6)*/
Step 7	Select diode mode MOSFET load	/* for current mode signal processing*/
Step 8	Compute $(W/L)_{load}$	/* using Equation (8)*/
Step 9	Compute $(W/L)_{LS}$	/*minimum size transistors*/
Step 10	Design tail transistor of MA	/*refer (13)*/
Step 11	Design tail transistor of CA	/*refer (14)*/
	END	

2.3. Analysis of the Circuit

The analysis of the circuit is given below:

In **Figure 2**, applying the square law to the transistors of MA and CA, which are biased in saturation region, the currents, I_1 and I_2 through load transistors of the cross-coupled amplifiers (MA-CA) are given by:

$$I_1 = I_{d1} + I_{d4} = \beta_{MA}\left(V_1 - V_{tune} - V_{P_{(MA)}} - V_{thn}\right)^2$$
$$+ \beta_{CA}\left(V_2 - V_{P_{(CA)}} - V_{thn}\right)^2 \quad (15)$$

$$I_1 = I_{d2} + I_{d3} = \beta_{MA}\left(V_2 - V_{tune} - V_{P_{(MA)}} - V_{thn}\right)^2$$
$$+ \beta_{CA}\left(V_1 - V_{P_{(CA)}} - V_{thn}\right)^2 \quad (16)$$

where $\beta = (1/2)\mu C_{ox}(W/L)$ is the transconductance parameter. $V_{P_{(MA)}}$ and $V_{P_{(CA)}}$ are the drain to source voltage across tail transistor of MA and CA respectively.

The differential output current, i_o is given by

$$i_0 = I_1 - I_2$$
$$= 2(v_{id})\left[\{(\beta_{MA} - \beta_{CA})(V_{DC} - V_P - V_{thn})\} - \beta_{MA}V_{tune}\right] \quad (17)$$

where $V_{P_{(MA)}} \cong V_{P_{(CA)}} = V_P$ is assumed.

Since "q" is taken as 2 to minimize HD$_3$:

$$\beta_{MA} = 2\beta_{CA} \quad (18)$$

Combining Equation (17) and Equation (18), one gets:

$$i_0 = (v_{id})\{\beta_{MA}(V_{DC} - V_P - V_{thn}) - 2\beta_{MA}V_{tune}\} \quad (19)$$

From Equation (19) the transconductance G_m is calculated as,

$$G_m = \frac{\partial i_0}{\partial v_{id}} = \beta_{MA}(V_{DC} - V_P - V_{thn}) - 2\beta_{MA}V_{tune} \quad (20)$$

Equation (20) shows linear behaviour of G_m with V_{tune}, as first part, $\beta_{MA}(V_{DC} - V_P - V_{thn})$ on the right hand side of the equation is almost constant. Thus from Equation (20) the tuning range is obtained and is given in Equation (21).

$$G_{m_{range}} = \left|2\beta_{MA}V_{tune}\right| \quad (21)$$

3. Simulation Results and Discussions

The proposed transconductor is simulated in Cadence VIRTUOSO environment using UMC 0.18 μm CMOS process technology. The transconductor is operated at 1.8 V and 27° Celsius. Bias currents $I_{Bias(MA)}$ and $I_{Bias(CA)}$ are kept at 200 μA and 25 μA, respectively to maintain $I_{Bias(MA)}/I_{Bias(CA)} = 8$. Channel length is taken as 0.9 μm which is five times the minimum as specified by the technology for all the MOSFETs of the transconductor to minimize channel length modulation effect [26]. The differential signal input voltage of 0.25 V is generated using voltage controlled voltage source (VCVS) as test bench setup.

The objective of the simulation is to demonstrate feasibility of power efficiency, linear tuning of G_m offering low harmonics with the help of separate bias control of cross-coupled amplifiers at 50 MHz and above. Different plots have been obtained to verify the designed aspects.

Plot in **Figure 3** shows the tunability of the proposed transconductor. The tuning voltage, V_{tune} is varied from 0.5 V to 1.0 V in steps of 0.1 V. The lower value (0.5 V) is kept slightly higher than the threshold voltage of input transistors M_5 and M_7 of LS and upper value is selected as per Equation (12) to keep them in saturation region. G_m is tuned between 390 μS to 195 μS. G_m is falling with increase in V_{tune} between ±0.25 V of v_{id} i.e. 1 V$_{p-p}$, However for higher values of v_{id}, (around ±0.5 V i.e. 2

V_{p-p}) the change in G_m w.r.t. V_{tune} is nonlinear and plots for different values of V_{tune} are almost merged at a point, indicates transconductance is independent of V_{tune}. The reason being that as per Equation (12),

$V_1\left(or\, V_2\right) < V_{DD} + V_{thn}$, but at higher values, this condition is violated. At $V_1\left(or\, V_2\right) = V_{DD} + V_{thn}$ transistor M_5 and M_7 of **Figure 2** are at the verge of saturation, and variation in drain to source voltage across it is small enough, making output of level shifter is almost constant, *i.e.* independent of tuning voltage.

As shown in **Figure 4** the variation of transconductance with respect to tuning voltage is linear validating Equation (20). The small deviation may be attributed to body effect in LS transistors (M_5 and M_7) and voltage drop in tail transistors.

Figure 5 shows HD$_3$ variation with respect to differential input signal amplitude for different values of tuning voltage. Distortion increases rapidly for the small values *i.e.* upto approximately 150 mV (0.6 V_{p-p}) of the differential input signal amplitude but after that it in creases

slowly due to cross-coupling effect. Harmonic distortion has also increased with the increase in tuning voltage due to decrease in DC current through MA. **Figure 6** shows variation of HD$_3$ with respect to V_{tune}.

Frequency response of the proposed transconductor for different values of tuning voltage is given in **Figure 7**. The 3 dB frequency of the transconductor is above 53 MHz for the complete range of variation of transconductance.

G_m, HD$_3$, P$_{Diss}$ and G_m/I_{DD} for the three different values of G_m obtained from the simulation are given in **Table 1**. It may be noted that at lower values of transconductance current efficiency reduces. The reasons are twofold: firstly, transconductance is low and secondly lower transconductance obtained at higher value of tuning voltage, gives high overdrive voltage to LS transistors which in turn draws higher current through LS.

The performance is compared on eight metric points with other reported circuits as given in **Table 2**. The proposed transconductor offers better current efficiency

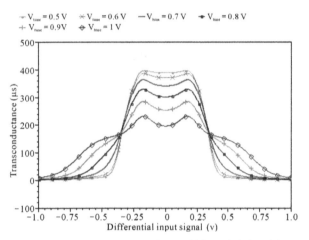

Figure 3. Transconductance (G_m) vs differential signal input (v_{id}) at different values of tuning voltage (V_{tune}).

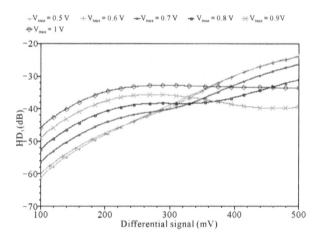

Figure 5. HD$_3$ vs differential signal input (v_{id}) at different tuning voltage (V_{tune}).

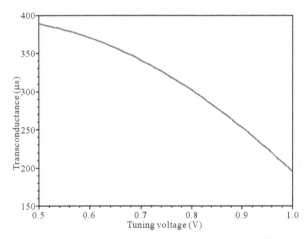

Figure 4. Transconductance (G_m) vs tuning voltage (V_{tune}) at differential signal input (v_{id}) = 0 V.

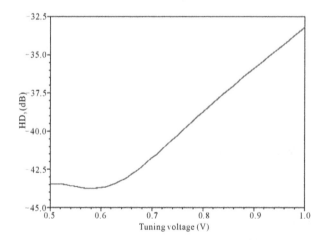

Figure 6. HD$_3$ vs Tuning voltage at differential signal input (v_{id}) = 0.25 V.

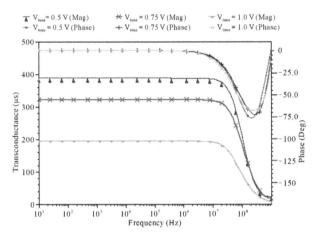

Legend:
- ⊥ V_{tune} = 0.5 V (Mag)
- ✳ V_{tune} = 0.75 V (Mag)
- ↝ V_{tune} = 1.0 V (Mag)
- ← V_{tune} = 0.5 V (Phase)
- + V_{tune} = 0.75 V (Phase)
- ◌ V_{tune} = 1.0 V (Phase)

Figure 7. Transconductance vs frequency at different tuning voltage (V_{tune}).

(1.18 V^{-1}) and transconductance (390 μS) with lower harmonics (–43.7 dB), at input swing of 1 V_{p-p} @50 MHz in comparison to the others. However, the transconductance reported in [9] is higher than the proposed at the cost of high supply voltage (5 V) and very low current efficiency (0.1 V^{-1} to 0.07 V^{-1}).

4. Conclusions

A power efficient linearly tunable high G_m, cross-coupled transconductor with separate bias currents (for low third harmonic distortion) is designed and analyzed in this paper. Results have been obtained with diode mode transistors as load extendable for MOTA, which is necessary for current mode signal processing. Transconductance is varied in linear manner. G_m is tuned between 195 to 390 μS when the tuning voltage is varied from 1.0 V to 0.5 V. Maximum current efficiency of 1.18 V^{-1} and minimum HD$_3$ less than –43.7 dB is obtained at 1 V_{p-p} @ 50 MHz at the tuning voltage of 0.5 V. Comparative study reveals that the proposed circuit consumes low power and gives high current efficiency, with low HD$_3$ and high tunable transconductance for high frequency of operation compared to others.

5. Acknowledgements

This work has been performed using the resources of VLSI Laboratory developed under Special Manpower Development Programme for VLSI Design and related software (SMDP-II) project funded by Department of

Table 1. Performance of proposed transconductor.

Performance Parameter	Simulation results		
Transconductance (G_m)	G_m = 390 μS (V_{tune}= 0.5 V)	G_m = 323 μS (V_{tune}= 0.75 V)	G_m = 195 μS (V_{tune}= 1.0 V)
(HD$_3$) at 1 V_{p-p}	– 43.7dB	– 40.5dB	– 33.2 dB
Power consumption (P_{diss})	0.60 mW	0.79 mW	1.20 mW
Current efficiency (G_m/I_{DD})	1.18 V^{-1}	0.74 V^{-1}	0.30 V^{-1}
3 dB Frequency	70 MHz	71 MHz	53 MHz

Table 2. Performance comparison of proposed transconductors with others.

Reference No.	[6]	[9]	[16]	[17]	[22]	[23]	Proposed
Supply voltage in V	1.8	5.0	3.3	2.5	1.8	1.8	1.8
Technology in μm	0.18	2.00	0.35	0.35	0.18	0.18	0.18
G_m in μS	8 to 131	166 to 575	160 to 340	3 to 30	110	310 to 100	390 to 195
Input Swing in V_{p-p}	1.0	1.0	1.4	1.0	0.1 – 0.9	1.0	1.0
HD$_3$/THD in dB	– 40	– 40	– 70	– 42 to –50	– 27 to – 43	– 30	– 43.7
Power consumption in mW	0.58$^{\$}$	8.24 to 41.50	6.60	0.38 to 0.24	0.42$^{\$}$	0.64$^{\$\$}$	0.60 to 1.20
#Current efficiency in V^{-1}	0.02 to 0.41	0.10 to 0.07	0.08 to 0.17	0.02 to 0.31	0.47	0.60	1.18 to 0.30
Frequency in MHz	10	10	26	1	50	50	50

Legend: # Calculated from the given data/average value in the references. $^{\$}$: Authors did not mention G_m at which the Power consumption values are reported. $^{\$\$}$: Power at a specific G_m.

Information Technology, Ministry of Communication and Information Technology Government of India.

REFERENCES

[1] B. Razavi, "Design of Analog CMOS Integrated Circuits," Tata McGraw-Hill Publishing Company Limited, 2002.

[2] D. A. Johns and K. Martin, "Analog Integrated Circuit Design," John Wiley and Sons, New York, 1997.

[3] P. E. Allen and D. R. Holberg, "CMOS Analog Circuit Design," Oxford University Press, New York, 2004.

[4] E. Sánchez-Sinencio and J. Silva-Martínez, "CMOS Transconductance Amplifiers, Architectures and Active Filters: A Tutorial," *IEE Proceedings Circuits, Devices & Systems*, Vol. 147, No. 1, 2000, pp. 3-12.

[5] J. Y. Kim and R. L. Geiger, "Characterisation of Linear MOS Active Attenuator and Amplifier," *Electronic Letters*, Vol. 31, 1995, pp. 511-513.

[6] X. Zhang and E. I. El-Masry, "A Novel CMOS OTA Based on Body-Driven MOSFETs and Its Applications in OTA-C Filters," *IEEE Transactions on Circuits and System-I Regular Papers*, Vol. 54, No. 6, 2007, pp. 1204-1211.

[7] J. Chen, E. Sanchez-Sinencio and J. Silva-Martinez, "Frequency Dependent Harmonic Distortion Analysis of a Linearized cross Coupled CMOS OTA and Its Application to OTA C-Filter," *IEEE Transactions on Circuits and System-I Regular Papers*, Vol. 53, No. 3, 2006, pp. 499-510.

[8] Z. Wang and W. Guggenbuhl, "A Voltage-Controlled Linear MOS Transconductor Using Bias Offset Technique," *IEEE Journal of Solid-State Circuits*, Vol. 25, 1990, pp. 315-317.

[9] Y. Sun, C. Hill and S. Szczepanski, "Large Dynamic Range High Frequency Fully Differential CMOS Transconductance Amplifier," *Analog Integrated Circuits and Signal Processing*, Vol. 34, 2003, pp. 247-255.

[10] D. V. Morozov and A. S. Kuroki, "Transconductance Amplifier with Low-Power Consumption," *IEEE Transactions on Circuits and System-II Express Briefs*, Vol. 52, No. 11, 2005, pp. 776-779.

[11] A. Lewinski and J. Silva-Martinez, "OTA Linearity Enhancement Technique for High Frequency Application With IM3 Below-65 dB," *IEEE Transactions on Circuits and System-II Express Briefs*, Vol. 51, No 10, 2004, pp. 542-548.

[12] S. Ouzounov, E. Roza, H. Hegt, G. V. D. Weide and A. V. Roermund, "Design of MOS Transconductors with Low Noise and Low Harmonic Distortion for Minimum Current Consumption," *Integration, the VLSI Journal*, Vol. 40, 2007, pp. 365-379.

[13] F. Krummenacher and N. Joehl, "A 4-MHz CMOS Continuous-Time Filter with On-Chip Automatic Tuning," *IEEE Journal of Solid-State Circuits*, Vol. 23, No. 3, 1988, pp. 750-758.

[14] J. Silva-Martinez, M. S. J. Steyaert and W. M. C. Sansen, "A Large-Signal Very Low-Distortion Transconductor for High-Frequency Continuous-Time Filters," *IEEE Journal of Solid-State Circuits*, Vol. 26, No. 7, 1991, pp. 946-954.

[15] M. Kachare, A. J. Lopez-Martin, J. Ramirez-Angulo, and R. G. Carvajal, "A Compact Tunable CMOS Transconductor with Linearity," *IEEE Transactions on Circuits and System-II Express Briefs*, Vol. 52, No. 2, 2005, pp. 82-84.

[16] W. Huang and E. Sanchez-Sinencio, "Robust Highly-Linear High-Frequency CMOS OTA with IM3 Below-70 dB at 26 MHz," *IEEE Transactions on Circuits and System-I Regular Papers*, Vol. 53, No. 7, 2006, pp. 1433-1447.

[17] F. A. P. Baruqui and A. Petraglia, "Linearly Tunable CMOS OTA With Constant Dynamic Range Using Source-Degenerated Current Mirrors," *IEEE Transactions on Circuits and System-II Express Briefs*, Vol. 53, No. 9, 2006, pp. 797-801.

[18] P. Monsurrò, S. Pennisi, G. Scotti and A. Trifiletti, "Linearization Technique for Source-Degenerated CMOS Differential Transconductors," *IEEE Transactions on Circuits and System-II*, Vol. 54, No. 10, 2007, pp. 848-852.

[19] K. Kuo and A. Leuciuc, "A Linear MOS Transconductor Using Source Degeneration and Adaptive Biasing," *IEEE Transactions on Circuits and System-II Express Briefs*, Vol. 48, No. 10, 2001, pp. 937-943.

[20] S. H. Yang, K. H. Kim, Y. You and K. R. Cho, "A Novel CMOS Operational Transconductance Amplifier Based on Mobility Compensation Technique," *IEEE Transactions on Circuits and System-II Express Briefs*, Vol. 52, No. 1, 2005, pp. 37- 42.

[21] S. Koziel and S. Szczepanski, "Design of Highly Linear Tunable CMOS OTA for Continuous-Time Filters," *IEEE Transactions on Circuits and System-II Analog and Digital Signal Processing*, Vol. 49, No. 2, 2002, pp. 110-122.

[22] A. A. Fayed and M. Ismail, "A Low Voltage, Highly Linear Voltage-Controlled Transconductor," *IEEE Transactions on Circuits and System-II Express Briefs*, Vol. 52 No. 12, 2005, pp. 831-835.

[23] V. Bhadauria and K. Kant, "A Novel Technique for Tuning Low Voltage Linear Transconductor," 2010 *International Conference on Electronic Devices, System and Application (ICEDSA2010)*, 12-13 April 2010, Kuala Lumpur, Malaysia, pp. 22-25.

[24] V. Bhadauria K. Kant and S. Banerjee, "A Tunable Transconductor with High Linearity," *Proceedings of Asia Pacific Conference on Circuits and Systems (APCCAS 2010)*, Kuala Lumpur, 6-9 December 2010, pp. 5-8.

[25] P. Bruschi, F. Sebastiano and N. Nizza, "CMOS Trans-

conductors with Nearly Constant Input Ranges over wide Tuning Intervals," *IEEE Transactions on Circuits and System-II Express Briefs*, Vol. 53, No. 10, 2006, pp. 1002-1006.

[26] R. J. Baker, "CMOS Circuit Design, Layout, and Simulation," IEEE Press, Wiley-Interscience, A John Wiley & sons, Inc., Publication, New York, 2005, Chapter 9, p. 291.

13

System-on-Chip Design Using High-Level Synthesis Tools

Erdal Oruklu[1*], Richard Hanley[1], Semih Aslan[2], Christophe Desmouliers[1],
Fernando M. Vallina[3], Jafar Saniie[1]

[1]Department of Electrical and Computer Engineering, Illinois Institute of Technology, Chicago, USA
[2]Ingram School of Engineering, Texas State University, San Marcos, USA
[3]Xilinx Inc., San Jose, USA

ABSTRACT

This paper addresses the challenges of System-on-Chip designs using High-Level Synthesis (HLS). HLS tools convert algorithms designed in C into hardware modules. This approach is a practical choice for developing complex applications. Nevertheless, certain hardware considerations are required when writing C applications for HLS tools. Hence, in order to demonstrate the fundamental hardware design concepts, a case study is presented. Fast Fourier Transform (FFT) implementation in ANSI C is examined in order to explore the important design issues such as concurrency, data recurrences and memory accesses that need to be resolved before generating the hardware using HLS tools. There are additional language constraints that need to be addressed including use of pointers, recursion and floating point types.

Keywords: System Level Design; High Level Synthesis; Field Programmable Gate Arrays; Fourier Transform

1. Introduction

In the past decade, there has been a substantial increase in the level of hardware abstraction that High-Level Synthesis (HLS) [1-5] tools offer, which has made designing a complete System-on-Chip (SoC) much more practical. By designing at the system level, it has become possible for hardware engineers to avoid gate-level semantics. HLS tools work by taking applications written in a subset of ANSI C, and translating it into a Register Transfer Level (RTL) module for Application-Specific Integrated Circuit (ASIC) or Field Programmable Gate Arrays (FPGAs) chip design. The design workflow requires knowledge of both software to write C applications and hardware to parallelize tasks, resolve timing and memory management issues. There has been significant previous work that discusses how to teach RTL concepts to students and design simple applications for SoCs [6,7]. Nevertheless, the learning curve for software engineers is relatively high since they need to use Hardware Descriptive Languages (HDL) such as Verilog and VHDL. By using HLS tools, software engineers can use their programming skills along with hardware knowledge to create complex embedded hardware/software co-design systems.

To demonstrate the critical hardware and software design issues, a Fast Fourier Transform (FFT) [8] case study is used as a guideline. In order to generate hardware modules satisfying predefined constraints such as

through-put and area, different modifications of the code required by HLS tools are presented step by step.

Section 2 of this paper provides a brief background of HLS tools, and the current pedagogical techniques. Section 3 presents an introduction of the FFT algorithm along with a software implementation. This software based FFT is then deconstructed in Section 4, where a fully synthesizable product is created. Section 5 analyzes the different results that can be produced depending on the constraints selected by the user such as speed, area, throughput, and targeted system.

For this paper, all designs are targeted for the Xilinx Virtex-5 FPGA platform [9] using the HLS tool called PICO, provided by Synfora Inc [10] (currently known as Synphony C Compiler by Synopsys [11]). However, the different code modifications presented in this paper are applicable to other HLS tools such as AutoESL [12] which targets primarily Xilinx FPGAs with architecture aware synthesis and Catapult C [13] which provides full-chip high-level synthesis for both ASIC and FPGA devices and automatic RTL verification.

2. High Level Synthesis Tools

This section outlines the important concepts that software developers need to know before entering the field of HLS. There is a special emphasis on how these concepts differ from the contemporary software environment familiar to the software engineers. Design of SoCs has historically

[*]Corresponding author.

been accomplished using Hardware Descriptive Languages such as VHDL or Verilog. Each expression in HDL represents a group of gates that operate in parallel, as opposed to machine instructions executed sequentially. This concept of instruction level parallelism is one of the first major hurdles when introducing hardware concepts.

Once an RTL module is designed, it can be compiled and simulated. The simulation is done by creating a series of pre-defined inputs, known as a testbench, and recording the outputs. If a module passes the simulation then a low level implementation can be created. This low level implementation then enters the verification process to ensure that all timing dependencies are met. In practice, simulating and verifying an implementation can take 50% - 60% of the development time, increasing the time-to-market (TTM) [14]. By automating the simulation and verification process, it is possible to greatly reduce the development time.

Integration of HLS tools into the FPGA or ASIC design flow, as shown in **Figure 1**, allows software designers to build hardware modules and speed up the TTM significantly. During the generation process of an RTL module from a software implementation, simulation and verification are done automatically by using a formal proof provided during the initial steps. Subsequently, by using synthesis tools, the RTL module is implemented and timing verification is done. An independent evaluation of HLS tools for Xilinx FPGAs has been done by Berkeley Design Technology [15]. It shows that using HLS tools with FPGAs can improve the performances of an application by an order of magnitude compared to DSPs. Moreover, this study shows that for a given application, HSL tools will achieve similar results compared to hand-written HDL code with a shorter development time.

HLS software based approach for simulation and verification is made possible by using SystemC, a language developed by Synopsys, University of California Irvine, Frontier Design and IMEC. SystemC is an extension of C++ that provides additional libraries to design an embedded system. The first version was released in 1999 and in 2005 it became IEEE standardized SystemC [16, 17] as the IEEE-1666-2005. These additional libraries make it possible to specify the hardware and software components in an embedded system using one unified paradigm and to generate testbenches.

Focusing further on HLS, the design flow is shown in **Figure 2**. Each module of a system is implemented using high level languages such as C, C++, Java, or Matlab [2,18], which can then be tested automatically with testbenches provided by the user. After verification of the complete system, the user can specify in the HLS tool which modules will be converted into hardware accelerators in order to speed up the application. This is one of the core elements of hardware/software co-design that software developers need to understand. There are inherent restrictions in the HDLs that are mirrored in the HLS tool. Therefore, the emphasis for teaching HDL to software developers is on its constraints and how it affects the HLS tools.

After generation of the hardware modules along with testbenches, the system is verified and can be implemented using synthesis tools.

This paper, as mentioned earlier, focuses on designing a Fast Fourier Transform. The concept of HLS is presented by using PICO (Program-In Chip-Out) Extreme from Synfora [10,19,20] to generate the RTL code of an FFT. To be specific, PICO takes a C-based description of an algorithm and generates: performance-driven device-dependent synthesizable RTL code, testbench files, application drivers, simulation scripts as well as SystemC based Transaction Level Models (TLM) [3,17,18,21]. PICO design flow is shown in **Figure 3**. With integration

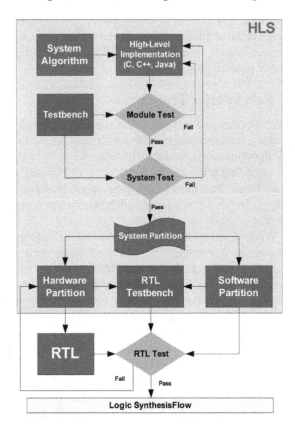

Figure 2. High level synthesis (HLS) design flow.

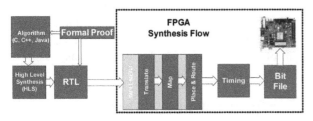

Figure 1. FPGA high level synthesis block diagram.

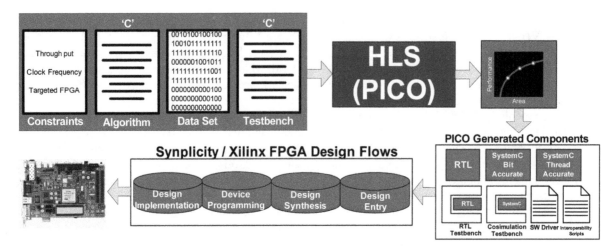

Figure 3. HLS (PICO) based design flow for hardware implementation.

of the PICO design tools to their FPGA flow, designers can create complex hardware [20] sub-systems from sequential untimed C algorithms. It allows designers to explore programmability, performance, power, area and clock frequency. This is achieved by providing a comprehensive and robust verification and validation environment. PICO is designed to explore different type of parallelism and will choose the optimal one transparently. Results in terms of throughput and area are given along with detailed reports that will help the user for code optimization. When the synthesized performances are satisfactory, RTL code is generated and can be implemented in the targeted platform. Because the testing is done in C, the verification time of the RTL module can be significantly reduced [20].

3. Fast Fourier Transform

In most cases, the first step when using an HLS tool is to create a reference implementation, which is used to verify the synthesized product. The reference code itself can be compiled using any C compiler, and is purely software based. This means that no new concepts have to be taught, making the reference implementation a logical starting point when using HLS.

When creating the reference code for FFT, there are few issues that need to be addressed when using HLS tools. The first issue is that arithmetic operations such as division can significantly decrease the performance of the design, and therefore should be avoided whenever possible. Nevertheless, division by a power of two is considered as a bit shift operation and hence can be used at no cost. The second issue, and more fundamental issue, is that pointers and recursion are not supported by the current HLS tools due to the fact that those concepts are purely software and can't be applied to hardware designs. Finally, HLS tools may not have the capability to synthesize software functions such as cosine and sine. As a re-

sult of these constraints, the reference code included in this section does not use divisions, is completely iterative, and has not pointer variables. However, before going into the details of the implementation, the mathematical background of the FFT is presented.

3.1. FFT Algorithm

The Fourier transform takes a signal x in time t and transforms it into a function X in frequency ω:

$$X(\omega) = \int_{-\infty}^{\infty} x(t) * e^{-2j\pi\omega t} dt \qquad (1)$$

The transform can be computed using a Discrete Fourier Transform (DFT).

$$X_k = \sum_{n=0}^{N-1} x_n e^{-2j\pi k \frac{n}{N}} \qquad (2)$$

where $k = 0, \cdots, N-1$.

The direct realization of DFT algorithm requires $O(N^2)$ computational time. To make this computation faster, an entire class of Fast Fourier Transforms (FFT) were developed [8]. However, in this paper a radix-2 FFT decimated in time is implemented. This algorithm divides the original DFT into two DFTs with half the length (*i.e.* decimation). The first step in decimation is shown below:

$$X_k = \sum_{m=0}^{\frac{N}{2}-1} x_{2m} e^{-\frac{2\pi j}{N}(2m)k} + \sum_{m=0}^{\frac{N}{2}-1} x_{2m+1} e^{-\frac{2\pi j}{N}(2m+1)k} \qquad (3)$$

Then the algorithm is recursively applied to each term until each DFT's length is 1. This recursive deconstruction of the DFT makes the computational time of $O(Nlog(N))$ [8].

3.2. Software Implementation of the FFT

In **Figure 4**, a 16-point radix-2 FFT is shown. A signal is

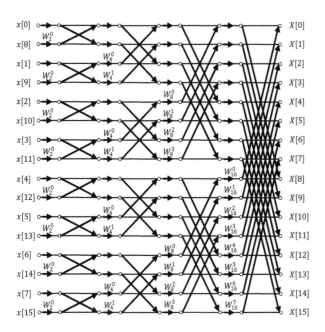

Figure 4. 16-point radix-2 FFT.

inputted into the FFT in a bit reversed order and then goes through $log_2(N)$ passes, where each pass has $N/2$ "butterfly" operations. These butterfly operations are defined as:

$W_N^k = e^{-2\pi jk/N}$ (called the Twiddle factor)

$$F = f + W_N^k \times g$$
$$G = f - W_N^k \times g$$

(4)

The butterfly operation requires complex number arithmetic additions and multiplications. Because of the programming constraints placed on the reference code, most complex number libraries are not useable. Hence, this reference code uses its own complex number representation shown below:

```
typedef struct{
    float x;
    float y;
}s _complex;
```

Moreover, in order to perform the butterfly operation, the W_N^k terms need to be calculated. Since we assume that HLS library does not support cosine and sine functions, the twiddle factors are pre-computed and stored in a table using the code below:

```
#include" fft.h"
#include < math.h >
#define pi2    (double)6.283185307179586476925286766655901
extern s _complex fix _float[N / 2];
void table _setup(void)
{
  double a = 0.0;
  double e = -pi2 / N;
  float cos _val, sin _val;
  int i;
  for(i = 0; i < N / 2; i ++){
    cos _val = cos(a);
    sin _val = sin(a);
    fix _float[i].x = cos _val;
    fix _float[i].y = sin _val;
    a = a + e;
  }
}
```

The particular implementation chosen for this reference FFT was provided by [22]. The exact code used is shown in **Figure 5**. N represents the length of the FFT and must be a power of 2. Before using the function *fft_ref*, the function *table_setup* must be executed in order to compute the twiddle factors and store them in the array *fix_float*. The FFT of an input z can then be executed. The first phase is the bit-reverse operation where the input data are rearranged as show in **Figure 4**. Then, for each passes, the butterfly operations are performed until the FFT is completed. In the next section this code will be made fully synthesizable by applying four modifications to it.

4. Code Modification for HLS

The objective of this section is to generate the hardware of a FFT block based on the reference C code using HLS tools. Multiple modifications are needed in order to generate an optimal hardware in term of resource usage and throughput. As an example, we generate an 8-bit 1024-point radix-2 FFT. The output is on 18 bits and will beavailable in natural order. The size of the data width inside the FFT has been chosen so that the HLS FFT gives the same results as the Xilinx FFT core [23].

4.1. Floating Point to Fixed Point Implementation

Since the reference C code is using floating point numbers, a fixed-point library is needed. For example, PICO, the HLS used in this demonstration, provides such library. The PICO fixed-point arithmetic library derives its semantics from the SystemC fixed-point library and it supports signed and unsigned arithmetic operations. Hence, the previous floating point complex structure must be modified as followed:

```
#include < math.h >
#include "fft.h"

s_complex fix_float[N/2];

int fft_ref (int n, int m, s_complex * z)
{
  int i, j, k, n1, n2;
  float c, s, t1, t2;
  j = 0;
  n2 = n / 2;
  for (i = 1; i < n - 1; i + +) {
    n1 = n2;
    while (j >= n1) {
      j = j - n1;
      n1 = n1 / 2;
    }
    j = j + n1;
    if (i < j) {
      s_complex t = z[i];
      z[i] = z[j];
      z[j] = t;
    }
  }
  n1 = 0;
  n2 = 1;
  for (i = 0; i < m; i + +) {
    n1 = n2;
    n2 = n2 + n2;
    int index = 0;
    int incr = n/(1 << (i + 1));
    for (j = 0; j < n1; j + +) {
      c = fix_float[index].x;
      s = fix_float[index].y;
      index = index + incr;
      if (index == N/2) { index = 0; }
      float temp, temp1;
      for (k = j; k < n; k = k + n2) {
        t1 = z[k + n1].x * c);
        temp = z[k + n1].y * s);
        t1 -= temp;
        t2 = z[k + n1].x * s;
        temp = z[k + n1].y * c;
        t2 += temp;
        z[k + n1].x = z[k].x - t1;
        z[k + n1].y = z[k].y - t2;
        z[k].x = z[k].x + t1;
        z[k].y = z[k].y + t2;
      }
    }
  }
  return 0;
}
```

Bit-reverse operation

Obtain cosine and sine values for the butterfly operation

Butterflycalculation

Figure 5. FFT reference C code.

```
typedef pico :: s_fixed < 22,18, pico :: S_RND, pico :: S_SAT, 0 > floatP;
typedef struct{
  floatP x;
  floatP y;
}s_complexP;
```

FFT is computed using 22-bit data width with 18 bits for the integer part and 4 bits for the fractional part. Rounding and saturation configuration is used. The effect of the number of bits allocated to the fractional part on the precision and resource usage of the FFT HLS is presented in Section V. The twiddle factors are pre-calculated with a precision of 16 bits and stored in an array eliminating the need of trigonometric functions.

4.2. Input Array to Stream of Input Data

In the reference C code, the input data are passed to the function as an array. This will be translated into memory accesses by the HLS tool which is not optimal for hardware implementation. Hence, a stream of input data is used. PICO supports two types of streams: external and internal. External streams are used to stream data from/to global memory and/or other blocks in the system. Internal streams are used to stream data between loops within a multi-loop accelerator designed by PICO. In PICO, streams are specified using explicit procedure calls that transmit a scalar value to an output stream or receive a scalar value from an input stream. These procedures are converted into special opcodes that receive (transmit) data from (to) actual streams. For the FFT application, four streams are needed: input/output streams for real and imaginary parts:

```
char pico_stream_input_xin();
char pico_stream_input_yin();
void pico_stream_output_xout(int);
void pico_stream_output_yout(int);
```

PICO synthesizes a FIFO (within the RTL) for each internal and external stream in the code. Different parameters such as the length of the FIFO can be configured using pragmas. The first step of the FFT will be the loading phase where input data are stored into a RAM called z as shown below:

```
for(h = 0; h < N; h + +){
  z[h].x = (floatP) pico_stream_input_xin();
  z[h].y = (floatP) pico_stream_input_yin();
}
```

Finally after the FFT is computed, the unloading phase is performed:

```
for(p = 0; p < N; p + +){
  pico_stream_output_xout(z[p].x);
  pico_stream_output_yout(z[p].y);
}
```

4.3. Bit-Reverse Operation

If we look at the reference C code, the next step would be the bit-reverse stage; this operation takes 1024 cycles. However, it can be integrated in the radix-2 FFT block, hence reducing the total number of cycles required to perform the calculations. This can be done using the *bit_swap* function:

```
unsigned short bit_swap(unsigned short in, unsigned short bits){
  unsigned short out = 0;
  unsigned short k;
  # pragma unroll
  for(k = 0; k < bits; k + +){
    out = (out << 1) | (in & 0x1);
    in = in >> 1;
  }
  return out;
}
```

In this function, we use the pragma *unroll* to specify to the HLS tool to unroll the loop and hence parallelize the operations to speed-up the process. This function is used to calculate the new address when performing the butterfly calculation on z as shown below:

```
.
.
.
for (k = j; k < n; k = k + n2) {
    unsigned short addr_k    = bit_swap(k,   m);
    unsigned short addr_k_n1 = bit_swap(k + n1, m);
    t1 = z[addr_k_n1].x * c);
    temp = z[addr_k_n1].y * s);
    t1 -= temp;
    t2 = z[addr_k_n1].x * s;
    temp = z[addr_k_n1].y * c;
    t2 += temp;
    z[addr_k_n1].x = z[addr_k].x - t1;
    z[addr_k_n1].y = z[addr_k].y - t2;
    z[addr_k].x = z[addr_k].x + t1;
    z[addr_k].y = z[addr_k].y + t2;
    }
  }
}
return 0;
}
```
— Bit-reverse operation

— Butterfly calculation

4.4. Memory Access Reduction

Each array of data in the reference C code will be implemented as a RAM by the HLS tool. We can see that multiple accesses of z are done which is not suitable for hardware implementation since only single or dual port RAMs/ROMs are available. In order to resolve this problem and obtain better performances, the first step is to use temporary variables. This step is shown below:

```
.
.
.
for (k = j; k < n; k = k + n2) {
    s_complex tmpz_n1, tmpz;
    s_complex outz_n1, outz;
    tmpz = z[k];
    tmpz_n1 = z[k + n1];
    t1 = (tmpz_n1.x * c - tmpz_n1.y * s);
    t2 = (tmpz_n1.x * s + tmpz_n1.y * c);
    outz_n1.x = (tmpz.x - t1);
    outz_n1.y = (tmpz.y - t2);
    outz.x = (tmpz.x + t1);
    outz.y = (tmpz.y + t2);
    z[k] = outz;
    z[k + n1] = outz_n1;
    }
  }
}
return 0;
}
```
— Butterfly calculation

Through this arrangement, the memory accesses are reduced to 2 read and 2 write operations. They can be reduced further using multi-buffering or ping-pong memories. Therefore, we use two RAMs z and $z1$ and we alternate read and write operations. For example, a read operation will be done on z (or $z1$) while the write operation will be done on $z1$ (or z):

```
.
.
.
for (k = j; k < n; k = k + n2) {
    s_complex tmpz_n1, tmpz;
    s_complex outz_n1, outz;
    if (i%2) {
        tmpz    = z1[k];
        tmpz_n1 = z1[k + n1];
    } else {
        tmpz    = z[k];
        tmpz_n1 = z[k + n1];
    }
    t1 = (tmpz_n1.x * c - tmpz_n1.y * s);
    t2 = (tmpz_n1.x * s + tmpz_n1.y * c);
    outz_n1.x = (tmpz.x - t1);
    outz_n1.y = (tmpz.y - t2);
    outz.x = (tmpz.x + t1);
    outz.y = (tmpz.y + t2);
    if (i%2) {
        z[k]      = outz;
        z[k + n1] = outz_n1;
    } else {
        z1[k]      = outz;
        z1[k + n1] = outz_n1;
    }
    }
  }
}
return 0;
}
```
— Multi-buffering

— Butterfly calculation

— Multi-buffering

By integrating the modifications presented in this section to the reference C code given in **Figure 5**, the HLS implementation of the FFT can be obtained as shown in **Figure 6**.

5. Hardware Synthesis Results

The HLS tool offers different configurations that will have an impact on the hardware generated. For example, the user can specify the desired frequency that may or may not be achieved by the tool depending on the system targeted and the complexity of the C code. As seen in

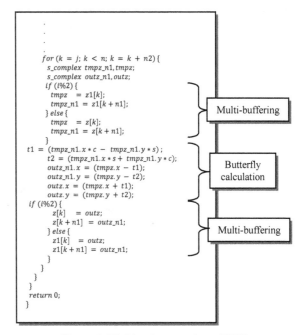

Figure 6. HLS implementation of FFT.

this section, increasing the frequency will increase the resources of the hardware generated by the HLS tool. The throughput (number of FFTs that can be done in one second) can also be specified. In order to achieve a high throughput, the HLS tool will parallelize tasks; hence increasing the hardware resources. Finally, the user can specify to implement arrays using block RAMs or look-up tables (LUTs). Hardware implementation results are obtained using Xilinx ISE 12.1 software with either speed or area optimization for Virtex-5 FPGA. The twiddle factors have been implemented using LUTs but can be also implemented using RAMs. By doing this, it will reduce the total number of slices LUTs but increase the number of blocks RAM/FIFO. **Table 1** shows the hardware usage of the HLS implementation of FFT with 22-bit data width for different targeted frequencies.

One can see a significant increase in terms of logic slices for 150 MHz operational frequency. This is due to the fact that we have selected optimization for speed in ISE in order to achieve the desired operational frequency after place and route. For frequencies lower than 150 MHz, optimization in terms of area has been selected. For frequencies from 50 MHz to 150 MHz, the total number of clock cycles achieved by PICO to perform the 1024-point FFT is 7168 but for 175 MHz it is increased to 12288 clock cycles. 7168 clock cycles is the minimum latency that can be obtained and is calculated as follow:

$$latency = loading + FFT + unloading$$

$$latency = N + \frac{N}{2} * \log_2(N) + N \tag{5}$$

$$lantecy = 1024 + 512 * 10 + 1024 = 7168 clock\ cycles$$

For frequencies higher than 150 MHz, PICO reduces the tasks' parallelism of the FFT in order to achieve the desired frequency. This results in an increase of the latency and a reduction of the hardware resources. The maximum frequency that can be obtained by PICO is around 270 MHz with a total of 17,408 clock cycles ($1024 + 3 \times 512 \times 10 + 1024$) to compute the FFT. Nevertheless, after place and route, the maximum frequency obtained is 180 MHz due to the FPGA targeted.

Area reduction in terms of slices and DSP48E blocks can be achieved by increasing the number of clock cycles required to perform the FFT. Hence, for equivalent throughput, it is better to choose a higher operational frequency and a higher number of clock cycles required to perform the FFT. **Table 2** shows the hardware usage of the FFT for a targeted frequency of 150MHz with different throughputs. For example, from **Table 1**, for a frequency of 75 MHz, the throughput is 10,463. Nevertheless, with a frequency of 150 MHz, a better throughput can be obtained using fewer DSP48E blocks (see **Table 2**, second row).

Figure 7 shows the error variation with respect to the width of the fractional part compared to the reference code shown in **Figure 5**. The relative error for the FFT is given using the formula below:

$$error = \frac{1}{100} \frac{1}{1024} \sum_{n=0}^{99} \sum_{k=0}^{1023} \left[\left| \frac{X_{ref}[n][k] - X_{HLS}[n][k]}{X_{ref}[n][k]} \right| + \left| \frac{Y_{ref}[n][k] - Y_{HLS}[n][k]}{Y_{ref}[n][k]} \right| \right] \tag{6}$$

where X and Y are real and imaginary parts respectively.

The relative error is calculated for 100 random input signals of 1024 samples each **Figure 7** shows that the relative error decreases linearly as the number of bit for the fractional part increases. For the implementation of the FFT, –40 dB is achieved giving the same results as the Xilinx FFT core. Nevertheless, the user can increase the precision at the expense of hardware usage. For 13 bits, the relative error achieved is –73 dB compared to the reference C code based on double precision floating point operations.

Table 3 shows the hardware usage with respect to the width of the fractional part for a desired operational frequency of 100 MHz. As expected, the resource usage increases with the number of bit for the fractional part. Nevertheless, the number of blocks RAM/FIFO used is the same. This is due to the architecture of the Virtex-5 FPGA selected.

Table 1. FFT hardware usage for different frequencies.

Targeted frequency	Resource usage				Achieved frequency
	Slices Registers	Slices LUTs	Block RAM/FIFO	DSP48E	
50 MHz	749	1700	2	4	50 MHz
75 MHz	765	1769	2	4	75 MHz
100 MHz	926	1967	2	4	100 MHz
125 MHz	1042	1714	2	4	125 MHz
150 MHz	1546	2004	2	4	150 MHz
175 MHz	1380	1849	2	2	165 MHz
270 MHz	1457	1989	2	2	180 MHz

Table 2. FFT hardware usage for different throughputs.

Targeted throughput	Resource usage			
	Slices Registers	Slices LUTs	Blocks RAM/FIFO	DSP48Es
20926	1546	2004	2	4
12207	1351	1693	2	2
8616	1186	1418	2	2
6658	1161	1404	2	1

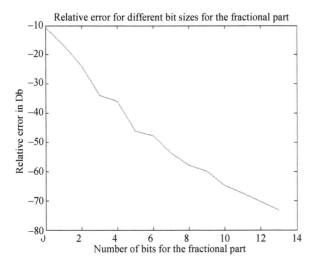

Figure 7. Relative error for different bit size for the fractional part.

Table 3. FFT hardware usage for different fractional sizes.

Fractional part number of bits	Resource usage			
	Slices Registers	Slices LUTs	Block RAM/FIFO	DSP48Es
0	767	1305	2	4
2	809	1474	2	4
4	926	1967	2	4
6	968	2184	2	4
8	1188	2309	2	4
10	1279	2405	2	8
13	1400	2607	2	8

6. Conclusion

In this paper, we have presented hardware considerations that software engineers need to apply when designing hardware modules using HLS tools. As a demonstration, the implementation of a radix-2 FFT unit has been presented. We have shown the different steps to achieve an optimized C code for HLS tools based on an ANSI C code. Results of the generated FFT for a Virtex-5 FPGA have been presented. FFT has a broad range of applications in digital signal processing, and multimedia. It is a key component that determines most of the design metrics in many signal processing communication applications. HLS tools facilitate complex algorithms to be realized at a higher level. They can reduce the design cycle significantly while successfully generating results very close to handmade HDL design.

7. Acknowledgements

The authors would like to thank the Xilinx, Inc. (www.xilinx.com) and Synopsys (www.synopsys.com) for their valuable support.

REFERENCES

[1] S. Dongwan, A. Gerstlauer, R. Domer and D. D. Gajski, "An Interactive Design Environment for C-Based High-Level Synthesis of RTL Processors," *IEEE Transactions on Very Large Scale Integration (VLSI) Systems*, Vol. 16, No. 4, 2008, pp. 446-475.

[2] S. Ramachandran, "Digital VLSI System Design," Chapter 11, Springer, New York, 2007.

[3] M. Glasser, "Open Verification Methodology Cookbook," Chapters 1-3, Springer, New York, 2009.

[4] E. Casseau and B. Le Gal, "High-Level Synthesis for the Design of FPGA-Based Signal Processing Systems," *International Symposium on Systems, Architectures, Modeling, and Simulation, SAMOS'09*, 20-23 July 2009, pp. 25-32.

[5] B. Bailey, G. Martin and A. Piziali, "ESL Design and Verification," Morgan Kaufmann, San Francisco, Chapters 1-6, 2007.

[6] V. Sklyarov and I. Skliarova, "Teaching Reconfigurable Systems: Methods, Tools, Tutorials, and Projects," *IEEE Transactions on Education*, Vol. 48, No. 2, 2005, pp. 290-300.

[7] L. E. M. Brackenbury, L. A. Plana and J. Pepper, "System-on-Chip Design and Implementation," *IEEE Transactions on Education*, Vol. 53, No. 2, 2010, pp. 272-281.

[8] J. G. Proakis and D. G. Manolakis, "Digital Processing 4th Edition," 4th Edition, Prentice Hall, New Jersey, 2006.

[9] Xilinx Inc., "XUPV5 Development Board," http://www.xilinx.com

[10] Synfora Inc, Website. http://www.synfora.com

[11] Synopsys, "Symphony C Compiler," http://www.synopsys.com/Tools/SLD/HLS/Pages/SynphonyC-Compiler.aspx

[12] AutoESL, Website. http://www.autoesl.com

[13] Mentor, Website. http://www.mentor.com

[14] P. Avss, S. Prasant and R. Jain, "Virtual Prototyping In-

creases Productivity—A Case Study," *IEEE International Symposium on VLSI Design, Automation and Test*, Hsinchu, 28-30 April 2009, pp. 96-101.

[15] Berkeley Design Technology, "An independent Evaluation of High-Level Synthesis Tools for Xilinx FPGAs," http://www.bdti.com

[16] K. L. Man, "An overview of SystemC^{FL}," *Research in Microelectronics and Electronics*, 2005 *PhD*, Vol. 1, 2005, pp. 145-148.

[17] P. Schumacher, M. Mattavelli, A. Chirila-Rus and R. Turney, "A Software/Hardware Platform for Rapid Prototyping of Video and Multimedia Designs," *Proceedings of Fifth International Workshop on System-on-Chip for Real-Time Applications*, 20-24 July 2005, pp. 30-33.

[18] W. Chen (Ed.), "The VLSI Handbook," 2nd Edition, Chapter 86, CRC Press LCC, Boca Raton, 2007.

[19] S. Van Haastregt and B. Kienhuis, "Automated Synthesis of Streaming C Applications to Process Networks in Hardware," *Proceedings of the Conference on Design Automation & Test in Europe*, April 2009, pp. 890-893.

[20] P. Coussy and A. Morawiec, "High-Level Synthesis: From Algorithm to Digital Circuits," Springer Science + Business Media, Chapters 1, 4, Berlin, 2008.

[21] N. Hatami, A. Ghofrani, P. Prinetto and Z. Navabi, "TLM 2.0 Simple Sockets Synthesis to RTL," *International Conference on Design & Technology of Integrated Systems in Nanoscale Era*, Vol. 1, 2000, pp. 232-235.

[22] D. L. Jones, "FFT Reference C Code," University of Illinois at Urbana-Champaign, 1992.

[23] Xilinx Inc., "CoreGen," http://www.xilinx.com

14

Experimental and Theoretical Considerations of Electrolyte Conductivity in Glucose Alkaline Fuel Cell

Lea Mor[1], Zeev Rubin[2]
[1]Department of Biotechnology Engineering, Ort Braude College, Karmiel, Israel
[2]Physics Unit, Ort Braude College, Karmiel, Israel

ABSTRACT

The paper focuses on the conductivity of the fuel cell electrolyte in a membraneless glucose-fueled alkaline fuel cell. The electrolyte conductivity is interpreted using simple physical models, considering either the empirical behavior of the solution's viscosity, or the consideration of ions and molecules colliding in solutions. The conductivity is expressed as a function of KOH and glucose concentrations. The physical properties of the species (*i.e.* radii, thermal velocity) and the chemical equilibrium constant of the reaction that glucose undergoes in an alkaline solution can be estimate by comparing the experimental results with the theory.

Keywords: Alkaline; Fuel Cell; Glucose; Electrolyte; Conductivity; Collision

1. Introduction

Fuel cell resistivity is one of the factors determining cell efficiency. The resistivity affects fuel cell power [1-3], efficiency and stability [4]. The resistivity of a glucose-fuelled alkaline fuel cell was previously found to depend linearly on the glucose concentration [5] dissolved in a constant KOH concentration of 0.35 M, and was shown to be seven times higher than the resistivity of a KOH-only solution [6].

The increase in resistivity of the alkaline glucose, or other carbohydrate's solutions, was also considered previously, to be due to the complexation of alkali ions with reducing and nonreducing carbohydrates [7].

The present study aimed to explain the relationship between the glucose and KOH concentrations and the changes in the fuel cell electrolyte resistivity over time.

The overall fuel cell resistance is defined as the sum of the resistances of the bulk solution (electrolyte), the diffusion layer [8] and the electrodes [3]. The electrolyte resistance was assumed to be larger than the electrodes' resistance [3]. Various authors have tried to develop theoretical and experimental methods for estimating the various components of fuel cell resistance [3,8]. Among these methods were: a micro-scale model for predicting contact resistance [8], a monodimensional simulation model of the overall electrical resistance due to ohmic losses and polarization phenomena in stationary conditions, assuming equilibrium of the chemical reactions [9], a dynamic model, based on experimental characteriza-tions of the anode and cathode equivalent resistance [3], and a transient model of the cathode catalyst layer [10].

This paper focuses on using experimental and theoretical considerations to study electrolyte conductivity of an alkaline glucose solution.

Two theories, explaining the behaviour of conductivity as function of glucose and KOH concentration, will be presented at the third section. The experimental behaveiour of conductivity in a test tube and in alkaline fuel cell will be introduced in the fourth section. Analysis of the experimental results using both theories is discussed in the 5th section.

2. Materials and Methods

The solutions investigated here were of glucose-KOH with various concentrations ranging from 0.05 M to 1 M for both the glucose and KOH. The solutions were prepared shortly before use by dissolving the glucose in water or in KOH solutions. KOH concentration was monitored before and during the experiments by titration with potassium biphthalate (Carlo Erba). It should be noted that measurement by titration with biphthalate gives the total OH⁻ concentration, but nonetheless, this measurement is referred to as the change in KOH concentration. The KOH is the main source of the ions in solution, and is responsible for the solution conductivity. The experiments include test tubes and open/closed circuit's fuel cell.

Test tube—A test tube of 50 ml volume, contained 25

ml glucose-KOH solution. The conductivity was measured in the test tube.

Open/closed circuit's fuel cell—The membraneless alkaline fuel cell, (purchased from Hong Kong University [11,12]), constructed with one reservoir including both the fuel glucose and the electrolyte KOH solution. Its cathode came into contact with the ambient air and its anode, with incorporated platinum particles, was immersed in fuel/electrolyte (25 ml glucose-KOH) solution. For close circuit's fuel cell experiments, the circuit was closed with a load resistance of 10 Ω. For electrolyte conductivity measurements the solution were temporarily transferred to a 50 ml test tube; after getting the conductivity result, the solution was returned to the fuel cell.

The temperature in both experiments was maintained in a water bath adjusted to 21 C.

Conductivity and KOH concentrations were measured every 20 minutes for the first five hours, and once a day for up to five days. Conductivity was measured with a Cyberscan 510 conductivity meter. Samples for HPLC analysis over time were conducted using an isocratic pump using eluting solvent acetonytrile:water 80:20 (v/v).

3. Theory

Equation (1) expresses the electrolyte conductivity, derived from the ions present in the electrolyte solution before and during the fuel cell operation, Using simplified kinetic theory considerations [13,14].

$$\sigma = e \sum_i |z_i| u_i c_i \tag{1}$$

here σ is the conductivity and e is the elementary charge. The summation index i refers to the ions that take part in electricity conduction in solution: K^+ and OH^- generated from the electrolyte, H^+ generated from the water, and g^- produced during a chemical reaction of glucose in the alkaline solution. z_i is the signed ionic charge of the ith ion, c_i is its concentration and u_i is its mobility coefficient, defined by:

$$u_i = v_{di}/E . \tag{2}$$

v_{di} is the drift velocity of the ions, induced by the electric field E. Equation (1) is composed of two parts: properties of the solution (e.g. concentrations and viscosity) and specific parameters of the ions (e.g. charge, velocity and effective size). The concentration of the ions derived from the electrolyte and water were assumed, for this presentation: The concentrations of K^+, OH^- and KOH are identical, and the concentration of H^+ is negligible comparared to the concentration of OH^-. The concentration of the ions produced during the chemical reactions (i.e. endiolate $(C_6H_{11}O_6)^-$ or gluconate $(C_6H_{11}O_7)^-$) were assumed to be $a_{g-} = k_{g-} c_g c_{OH-}$, where K_{g-} was the equi-

librium constant for the ions generated from the glucose in the alkaline solution.

3.1. Conductivity-Viscosity Empirical Evaluation

The mobility coefficient is often expressed by the Stokes-Einstein equation [13]:

$$u_i = \frac{|z_i| e}{6 \pi \eta r_i} . \tag{3}$$

Here, η is the solvent viscosity (in this case, of an aqueous glucose solution) and r_i is customarily called the (hydrated) ionic radius of the ith ion. Equation (3) appears to describe a sphere with charge $z_i e$, moving at a terminal velocity v_{di} under the influence of an electrical field E and a Stokes-Law drag force (i.e., a drag force in a creeping flow around a sphere). However, this is not the physical picture: Given that the ions and the water (and glucose) molecules are of similar orders of magnitude, the ions are not surrounded by an inter-molecular fluid and no drag whatsoever acts on them. Consequently, Equation (3) is used as an empirical approximation, rather than as a statement of a force balance on an ion. In this context, $1/\eta$ represents the notion that sluggishly flowing solvents do hinder the mobility of the ions in them and $e/(6\pi r_i)$ is a coefficient, characteristic of the ith ion. Consequently, substituting Equation (3) into Equation (1), and introducing all the definitions and assumptions, yields:

$$\frac{1}{\sigma} = \frac{6\pi\eta}{e^2 \left(\dfrac{c_{OH^-}}{r_{OH^-}} + \dfrac{c_{K^+}}{r_{K^+}} + \dfrac{K_{g-} c_g c_{OH^-}}{r_{g-}} \right)} \tag{4}$$

We now introduce the concept of normalized conductivity:

$$\bar{\sigma} = \sigma / [\text{KOH}] \tag{5}$$

Since KOH is the major contributor to the conductivity, this normalization reveals the changes in conductivity undergone by the other factors in the solution, with the exception of KOH.

Equation (4) leads to:

$$\frac{1}{\bar{\sigma}} = \frac{6\pi\eta}{e^2 N_A \left(\dfrac{1}{r_{OH^-}} + \dfrac{1}{r_{K^+}} + \dfrac{K_{g-} c_g}{r_{g-}} \right)} . \tag{6}$$

This completes the inclusion of the Stokes-Einstein Equation (3) in expression (1). Empirical expressions (4) and (6) can be used for processing the measured conductivity values. These two expressions include the assumption in expression (1) of constant u_i values, which may prove suitable when only the ionic concentrations affect the conductivity, and the assumption in expression (3), which can handle some of the glucose concentration's effect, because η varies with the glucose concentration in the solvent [15].

3.2. Conductivity-Collision Evaluation

Let us now define the acceleration under the influence of an electric field, v_{di}/τ_i. Introducing Newton's second law gives:

$$E = v_{di}m_i/q_i\tau_i . \tag{7}$$

τ_i is the mean average characteristic time of successive collisions between the ith ion and glucose molecules $\tau_i = 1/c_g\sigma_{gi}v_i$. σ_{gi} is the cross-section of collision $\pi\left(r_i^2 + r_g^2\right)$ [16], v_i is the thermal velocity of the ith ion in the solution, c_g is the glucose concentration and r_i and r_g are the hydrated radii of the ions and glucose in the solution. Introducing the definitions and assumptions of Equation (1) yields:

$$\frac{1}{\sigma} = \frac{c_g}{\left[e^2\left(\dfrac{c_{KOH}}{\sigma_{gK^+}v_{K^+}m_{K^+}} + \dfrac{c_{KOH}}{\sigma_{gOH^-}v_{OH^-}m_{OH^-}} + \dfrac{K_{g-}c_g * c_{KOH}}{\sigma_{gg-}v_{g-}m_{g-}}\right)\right]} \tag{8}$$

Introducing the normalized conductivity definition (5) to Equation (8) leads to

$$\frac{1}{\bar{\sigma}} = \frac{c_g}{\left[e^2\left(\dfrac{1}{\sigma_{gK^+}v_{K^+}m_{K^+}} + \dfrac{1}{\sigma_{gOH^-}v_{OH^-}m_{OH^-}} + \dfrac{K_{g-}c_g}{\sigma_{gg-}v_{g-}m_{g-}}\right)\right]} \tag{9}$$

The theoretical expressions (8) and (9) can be used for processing of measured conductivity values. They include the assumption in equation (1) of constant u_i values, which may prove suitable when the colliding species are hard, not interacting spheres, as in dilute gases [17].

4. Results

4.1. Conductivity Measurements in the Test Tube

Since electrolytes play a major part in fuel cell resistance, the first step in studying glucose-fuelled alkaline fuel cell resistance changes over time is to investigate the instantaneous conductivity of an alkaline glucose solution in a test tube. The conductivity of KOH solutions (0.05 M to 1 M) with various glucose concentrations, up to 1 M, was measured shortly after preparation. The resistivity

ρ (the reciprocal of conductivity) for each initial KOH concentration was plotted against the glucose concentration in **Figure 1**. It can be seen that for each initial KOH concentration the glucose, a nonionic compound, increased the solution's resistivity (decreased the solution conductivity). To discern the changes in the solutions' conductivity caused by factors other than KOH—which is the major contributor to the conductivity—the normalized resistivity ρ (reciprocal of normalized conductivity) was plotted against the glucose concentration in **Figure 2**. Once all the graphs of the different KOH concentrations were combined into one graph, the data indeed showed that the glucose concentration was responsible for the conductivity changes. To demonstrate the effect of time on fuel cell electrolyte conductivity, the conductivity was monitored in three solutions, representing high (0.8 M), medium (0.25 M) and low (0.05 M) KOH concentrations. The data shows that normalized resistivity was linear with the glucose concentration for both instantaneous and subsequent measurements (after 3 - 4 days).

4.2. Changes in Normalized Conductivity over Time

Since the changes in normalized conductivity over time is function of both KOH concentration and solution conductivity, both KOH concentration and solution conductivity were measured over time in two solutions, representing high (0.35 M KOH, 1 M glucose) and low (0.1 M KOH, 0.1 M glucose) concentrations. Two experiments per solution were conducted.

4.2.1. KOH Concentration Changes over Time

The mean KOH concentration decreased with time both in the test tube and in the open/closed fuel cell during the five days of the experiment (**Figure 3**).

The concentration changes in the test tube were higher

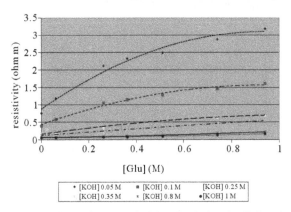

Figure 1. The resistivity of glucose solution in KOH, for each KOH concentration, is plotted against glucose concentration. Measurements were taken in the test tube shortly after preparing the solution.

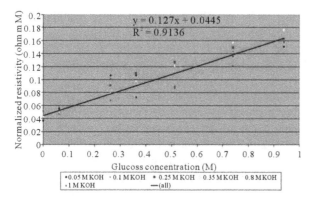

Figure 2. Normalized resistivity, as a function of glucose concentration at various KOH concentrations. Measurements were taken in the test tube shortly after preparing the solution.

when the KOH concentration was high (0.35 M) as opposed to low (0.1M). Significant changes between the KOH concentration in the test tube and in the fuel cell, for both KOH concentrations, were evident. The decrease in KOH concentration over time in the low (0.1 M) KOH concentration resulted from the reaction of KOH with CO_2, which already existed, and was continuously dissolving in the water. In the high (0.35 M) KOH concentration, the higher decrease may result from the isomerization reactions of glucose, catalyzed by the high KOH concentration, producing endiolate ions. In the fuel cell, the fuel cell electrode can, in addition, catalyzes electrochemical reaction, in both KOH concentrations, yealding gluconate ions, which contributed to the lower KOH concentration in the fuel cell [18].

4.2.2. Conductivity Changes over Time

4.2.2.1. Test Tube

The reduction of the solution's mean conductivity measured in the test tube depended on the amount of time that had elapsed (**Figure 4**). For the first few hours, the effect was high, and thereafter remained stable for the next few days. Comparing changes in the KOH concentration (**Figure 3**) and conductivity (**Figure 4**), led to the following inferences: The rate of KOH concentration changed during the first day; at a concentration of 0.1 M KOH, it was similar to the rate of the conductivity change. In opposition, when the KOH concentration was 0.35 M, the rate of the KOH concentration change was much larger than the rate of the conductivity change. This effect can be clearly expressed by the normalized resistivity ([KOH]/σ) (**Figure 5**). The normalized resistivity in solution was almost constant at 0.1 M KOH, whereas it dropped significantly in a concentration of 0.35M KOH, because of the reaction took place in a solution, catalyzed by a high KOH concentration. Ionic compounds generated by this reaction contributed to the conductivity, and kept it almost constant in spite of the

reduction in OH$^-$ concentration.

4.2.2.2. Fuel Cell

The situation was different in the fuel cell. Here, under both KOH concentrations, despite the high reduction in KOH concentration over time (**Figure 3**), the reduction in conductivity is less profound (**Figure 4**). Consequently, the normalized resistivity (**Figure 5**) decreased over time for both KOH concentrations. This can be explained by generation of ionized compounds g$^-$ by the electrochemical reaction.

4.2.3. Normalized Resistivity Changes with Glucose Concentration

The normalized resistivity in two glucose concentrations are shown in **Figure 6(a)** for the test tube, and in **Figure**

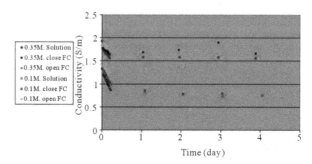

Figure 3. KOH concentration changes in open/closed fuel cell, compared to test tube.

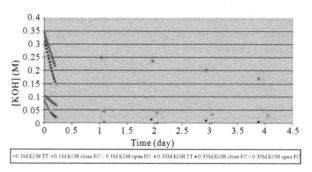

Figure 4. Conductivity changes in open/closed fuel cell, compared to test tube.

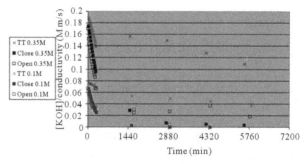

Figure 5. Normalized resistivity ([KOH]/conductivity) changes in open/closed fuel cell, compared to test tube.

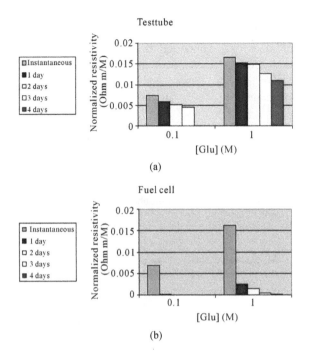

(a)

(b)

Figure 6. Effect of time on normalized resistivity under two glucose concentrations, [Glu]. (a) Test tube; (b) Fuel cell.

6(b) for the fuel cell. It can clearly seen that in the test tube, there was a slow and graduated decrease in normalized resistivity in both glucose concentrations (high and low). In the fuel cell, there was a dramatic drop in normalized resistivity beginning from the first day onward.

4.3. HPLC Analysis of the Glucose-KOH Solution

To observe the chemical changes in an alkaline glucose solution, HPLC analysis of glucose (0.1 M) in KOH (0.1 M) was done (**Figure 7**). Two dominant species (Rt 9.6 - 9.8 and 13), had no significant change in concentration over time, were evident in the test tube (**Figure 7(b)**). In the fuel cell, these species concentrations change (either increase or decrease over time). In the fuel cell, there was additional specie (Rt 10.5), which increase in concentration over time (**Figure 7(a)**). Other species (Rt 7.1, 8 and 8.9), having low concentration, exist in both test tube and fuel cell with no significant changes over time. These findings prove that there are differences between the chemical reactions occurring in the fuel cell (the electrochemical reaction and isomerization) and in test tube (only isomerization).

5. Discussion

5.1. Analysis of the Experimental Results Using the Conductivity-Viscosity Empirical Evaluation for Low Glucose Concentration

Assuming low glucose concentrations

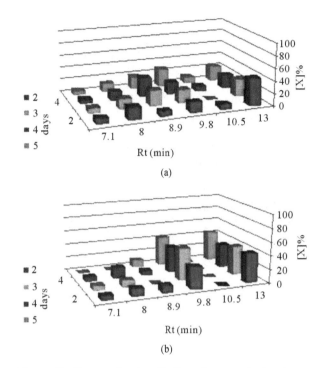

(a)

(b)

Figure 7. Changes in the alkaline glucose solution in: (a) fuel cell, (b) test tube. [Glu] 0.1 M, [KOH] 0.1 M, elution solvent AcN:H$_2$O 80:20.

$$\left(1/r_{OH^-} + 1/r_{K^+}\right) \cdot \left(r_{g^-}/K_{g^-}\right) >> c_g, \qquad (10)$$

and assuming

$$r_{OH^-} = r_{K^+} = r_i, \qquad (11)$$

the normalized conductivity (Equation (6)) is simplified to:

$$\frac{1}{\bar{\sigma}} = \bar{\rho} = \frac{3\pi\eta r_i}{e^2 N_A}. \qquad (12)$$

The viscosity has a linear dependence on the glucose concentration (Equation (13)) [15]:

$$\eta = 0.7308E-3[G] + 0.9307E-3, Pas. \qquad (13)$$

Exploring (Equation (13)) and (Equation (12)), it is evidence that the normalized resistivity is a linear function of the glucose concentration, in agreement with the experimental results (Equation (14)), **Figure 2**):

$$\bar{\rho} = 0.1271[G] + 0.0445. \qquad (14)$$

By fitting the experimental results (Equation (14)) to Equation (12,13), two values of r_i were found: 2.84E–10 m (2.84 Å), and 0.78Å. The error in estimating r_i here is approximately 57% relative to its mean value. Both values of r_i are in agreement with the range of (1.37 - 10) Å obtained from the estimated hydrated and unhydrated ion radii [19]. The minimal value of r_i, taking into account the ion radii in crystals and solutions [15], cannot be below 1.37 Å. Hence, the model predicted that the ions were in hydrated form.

The experimental results showed a drop in normalized resistivity over time in a fuel cell (**Figure 5**).The model explains the experimental time effect by assuming increase in g- over time. This finding agrees with the HPLC data showing the production of a chemical species in the fuel cell, which was not present in the test tube.

5.2. Analysis of the Experimental Results Using the Conductivity-Collision Equation Assuming a Low Glucose Concentration

For low glucose concentrations,
$c_g \ll \sigma_{gg^-} v_{g^-} m_{g^-} / K_{g^-} \sigma_{gi} v_i m_i$, Equation (9) can be simplified and expressed in Equation (15), in terms of the normalized resistivity as a function of glucose concentration.

$$\bar{\rho} = \frac{c_g}{\left[e^2 \left(\dfrac{1}{\sigma_{gK^+} v_{K^+} m_{K^+}} + \dfrac{1}{\sigma_{gOH^-} v_{OH^-} m_{OH^-}} \right) \right]} . \quad (15)$$

Equation (15) shows that the normalized resistivity is linear with the glucose concentration, thus agreeing with the experimental results (**Figure 2**). However, it does not describe the resistivity of the pure KOH solution, in the absence of glucose, which is expressed by the intercept in **Figure 2**.

5.3. The Viscosity

The viscosity expression (Equation 16) was evaluated using the mobility definition (Equation (2)) in both the models (Equations (3) and (7)).

$$\eta = \sum \frac{m_i \sigma_{ji} v_i}{6\pi r_i} \cdot c_g \quad (16)$$

Equation (16) shows that the solution's viscosity, an empirical characteristic of the solution, is basically a function of parameters influencing the collision in the solution, and is linear with the solute (glucose) concentration. This explains the mechanism by which the viscosity influences the solution resistivity.

6. Conclusion

Glucose increases the resistivity of a KOH solution. Two simple physical models were used to explain the contribution of glucose to fuel cell resistivity, based on the solution viscosity or collisions between ions and glucose molecules in solution. The simple collision model proposed here is also applicable to solutions. It predicts the species parameters. Glucose degrades under alkaline conditions in fuel cells, which can increase fuel cell resistivity.

7. Acknowledgements

This study was supported by a grant from the ORT Braude College research committee. The technical assistance of Mrs. J. Bassan and Mrs. R. Asakla are acknowledged.

REFERENCES

[1] S. V. Alferov, L. G. Tomashevskaya, O. N. Ponamoreva, V. A. Bogdanovskaya and A. N. Reshetilov, "Biofuel Cell Anode Based on the Gluconobacter Oxydans Bacteria Cells and 2,6-Dichlorophenolindophenol as an Electron Transport Mediator," *Russian Journal of Electrochemistry*, Vol. 42, No. 4, 2006, pp. 403-404.

[2] M. Shibazaki and T. Taniuchi, "Jpn. Kokai Tokkyo," JP Patent No. 2005166356 A2 20050623, 2005.

[3] X. Xue, J. Tang, N. Sammes and Y. Du, "Dynamic Modelling of Single Tubular SOFC Combining Heat/Mass Transfer and Electrochemical Reaction Effects," *Journal of Power Sources*, Vol. 142, 2005, pp. 211-222.

[4] K. Nakafuji and A. Muneuchi, "Jpn. Kokai Tokkyo Koho," JP Patent No. 2006032275 A 20060202 CAN 144: 174271 AN 2006:97621, 2006.

[5] Z. Rubin and L. Mor, "Electrode Resistance Dependence on Alkaline Glucose Fuel Cell Electrolyte Concentration," *Proceedings of the International Conference of Fundamentals and Developments of Fuel Cells*, December 2008, Nancy, pp. 115-116.

[6] E. Bubis, L. Mor, N. Sabag, Z. Rubin, U. Vaysban, *et al.*, "Electrical Characterization of a Glucose-Fueled Alkaline Fuel Cell," *Proceedings of the 4th International ASME Conference on Fuel Cell Science, Engineering and Technology, FuelCell2006*, Irvine, Vol. 2006, 2006, 8 Pages.

[7] S. P. Moulik and D. P. Khan, "Complexation of Reducing and Nonreducing Carbohydrates with Hydroxides of Some Alkali and Alkaline-Earth Metals," *Carbohydrate Research*, Vol. 41, 1975, pp. 93-104.

[8] Y. Zhou, G. Lin, A. J. Shih and S. J. Hu, "A Micro-Scale Model for Predicting Contact Resistance between Bipolar Plate and Gas Diffusion Layer in PEM Fuel Cell," *Journal of Power Sources*, Vol. 163, No. 2, 2007, pp 777-783.

[9] P. Costamagna, E. Arato, P. L. Antonucci and V. Antonucci, "Partial Oxidation of CH_4 in Solid Oxide Fuel Cells: Simulation Model of the Electrochemical Reactor and Experimental Validation," *Chemical Engineering Science*, Vol. 51, No. 11, 1996, pp. 3013-3018.

[10] D. B. Genevey, M. R. Spakovsky, M. W. Ellis, D. J. Nelson, B. Olsommer, *et al.*, "Transient Model of Heat, Mass, and Charge Transfer as Well as Electrochemistry in the Cathode Catalyst Layer of a PEMFC," *Proceedings of the ASME Advanced Energy Systems Division*, New York, November 2002, pp. 393-406.

[11] K. Y. Chan, *et al.*, "Methods and Apparatus for the Oxi-

dation of Glucose Molecules," United States Patent No. 20020125146, 2002.

[12] W. Chan, "Fuel Cell Research Laboratory," Hong Kong University, Hong Kong, 2003. http://chem.hku.hk/%7Efuelcell/demo.htm

[13] A. J. Bard and L. R. Faulkner, "Electrochemical Methods," 2nd Edition, John Wiley & Sons Ltd, New York, 2001.

[14] D. Halliday, R. Resnick and K. Krane, "Physics," Vol. 2, John Wiley & Sons, New York, 2002.

[15] D. R. Lide, "Handbook of Chemistry and Physics," 83rd Edition, CRC Press, Boca Raton, 2002-2003.

[16] F. Raif, "Statistic Physics, The Berkeley Course of Phys-ics," Vol. 5, McGraw Hill, New York, 1968.

[17] J. P. Hansen and I. R. McDonald, "Theory of Simple Liquids," 3rd Edition, University of Cambridge, Amsterdam, 2007.

[18] L. Mor, Z. Rubin and P. Schechner, "Measuring Open Circuit Voltage in Glucose Alkaline Fuel Cell Operated as a Continuous Stirred Tank Reactor," *Journal of Fuel Cell Science and Technology*, Vol. 5, No. 1, 2008, Article ID 014503.

[19] T. I. Berlidze and K. L. Magleby, "Probing the Geometry of the Inner Vestibule of BK Channels with Sugars," *Journal of General Physiology*, Vol. 126, No. 105, 2005, pp. 105-121.

Nomenclature

Latin Symbols

C_i: Molar concentration of the ith chemical species, $kmol/m^3$

c_i: concentration of the ith chemical species, $1/m^3$

e: Elementary charge, 1.602×10^{-19} C

K_{g-}: Equilibrium constant for ions generated from glucose, $m^3/kmol$

m_i: Ion mass, kg

r_i: Length coefficient (also called the "hydrated ion radius") for the ith ion, m

v_{di}: Drift velocity, m/sec

v_{mi}: v_i is a thermal velocity, m/sec

u_i: Mobility coefficient of the ith ion, $m^2 \cdot sec^{-1} \cdot V^{-1}$

z_i: Signed ionic charge, expressed as the number of elementary charges

Greek symbols

η: Viscosity, $Kg \cdot m^{-1} \cdot sec^{-1}$

ρ: Electrical resistivity, $\Omega \cdot m$

$\bar{\rho}_{KOH} = 1/\bar{\sigma}_{KOH}$: Normalized resistivity, $\Omega \cdot m \cdot kmol/m^3$

σ: Electrical conductivity, $\Omega^{-1} \cdot m^{-1}$

σ_{ij}: Cross section collision between two species i with j, m^2

$\bar{\sigma}_{KOH} = \dfrac{\sigma}{[KOH]}$: Normalized conductivity, $\Omega^{-1} \cdot m^{-1} \cdot m^3/kmol$

τ_{ij}: Time between collisions, sec

Subscripts

$g.G$: Glucose

I: The ith collide species

J: The jth species collided with

Abbreviations

Å: 10^{-10} m

g^-: Glucose ions $(C_6H_{11}O_6)^-$

mol: Gram molecular weight

Rt: Retention time, min

TT: Test tube

[X]: Molar concentration (M) of the X chemical species, $kmol/m^3$

15

A High Color Rendering Index on Multichip LED Light Source

Jen-Yu Shieh[1], Luke K. Wang[2], Ming-Lei Chiu[3]

[1]Department of Electro-Optics Engineering, National Formosa University, Yunlin County, Chinese Taipei
[2]Department of Electrical Engineering, National Kaohsiung University of Applied Sciences, Kaohsiung, Chinese Taipei
[3]Chung Hua-Chin Kong Optoelectronics Co., Ltd., Chung Hwa County, Chinese Taipei

ABSTRACT

Light source carrying a high color rendering index (CRI) finds potential applications in people's everyday life as well as lighting industry. Combination of multi-wavelength LED light sources with designated direct emission sources can achieve warm-white and cool-white light. A generic design of high CRI multi-wavelength light-emitting-diode (LED) light source, using flyback converter, pulse width modulation (PWM) voltage control, variable resistor, and timer, is proposed. The PWM pulse is for the voltage control of cascade LEDs, while variable resistor manipulates the current flowing through LEDs. A design of dimming drive with cascade-connected electronic switch is also proposed. By adjusting the width of the dimming signal, the average value of forward current pulse can be changed, and therefore the objective, the tuning of the amount of light output, can be fulfilled. The advantage of the proposed design is its short response time.

Keywords: CRI; PWM Dimming; LED; Flyback Converter

1. Introduction

The use of LED in lighting applications is overwhelming. The traditional light sources using either incandescent or fluorescent have been shifted to the solid-state's due to their intrinsic limitations/factors, almost impossible to overcome or to be substituted.

Smart lighting nowadays may be fulfilled by the employment of digitally controlled multi-chip LED systems, belonging to the category of solid state lighting (SSL). SSL offers many advantages such as control of color rendering, chromaticity control, better light quality, and energy-saving; controllability of spectral power distribution, color temperature, temporal modulation, spatial distribution, and polarization properties are feasible [1]. Meanwhile, a trade-off must be made between color rendering and luminous efficacy of the radiation of LEDs. The most significant property of SSL is associated with the development of artificial light sources. Two approaches for white LEDs are phosphor-conversion LED lamp and multi-chip polychromatic LED lamp. The output light emission and forward voltage of LED vary with the temperature and current passing through it. The performance of LED diodes is always fluctuating with the thermal condition of the LED device/system [2]. The control of color rendering is through the introduction of multi-chip LED light source in this analysis.

A prototype of LED light source with 9 different LED chips is constructed. The effects of light mixture with different color temperatures are visualized. We can take the advantage of LED's small full-width-half-max (FWHM) attribute, having a CRI of 98% and higher. The mixture of color spectral distribution functions can be obtained by the linear combination of each LED spectrum. The mimics of natural light sources with the proposed multi-wavelength LED light source are demonstrated via the comparisons of the measured color temperatures and the computed ones as well as corrected color temperature (CCT).

2. Led Light Source Fundamentals

2.1. CIE Color Definition

First, the color rendering index is defined by CIE color definition.

2.2. Color Temperature

The color temperature of a light source is the temperature of an ideal black-body radiator that radiates light of comparable hue to that light source. The temperature is conventionally expressed in terms of absolute temperature, kelvin (K) [3]. Higher color temperatures (5000 K or more) are called cool colors (blueish white); lower color temperatures (2700 - 3000 K) are called warm colors (yellowish white through red) [4]. The polynomial formula for corrected color temperature (CCT) T is [5]

$$T = -437n^3 + 3601n^2 - 6861n + 5514.31 \qquad (1)$$

with inverse line slope n,

$$n = \frac{(x-0.3320)}{(y-0.1858)} \qquad (2)$$

where (x, y) is the chromaticity coordinates. The chromaticity coordinates is based on standard tristimulus (X, Y, Z), defined by the International Commission on Illumination (CIE). The transformation from RGB to CIE color space (X, Y, Z) is

$$\begin{bmatrix} X \\ Y \\ Z \end{bmatrix} = \begin{bmatrix} 2.7689 & 1.7517 & 1.1302 \\ 1 & 4.5907 & 0.0601 \\ 0 & 0.0565 & 5.5943 \end{bmatrix} \begin{bmatrix} R \\ G \\ B \end{bmatrix} \qquad (3)$$

The transformation from (X, Y, Z) to chromaticity coordinates is $x = X/(X+Y+Z)$ and $y = Y/(X+Y+Z)$.

2.3. Color Rending Index (CRI)

The color rendering index (CRI) is a quantitative measure of the ability of a light source to reproduce the colors of various objects faithfully in comparison with an ideal or natural light source [4].

2.4. Multiwavelength LED Spectrum

A composite light spectrum is a linear combination of each LED spectrum, $S_i(\lambda)$,

$$S(\lambda) = \sum_i \alpha_i S_i(\lambda) \qquad (4)$$

where α_i is the proportion under equivalent power assumption. The goal is to make $S(\lambda)$ close to those CIE-defined standard light spectrum of D50, D65, and D75, choosing color temperatures of 5000 K, 6500 K, and 7500 K, respectively. An objective function E can be defined in order to compute those optimums of α_i,

$$E = \sum_j \left[S_j(\lambda) - D_j(\lambda) \right]^2 \qquad (5)$$

where color temperature 5000 K, 6500 K, and 7500 K are for $j = 1$, 2, and 3, respectively and $D_j(\lambda)$ is the spectrum of the CIE-defined standard light source.

2.5. LED Power Source with Power Factor Correction Functionality

The most attractive and beneficial attribute of LED lighting technology is its energy efficiency. LED power supply may come from a DC power source or, alternatively, transforming from AC power source after passing

through a rectifier; basically, a DC power source may not provide any power factor correction (PFC) functionality as well as dimming capability for LED. Therefore, a flyback converter is included in the proposed LED power source module. The proposed LED drive with PFC is shown in **Figure 1**.

2.6. LED Dimming Design

Varying the forward drive current can dim an LED array; using a voltage regular or a variable resistor will accomplish the dimming requirement. An alternative way is to employ PWM. Two key factors, pulse width and duty cycle, can make LED light to vary its intensity. By turning the LED off for a short period of time will illude the human eyes, perceiving the LED as a continuous light stream. Therefore a LED drive circuitry is required to produce appropriate pulse width and frequency. The propose LED dimming design uses LM555 timer and variable resistor for the control of output pulse width. **Figure 2** shows the design of dimming circuitry.

3. Simulation and Experiment

A flyback converter with power factor correction functionality in combination with LM555 timer generating PWM signal is made to implement on a LED array, consisting of three cascade LEDs. The output of the flyback converter is connected to the input of the LM555. These three cascade LEDs play the role of load. By varying the duty cycle and the ratio of the variable resistor, the PWM pulse width can be changed accordingly.

The input DC voltage range is 5 ~ 15 V; the load to the LED module is consisted of 4 cascade LEDs. LED dim-

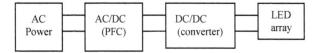

Figure 1. LED power source with PFC functionality.

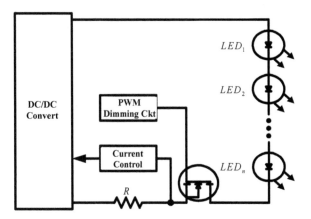

Figure 2. The schematics of cascade-connected switch dimming design.

ming drive is fulfilled via the tuning of variable resistor, width of PWM pulses, on/off timing of control/triggering of electronic switch. An example using resistor ratio (0.2, 0.5, 0.8) associated with duty cycle (0.2, 0.5, 0.8) and 5K Hz for the switching frequency of PFC is conducted to simulate the corresponding voltage output across LEDs and the forward current through LEDs. Simulation results show that the larger the duty cycle, the larger the output voltage; the forward current and output voltage are propositional to the variable resister ratio, as expected. Simulation also shows that a duty cycle of 0.8 or higher will always make the output quantities diverge.

Nine different kinds of LED chips, AlGaInP and In-GaNA, are introduced in all constructed LED modules, being packaging with 4 parallel-arranged LED chips in order to increase their brightness level and emission area. A prototype of multi-wavelength LED light source with dimming capability is constructed, and is shown in **Figure 3**.

The wavelengths and nomenclatures are listed in **Table 1**. Three designated mix of color and their associated percentage of emission are listed in **Table 2**.

Table 3 records the mimic of the color temperature/chromaticity coordinates of natural light sources. Therefore the proposed multi-wavelength LED light source can mimic a variety of natural light sources ranging from outdoor to indoor. The performance of the proposed LED light source is also evaluated using the NIST's scenario. The values of R_a, the general color rendering index, as well as the corresponding computed color temperature for all 14 samples are listed in **Table 4**, illustrating the performance of the proposed LED light source via R_a. u'

Figure 3. The emission of the multiwavelength of the LED light source module.

Table 1. Wavelenght of led chips.

No.	Color assignment	Wavelength(nm)
1	B1	455.0 ~ 457.5 nm
2	B2	470.0 ~ 472.5 nm
3	G	520.5 ~ 522.5 nm
4	Y1	561.0 ~ 563.3 nm
5	Y2	568.8 ~ 571.0 nm
6	O1	586.0 ~ 590.0 nm
7	O2	590.1 ~ 592.0 nm
8	R1	617.9 ~ 619.8 nm
9	R2	620.0 ~ 622.6 nm

Table 2. Mix of led light.

No.	Color Assignment	Emission (%)
1	B1 + B2	41.6%
2	G	33.4%
3	Y1 +Y2 + O1 + O2 +R1 +R2	25%

Table 3. Mix of led light.

No.	x	y	Color Temperature (T) (measured)	N	T (computed)	Mimic of different light sources
1	0.2998	0.303	7674	−0.27474403	7680	White-light
2	0.3005	0.3101	7486	−0.25341915	7491	White-light
3	0.303	0.3001	7489	−0.25371829	7494	White-light
4	0.2981	0.298	7921	−0.30213904	7928	White-light
5	0.2961	0.2961	8136	−0.32547597	8144	White-light
6	0.2865	0.2973	8933	−0.40807175	8943	Morning
7	0.2857	0.3423	7864	−0.29584665	7871	Outdoor shade region
8	0.3332	0.3461	5466	0.007485964	5463	Noon daylight, Direct sun
9	0.3649	0.3813	4467	0.168286445	4460	Afternoon
10	0.3605	0.3937	4647	0.137085137	4640	Afternoon
11	0.3877	0.399	3970	0.261257036	3960	Late afternoon
12	0.4338	0.426	3235	0.423813489	3220	Sunrise or sunset
13	0.4703	0.4512	2973	0.521100226	2855	Sunrise or sunset; household light bulbs
14	0.247	0.2651	17514	−1.07187894	17544	North light, blue sky

Table 4. Measurements (based on D65).

No.	x	y	Color Temperature (measured)	Color Temperature (computed)	u' (CIE)	v' (CIE)	$\Delta u'v'$	R_a
1	0.2998	0.303	7674	7680	0.1987	0.3031	0.0191	99.91
2	0.3005	0.3101	7486	7491	0.1964	0.3098	0.0124	99.94
3	0.303	0.3001	7489	7494	0.2022	0.2986	0.0240	99.89
4	0.2981	0.298	7921	7928	0.1994	0.2989	0.0233	99.89
5	0.2961	0.2961	8136	8144	0.1987	0.2980	0.0242	99.89
6	0.2865	0.2973	8933	8943	0.1912	0.3041	0.0192	99.91
7	0.2857	0.3423	7864	7871	0.1748	0.3507	0.0366	99.83
8	0.3332	0.3461	5466	5463	0.2055	0.3280	0.0096	99.96
9	0.3649	0.3813	4467	4460	0.2132	0.3441	0.0268	99.88
10	0.3605	0.3937	4647	4640	0.2059	0.3576	0.0364	99.83
11	0.3877	0.399	3970	3960	0.2211	0.3481	0.0349	99.84
12	0.4338	0.426	3235	3220	0.2395	0.3483	0.0492	99.77
13	0.4703	0.4512	2973	2855	0.2517	0.3514	0.0613	99.72
14	0.247	0.2651	17514	17544	0.1737	0.2908	0.0396	99.82

and u' are defined by Equations (6) and (7).

$$u' = \frac{4x}{(-2x + 12y + 3)} \qquad (6)$$

$$v' = \frac{6y}{(-2x + 12y + 3)} \qquad (7)$$

transforming CIE's chromaticity (x, y) into u' and u'. $\Delta u'v'$ is the Euclidean distance between the CIE 1960 target chromaticity and the Planckian chromaticity coordinates [6,7].

4. Conclusion

An artificial multiwavelength/multichip LED light source with dimming control, consisting of 9 different LED chips, is implemented to achieve the goal of this paper, i.e., obtaining high CRI value. The key feature is to introduce PWM, power factor correction, and an electronic switch in the design of circuitry; dimming function is also included in the design. The verification of the proposed LED light source to mimic the natural light source is conducted through the comparisons of the measurements of color temperature with the computed ones. The manipulation of color rendering, a figure of merit for any white light source, is fulfilled as well, and the performance of the proposed LED light source is visualized via those high CRI values, which in average are greater or equal to 98%.

5. Acknowledgements

We would also like to thank National Formosa University for granting us the subsidies in 2010 Excellence in Teaching Project, giving us the opportunity to work this project.

REFERENCES

[1] E. F. Schubert and J. K. Kim, "Solid-State Light Sources Getting Smart," *Science*, Vol. 38, 2005, pp. 1274-1278.

[2] C. Biber, "LED Light Emissions as a Function of Thermal Conditions," 24*th IEEE SEMI-THERM Symposium*, 2008, pp. 180-184.

[3] http://www.handprint.com/HP/WCL/color12.html

[4] C. S. McCamy, "Correlated Color Temperature as an Explicit Function of Chromaticity Coordinates," *Color Research & Application*, Vol. 17, No. 2, 1992, pp. 142-144.

[5] http://en.wikipedia.org/wiki/Color_temperature.

[6] http://en.wikipedia.org/wiki/Color_rendering_index.

[7] Improvement to Industrial Color Difference Evaluation, CIE 141-2001, Technical Report, ISBN: 9783901906084.

16

An Analytical Approach for Fast Automatic Sizing of Narrow-Band RF CMOS LNAs[*]

Jin Young Choi

Electronic & Electrical Engineering Department, Hongik University, Jochiwon, South Korea

ABSTRACT

We introduce a fast automatic sizing algorithm for a single-ended narrow-band CMOS cascode LNA adopting an inductive source degeneration based on an analytical approach without any optimization procedure. Analytical expressions for principle parameters are derived based on an ac equivalent circuit. Based on the analytical expressions and the power-constrained noise optimization criteria, the automatic sizing algorithm is developed. The algorithm is coded using Matlab, which is shown capable of providing a set of design variable values within seconds. One-time Spectre simulations assuming usage of a commercial 90 nm CMOS process are performed to confirm that the algorithm can provide the aimed first-cut design with a reasonable accuracy for the frequency ranging up to 5 GHz. This work shows one way how accurate automatic synthesis can be done in an analytical approach.

Keywords: Automatic Synthesis; Analytical Approach; CMOS LNA; Narrow Band; Cascode

1. Introduction

In the field of RF transceiver design, there is a strong demand to digitalize even RF analog parts to mount a transceiver on a single chip [1,2] to utilize the capability of automatic synthesis in digital circuit design. However, the low noise amplifier (LNA), which is a critical building block in any RF front-end, is not ready for digitalization yet. Many efforts have been done for design automation of LNA beforehand since the design of LNA is a time-consuming task that typically relies heavily on the experience of RF designers. LNA design automation can significantly simplify the design task, and also opens a possibility towards digitalization.

There are two basic methods for LNA design automation: simulation based or equation based. Although the simulation-based methods [3,4] are more accurate, they are time consuming due to optimization procedures. On the other hand, equation-based methods [5-7] are faster, but are dependent on the accuracy of the models used. To overcome the disadvantages in some extent, advanced methods using both of equation-based and simulation-based approaches [8-10] have been also suggested.

The difficulties in design automation of LNA lie in several aspects. It is topology dependent, and the design itself is difficult involving trade-offs among critical figures of merits such as NF, power gain, impedance matching, power consumption, linearity, and stability. Mentioning the difficulties in a manual design, for example, even only for input and output matching, many iteration steps are needed. It should be also redesigned every time when the fabrication process is changed. Therefore it is desirable if the first-cut design synthesis can be done automatically and fast with an acceptable accuracy.

The purpose of this work is to suggest a methodology for providing a set of first-cut design variables for a narrow-band LNA with a reasonable accuracy once design and process specifications are given.

We introduce a speedy automatic sizing algorithm for a single-ended narrow-band cascode LNA adopting inductive source degeneration based on an analytical approach without any optimization procedure. In Section 2, design assumptions are discussed. In Section 3, analytical expressions for principle parameters are derived based on an ac equivalent circuit assuming a resistive output termination. In Section 4, the developed automatic sizing algorithm is explained in detail. In Section 5, verifications are given to check the accuracy of the automatic sizing results.

2. Design Assumptions

There are many topologies for narrow-band LNAs, however, typical topologies include cascode, common source, and differential configurations, and the cascode

[*]This work was supported by 2011 Hongik University Research Fund (sponsors).

structure with an inductive source degeneration shown in **Figure 1** is the most attractive one in single-ended topologies since it gives smaller input capacitance and larger in-out isolation [11]. In this work, the cascode LNA topology shown in **Figure 1** is chosen as the objective circuit for automatic sizing even though the same approach can be applied to the other topologies.

There are several assumptions made in this work as follows:

1) Narrow-band LC matching networks are used for input and output as shown in **Figure 1**. R_1 is used to provide capability for adjusting power gain. As the output termination, two cases are considered: resistive or capacitive termination.

2) For sizing of the MOS transistors M_1 and M_2, the power-constrained noise optimization (PCNO) criteria [11] is adopted to trade off noise performance against power consumption.

3) Ideal inductors and capacitors are used by assuming usage of off-chip components. The series resistances of the on-chip inductors can be considered as well, but we choose a simpler case.

4) A current-mirror biasing is adopted as shown in **Figure 1**.

5) The widths of M_1 and M_2 are set as same.

6) The design specifications include operating frequency, input and output terminations, power consumption, power gain, and sufficiently low input and output reflection coefficients S_{11} and S_{22}.

7) The design variables include L_g, L_s, L_1, C_i, C_o, R_1, R_{DB}, and R_B including the widths of M_1, M_2, and M_B in **Figure 1**.

3. Derivation of Analytic Expressions for Principal Parameters

3.1. Input Impedance

Figure 2 is the whole ac equivalent circuit for the cascode LNA shown in **Figure 1** including the input signal source and the output resistive termination. We note that, compared to the complete equivalent circuit of the BSIM4 NMOS transistor in SPICE, only the back-gate transconductance g_{mb} and the gate-body capacitance C_{gb} in the transistor model are ignored to simplify the analysis. The distributed resistances including R_s, R_d, R_g, and R_{sub}, which are included in the BSIM 4 transistor model, are also ignored since they are negligible in large transistors.

In **Figure 2**, g_{m1} and g_{m2} denote the transconductances of M_1 and M_2, respectively. C_{gs}, C_{gd}, and C_{ds} denote the gate-source, gate-drain, and drain-source capacitances of the NMOS transistors, respectively. C_{js} and C_{jd} denote the source-body and drain-body junction capacitances, and C_L is equal to the sum of C_{dg2} and C_{jd2}, which are the

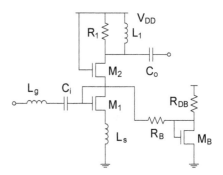

Figure 1. Assumed cascode LNA circuit.

capacitances present at the drain node of M_2 in **Figure 1**.

The impedances Z_{in}, Z_{in1}, Z_{in2}, Z_o, Z_{out}, Z_{out1}, and Z_{out2} are self-defined in the circuit. We first consider the resistive output termination case and discuss the capacitive output termination case later in Section 6. We note that C_{gs}, C_{gd}, and C_{ds} are replaced by C_{sg}, C_{dg}, and C_{sd}, respectively, in some part of our derivations for input and output impedances considering the non-reciprocal nature of gate-oxide capacitances in the BSIM4 MOSFET capacitance model [12].

First, we derive Z_{in} by deriving Z_o, Z_{in2}, and Z_{in1} in order. We note that, we use s and $j\omega$ without differentiation since we are dealing with ac response only.

To derive Z_o at the operating frequency, the series C_o and R_{so} in **Figure 2** can be transformed to the parallel equivalents, C_p and R_p [11]. Then $Y_o = 1/Z_o$ is simply expressed as

$$Y_o = \frac{1}{sL_1} + sC_p + \frac{1}{R_p}, \tag{1}$$

where $R_p = R_{so}(Q^2 + 1)$, $C_p = C_oQ^2/(Q^2 + 1)$, and $Q = 1/(\omega R_{so}C_o)$.

Figure 3 shows the ac equivalent circuit to derive an expression for Z_{in2}. Notice that, in the circuit shown in **Figure 3**, the non-reciprocal capacitance C_{sd2} is used instead of C_{ds2}, since we are looking into the source of M_2.

By neglecting the parallel $(C_{sg2} + C_{js2})$ branch, we derive the input admittance Y_{in21} first, and add $s(C_{sg2} + C_{js2})$ to find $Y_{in2} = 1/Z_{in2}$. When the $(C_{sg2} + C_{js2})$ branch is neglected, the circuit can be characterized by (2) and (3).

$$v_o = \left[g_{m2}v_{s2} + (v_{s2} - v_o)(g_{ds2} + sC_{sd2}) \right] \cdot \left(\frac{1}{sC_L} // R_1 // Z_o \right) \tag{2}$$

$$i = g_{m2}v_{s2} + (v_{s2} - v_o)(g_{ds2} + sC_{sd2})$$
$$= (g_{m2} + g_{ds2} + sC_{sd2})v_{s2} - (g_{ds2} + sC_{sd2})v_o \tag{3}$$

By eliminating v_o in (2) and (3), we can express Y_{in21} as

$$Y_{in21} = \frac{i}{v_{s2}} = \frac{(g_{m2} + g_{ds2} + sC_{sd2})}{1 + (g_{ds2} + sC_{sd2})Z_p}, \tag{4}$$

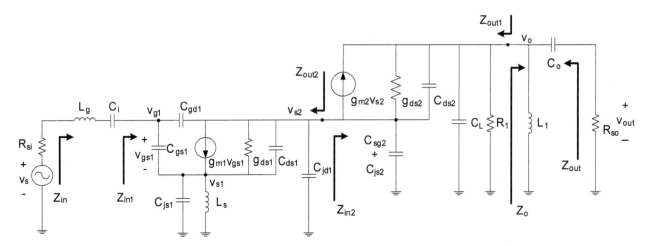

Figure 2. AC equivalent circuit of the cascode LNA in Figure 1.

where $Z_p = (1/sC_L)//R_1//Z_o$.

Then Y_{in2} are expressed as

$$Y_{\text{in2}} = Y_{\text{in21}} + s\left(C_{sg2} + C_{js2}\right). \qquad (5)$$

Figure 4 shows the ac equivalent circuit to derive an expression for Z_{in1}. The circuit can be characterized by (6), (7), and (8).

$$v_{s1} = \left[sC_{gs1}\left(v_{g1} - v_{s1}\right) + g_{m1}v_{gs1}\right.$$
$$\left. + \left(v_{s2} - v_{s1}\right)\left(g_{ds1} + sC_{ds1}\right)\right] \cdot \left(sL_s // \frac{1}{sC_{js1}}\right) \qquad (6)$$

$$v_{s2} = -\left[sC_{gd1}\left(v_{s2} - v_{g1}\right) + g_{m1}v_{gs1}\right.$$
$$\left. + \left(v_{s2} - v_{s1}\right)\left(g_{ds1} + sC_{ds1}\right)\right] \cdot Z_L \qquad (7)$$

$$i = sC_{gs1}\left(v_{g1} - v_{s1}\right) + sC_{gd1}\left(v_{g1} - v_{s2}\right), \qquad (8)$$

where $Z_L = (1/(sC_{jd1}))//Z_{\text{in2}}$.

By eliminating v_{s1} and v_{s2} in (6), (7) and (8), $Y_{\text{in1}} = 1/Z_{\text{in1}}$ is expressed as

$$Y_{\text{in1}} \equiv \frac{i}{v_{g1}} = Y_{\text{in11}} + Y_{\text{in12}} + Y_{\text{in13}}, \qquad (9)$$

where $Y_{\text{in11}} = \left(sC_{gs1} + sC_{gd1}\right),$

$$Y_{\text{in12}} = \frac{\left[\left(sC_{gs1} + g_{m1}\right)\left(g_{m1} + g_{ds1} + sC_{ds1}\right) + \left(sC_{gd1} - g_{m1}\right)e_1\right] \cdot sC_{gd1}}{\left(g_{ds1} + sC_{ds1}\right)\left(g_{m1} + g_{ds1} + sC_{ds1}\right) - e_1 e_2},$$

$$Y_{\text{in13}} = \frac{\left[\left(sC_{gs1} + g_{m1}\right)e_2 + \left(sC_{gd1} - g_{m1}\right)\left(g_{ds1} + sC_{ds1}\right)\right] \cdot sC_{gs1}}{\left(g_{ds1} + sC_{ds1}\right)\left(g_{m1} + g_{ds1} + sC_{ds1}\right) - e_1 e_2},$$

$$e_1 = \frac{1}{sL_s // \dfrac{1}{sC_{js1}}} + sC_{gs1} + g_{m1} + g_{ds1} + sC_{ds1}$$

and $e_2 = \dfrac{1}{Z_L} + sC_{gd1} + g_{ds1} + sC_{ds1}$.

Then Z_{in} is expressed as

$$Z_{\text{in}} = Z_{\text{in1}} + sL_g + \frac{1}{sC_i}. \qquad (10)$$

3.2. Output Impedance

Z_{out} derivation can be done similarly as the Z_{in} derivation using the equivalent circuit in **Figure 2** assuming R_{si} input termination. We present the results only here.

$Y_{\text{out2}} = 1/Z_{\text{out2}}$ is expressed as

$$Y_{\text{out2}} \equiv \frac{i}{v_{s2}} = Y_{\text{out21}} + Y_{\text{out22}} + Y_{\text{out23}} + Y_{\text{out24}}, \qquad (11)$$

where $Y_{\text{out21}} = g_{ds1} + sC_{ds1} + sC_{dg1},$

$$Y_{\text{out22}} = \frac{\left[sC_{sg1}\left(g_{ds1} + sC_{ds1}\right) + sC_{dg1}d_1\right] \cdot \left(g_{m1} - sC_{dg1}\right)}{d_1 d_2 - sC_{sg1}\left(sC_{sg1} + g_{m1}\right)},$$

$$Y_{\text{out23}} = -\frac{\left[\left(g_{ds1} + sC_{ds1}\right)d_2 + sC_{dg1}\left(sC_{sg1} + g_{m1}\right)\right]\left(g_{m1} + g_{ds1} + sC_{ds1}\right)}{d_1 d_2 - sC_{sg1}\left(sC_{sg1} + g_{m1}\right)},$$

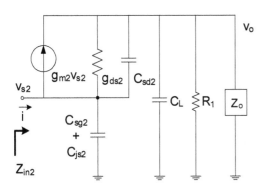

Figure 3. AC equivalent circuit to find Z_{in2}.

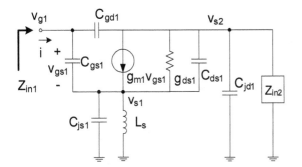

Figure 4. AC equivalent circuit to find Z_{in1}.

$$Y_{out24} = sC_{jd1},$$

$$d_1 = \frac{1}{\dfrac{1}{sC_{js1}} //sL_s} + sC_{sg1} + g_{m1} + \left(g_{ds1} + sC_{ds1}\right),$$

$$d_2 = \frac{1}{Z_i} + sC_{dg1} + sC_{sg1},$$

and $Z_i = R_{si} + sL_g + \dfrac{1}{sC_i}$.

$Y_{out1} = 1/Z_{out1}$ is expressed as

$$Y_{out1} = \frac{1}{Z_2} + sC_L + \frac{1}{R_1}, \tag{12}$$

where $Z_2 = \dfrac{1}{g_{ds2} + sC_{ds2}} + Z_1\left(1 + \dfrac{g_{m2}}{g_{ds2} + sC_{ds2}}\right)$ and

$Z_1 = Z_{out2} // \dfrac{1}{s\left(C_{sg2} + C_{js2}\right)}$.

Then Z_{out} is expressed as

$$Z_{out} = \frac{1}{sC_o} + Z_{out1} //sL_1. \tag{13}$$

3.3. Power Gain

To derive the LNA voltage gain, the equivalent circuit in **Figure 2** is simplified into the one shown in **Figure 5**,

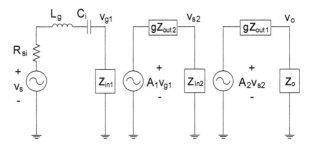

Figure 5. Equivalent circuit to find the voltage gain.

where the whole circuit is expressed as a 3-stage cascaded amplifier.

Z_{in1}, Z_{in2} and Z_o in **Figure 5** are already derived in (9), (5) and (1), respectively. Notice that A_1v_{g1}, gZ_{out2}, A_2v_{s2}, and gZ_{out1} are the Thevenin equivalent voltages and impedances of the 2nd and 3rd gain stages in **Figure 2**. Therefore gZ_{out2} and gZ_{out1} differ from Z_{out2} and Z_{out1} in (11) and (12), respectively, and can be derived as follows.

By definition, gZ_{out2} corresponds to the impedance seen to the left of the v_{s2} node when $v_{g1} = 0$ in **Figure 2**, and can be derived using the equivalent circuit shown in **Figure 6**.

The circuit can be characterized by the Equations (14) and (15).

$$v_{s1} = \left[-g_{m1}v_{s1} + \left(g_{ds1} + sC_{ds1}\right)\left(v_{s2} - v_{s1}\right)\right]$$
$$\cdot \left(\frac{1}{s\left(C_{sg1} + C_{js1}\right)} //sL_s\right) \tag{14}$$

$$i = -g_{m1}v_{s1} + \left(g_{ds1} + sC_{ds1}\right)\left(v_{s2} - v_{s1}\right) \tag{15}$$

By eliminating v_{s1} in (14) and (15), gY_{out21} is expressed as

$$gY_{out21} \equiv \frac{i}{v_{s2}}$$
$$= \frac{\left(g_{ds1} + sC_{ds1}\right)\left[s\left(C_{sg1} + C_{js1}\right) + \dfrac{1}{sL_s}\right]}{s\left(C_{sg1} + C_{js1}\right) + \dfrac{1}{sL_s} + g_{m1} + g_{ds1} + sC_{ds1}}. \tag{16}$$

Then $gY_{out2} = 1/gZ_{out2}$ is expressed as

$$gY_{out2} \equiv \frac{i_{s2}}{v_{s2}} = gY_{out21} + s\left(C_{dg1} + C_{jd1}\right). \tag{17}$$

By definition, A_1 corresponds to the voltage gain v_{s2o}/v_{g1}, where v_{s2o} is the v_{s2} node voltage when open, and can be derived using the equivalent circuit shown in **Figure 7**. The circuit can be characterized by the Equations (18) and (19).

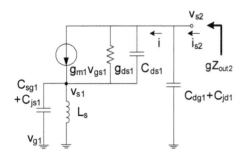

Figure 6. AC equivalent circuit to find gZ_{out2}.

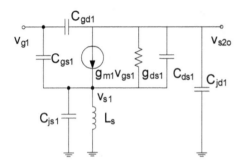

Figure 7. AC equivalent circuit to find A_1.

$$v_{s1} = \left[sC_{gs1}\left(v_{g1} - v_{s1}\right) + g_{m1}v_{gs1} \right.$$
$$\left. + \left(v_{s2o} - v_{s1}\right)\left(g_{ds1} + sC_{ds1}\right) \right] \cdot \left(sL_s // \frac{1}{sC_{js1}} \right) \quad (18)$$

$$v_{s2o} = -\left[sC_{gd1}\left(v_{s2o} - v_{g1}\right) + g_{m1}v_{gs1} \right.$$
$$\left. + \left(v_{s2o} - v_{s1}\right)\left(g_{ds1} + sC_{ds1}\right) \right] \cdot \frac{1}{sC_{jd1}} \quad (19)$$

By eliminating v_{s1} in (18) and (19), we get

$$A_1 \equiv \frac{v_{s2o}}{v_{g1}}$$
$$= -\frac{\left(sC_{gs1} + g_{m1}\right)\left(g_{m1} + g_{ds1} + sC_{ds1}\right) + \left(sC_{gd1} - g_{m1}\right)f_1}{\left(g_{ds1} + sC_{ds1}\right)\left(g_{m1} + g_{ds1} + sC_{ds1}\right) - f_1 f_2}, \quad (20)$$

where $f_1 = \dfrac{1}{sL_s // \dfrac{1}{sC_{js1}}} + sC_{gs1} + g_{m1} + g_{ds1} + sC_{ds1}$ and

$f_2 = sC_{jd1} + sC_{gd1} + g_{ds1} + sC_{ds1}$.

gZ_{out1} corresponds to the impedance seen to the left of the v_o node with $v_{s2} = 0$ in **Figure 2**. Since $g_{m2}v_{s2}$ and $\left(C_{gs2} + C_{js2}\right)$ do not function when $v_{s2} = 0$, $gY_{out1} = 1/gZ_{out1}$ is simply expressed as

$$gZ_{out1} = g_{ds2} + sC_{ds2} + sC_L + \frac{1}{R_1}. \quad (21)$$

A_2 corresponds to the voltage gain v_{oo}/v_{s2}, where v_{oo} is the v_o node voltage when open, and A_2 derivation can be

done in the similar fashion to the one for A_1 derivation. The resulting A_2 is expressed as

$$A_2 \equiv \frac{v_{oo}}{v_{s2}} = \frac{g_{m2} + g_{ds2} + sC_{sd2}}{g_{ds2} + sC_{sd2} + 1 \Big/ \left(\dfrac{1}{sC_L} // R_1 \right)}. \quad (22)$$

In **Figure 2**, the available input power P_i, which is supplied to the LNA when impedance matched, is defined as

$$P_i = \frac{v_s^2}{4R_{si}}. \quad (23)$$

The maximum output power P_o, which is supplied to the resistive load R_{so} when impedance matched, is expressed as

$$P_o = \frac{v_o^2}{R_p} = \frac{v_{out}^2}{R_{so}}, \quad (24)$$

where v_o and v_{out} are defined in **Figure 2**, and R_p is the transformed parallel resistance of R_{so}, which is already defined relating (1).

Then the available power gain G is expressed as

$$G = \frac{P_o}{P_i} = \frac{4R_{si}}{R_p}\left(\frac{v_o}{v_s}\right)^2$$
$$= \frac{4R_{si}}{R_p}\left(\frac{v_{g1}}{v_s}\frac{v_{s2}}{v_{g1}}\frac{v_o}{v_{s2}}\right)^2 \equiv \frac{4R_{si}}{R_p}A_{v1}^2 A_{v2}^2 A_{v3}^2, \quad (25)$$

where A_{v1}, A_{v2}, and A_{v3} can be easily derived from **Figure 5** as follows.

$$A_{v1} \equiv \frac{v_{g1}}{v_s} = Z_{in1}\Big/\left(R_{si} + sL_g + \frac{1}{sC_i} + Z_{in1} \right) \quad (26)$$

$$A_{v2} \equiv \frac{v_{s2}}{v_{g1}} = A_1 Z_{in2}\Big/\left(gZ_{out2} + Z_{in2}\right) \quad (27)$$

$$A_{v3} \equiv \frac{v_o}{v_{s2}} = A_2 Z_o\Big/\left(gZ_{out1} + Z_o\right) \quad (28)$$

4. Automatic Sizing Algorithm

Figure 8 shows the automatic sizing algorithm developed in this work. The inputs to the algorithm include design and process specifications, and the outputs include synthesized design variable values are for R_{DB}, W, nfb, L_s, L_g, C_i, R_1, L_1, C_o. Here, we explain the procedures from top to bottom in accordance with each step, which is explicitly indicated in **Figure 8**.

4.1. 1st Step: Entering Design and Process Specifications

The 1st step in the automatic sizing is to enter the design

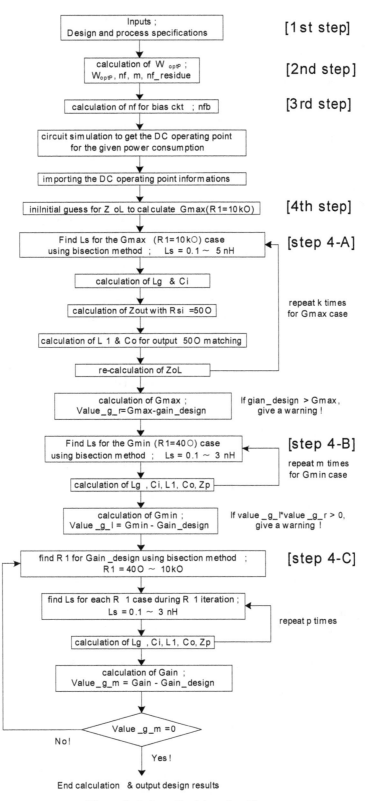

Figure 8. Automatic sizing algorithm.

and process specifications. The design specifications include the operating frequency f, the input output terminations R_{si} and R_{so}, the supply current I_{DD}, the desired power gain Gain_design. Instead of I_{DD}, the power consumption PWR and the supply voltage V_{DD} can be entered to calculate I_{DD} by PWR/V_{DD}. The process specifications include the transistor channel length L, the transistor channel width per finger WF, and the maximum finger number nf_max defined for one unit of transistors.

4.2. 2nd Step: Calculation of Optimum Transistor Width

The next step is to calculate the transistor channel width W for optimum noise performance. The width for optimum noise performance is usually too large for practical use, and therefore the power-constrained noise optimization (PCNO) device width W_{optP} [11] is adopted as W in this work. W_{optP} is calculated according to the last rough equation in (29).

$$W_{optP} = \frac{3}{2} \frac{1}{\omega L C_{ox} R_{si} Q_{sp}} \approx \frac{1}{3\omega L C_{ox} R_{si}} \qquad (29)$$

As shown in (29), W_{optP} increases continuously as the frequency decreases. Therefore it may be necessary to define a maximum value for W considering lower frequency design. We suggest to limit W below 1000 μm.

If W_F and nf_max are defined, the finger number nf is first calculated as W/W_F, and the number of the maximum-fingered units m is calculated as the integer value of nf/nf_max, and the residual finger number nf_residue is determined as the residue to give an information for the transistor layout. Then the final W is determined by $W = W_F \times (m \times$ nf_max + nf_residue). We note that W_F and nf_max are usually defined in most of recent processes.

4.3. 3rd Step: Calculation of Bias Circuit Design Variables and Getting DC Operating Point Information

The next step is to determine the bias circuit variable values and to get the dc operating point information.

The finger number for the bias transistor nfb and the drain bias resistance R_{DB} in **Figure 1** should be determined. By limiting the bias circuit current around 100 μA, for example, we can determine nfb by nfb = (100 μA/I_{DD}) × nf. For the decoupling resistor R_B, we can simply use 5 kΩ, which is a reasonable value.

The next procedure is to determine R_{DB}, which, however, is very difficult to determine by calculation. Since I_{DD} is sensitive to the value of R_{DB}, it should be manually determined to give the specified I_{DD} value by dc circuit simulations. This procedure is one obstacle against full design automation in this work. However, it is an essential procedure since it provides the accurate operating point information to proceed with the remaining part of the design automation. The needed operating point information include the values of g_m, g_{ds}, C_{gs}, C_{sg}, C_{gd}, C_{dg}, C_{ds}, C_{sd}, C_{js}, and C_{jd} of M_1 and M_2 in **Figure 1**, which should be imported into the automatic sizing algorithm.

4.4. 4th Step: Iterations to Determine Design Variable Values

There are three main iteration loops in the automatic sizing algorithm as shown in **Figure 8**. The 1st loop finds G_{max}, which corresponds to the case with the upper limit of R_1, which is chosen arbitrarily large enough as 10 kΩ in this work. To find G_{max}, we need to find all the design variable values for the G_{max} case simultaneously. Iteration is needed since the input and output matching designs affect each other. The 2nd loop finds G_{min}, which corresponds to the case with the lower limit of R_1, which is arbitrarily chosen small as 40 Ω in this work to allow a larger allowable gain range. This iteration is also needed for the same reason explained for the G_{max} case. The 3rd loop finds the proper R_1 value for the desired gain Gain_ design by the bisection method, which lies within the lower and upper boundaries G_{min} and G_{max}, and its inner loop finds the corresponding design variable values for the present gain value during iteration similarly as in the 1st and 2nd iteration loops.

4.4.1. Iterations to Solve for the G_{max} Case

As explained above, Z_{in1} is affected by output matching design, and Z_{out} is affected by input matching design. Therefore we need some iteration to determine L_s. Since Z_{in2} is affected by Z_o, which is unknown yet, we need an initial guess for Z_o to find the 1st L_s value. As shown in **Figure 8**, an initial guess for $Z_{oL} = Z_o//(1/sC_L)$ is given as 50/g·m², which is shown to be large enough for all possible situations in the procedure, to solve for Z_{in2} by (5).

The impedance seen at the gate of M_1 is equal to Z_{in1}, which is derived in (9). By setting the real part of Z_{in1} Re(Z_{in1}) equal to R_{si} for input impedance matching, we can find L_s. However this equation Re(Z_{in1}) = R_{si} is too complicated to get the solution directly with the other present design variables values given, and therefore L_s is solicited numerically within the lower and upper boundaries of 0.1 nH and 5 nH. We use the bisection method for this purpose.

The next procedure is to calculate L_g and C_i, which nullify the imaginary part of Z_{in1} Im(Z_{in1}) in **Figure 2**. Z_{in1} is usually capacitive to give a negative value for Im(Z_{in1}), and therefore L_g can be calculated using the equation Im(Z_{in1}) − 1/(ωC_i) + ωL_g = 0, where C_i is simply a large dc blocking capacitor. We first calculate L_{g1}, which nullifies Im(Z_{in1}) using Im(Z_{in1}) + ωL_{g1} = 0. Although C_i is larger the better, considering the layout size, 1/(ωC_i) = ωL_{g1}/10 is used to determine C_i. L_g is then recalculated using Im(Z_{in1}) − 1/(ωC_i) + ωL_g = 0.

Depending on to the operating frequency and the desired gain, Z_{in1} may happen to be inductive, or this situation can happen in the middle of the iterations. For this case, a nominal single bond wire inductance of 1 nH is assumed for L_g and $\text{Im}(Z_{in1}) - 1/\omega C_i + \omega L_g = 0$ is used to calculate the required C_i value.

In the next procedure, the design variables L_1 and C_o are determined using the equations $\text{Re}(Z_{out}) = R_{so}$ and $\text{Im}(Z_{out}) = 0$ for output impedance matching to R_{so}, where $\text{Re}(Z_{out})$ is the real part of Z_{out} expressed in (13).

If we let Z_{out1} in (12) equal to $A + jB$, the real and imaginary parts of $Z_{out1}//j\omega L_1$ in (13) are expressed as

$$\text{Re}\left(Z_{out1}//j\omega L_1\right) = \frac{A\omega^2 L_1^2}{A^2 + \left(B + \omega L_1\right)^2} \text{ and}$$

$$\text{Im}\left(Z_{out1}//j\omega L_1\right) = \frac{\left(A^2 + B^2\right)\omega L_1 + B\omega^2 L_1^2}{A^2 + \left(B + \omega L_1\right)^2}. \tag{30}$$

Then by letting $\text{Re}(Z_{out}) = \text{Re}(Z_{out1}//j\omega L_1) = R_{so}$, L_1 is expressed as

$$L_1 = \frac{R_{so}B + \sqrt{R_{so}^2 B^2 + \left(A - R_{so}\right)\left(A^2 + B^2\right)R_{so}}}{\omega\left(A - R_{so}\right)} \tag{31}$$

By letting $\text{Im}(Z_{out}) = \text{Im}(Z_{out1}//j\omega L_1) - 1/(\omega C_o) = 0$, C_o is expressed as

$$C_o = \frac{1}{\omega \cdot \text{Im}\left(Z_{out1}//j\omega L_1\right)}. \tag{32}$$

Using (31) and (32), L_1 and C_o can be simply calculated.

Now the 1st set of the design variable values are ready to update Z_{oL} and the remaining iterations are performed to find the final design variable values for the G_{max} case. It was found that the iteration number for this loop should be larger than 10.

Right after the iteration loop, A_1, gZ_{out2}, A_2, and gZ_{out1} are calculated using (20), (17), (22), and (21), respectively, and G_{max} is calculated using (25).

If the G_{max} value is smaller than the desired gain, the routine gives a warning and stops.

4.4.2. Iterations to Solve for the G_{min} Case

The 2nd loop finds the design variable values for the G_{min} case. The same iteration as above with the last Z_{oL} value as an initial guess is performed to find G_{min} using (25) again.

4.4.3. Iterations to Solve for the Gain_Design Case

The 3rd loop finds the proper R_1 value for the desired gain Gain_design using the bisection method while the inner loop finds the corresponding design variable values for the present gain value. This inner iteration loop is exactly same as the 1st and 2nd loops. After all the design variables are determined for the present gain value, the gain is calculated using (25) again. If the calculated gain is equal to Gain_design within the allowed tolerance, the

calculation stops to output the final set of the design variable values, which include W, nf, m, nf_residue, nfb, L_s, L_g, C_i, R_1, L_1, and C_o.

5. Verifications

The automatic sizing algorithm explained in Section 4 was coded using Matlab (Version 7.9.0.529) assuming usage of a 90 nm commercial CMOS process. The design variable sets for seven different operating frequencies ranging from 0.7 GHz to 5 GHz were synthesized, and verifications were done by one-time Spectre circuit simulations with the corresponding BSIM4.5.0 MOSFET model [12] for the assumed process.

The design specifications include $I_D = 5$ mA, $V_{DD} = 1.2$ V, Gain_design = 21 dB, and $R_{si} = R_{so} = 50$ Ω. The process specifications include $L = 75$ nm, $W_F = 3$ μm, and nf_max = 64, where 75 nm for L is the effective channel length in this process. The maximum transistor width was set as $W_{max} = $ nf_max $\times m \times W_F = 64 \times 5 \times 3$ μm $= 960$ μm, which is below 1000 μm as we suggested.

As examples of the verifications, **Figures 9** and **10** show the simulated LNA characteristics without any tuning for the operating frequency of 1 GHz and 5 GHz, respectively, when the corresponding sets of the design variable values obtained using the automatic sizing algorithm are used for the simulations. The synthesized design variable values are as follows;

For 1 GHz design, $R_{DB} = 12.7$ kΩ, $W = 960$ μm ($m = 5$, nf_residue = 0), nfb = 6, $L_s = 1.382$ nH, $L_g = 19.557$ nH, $C_i = 14.25$ pF, $R_1 = 497.1$ Ω, $L_1 = 11.904$ nH, $C_o = 1.447$ pF.

For 5 GHz design, $R_{DB} = 5.96$ kΩ, $W = 231$ μm ($m = 1$, nf_residue = 13), nfb = 2, $L_s = 0.5383$ nH, $L_g = 2.690$ nH, $C_i = 4.142$ pF, $R_1 = 1.752$ kΩ, $L_1 = 2.813$ nH, $C_o = 0.190$ pF.

Table 1 summarizes the simulated results of the seven designs, which reside in the frequency range, where the automatic sizing program could provide the design variable set for Gain_design of 21 dB. Notice that, for the operating frequencies below 1 GHz, the synthesized W values are restricted to below 960 μm, which is equal to the value for W_{max}.

In **Table 1**, we can see that the input and output matchings (S_{11} and S_{22}) are pretty good for all the designs, and the noise figure is pretty close to the noise figure minimum, which demonstrates the adequacy of the designs.

We note that power gain values are about the same with S_{21} values. The S_{21} values in **Table 1** are smaller than the desired gain of 21 dB. This seems to be caused by neglecting g_{mb}, C_{gb}, R_s, R_d, R_g, and R_{sub} in the equivalent circuit in **Figure 2**. However we believe that the result is pretty good for the first-cut quick design.

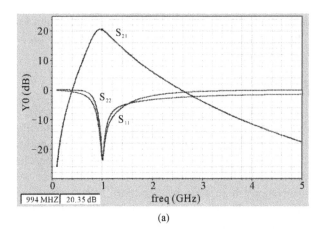

(a)

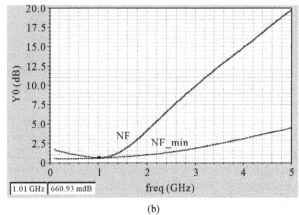

(b)

Figure 9. Simulated (a) s parameter and (b) noise charac-teristics for f = 1 GHz: S_{21} = 20.31 dB, NF = 0.660 dB, NF_{min} = 0.585, S_{11} = –23.6 dB, S_{22} = –23.0 dB.

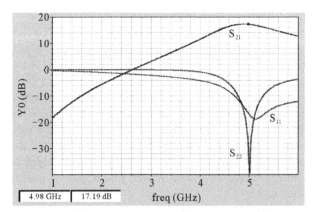

Figure 10. Simulated s parameters for f = 5 GHz: S_{21} = 17.16 dB, S_{11} = –16.9 dB, S_{22} = –34.8 dB.

Table 2 summarizes the synthesized available gain ranges with the corresponding R_1 values for each design. We can see that a wide range of power gain can be obtained by varying the R_1 values as expected.

6. Conclusions

The analytical expressions for the principle parameters

Table 1. Simulation summary for the desired gain Gain_design of 21 dB.

f [GHz]	W [μm]	S_{21} [dB]	S_{11} [dB]	S_{22} [dB]	NF [dB]	NF_{min} [dB]
0.7	960	20.29	–24.0	–23.2	0.826	0.556
0.8	960	20.42	–24.8	–22.9	0.734	0.562
1	960	20.31	–23.6	–23.0	0.660	0.585
2	576	19.10	–20.3	–22.7	0.783	0.728
3	384	18.41	–19.0	–24.9	0.933	0.856
4	291	17.78	–17.5	–29.8	1.032	0.948
5	231	17.16	–17.0	–34.8	1.183	1.073

Table 2. Synthesis summary for the available gain ranges with the corresponding R_1 values.

f [GHz]	W [μm]	S_{21} [dB]	R_1 [Ω]
0.7	960	17.4 - 22.0	55.9 - 218
0.8	960	16.8 - 23.3	59.8 - 1.2 k
1	960	14.0 - 23.2	54.6 - 6.5 k
2	576	12.7 - 23.3	55.8 - 9.1 k
3	384	12.0 - 23.2	55.8 - 8.4 k
4	291	12.0 - 23.0	68.0 - 9.8 k
5	231	11.0 - 22.9	55.8 - 9.1 k

were derived using the ac equivalent circuit of the single-ended narrow-band cascode CMOS LNA adopting the inductive source degeneration. Based on the expressions, the automatic sizing algorithm was developed by adopt-ing the power-constrained noise optimization criteria. The algorithm was coded using Matlab, and could pro-vide a set of design variable values within seconds. One-time Spectre simulations without any tuning assum-ing usage of a commercial 90 nm CMOS process were performed to confirm that the automatic sizing program can synthesize the aimed first-cut design with a reason-able accuracy for the frequency range reaching up to 5GHz.

This work showed in detail how the accurate auto-matic sizing can be done in an analytical approach. The approach can be applied to a common source LNA more easily since the derivation of principal parameters will be simpler with a fewer gain stages. It can be also applied to a differential LNA easily since the derivation will be basically same. The approach seems applicable to more complicated designs even though the derivation proce-dures will contain enhanced complexity.

The automatic sizing program may be utilized effi-ciently for additional tuning purpose. For example, after examining the first-cut synthesis result with verifying circuit simulations, a smaller value for W_{M2} compared to the synthesized one for W_{M1} can be entered into the automatic sizing program to obtain another design variable set for better linearity.

REFERENCES

[1] K. Muhammad, R. B. Staszewski and D. Leipold, "Digital RF Processing: Toward Low-Cost Reconfigurable Radios," *IEEE Communications Magazine*, Vol. 43, No. 8, 2005, pp. 105-113.

[2] A. A. Abidi, "The Path to the Software-Defined Radio Receiver," *IEEE Journal of Solid-State Circuits*, Vol. 42, No. 5, 2007, pp. 954-966.

[3] G. Zhang, A. Dengi and L. R. Carley, "Automatic Synthesis of a 2.1 GHz SiGe Low Noise Amplifier," *Proceedings of IEEE Radio Frequency Integrated Circuits Symposium*, Seattle, 2-4 June 2002, pp. 125-128.

[4] M. Chu and D. J. Allstot, "An Elitist Distributed Particle Swarm Algorithm for RFIC Optimization," *Proceedings of Asia and South Pacific Design Automation Conference*, Shanghai, 18-21 January 2005, pp. 671-674.

[5] P. Vancorenland, C. De Ranter, M. Steyaert and G. Gielen, "Optimal RF Design Using Smart Evolutionary Algorithms," *Proceedings of Design Automation Conference*, Los Angeles, 4-8 June 2000, pp. 7-10.

[6] G. Tulunay and S. Balkır, "A Compact Optimization Methodology for Single-Ended LNA," *Proceedings of IEEE International Symposium Circuits and Systems*, Geneva, 23-26 May 2004, pp. V-273-V-276.

[7] T.-K. Nguyen, C.-H. Kim, G.-J. Ihm, M.-S. Yang and S.-G. Lee, "CMOS Low-Noise Amplifier Design Optimization Techniques," *IEEE Transactions on Microwave Theory and Technique*, Vol. 52, No. 5, 2004, pp. 1433-1442.

[8] G. Tulunay and S. Balkır, "Automatic Synthesis of CMOS RF Front-Ends," *Proceedings of IEEE International Symposium Circuits and Systems*, Island of Kos, 21-24 May 2006, pp. 625- 628.

[9] A. Nieuwoudt, T. Ragheb and Y. Massoud, "SOC-NLNA: Synthesis and Optimization for Fully Integrated Narrow-Band CMOS Low Noise Amplifiers," *Proceedings of Design Automation Conference*, San Francisco, 24-28 July 2006, pp. 879-884.

[10] W. Cheng, A. J. Annema and B. Nauta, "A Multi-Step P-Cell for LNA Design Automation," *Proceedings of IEEE International Symposium Circuits and Systems*, Seattle, 18-21 May 2008, pp. 2550-2553.

[11] T. H. Lee, "The Design of CMOS Radio-Frequency Integrated Circuits," 2nd Edition, Cambridge University Press, Cambridge, 2004.

[12] BSIM4.5.0 MOSFET Model, User's Manual, University of California, Berkeley, 2004.

17

A Hybrid GA-SQP Algorithm for Analog Circuits Sizing

Firas Yengui, Lioua Labrak, Felipe Frantz, Renaud Daviot, Nacer Abouchi, Ian O'Connor
The Lyon Institute of Nanotechnology (INL), University of Lyon, Lyon, France

ABSTRACT

This study presents a hybrid algorithm obtained by combining a genetic algorithm (GA) with successive quadratic sequential programming (SQP), namely GA-SQP. GA is the main optimizer, whereas SQP is used to refine the results of GA, further improving the solution quality. The problem formulation is done in the framework named RUNE (fRamework for aUtomated aNalog dEsign), which targets solving nonlinear mono-objective and multi-objective optimization problems for analog circuits design. Two circuits are presented: a transimpedance amplifier (TIA) and an optical driver (Driver), which are both part of an Optical Network-on-Chip (ONoC). Furthermore, convergence characteristics and robustness of the proposed method have been explored through comparison with results obtained with SQP algorithm. The outcome is very encouraging and suggests that the hybrid proposed method is very efficient in solving analog design problems.

Keywords: Genetic Algorithm; Sequential Quadratic Programming; Hybrid Optimization; Analog Circuits; Transimpedance Amplifier; Optical Driver

1. Introduction

Since their appearance, the EDA (Electronic Design Automation) tools have helped to minimize the cost of production of very large scale integration (VLSI) elec- tronics. This improvement is achieved thanks to the re- duction of development time and to the relationship between sizes of circuits on the one hand and the complexity of performed functions on the other hand. EDA tools allow designing automatically digital circuits from specifications of design masks. However, the development of these tools dedicated to analog circuits is perceived as a very difficult activity.

Analog components constitute an important part of integrated electronic systems. This importance is manifested in terms of elements and area in mixed-signal systems and also as a vital part in digital systems. The nature of analog circuits makes their design complex.

It does not consist only of topology and layout synthesis but also of component sizing. This sizing is an iterative process, which, for analog circuits, is often manual and strongly relies on the designer's intuition and experience to succeed. In manual procedures, it is common that the designer varies only one parameter of the circuit while keeping all the others fixed until obtaining the desired solution. Optimizing the sizes of the analog components automatically is an important issue towards being able to rapidly design true high performance circuits.

The problem of sizing an analog circuit can, indeed, be formulated as an optimization problem. Evolutionary algorithms, as a general purpose optimization technique, have proven strong efficiency for solving complex optimization problems. In this family of evolutionary algorithms, we find the Genetic Algorithms (GA) [1-3]. It remains the most recognized and practiced form of Evolutionary Algorithms. These are stochastic optimization techniques that mimic Darwin's principles of natural selection and survival of the fittest. The main strength of GA is its fast convergence. However, GA performs better in a global search than in a localized one. In the last period of the evolution and when reaching a near optimal solution, the convergence rate decreases considerably, the algorithm stops optimizing, and thus the achieved accuracy of algorithm becomes limited [4].

This work deals with optimal sizing of the analog electronic parts of an Optical Network-on-Chip (ONoC). We mention the example of a TransImpedance Amplifier (TIA) and that of an optical driver (Driver) to which we apply a hybrid optimization approach, namely GA-SQP. GA is the main optimizer, whereas SQP (Sequential Quadratic Programming) [5] is used to fine tune the re- sults of GA. At first, GA searches the global optimum in the whole solution region in order to obtain a quasi-op- timal solution. It provides means to explore efficiently the design space. Then the global optimal solution can be obtained by SQP. This SQP significantly increases the power of the GA in terms of solution quality and speed of convergence to the optimal. Therefore, we used a framework, named RUNE (fRamework for aUtomated aNalog dEsign), to optimize a TIA and an Optical Driver circuits.

The remainder of the paper is organized as follows: Section 2 gives an overview of the RUNE framework. In Section 3, we recall the working principles of genetic and SQP algorithms and propose our hybrid approach GA-SQP. In Section 4, two application examples are given. The first application is a mono-objective problem that deals with optimizing the sizing of an optical driver circuit to meet fixed specifications. The second application is a multiobjective problem with two conflicting objecttives of a TIA circuit. Optimization results for the TIA circuit with proposed hybrid algorithm are compared with results obtained with SQP algorithm. Finally, we give a conclusion in Section 5.

2. The Framework RUNE

2.1. Overview of RUNE

RUNE (fRamework for aUtomated aNalog dEsign) [6,7] is an Analog/Mixed-Signal (AMS) synthesis framework. As shown in **Figure 1**, the main inputs are the hierarchical description of the system and associated system level performances. From the user's point of view, there are two main phases leading to the synthesis of an (*Intellectual Property*) IP block:

- Definition of AMS *soft-IP*, described in the Extended Markup Language (XML) format (directly into an XML file or through the graphical user interface, GUI). In this step, all information related to the system must be provided (hierarchy, models, variables, performances specifications, etc.).
- Configuration of the AMS *firm-IP* synthesis method. In this step, the user must define an optimization strategy, *i.e.* a numerical method or algorithm and the formulation of the problem according to the specifications.

In RUNE, different kinds of models describing the whole or part of the system at a given representational abstraction level can be entered. These models are stored in a database allowing each *soft-IP* to be used as part of a system. Also, in order to evaluate the performance of these domain-specific models, a simulation Application Programming Interface (API) has been developed in order to plug in several external simulators. In this way, the user can select the external simulators to use in the specification evaluation phase.

2.2. Optimization Process

The optimization process can be used at each abstraction level and for every structural (sub-)component. Three main steps are followed (**Figure 2**):

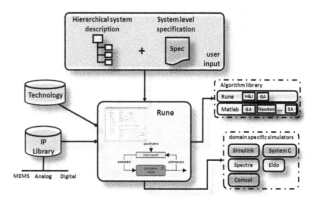

Figure 1. RUNE block diagram functions.

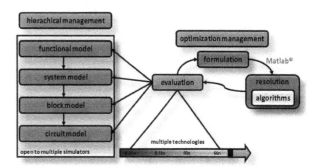

Figure 2. RUNE optimization steps.

- A cost function is formulated from specifications and design parameters set and stored in XML files.
- A design plan is set to define which optimization algorithms will be used to perform synthesis.
- A model at a given abstraction level for each specification must be defined for the performance evaluation during optimization process.

From the set of information provided by the designer, a multi-objective optimization problem is automatically formulated and run using the aggregation approach [8]. This is the formulation step, which consists in defining the objectives and the constraints of the problem, as well as the variables and parameters, their ranges and initial values. The implementation of this step is set up to use either Matlab® or an algorithm directly implemented in RUNE such as genetic algorithms, simulating annealing, Hooke and Jeeves, sequential quadratic optimization and pattern search algorithm. The evaluation method called during the optimization process can use a model from any abstraction level, since RUNE can call various simulators to perform an evaluation through its standard API. For example in the electrical domain, a given block can be described at circuit level (schematic representation) and its performance metrics can be evaluated with electrical simulation tools such as Spectre or Eldo, with various target technologies. The ability to use different models and tools, and to manage heterogeneity, plays an important role in the definition of complex design, as will be seen in the following section describing an application example.

3. Hybrid GA-SQP Algorithm

We have seen in the previous section that RUNE platform allows selection of several algorithms to perform optimization of complex circuits. We describe in the following part the candidate algorithms that will be used in our hybrid approach.

3.1. Genetic Algorithm

Genetic Algorithms are based on natural genetic and natural selection mechanism and some fundamental ideas are borrowed from Genetics in order to artificially construct an optimization procedure. The GA acts over a population of potential solutions, applying intensification (crossover) and diversification (mutation) operators to explore the problem space. The fittest individuals are selected and give birth to a new population, in the hope of improving the solution quality. GA is extensively discussed in the literature and details on its mechanisms can be found in [1]. The GA used in this study is part of the MATLAB optimization toolbox. The GA is configured to use heuristic crossover, roulette wheel selection and adaptive feasible mutation (detailed in the **Table 1**). The generation and the population values used for GA are set respectively to 5 and 10.

3.2. Sequential Quadratic Programming (SQP)

Sequential quadratic programming (SQP) [5,9] is one of the most popular and robust algorithms for nonlinear continuous optimization. It starts from a single point and finds a solution using the gradient information. SQP requires a reasonable starting solution to increase the opportunity to achieve an acceptable solution and to avoid the local optima. This algorithm allows to closely mimic Newton's method for constrained optimization just as is done for unconstrained optimization. Each iteration contains an approximation made of the Hessian of the Lagrangian function which uses a quasi-Newton updating method. This is then used to generate a Quadratic Programming (QP) subproblem whose solution is used to form a search direction for a line search procedure. Sequential Quadratic Programming is an iterative method. It allows solving at the kth iteration a QP of the following form:

$$\text{Minimize } 0.5d^t \, H_k d + \nabla f\left(x_k\right)^t d \quad (1)$$

subject to: $\nabla h_i\left(x_k\right)^t d + h_i\left(x_k\right) = 0, i = 1, \cdots, p,$

$$\nabla g_i\left(x_k\right)^t d + g_i\left(x_k\right) = 0, i = 1, \cdots, p,$$

d is defined as the search direction and H_k is a positive

Table 1. GA configuration.

Option	Type	Description
Crossover	Heuristic	Returns a child that lies on the line containing the two parents, a small distance away from the parent with the better fitness value in the direction away from the parent with the worse fitness value. We specify how far the child is from the better parent by the parameter Ratio. In our configuration Ratio is set to 1,2.
Selection	Roulette wheel	Roulette selection chooses parents by simulating a roulette wheel, in which the area of the section of the wheel corresponding to an individual is proportional to the individual's expectation. The algorithm uses a random number to select one of the sections with a probability equal to its area.
Mutation	Adaptive Feasible	Randomly generates directions that are adaptive with respect to the last successful or unsuccessful generation. The feasible region is bounded by the constraints and inequality constraints. A step length is chosen along each direction so that linear constraints and bounds are satisfied.

definite approximation to the Hessian matrix of Lagrangian function of the problem. The Lagrangian function can be described as:

$$L\left(x, y, \beta\right) = f\left(x\right) + \sum_{i=1}^{p} \gamma_i h_i\left(x\right) + \sum_{j=p+1}^{p} \beta_j g_j\left(x\right) \quad (2)$$

where γ, β are the Lagrangian multipliers. The active set strategy allows to solve the developed QP.

According to Equation (3), the solution x_k is updated at each iteration.

$$X_{k+1} = x_k + \alpha_k d_k \quad (3)$$

α is defined as the step size and takes values in the interval [0, 1]. After each iteration the matrix H_k is updated based on the Newton Method. The SQP used in this study is part of MATLAB tools.

3.3. Proposed Hybrid Approach: GA-SQP

Most of the studies on analog design automation process have focused on many optimization algorithms that have insisted on global search heuristics. However, the simultaneous use of local and global search techniques considerably improve the accuracy of results while reducing computational effort. Our proposed method therefore is an optimization algorithm combining a GA with a SQP algorithm, in order to solve analog circuit sizing problems. The GA algorithm is a global algorithm, which is well for a global search but performs very slow and very poor in a localized search. The SQP algorithm, on the contrary, has a strong ability to find local optima for constrained nonlinear optimizations problems, but it cannot guarantee that the solution is the global optimum of the problem. It ensures computational robustness when it starts from a feasible initial solution. By combining the GA with SQP, a new algorithm referred to as GA-SQP hybrid algorithm is formulated in this paper. First, GA searches the global optimum in the whole solution region in order to obtain a quasi-optimal solution. Then the global optimal solution can be obtained by SQP. This SQP significantly increases the power of the GA in terms of solution quality and speed of convergence to the best solution. The proposed hybrid method allows eliminating the need to provide a suitable starting point and allows ensuring a faster convergence speed and a higher convergence accuracy to find the optimal solution. The flow chart of the proposed GA-SQP algorithm can be summarized as follows (**Figure 3**).

4. Optimization Results of the TIA and Driver Circuits

Optical Network-on-Chip (ONoC) is a technology for high speed communication inside a single chip (a system-on-chip) [10]. Instead of transmitting data via metallic routes, an ONoC converts electrical signals to light pulses and transmits them through a dedicated network of optical waveguides (λ-router). An ONoC is a multi-domain system, composed of digital elements for data flow control and analog and optical blocks to convert and modulate data as light impulsions. Together, these blocks compose transmission and reception interfaces with whom processors, memories and other intellectual property (IP) blocks can communicate.

In this paper we are interested only in the synthesis of the analog circuits of ONoC such as a transimpedance amplifier (TIA) used for reception and an optical driver (Driver) used in transmission, as illustrated in **Figure 4**. We used RUNE to optimize these circuits. The type of evaluation used for each performance, is based on equations and electrical simulations. The technology used for the design of both the circuits is a CMOS 0.35 µm.

These two examples of application are given in order to show the effectiveness of the proposed GA-SQP to solve analog circuits design problems. The first application concerns a mono-objective problem. That issue deals with optimizing the sizing of driver circuit to meet fixed specifications with two nonlinear equality constraints. The second application is about a multi-objective problem using the aggregation approach, and consists of sizing a TIA circuit with nonlinear inequality and nonlinear

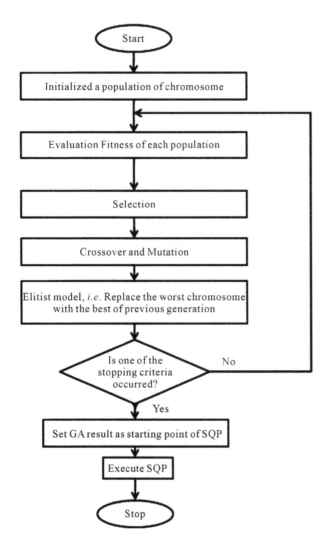

Figure 3. Flow chart of the proposed hybrid method.

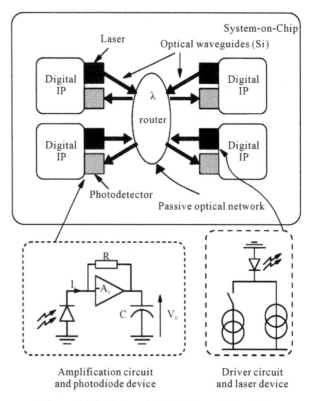

Figure 4. Multi-domain ONoC description [10].

equality constraints. Then, the performance of the proposed GA-SQP algorithm is compared to SQP. All the experiments were run under a Linux environment on an Intel Xeon machine (2.6 GHz, 8 GB of RAM, 4 CPU).

4.1. Optical Driver

An optical driver is a circuit used to modulate information as a light signal. In the case of our ONoC system, the driver circuit (**Figure 5**) converts binary data into two current intensities, which in turn drive a laser beam.

The design problem of this circuit consists of minimizing the area of the transistors, while keeping the output current at levels required by the laser (bias and modulation currents). The optimization variables are the width (W_i) and length (L_i) of each transistor (M_i), which dictate their electrical behaviour. The area objective can be calculated by the product of the widths and lengths of each transistor, while the output current values come from the electrical simulator. In this case study, the problem is formulated as follows, with two equality constraints and that ensure proper functioning of the circuit in our target technology.

$$\min : \text{Area}(X)$$

$$s.t : \begin{cases} I_{\text{Bias}}(X) = 100\ \mu\text{A} \\ I_{\text{Modulation}}(X) = 1\ \text{mA} \end{cases}$$

where X is the vector composed by the input variables ($W1$, $L1$, $W2$, $L2$, $W3$, $L3$, $W4$ and $L4$). The variation range of the optimization variables of the vector X are set as shown in **Table 2**.

The results obtained with GA-SQP are shown in **Table 3**. The transistor sizes for this optimal solution are listed in **Table 4**. Results show that the algorithm allows reaching the objective while respecting the nonlinear equality constraints.

4.2. Transimpedance Amplifier (TIA)

The Transimpedance Amplifier (TIA) is used in the receiver side of the ONoC. The incoming light signal is

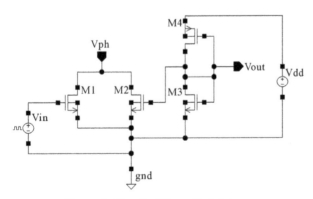

Figure 5. Circuit of the optical driver.

Table 2. Parameters values of the driver.

Variable parameters	Variation range
$W1$	[0.45 μm, 50 μm]
$L1$	[0.35 μm, 30 μm]
$W2$	[0.35 μm, 30 μm]
$L2$	[0.45 μm, 50 μm]
$W3$	[0.45 μm, 50 μm]
$L3$	[0.35 μm, 30 μm]
$W4$	[0.45 μm, 50 μm]
$L4$	[0.35 μm, 30 μm]

Table 3. Driver specifications and results.

Performance	Area (μm²)	Bias current (μA)	Modulation current (mA)	CPU Time (mn)
Specification	Min.	=100	=1	-
GA-SQP results	4.3559	100	1	42

Table 4. Results of parameters sizing.

Parameters	Size
$W1$	9.37 μm
$L1$	0.35 μm
$W2$	1.9 μm
$L2$	0.35 μm
$W3$	0.45 μm
$L3$	0.523 μm
$W4$	0.494 μm
$L4$	0.35 μm

converted to current by a photodetector, and the role of the TIA is to convert this weak current signal to a voltage level that can be used in a digital circuit. The structure of the TIA, with its internal inverter amplifier, is illustrated in **Figure 6**.

The desired TIA performance criteria are: the transimpedance gain Zg, the bandwidth BW, the quality factor Q, the power consumption pwr and the transistors surface Area. Zg, BW and pwr are evaluated with the electrical simulator "Spectre". Q and Area are evaluated with respectively the Equations (4) and (5).

$$Q = \sqrt{\frac{\dfrac{Rf}{Rout} * \dfrac{Cd}{Cl} * (1 + Av)}{1 + \dfrac{Cd}{Cl} * \left(1 + \dfrac{Rf}{Rout}\right)}} \qquad (4)$$

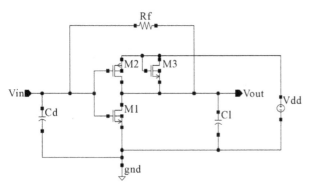

Figure 6. Circuit of the TIA.

$$Area = L1*W1 + L2*W2 + L3*W3 \qquad (5)$$

where, *Rout* and *Av* are, respectively, output resistance and gain of internal amplifier. They are evaluated with electrical simulations.

The purpose consists in optimally sizing TIA circuit with maximizing *Zg* and *BW*. We transformed these multi-objective problems into a mono-objective using the aggregation approach. There are two nonlinear inequality constraint such as pwr and Area and one nonlinear equality constraint such as *Q*.

The problem can be formulated as follows:

$$\underset{X}{\text{Max}} : Zg(X), BW(X)$$

$$s.t : \begin{cases} Q(X) = 0.707 \\ Pwr(X) \le 4 \text{ mW} \\ \text{Area}(X) \le 17 \ \mu m^2 \end{cases}$$

where X is the vector composed by the input variables (*W1*, *W2*, *W3*, *Rf*, *Cd* and *Cl*). The transistor length is fixed at 0.35 μm for all transistors and the variation range of the optimization variables of the vector X are set as shown in **Table 5**.

Table 6 presents TIA specification and best results of GA-SQP algorithm for 52 runs. Results of parameters sizing with GA-SQP algorithm are shown in **Table 7**. Results show that the algorithm allows reaching the objectives while respecting the nonlinear inequality and equality constraints.

4.3. Comparing GA-SQP to SQP

To show the effectiveness of hybrid optimization method, the proposed GA-SQP algorithm is compared to SQP. For this analysis we have collected, for both algorithms, runtime and fitness data over several independent runs of the TIA circuit optimization problem. A random multi start approach is used with the SQP algorithm to make comparison with GA-SQP which does not depend on its starting point. In all experiments, the stopping criteria of both algorithms are set to the same value. It takes into

Table 5. Parameters values of the TIA.

Variable parameters	Variation range
W1	[1 μm, 20 μm]
W2	[1 μm, 20 μm]
W3	[1 μm, 20 μm]
Rf	[1 kΩ, 3 kΩ]
Cd	[100 fF, 500 fF]
Cl	[100 fF, 200 fF]

Table 6. TIA specifications and results.

Perf.	Zg (Ω)	BW (GHz)	Area (μm²)	pwr (mW)	Q
Spec.	Max.	Max.	<17	<4	=0.707
GA-SQP results	966	0.713	15.78	3.79	0.707

Table 7. Results of parameters sizing with GA-SQP.

Parameters	size
W1 (μm)	11.3
W2 (μm)	33.3
W3 (μm)	0.5
Rf (kΩ)	1.5
Cl (nF)	0.1
Cd (nF)	0.4

account the maximum number of iterations, the termination tolerance for the objective function value and the termination tolerance for the nonlinear constraints. The main input parameters of SQP and GA-SQP are indicated in **Table 8**.

GA-SQP and SQP algorithms have been executed 52 times. As shown in **Table 9**, GA-SQP algorithm allows to obtain 82.76% success solution and SQP algorithm allows to obtain only 18.29% success solution. **Table 10** shows that the GA-SQP outperforms SQP in terms of the best and mean cost for success solution obtained during our tests. The gain of GA-SQP compared to SQP in terms of mean and minimum are respectively 25% and 13%. It clearly shows that the GA provides a good starting point to the SQP method more efficiently than a simple random start. Moreover, **Table 11** shows that the GA-SQP consumes less time compared to SQP, because it requires less iteration to find the optimal solution.

In the hybrid GA-SQP, the initial search based on the use the GA does not require the user to provide such a starting value as the search is performed automatically. The results demonstrate that the proposed hybrid method

Table 8. SQP and GA-SQP input parameters.

Algorithms	Input parameters	Value
GA-SQP	Population size	10
	Generations	5
	Max SQP iterations	50
SQP	Max SQP iterations	50

Table 9. Success rate of GA-SQP and SQP.

Algorithms	Run numbers	Success solution numbers	% Success rate
GA-SQP	52	42	80.76%
SQP	52	12	18.29%

Table 10. Minimum and mean cost comparison.

Performances	SQP	GA-SQP	GA-SQP Gain
Mean cost	6.68	5.03	25%
Minimum cost	1.94	1.68	13%

Table 11. Mean execution time comparison.

	SQP	GA-SQP
Mean time (second)	866	749
Mean evaluation number	255	236

outperforms the SQP in terms of better optimal solution and significant reduction of computing times. The result for computational run time is impressive, because the combination of two algorithms consumes less than one. This explains that the genetic algorithm converges quickly to a near optimal solution, which allows to the SQP algorithm to find the optimum result with less effort.

5. Conclusion

We proposed a method based on a combination of GA algorithm and successive SQP algorithm, namely GA-SQP. It is implemented in the framework RUNE to optimize performances of analog circuits. GA-SQP seems to be suitable for solving both nonlinear mono-objective and multiobjective optimization problems. The results of the proposed hybrid method were compared with SQP algorithms to solve a TIA sizing problem. The results show that the proposed hybrid method outperforms the SQP in terms of better optimal solutions and signficant reduction of computing time. Furthermore, the hybrid GA-SQP algorithm does not require the user to specify the starting point. Finally, the proposed approach let us

conclude that depending on the nature of our analog sizing problem (degrees of freedom, number of performances), efficient hybrid combination between an evolutionary approach and a direct search can be found.

REFERENCES

[1] G. Renner and A. Ekárt, "Genetic Algorithms in Computer Aided Design," *Computer-Aided Design*, Vol. 35, No. 8, 2003, pp. 709-726.

[2] M. Taherzadeh-Sani, R. Lotfi, H. Zare-Hoseini and O. Shoaei, "Design Optimization of Analog Integrated Circuits Using Simulation-Based Genetic Algorithm," *Proceedings of International Symposium on Signals, Circuits and Systems*, Iasi, 10-11 July 2003, pp. 73-76.

[3] A. Jafari, M. Zekri, S. Sadri and A. R. Mallahzadeh, "Design of Analog Integrated Circuits by Using Genetic Algorithm," *Proceedings of International Conference on Computer Engineering and Applications*, Bali Island, 19-21 March 2010, pp. 578-581.

[4] C. Wang, Q. Wang, H. Huang, S. Song, Y. Dai and F. Deng, "Electromagnetic Optimization Design of a HTS Magnet Using the Improved Hybrid Genetic Algorithm," *Proceedings of Asian Conference on Applied Superconductivity and Cryogenics*, Miyazaki, 12 December 2004, pp. 349-353.

[5] N. Menezes, R. Baldick and L. T. Pileggi, "A Sequential Quadratic Programming Approach to Concurrent Gate and Wire Sizing," *Proceedings of International Conference on Computer-Aided Design*, San Jose, 5-9 November 1995, pp. 867-881.

[6] L. Labrak and I. O'Connor, "Heterogeneous System Design Platform and Perspectives for 3D Integration," *Proceedings of 21st IEEE International Conference on Microelectronics*, Marrakech, 19-22 December 2009, pp. 161-164.

[7] F. Tissafi-Drissi, I. O'Connor and F. Gaffiot "RUNE: Platform for Automated Design of Integrated Multi-Domain Systems Application to High-Speed CMOS Photoreceiver Front-Ends," *IEEE Proceedings of Design, Automation and Test in Europe Conference*, Paris, 16-20 February 2004, pp. 16-21.

[8] E. G. Talbi, "Metaheuristics: From Design to Implementation," John Wiley and Sons Ltd., Hoboken, 2009.

[9] P. T. Boggs and J. W. Tolle, "Sequential Quadratic Programming for Large-Scale Nonlinear Optimization," *Journal of Computational and Applied Mathematics*, Vol. 124, No. 1-2, 2000, pp. 123-137.

[10] E. Drouard, M. Briere, F. Mieyeville, I. O'Connor and X. Letartre, "Optical Network On-Chip Multi-Domain Modeling Using System C," *Proceedings of the Forum on Specification and Design Languages*, Lille, 13-17 September 2004, pp. 123-135.

18

A Parallel Circuit Simulator for Iterative Power Grids Optimization System

Taiki Hashizume[1], Masaya Yoshikawa[2], Masahiro Fukui[1]
[1]Department of VLSI System Design, Ritsumeikan University, Kusatsu, Japan
[2]Department of Information Engineering, Meijo University, Nagoya, Japan

ABSTRACT

This paper discusses a high efficient parallel circuit simulator for iterative power grid optimization. The simulator is implemented by FPGA. We focus particularly on the following points: 1) Selection of the analysis method for power grid optimization, the proposed simulator introduces hardware-oriented fixed point arithmetic instead of floating point arithmetic. It accomplishes the high accuracy by selecting appropriate time step of the simulation; 2) The simulator achieves high speed simulation by developing dedicated hardware and adopting parallel processing. Experiments prove that the proposed simulator using 80 MHz FPGA and eight parallel processing achieves 35 times faster simulation than software processing with 2.8 GHz CPU while maintaining almost same accuracy in comparison with SPICE simulation.

Keywords: Dedicated Hardware Accelerator; Power Grids Optimization; Parallel Circuit Simulator

1. Introduction

With the deep submicron technologies, it has become possible to mount a large and high performance system on one VLSI chip. However, the power supply voltage is lowering along with shrinking of the device size. On the other hand, the power consumption is increasing because the number of transistors and the clock frequency increase. Therefore, IR-drop and electro-migration (EM) in the power grids make functions and devices unreliable. It becomes more serious problem than ever. The power grid optimization has become very important for ensuring the reliability, correctness and stability of the design. In recent years, many prior researches [1-6] have been proposed to solve the problem. A heavy simulation time is required to analyze the problem of heat and electromagnetic field [3]. Moreover, a high speed and high accurate circuits simulator is required for iterative optimization which includes execution of the simulation many times for its evaluation.

Thus, several hardware accelerator approaches have been reported [7-12]. Lee *et al.* achieved 25 times high speed processing in the timing verification using multi CPU [7]. Nakasato *et al.* demonstrated particle simulation by floating point arithmetic on an FPGA [8]. Watanabe *et al.* introduced parallel-distributed time-domain circuit simulation of power distribution networks by multiple PC [9]. However, no research of hardware accelerator to optimize power grids of VLSI has been reported.

This paper aims at estimating the performance improvement by hardware implementation of the circuit simulation in the power supply wiring. We have analyzed accuracy, speed, and hardware resources to implement typical numerical analysis algorithms of circuit simulation, in cases of floating point and fixed point variables, software and hardware. Moreover, we propose an efficient hardware circuit simulator for power grid optimization. It achieves high speed simulation by adopting pipeline and parallel processing. The proposed simulator introduces hardware-oriented fixed point arithmetic instead of floating point arithmetic. The hardware-oriented fixed point arithmetic realizes the high area-efficiency by reducing hardware resources, and it also accomplishes the high accuracy by controlling intervals of simulation.

2. Power Grid Optimization System

2.1. Power Grid Optimization Algorithm

The power grid consists of two vertical and horizontal layers. Those are interconnected by contacts at the intersection. The equivalent circuit model for proposed power grid optimization system is shown in **Figure 1**.

Decoupling capacitors are inserted to decrease dynamic IR-drop and inductor noise to the power grid. At each grid area, four edges of resistances are placed. The capacitance which connected to each node represents the sum of the decoupling capacitance and the wiring capacitance.

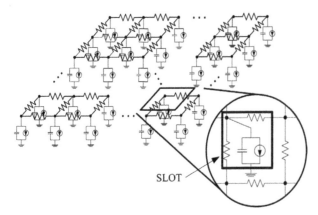

Figure 1. Equivalent circuit model for power grids.

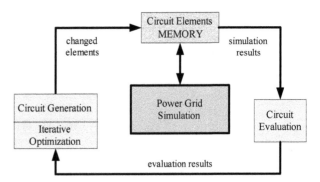

Figure 2. Power grid optimization system.

Current source which connected to each node corresponds to the current consumption of functional block of VLSI. These circuit elements connected with a grid are defined as SLOT. The power grid optimization is defined as a multi-objective optimization problem. First objective is to reduce the risk of timing error which is caused by transient and local IR-drop. Second objective is to reduce the risk of wire break which is caused by excess of electric current density at a portion of a wiring. Third objective is to reduce the risk of failing signal wiring which is caused by local congestion of wires. We have already proposed an algorithm to solve these trade-off problems [13-15]. It defines the optimization problem by using an evaluation function which unifies the risks of multiple objectives. The optimization is scheduled by an iterative improvement. Iterative operation consists of circuit simulation, evaluation of risks, and small modification of wire width or decupling capacitance.

2.2. Organization of Power Grid Optimization System

The power grid optimization system consists of three parts, the simulation part, the evaluation part and the optimization part, as shown in **Figure 2**. A new repetitive optimization and evaluation function is introduced to improve the multiple physical issues [13]. To evaluate circuits, an original metrics, RISK, is defined. The proposed power grid optimization system adopts the algorithm as a base algorithm of the optimization part. Effectiveness of the power grid optimization system is determined by communication-overhead between each part, in addition to the simulation accuracy and the processing speed.

The simulation part is the most time consuming. It simulates the circuit behavior and calculates the electric current of each edge and the voltage of the each node. It takes more than 99% of the total computation time. Therefore, reduction of processing time of the simulation part is most important from the point of high speed opti-

mization processing. The evaluation part defines a risk function for each design metric, *i.e.*, IR-drop, EM, and wiring congestion, from simulation results. IR-drop RISK is defined as a probability of causing the timing error. An increase of current density raises the EM RISK and it cause a deterioration and disconnection of wires to be unable to operate. As a result, the circuit doesn't operate. The wiring congestion RISK represents the proportion of the wiring resource in a SLOT area. It is a restriction of preventing from an excessive wiring and state that cannot be wired. Because each grid is composed of the power grid, decoupling capacitor and signal wire, totals of those areas are compared with the grid area.

The optimization part improves IR-drop, EM and wiring congestion by changing wiring width and decoupling capacitance. Performance of the power grid optimization system is determined by communication overhead between each part, in addition to the simulation accuracy and the processing speed.

2.3. Simulation Algorithm

2.3.1. Circuit Analysis Method

This section summarizes typical numerical analysis methods which can be used for the power grid simulation. Euler method and Runge-Kutta method are typical numeric method to solve differential equations. Generally, small time step must be selected to analyze steadily by Forward Euler method (FE).

The computation algorithm is simple and needs smaller hardware resources, but it may easily diverge. Runge-Kutta methods require complex calculation, but the simulation is more stable even though we select a larger time step than FE. Thus, we must carefully select the numerical algorithm for the given problem. We have examined 100 or more variations of power grids and evaluated.

The test data is composed of four size variations, 50 × 50, 100 × 100, 200 × 200, 500 × 500. Also, it is composed of five RC distributions, regular, random, two types of hand-specified, extracted from real chips. The largest RC time constant was about 20 times larger than the minimum one.

As the results, the accuracy is almost same for each numerical method and we have selected FE. For the evaluation of numerical methods see the next section.

2.3.2. Evaluation of the Accuracy by Comparing with SPICE

This In order to verify the proposed algorithm's validity, comparative experiments are performed using the following two types of circuit simulations: 1) Accuracy comparison between double-precision floating point arithmetic and SPICE; and 2) Accuracy comparison between single-precision fixed point arithmetic and double-precision floating point arithmetic. The power grid which is used for the analysis is a structure of uniform RC distribution, and R and C in the power grid were randomly set from predefined three values. The power grid scale is 10 × 10 grids. The dynamic current consumption is changed in every 10 [μsec]. In conversion into the fixed point, the fraction part of all variables was set to 22-bit. Since 32-bit adders and multipliers are used for experiment, the overflow happened in 23-bit or more.

Firstly, the result of experiments on each simulation with double-precision arithmetic is shown in **Figures 3** and **4**. The step size is an important point in the transition analysis, and it is necessary to set it to small step to execute an accurate analysis. The small step is set 0.63 [μsec]. The smallest RC was 20 [μsec]. All the analysis methods have been achieved high accuracy compared with SPICE.

Next, experiments on fixed point arithmetic are executed by various step sizes, and the error is verified with the floating point arithmetic. In small step size, the maximum error margin and the average error margin are shown in **Tables 1** and **2**.

In the uniform RC distribution, all nine patterns, the

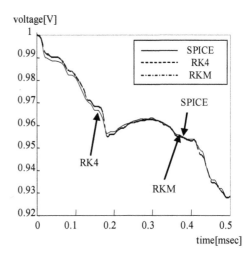

Figure 4. Simulation result by Euler method with small step size.

Table 1. Error by fixed point arithmetic for uniform RC circuit.

	FE	ME	RK4	RKM
max [%]	0.11	0.11	0.11	0.11
Ave [%]	0.021	0.021	0.020	0.020

Table 2. Error by fixed point arithmetic for random RC circuit.

	FE	ME	RK4	RKM
max [%]	0.057	0.057	0.058	0.057
Ave [%]	0.0083	0.0083	0.0083	0.0082

combination of the wiring resistance and the capacitance, are executed. **Table 2** shows the maximum error and the average error of 100 kinds of circuit selected at random. The high accurate simulation has been achieved with a small time step.

In fixed point arithmetic, fourth order Runge-Kutta Method (RK4) and Runge-Kutta marsun method (RKM) obtain a good result. In addition, the error of uniform RC distribution is larger than that of random circuit. The computational complexity of FE and Modified Euler method (ME) are small. In contrast, RK4 and RKM are complex for computation, though they can execute an accurate analysis.

In our preliminary experiments, FE and RK4 diverged on the same time step. Therefore, FE is superior to RK4 in case of the power grid optimization problem.

2.3.3. Simulation Flow

Voltage and current change in each node at small time step is analyzed based on information of the RC distribution, the current consumption distribution, and the supply

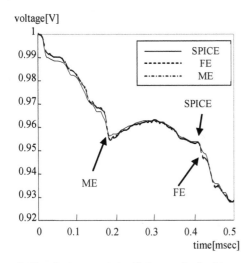

Figure 3. Simulation result by Euler method with small step size.

voltage, etc. The simulation flow is shown in **Figure 5**, and a part of the equivalent circuit is shown in **Figure 6**.

In the simulation part, the current of each wiring is calculated from voltage distribution and the wiring resistance. Then, the charge which accumulates in the capacitance connected with each node is calculated, and the voltage is derived every small time step dT. These processing are iterated during simulation time for entire power grid T_m, and assumed to be end of simulation. To obtain the voltage at each node, the charge is changed by the inflow current I_{left} and I_{up}, the outflow current I_{right} and I_{down}, and the current consumption I_{con}. Voltage and current change in each node are computed based on RC distribution at small time step.

For more high speed simulation, the simulation with hardware is effective, but the achievement of the hardware simulator is not easy according to the restriction of the error margin and the hardware resource. To examine whether it is feasible to make the present simulation hardware, the accuracy of the analysis by the double-precision floating point arithmetic and by the single-precision fixed point arithmetic are verified. The error margin is caused by replacing with fixed point arithmetic. It is because the fixed point arithmetic can be processed at the same speed as the integer operation. Additionally, the area of the fixed point arithmetic unit is far smaller compared with the floating point arithmetic unit.

3. Hardware Architecture for Power Grid Simulation

The proposed simulation algorithm adopts fixed point arithmetic. It achieves the same processing speed as the integer operation, and has an advantage of area-efficiency when implementing on hardware. Fixed point arithmetic includes a risk of overflow; however, this risk is reduced by correction processing and bit shift. The simulation part computes the voltage and the current of each node of power grid, and stores the simulation results into memory. Furthermore, it is necessary to control the simulation and the memory behavior to achieve high speed simulation. **Figure 7** shows the block diagram of the power grid simulation which corresponds to simulation module and memory access as shown in **Figure 2**. Control module controls state transition and timing of each module. Each circuit variables are stored in each memory. Wiring resistance and capacitance are updated when changing the circuit design.

The voltage and the charge are updated whenever advancing at a small time step. Therefore, these are stored in RAM. Circuit variables are fetched from the memory into the simulation module, and the results are written into memory.

The simulation module is composed by adder, subtractor, and multiplier, and doesn't use divider. Current is calculated by dividing potential difference of wiring resistance, however divider needs a lot of implementation areas. Therefore, divider is converted into multiplier by storing each reciprocal when wiring resistance and capacitance are stored in the memory. **Figure 8** shows the calculation procedure in the simulation module.

Input variables, "G_{right}", "G_{down}" and "Z" show the reciprocal of wiring resistance and capacitance respectively. In the current calculation of the hardware algorithm, only outflow current is computed as shown in **Figure 4**. Because inflow current of a point corresponds to outflow current of the adjacent point (left side or upper side).

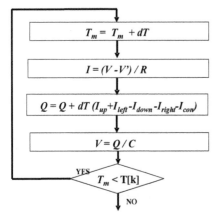

Figure 5. Simulation flow.

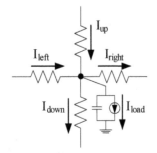

Figure 6. A part of equivalent circuit.

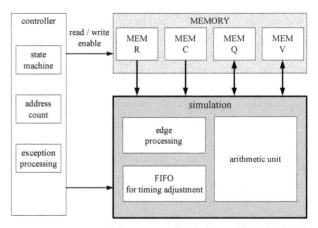

Figure 7. Block diagram of the power grid simulation.

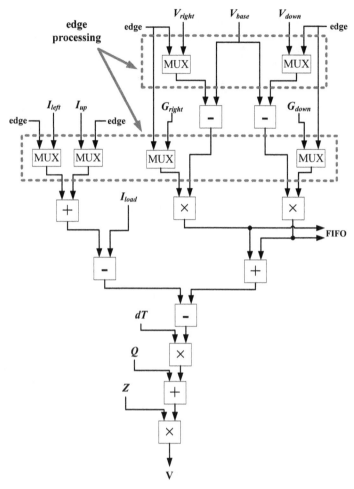

Figure 8. Calculation procedure in the simulation module.

The simulation module processes the circuit variables from memory, and writes simulation result into the memory. The variables written in the memory are the current, the charge, and the voltage. The current is used to calculate the RISK, the charge is necessary for each grid simulation, and the voltage is both. When the edge of the power grid is simulated, the variable is switched to the exception parameter by multiplexer (MUX) because the adjacent SLOT doesn't exist.

4. Hardware Algorithm

4.1. Pipeline Processing

Registers are inserting between each arithmetic unit to achieve pipeline processing. The proposed pipeline processing is composed of eight stages, and the data of each SLOT is transferred to the simulation module per clock cycle. The simulation flow by pipeline processing is as follows.

1) Each variable is stored from the memory to register.
2) Calculation of potential difference.
3) Calculation of each current.

4) Addition of each current (I_{right}, I_{down}, I_{left} and I_{up}).
5) Addition of Stage 4 and current source.
6) Calculation of inflow/outflow currents in small time step.
7) Computation of charge.
8) Computation of voltage.

Figure 9 shows the pipeline stage in the simulation module. All nodes of the power grid are sequentially simulated in the simulation module.

Because current calculation of a node require the voltage of the adjacent node, it is necessary to wait until the adjacent node finishes simulating, even if the node finishes simulating. Horizontal size and vertical size of power grid are defined as H_SIZE and V_SIZE. In an ideal pipeline processing, H_SIZE times V_SIZE clocks are needed for the simulation of all nodes. Moreover, 8 + H_SIZE clocks are needed to finish eight stage pipeline processing of a node and the adjacent node.

4.2. Parallel Processing

Figure 10 shows an example of which a circuit is divided

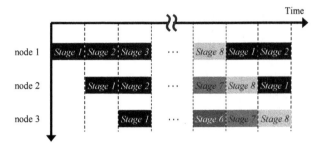

Figure 9. Pipeline stage of each node.

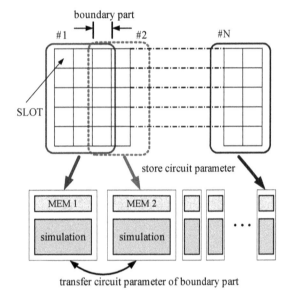

Figure 10. Circuit partitioning for parallel processing.

into N parts to perform parallel processing. The memory and the simulation module are regarded as one functional block, and all the functional blocks are operated in parallel. The boundary of sub-circuit is overlapped, and the data of boundary part is stored in each memory. There is a point that should be considered in parallelization. For example, when simulating the sub-circuit No. 2, voltage is referred from right-hand memory to compute the outflow current of right boundary part. The inflow current is considered to simulate the left boundary part, however the inflow current quotes the outflow current of the left node as shown in **Figure 4**. However, referring to the inflow current, it is necessary to adjust timing at Stage 2. Then, simulation results are referred from left-hand circuit, and the process of timing adjustment is omitted to prevent performance deterioration. Therefore, the results of boundary part must be stored into each memory.

In massively parallel computing approach, e.g. GPGPU, similar synchronization technique is discussed to hold the important data in shared memories. In our FPGA approach, the structure of the shared memories are structured as we like, thus, in general, more efficient data communications are possible.

5. Experimental Results

5.1. Evaluation of Pipeline Processing

To evaluate the speed of the proposed hardware simulator, FE is described in C language with fixed point, which is functionally equal to the hardware simulator. Bit shift is executed to prevent overflow after multiply operation. The simulation is executed with fixed time step. The FE program in C language is executed on HP xw9400Workstation with Dual-Core AMD Opteron Processor2220 2.8 GHz and 8 GB RAM. The test data for accuracy evaluation is given by an RC circuit as shown in **Figure 1**, and the circuit scale is 100 × 100 grids. The value of resistance is selected from 2, 3, 4 [mΩ], and the value of each capacitance is selected from 10, 30, 60 [μF].

The supply voltage is 1 [V]. The results of SPICE simulation by the same circuits are used for the reference data. SPICE performs Backward Euler method and Trapezoidal method [14]. These analytical methods realize high accuracy, however take a lot of processing time, in general. For speeding up the simulation, SPICE dynamically selects the time step size. The maximum error ratio in the all node voltage is evaluated by comparing the FE and SPICE.

First, pipeline processing is achieved as one of the speed-up techniques with hardware. The architecture described in Section 4 is achieved with Verilog HDL. Then, the speed performance of the power grid simulation by three processing, software, non-pipeline, pipeline, are compared as shown in **Table 3**. The processing time of software shows the result of single thread execution. That of HDL is calculated by number of clock times multiplied by the clock period of the FPGA. Target FPGA for logic synthesis is "EP2S180F1020C3, Stratix II, ALTERA". Quartus II 7.1 is used as a logic synthesis tool. Non-pipeline processing is achieved about 1.2 times faster than software. As a result, the maximum frequency, 26 [MHz], was low because some operations had been executed with one clock. Inserting the register between each arithmetic unit, pipeline processing achieved about three times faster than non-pipeline processing. The maximum clock frequency and the latency are 80 [MHz] and 101 [nsec] by pipeline processing. In this experiment, 32-bit multiplication has become critical path because the pipeline stage was delimited between each arithmetic unit. About dividing the pipeline stage, there is leeway for improvement.

Next, the circuit scale has been changed. **Table 4** shows the speed gain by the hardware implementation. Experiment has been executed on large power grid to compare simulation time. The speed gain tends to be high in large scale circuit, and the hardware simulator has achieved 4.5 times faster processing speed than software.

Table 3. Speed gain by pipeline processing.

	Time [sec]	Frequency [MHz]
C	8.0	[N/A]
Non-pipeline	6.4	26
Pipeline	2.1	80

Table 4. Speed estimation by changing circuit scale.

Circuit scale	C [sec]	HDL [sec]
100 × 100	8.0	2.1
200 × 200	38	8.3
300 × 300	85	18
500 × 500	252	52

5.2. Evaluation of Parallel Processing

This section described parallel processing of the power grid simulation. The simulation module by pipeline processing in previous section is connected in parallel. The entire circuit scale is changed from 50 × 50 to 500 × 500, and the speeding gain by the parallel processing is shown in **Table 5**. **Figure 11** shows the processing time and speed ratio when the circuit scale is set to 500 × 500 grids. The bar chart indicates the processing time. The line charts and shows the speeding up ratio when the number of partitions is expanded.

The speeding up ratio is set on the basis of the processing time at one block. A high parallelism have achieved without saturation even if the number of partitions increased. About 7.9 times speeding up has been achieved when the power grid had been divided into eight. When the number of division circuits is defined as N, the speed improvement of proposal algorithm expect as shown in (1).

$$1+(N-1)\times(\text{H\_SIZE}-1)/\text{H\_SIZE} \qquad (1)$$

Increasing the number of division circuit influence speed improvement because the boundary parts are overlapped. **Table 6** shows the result of logic synthesis when simulating 100 × 100 grids and divided into eight. The usage rate of DSP is comparatively high. Therefore, it is necessary for higher parallel processing to improve the algorithm or apply to larger scale FPGA.

6. Conclusions

In this paper, we have proposed an efficient hardware circuit simulator for power grid optimization. The proposal technique achieves high accuracy and high speed simulation by adopting fixed point arithmetic and parallel processing.

In the evaluation experiment of accuracy, we have evaluated four type's analysis method by comparing the

Table 5. Speed gain by changing the number of partitions.

	2	3	4	5	6	7	8
50 × 50	2.0	2.9	3.8	4.6	5.5	6.3	7.1
100 × 100	2.0	2.9	3.8	4.8	5.6	6.2	7.1
200 × 200	2.0	3.0	3.9	4.9	5.9	6.8	7.7
500 × 500	2.0	3.0	4.0	5.0	5.9	6.9	7.9

Table 6. Result of logic synthesis of eight parallel simulation modules.

Logic	14,546 [LEs] (10%)
Memory	4.3 [Mbit] (45%)
DSP (9-bit)	524 (68%)
Max frequency.	80 [MHz]

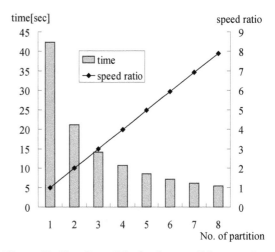

Figure 11. Circuit partitioning for parallel processing.

functionally equal program and SPICE. The FE achieves high accuracy simulation by several different experiments, *i.e.*, in different time steps, floating point or fixed point.

Next, we have evaluated the speed gain by pipeline processing and parallel processing. The proposed power grid simulation algorithm performs 4.5 times faster processing than software processing. In addition, eight parallel processing achieves 7.9 times higher speed than one unit processing. Therefore, the proposed power grid simulation using 80 MHz FPGA achieves 35 times higher speed than software processing with 2.8 GHz CPU while maintaining the high accuracy.

In the future, we will implement the proposed hardware algorithm onto a Compute Unified Device Architecture (CUDA) platform.

REFERENCES

[1] D. A. Andersson, L. J. Svensson and P. Lasson-Edefors,

"Noise-Aware On-Chip Power Grid Considerations Using a Statistical Approach," *Proceedings of International Symposium on Quality Electronic Design*, San Jose, 17-19 March 2008, pp. 663-669.

[2]   S. W. Wu and Y. W. Chang, "Efficient Power/Ground Network Analysis for Power Integrity-Driven Design Methodology," *Proceedings of Design Automation Conference*, San Diego, 7-11 June 2004, pp. 177-180.

[3]   A. Muramatsu, M. Hashimoto and H. Onodera, "Effects of On-Chip Inductance on Power Distribution Grid," *IEICE Transactions on Fundamentals of Electronics, Communications and Computer Sciences*, Vol. E88-A, No. 12, 2005, pp. 3564-3572.

[4]   Y. Zhong and M. D. F. Wong, "Thermal-Aware IR Drop Analysis in Large Power Grid," *Proceedings of International Symposium on Quality Electronic Design*, San Jose, 17-19 March 2008, pp. 194-199.

[5]   B. Yu and M. L. Bushnell, "Power Grid Analysis of Dynamic Power Cutoff Technology," *Proceedings of International Symposium on Circuits and Systems*, New Orleans, 27-30 May 2007, pp. 1393-1396.

[6]   C. Mizuta, J. Iwai, K. Machida, T. Kage and H. Matsuda, "Large-Scale Linear Circuit Simulation with an Inversed Inductance Matrix," *Proceedings of Asia and South Pacific Design Automation Conference*, Kanagawa, 27-30 January 2004, pp. 511-516.

[7]   P. M. Lee, S. Ito, T. Hashimoto, J. Sato, T. Touma and G. Yokomizo, "A Parallel and Accelerated Circuit Simulator with Precise Accuracy," *Proceedings of International Conference on VLSI Design*, Bangalore, 7-11 August 2002, pp. 213-218.

[8]   N. Nakasato and T. Hamada, "Acceleration of Hydrosynamical Simulations Using a FPGA Board," *Institute of Electronics, Information and Communication Engineers Technical Report*, Vol. 105, No. 515, 2006, pp. 19-24.

[9]   T. Watanabe, Y. Tanji, H. Kubota and H. Asai, "Parallel-Distributed Time-Domain Circuit Simulation of Power Distribution Networks with Frequency-Dependent Parameters," *Proceedings of Asia and South Pacific Conference on Design Automation*, Yokohama, 24-27 January 2006, pp. 832-837.

[10] Y. Gu, T. Vancourt and M. C. Herbordt, "Improved Interpolation and System Integration for FPGA-Based Molecular Dynamics Simulations," *Proceedings of International Conference of Field Programmable Logic and Applications*, Madrid, 28-30 August 2006, pp. 1-8.

[11] L. Zhuo and V. K. Prasanna, "High-Performance and Parameterized Matrix Factorization on FPGAs," *Proceedings of International Conference of Field Programmable Logic and Applications*, Madrid, 28-30 August 2006, pp. 363-368.

[12] M. Yoshimi, Y. Osana, Y. Iwaoka, Y. Nishikawa, T. Kojima, A. Funahashi, N. Hiroi, Y. Shibata, N. Iwanaga, H. Kitano and H. Amano, "An FPGA Implementation of Throughput Stochastic Simulator for Large-scale Biochemical Systems," *Proceedings of International Conference of Field Programmable Logic and Applications*, Madrid, 28-30 August 2006, pp. 227-232.

[13] H. Ishijima, T. Harada, K. Kusano, M. Fukui, M. Yoshikawa and H. Terai, "A Power Grid Optimization Algorithm with Consideration of Dynamic Circuit Operations," *Proceedings of Synthesis and System Integration of Mixed Information*, Nagoya, 3-4 April 2006, pp. 446-451.

[14] Y. Kawakami, M. Terao, M. Fukui and S. Tsukiyama, "A Power Grid Optimization Algorithm by Observing Timing Error Risk by IR Drop," *IEICE Transactions on Fundamentals*, Vol. E91-A, No. 12, 2008, pp. 3423-3430.

[15] T. Hashizume, H. Ishijima and M. Fukui, "An Evaluation of Circuit Simulation Algorithms for Hardware Implementation," *Proceedings of Synthesis and System Integration of Mixed Information*, Hokkaido, 15-16 October 2007, pp. 322-327.

19

A New Current-Controlled-Power Technique for Small Signal Applications

Adisak Monpapassorn

Department of Electronic Engineering, South-East Asia University, Bangkok, Thailand

ABSTRACT

In this paper, a new current-controlled-power technique for small signal applications is presented. The proposed technique needs no passive devices (a resistor and a capacitor) but the well-known SCR technique needs, thus the proposed technique is very suitable for an IC process. An example application as a new current-controlled-power CMOS full-wave rectifier is also given. The example application is simulated by using the SPICE program. Simulation results show that the proposed technique can work well; the controlled-current from 0 μA to 5.5 μA produces the peak area amplitude from 100 mV to 0 mV to the load.

Keywords: Current-Controlled-Power; Full-Wave Rectifier; Analog Signal Processing

1. Introduction

As is well known, it is hard to find the device that operates as a silicon-controlled rectifier (SCR) [1] for controlling the power in small signal applications. In this paper, the author presents a new current-controlled-technique for small signal applications. The proposed technique yields the advantages:

- The proposed technique needs no a capacitor and a resistor but the well-known SCR technique needs; therefore, without passive devices, the proposed technique uses a much smaller chip area in the IC process [2].
- The proposed technique works with a small signal but the SCR technique cannot work because of the threshold voltage of the SCR [1].
- The proposed technique can also work with a large signal by driving a power bipolar transistor.
- The proposed technique with current-controlled is very suitable for an automatic control system by the current feedback. Whereas the SCR technique uses the RC time constant for clipping time [1], it is hard for the automatic control system.

The example application as a new current-controlled-power CMOS full-wave rectifier is also presented. It provides the advantages as follows.

- The new full-wave rectifier works both full-wave rectification and current-controlled-power operation. But the previous proposed full-wave rectifiers cannot control the output power.
- The new rectifier uses all MOSs with typical structure

thus it is very suitable for IC processes [3].
- The new rectifier, its core operates in balanced mode resulting in a low noise output [4].
- Using the new rectifier, one can independently control the positive part and the negative part of the input signal, this yields more precision control.

2. Proposed Current-Controlled-Power Technique

The proposed technique is shown in **Figure 1(a)** and its signals are shown in **Figure 1(b)**. The operation is as follows. I_{CL1} is fed to shift down the input differential current signal (I_{in+}). It will decrease the amplitude and area of the positive signal and will increase those of the negative signal. The bias source (V_b) is the voltage or current, for turning-on the current mirror (MN1 and MN2) all the time for very small signal operation. The V_b must be the minimum voltage or current to make the minimum offset at the output (I_{out}). The I_{out} is the positive signal rectified by the current mirror. Because the input signal is shifted down, one must compensate this for (I_{in-}) by feeding I_{CL2} for balancing the input signal.

Note the proposed technique that the output is a horizontal clipped signal but the well-known SCR technique the output is a vertical clipped signal. The proposed technique with all active devices is better than the SCR technique with the resistor and capacitor devices in view of IC fabrication. Additionally, the proposed technique with current-controlled is very suitable for automatic control system by a current feedback. Whereas the SCR

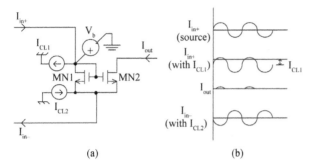

(a)   (b)

Figure 1. Proposed technique: (a) circuit and (b) operation.

technique uses the RC time constant for clipping time, it is hard for automatic control system. Moreover, the proposed technique can be used in high power applications; it can drive the high current bipolar transistor.

3. Application Example as a New Current-Controlled-Power Full-Wave Rectifier

The circuit in **Figure 2** operates as a full-wave rectifier where $I_{CL+1} = I_{CL+2} = I_{CL-1} = I_{CL-2} = 0$. Its operation is as follows. The constant current source I_C is mirrored by MI1 and MI3 to the drain of M3 (I_{D3}); and is mirrored by MI1, MI2, MI4 and MI5 to the drain of M1 (I_{D1}). The W/L ratios of MI1 to MI5 are equal, making $I_{D1} = I_{D3}$. Moreover, using matched MOS transistors M1 to M4 [5], the input voltage is thus followed to a MOS resistor (R_A) [6], the resistance of which is given by

$$R = \frac{1}{2KV_{DT}} \quad (1)$$

where MA1 and MA2 have the same characteristics; $K = \mu C_{ox}W/L$, μ is the carrier mobility, C_{ox} is the gate capacitance per unit area, W and L are the channel width and length respectively; $V_{DT} = V_{DD} - V_T = -(V_{SS} + V_T)$, $V_{DD} = -V_{SS}$, V_T is the threshold voltage.

Equation (1) is valid when both MA1 and MA2 maintain in the saturation region, which is true if

$$|V_A| \le V_{DT} \quad (2)$$

This input voltage creates the current I_{in} flowing through R_A.

$$I_{in} = V_{in} 2KV_{DT} \quad (3)$$

In **Figure 2**, I_{in} is mirrored by M5, M6, M9, and M10 as I_1; and is mirrored by M5, M7, M9, and M11 as $I_4 = -I_1$. Furthermore, I_{in} is mirrored by M5, M8, M9, M12, M13, M14, M16, and M17 as I_2; and is mirrored by M5, M8, M9, M12, M13, M15, M16, and M18 as I_3. One assumes that the gain of all current mirrors is unity, thus

$$\left. \begin{array}{l} I_1 = I_2 \\ I_3 = I_4 \end{array} \right\} \quad (4)$$

When the input voltage is positive, the current mirror (M19 and M20) turns on and the current mirror (M21 and M22) turns off. Inversely, when the input voltage is negative, the current mirror (M19 and M20) turns off and the current mirror (M21 and M22) turns on, resulting in

$$\left. \begin{array}{l} V_{in} > 0; I_1 = I_2 = I_{in}; I_3 = I_4 = 0 \\ V_{in} < 0; I_1 = I_2 = 0; I_3 = I_4 = I_{in} \end{array} \right\} \quad (5)$$

The drain currents of M20 and M22 are finally mirrored by M23 and M24 and then are converted to the voltage by R_B. Using $R_A = R_B$ by setting MA1 = MA2 = MB1 = MB2, the relation between input and output voltages (full-wave rectification) can be written as

$$\left. \begin{array}{l} V_{in} > 0; V_{out} = V_{in} \\ V_{in} < 0; V_{out} = -V_{in} \end{array} \right\} \quad (6)$$

The bias sources (V_{b1} and V_{b2}) in **Figure 1** may be the voltage or current source. This bias source makes the MOSs in core 1 and core 2 (M19, M20, M21, and M22) turning-on all the time, to reduce the error at zero-crossing of the full-wave output signal.

Three main errors of the operation of the proposed rectifier can be considered. Assume that the error of W/L ratios of MOS transistors is ignored since it is very small in the present technology.

The first error is for transferring an input voltage to node A [5] because the currents I_{D1} and I_{D3} are slid resulting from the error of simple current mirrors (MI1 to MI5). This error can be minimized by using the better current mirrors (cascode or Wilson type); however, it requires higher supply voltage [7].

The second error is for mirroring the input current from R_A to core 1 and core 2. And the last error is the error of core 1 and core 2. The second and the last errors can be reduced by using the better current mirrors as mentioned above.

The best way for setting three above errors to minimize, is compensation. The compensation can be done by adjusting the gain of core 1 and core 2 through the W/L ratios (of M20 for positive input and of M22 for negative input). In addition, adjusting the resistant of R_B through W/L ratios of MB1 and MB2 is also compensation.

M2 and M4 must be in the saturation mode as M1 and M3; this yields the input operation range,

$$\left. \begin{array}{l} V_{in(min)} = \dfrac{V_{SS} + |V_{eff4}| + |V_{eff9}| + |V_{TP}| + |V_{TN}|}{\alpha} \\ V_{in(max)} = \dfrac{V_{DD} - |V_{eff2}| - |V_{eff5}| - |V_{TN}| - |V_{TP}|}{\alpha} \end{array} \right\} \quad (7)$$

where $V_{eff} = V_{GS} - V_T = \sqrt{\dfrac{2I_D}{\mu C_{OX}(W/L)}}$ [7], and α is the

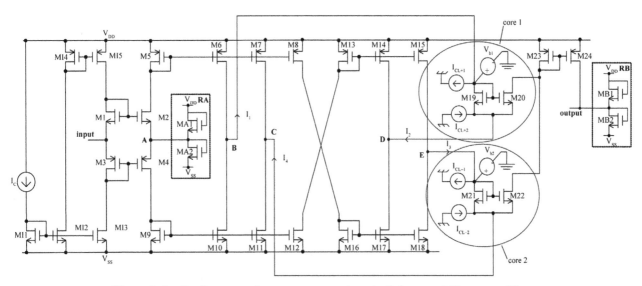

Figure 2. Application example as a new current-controlled-power full-wave rectifier.

voltage gain between input and node A, ideally it must be unity.

In the same way, M6, M7, M8, M10, M11, M12, M14, M15, M17, and M18 have to be in the saturation mode. If these MOSs have the same parameters, one can write the operation range of signals at nodes B, C, D, and E as

$$
\left.
\begin{aligned}
V_{B,C,D,E(\min)} &= V_{SS} + \left|V_{effN}\right| + \left|V_{TN}\right| \\
V_{B,C,D,E(\max)} &= V_{DD} - \left|V_{effP}\right| - \left|V_{TP}\right|
\end{aligned}
\right\}
\tag{8}
$$

Using the same characteristics M5 to M18, considering Equations (2), (7), and (8), the operation range of the proposed full-wave rectifier is considered as (7).

Note that two signals of core 1 at nodes B and D, two signals are 180 degrees out-of-phase; hence, some in-phase outside noise around the core will be cancelled, as well-known. It is also for core 2. This indicates that the proposed rectifier operates in a balanced mode, canceling some outside noise around the core.

As mentioned above, if we feed the control current ($I_{CL+1} = I_{CL+2}$), we can control the peak area of the positive input signal (see **Figure 1(b)**). Moreover, by feeding $I_{CL-1} = I_{CL-2}$, we also can control the peak area of the negative input signal. It is evident that we can independently control the positive part and the negative part of the input signal, this yields more precision control.

At this point, we can see that one application example of the new current-controlled-power technique is the new full-wave rectifier. The new rectifier can be realized by using all MOS transistors with typical structure. It is very suitable for the process of IC fabrication. Furthermore, not only full-wave rectification but also current-controlled-power operation, the proposed rectifier can work. The previous proposed rectifiers cannot operate this current-controlled-power function. Additionally, the balanced

mode operation of the core gains a lower noise output.

4. Results

To verify the theoretical design, the application example as a new current-controlled-power full-wave rectifier was simulated by using parameters extracted from its layout (including parasitic capacitance) in a 0.5 μm AMI MOS transistor technology, through a level-49 model.

The supply voltage is ±1.2 V. For full-wave rectifier simulation, I_C is 20 μA, $V_{b1} = V_{b2}$ are the current sources of 5 μA, $I_{CL+1} = I_{CL+2} = I_{CL-1} = I_{CL-2}$ are 0 μA. The W/L ratios of MA1 = MA2 = 1.5 μm/1.5 μm, MB1 = MB2 = 1.5 μm/3.9 μm, and other MOSs = 20 μm/0.6 μm, were chosen.

Figure 3 shows the output of the proposed full-wave rectifier with a sine wave input signal (100 mV$_{peak}$, 100 kHz). The amplitude error of the output signal is almost zero because of compensation by using $R_B > R_A$, by adjusting their W/L ratios as mentioned in Section 3. Also, the gain compensation can be done through the W/L ratios of M20, M22, and M24. The author tried to decrease the amplitude of the input signal; one found that the proposed rectifier can rectify a minimum voltage of 350 μV$_{peak}$. Changing frequency was done, the maximum operation frequency of the proposed rectifier was 30 MHz (–3 dB point).

For current-controlled-power operation, the author set $I_{CL+1} = I_{CL+2} = I_{CL-1} = I_{CL-2}$ following to the left column of **Table 1**, the right column shows the rectified output peak area amplitude. According to the theory, it was (namely, more $I_{CL+1} = I_{CL+2} = I_{CL-1} = I_{CL-2}$, more shifted-down signal, less output peak area amplitude).

As mentioned in Section 3 that we can independently control the positive part and the negative part of the input signal, this yields more precision control. We will show it here. The rectifier output can be divided to two parts for controlling (*A*. the positive input part and *B*. the negative input part shifted the phase by 180 degrees, by rectifier). *A* is controlled by $I_{CL+1} = I_{CL+2}$ and *B* is controlled by $I_{CL-1} = I_{CL-2}$. **Figure 4** shows the full-wave rectified output with $I_{CL+1} = I_{CL+2} = 1$ μA and $I_{CL-1} = I_{CL-2} = 3.5$ μA (changing the frequency to 1 MHz). It also shows that we can independently control the positive part and the negative part of the input signal, giving more precision control. Moreover, the proposed current-controlled- power full-wave rectifier is very suitable for an automatic control system by the current feedback. Whereas the SCR technique uses the RC time constant for clipping time, it is hard for the automatic control system.

Absolutely, not only full-wave rectification but also current-controlled-power operation, the proposed recti-

fier can work. The previous proposed rectifiers cannot operate this current-controlled-power function.

5. Conclusions

In this paper, the author has reported a new current-controlled-power technique that can be useful in analog small signal processing. The proposed technique needs no passive devices; it is very suitable for the IC process. The proposed technique can also work with a large signal by driving a power bipolar transistor. The proposed technique is very suitable for an automatic control system by the current feedback.

An application example as a new current-controlled-power full-wave rectifier has also been proposed. The new full-wave rectifier works both full-wave rectification

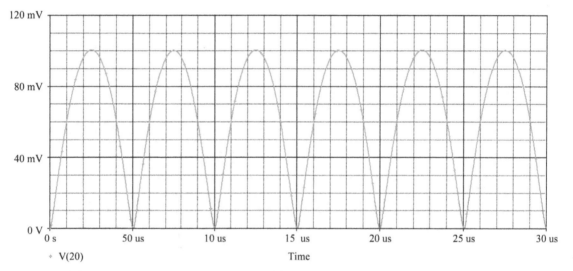

Figure 3. Output of the proposed current-controlled-power full-wave rectifier ($I_{CL+1} = I_{CL+2} = I_{CL-1} = I_{CL-2} = 0$) with an input sine wave of 100 mV$_{peak}$, 100 kHz.

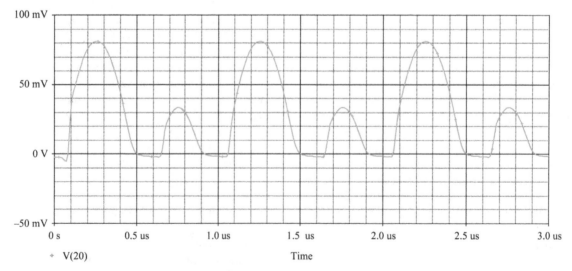

Figure 4. Output of the proposed current-controlled-power full-wave rectifier with an input sine wave, 100 mV$_{peak}$, 1 MHz, ($I_{CL+1} = I_{CL+2} = 1$ μA and $I_{CL-1} = I_{CL-2} = 3.5$ μA).

Table 1. Relation between the controlled current and the output.

$I_{CL+1} = I_{CL+2} = I_{CL-1} = I_{CL-2}$ (μA)	Output peak area amplitude (mV)
0	100
0.5	91
1	81.7
1.5	72.3
2	62.8
2.5	53.1
3	43.3
3.5	33.4
4	23.4
4.5	13.5
5	1.9
5.5	0

and current-controlled-power operation. The new rectifier uses all MOSs with typical structure thus it is very suitable for the IC process. The new rectifier, its core operates in balanced mode resulting in a low noise output. Using the new rectifier, one can independently control the positive part and the negative part of the input signal, this yields more precision control.

It should be noted on the use of the new rectifier that it is suitable for a high impedance load. If the low impedance load is applied, it needs a voltage buffer at the output.

REFERENCES

[1] G. B. Rutkowski and J. E. Oleksy, "Solid-State Electronics," McGraw-Hill, Singapore, 1992.

[2] A. Hastings, "The Art of Analog Layout," Prentice-Hall, Upper Saddle River, 2006.

[3] B. Razavi, "Design of Analog CMOS Integrated Circuits," McGraw-Hill, Singapore City, 2001.

[4] F. W. Hughes, "Op Amp Handbook," Prentice-Hall, Upper Saddle River, 1993.

[5] E. Bruun, "CMOS High Speed, High Precision Current Conveyor and Current Feedback Amplifier Structures," *International Journal of Electronics*, Vol. 74, No. 1, 1993, pp. 93-100.

[6] Z. Wang, "2-MOSFET Transresistor with Extremely Low Distortion for Output Reaching Supply Voltages," *Electronics Letters*, Vol. 26, No. 13, 1990, pp. 951-952.

[7] D. Johns and K. Martin, "Analog Integrated Circuit Design," John Wiley & Sons, New York, 1997.

20

Optimizing the Stage Resolution of a 10-Bit, 50 Ms/Sec Pipelined A/D Converter & Its Impact on Speed, Power, Area, and Linearity

Perala Prasad Rao[*], **Kondepudi Lal Kishore**

Department of Electronics and Communication Engineering, Jawaharlal Nehru
Technological University, Hyderabad, India

ABSTRACT

At high speeds and high resolution, the Pipeline ADCs are becoming popular. The options of different stage resolutions in Pipelined ADCs and their effect on speed, power dissipation, linearity and area are discussed in this paper. The basic building blocks viz. Op-Amp Sample and Hold circuit, sub converter, D/A Converter and residue amplifier used in every stage is assumed to be identical. The sub converters are implemented using flash architectures. The paper implements a 10-bit 50 Mega Samples/Sec Pipelined A/D Converter using 1, 1.5, 2, 3, 4 and 5 bits/stage conversion techniques and discusses about its impact on speed, power, area, and linearity. The design implementation uses 0.18 μm CMOS technology and a 3.3 V power supply. The paper concludes stating that a resolution of 2 bits/stage is optimum for a Pipelined ADC and to reduce the design complexity, we may go up to 3 bits/stage.

Keywords: Switched Capacitor Sample and Hold Circuit; 1.5 Bits/Stage; Linearity; Power; Redundancy; Folded Cascode Op-Amp

1. Introduction

Although many Pipelined ADC architectures are discussed in literature, the number of bits/stage conversion was always a designer's choice. Many designers preferred a stage resolution of 3 bits just to reduce the design complexity. This paper discusses the options of number of bits/stage conversion techniques in Pipelined ADCs and their effect on area, speed, power dissipation and linearity. The paper examines 1, 1.5, 2, 3, 4 and 5 bits/stage conversion to implement a 10-bit Pipelined ADC. In the analysis, all the basic blocks are assumed to be identical.

The rapid advancements in electronics has resulted in digital revolution with telephony switching systems in 1970's and continued with digital audio in 1980's and digital video in 1990's. This is expected to prevail in the present multimedia era and even can influence in future systems. Since all electrical signals are analog in nature and since most signal processing is done in the digital domain therefore, A/D and D/A Converters have become a necessity. Flash ADC makes all bit decisions in a single go while successive approximation ADC makes single bit decision at a time. Flash ADCs are faster but area increases exponentially with bit length while successive

approximation ADC is slow and occupies less area.

Between these two extremes many other architectures exist deciding a fixed number of bits at a time such as pipeline and multi step ADCs. They balance circuit complexity and speed. **Figure 1** shows recently published high speed ADC architecture applications and resolution versus speed. In general, three architectures are suitable for three important areas of usage. For example, over sampling converter is used exclusively to achieve high resolution (greater than 12 bits at low frequencies). For medium speed with high resolution multi step and Pipeline ADCs are promising. At extremely high frequencies, flash ADCs survive but only at low resolution.

Figure 2 shows resolution versus speed depicting this trend. Most architecture known to date is not likely to achieve a resolution of 12 bits at over 100 MHz using even 180 nm to 90 nm technologies. However, two high speed architectures, namely multi step, pipelined and folding are potential architectures to challenge in times to come.

1.1. Flash ADC

The straightforward approach for A/D Conversion is to compare the input with all divided levels of the reference voltage and this is used in flash ADC. The conversion

---

[*]Corresponding author.

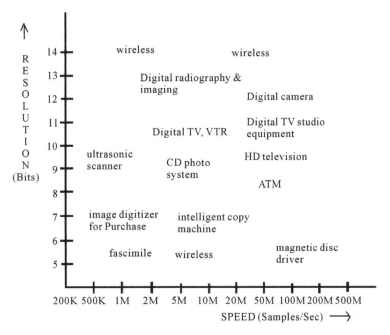

Figure 1. Speed versus resolution.

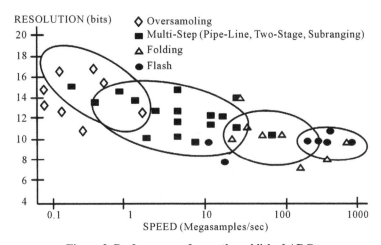

Figure 2. Performance of recently published ADCs.

completes in a single step. Therefore, flash ADC is the fastest of all ADCs. **Figure 3** shows flash ADC technique. As the output of comparator set is thermometer coded, the priority encoder is required. The performance is decided by the comparator resolution and the accuracy of voltage divisions. Practically, the exponential growth of the number of comparators and resistors with increased bit size limits the usage of flash ADCs. An N bit flash ADC requires 2^{N-1} comparators and 2^N resistors. Also with increased bit length, the comparators present significant capacitive loading on the Sample and Hold circuit thus reducing the speed of conversion.

As the comparators number increases and also the capacitive loading, the power consumption also becomes high. Therefore, flash converters are preferred for bit length less than 8 only. Flash ADCs are preferred as

coarse and fine quantizers in multi step and Pipeline ADCs.

1.2. Multi Step ADC

Instead of making all bit decisions at a time as in flash ADC or single bit decision at a time as in successive approximation ADC, we can resolve a few bits at a time as it makes the system simpler and easily manageable [1].

It also allows us to use digital error correction mechanism. This is adopted by the multi step ADC architecture. Here only a single Sample and Hold circuit is used and every stage requires a coarse ADC, DAC and a residue amplifier as shown in **Figure 4**. We need to use multi phase clocking scheme to complete conversion in one clock cycle. In the multi step architecture, number of

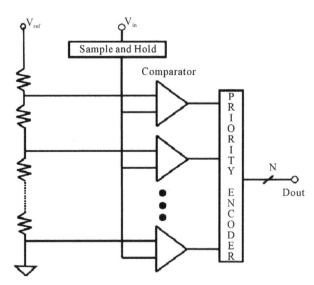

Figure 3. Flash ADC architecture.

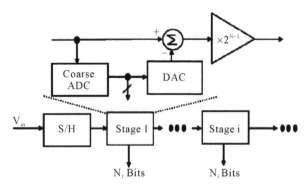

Figure 4. Multi step ADC architecture.

steps are usually limited to two due to the difficulty in multiphase clocking. Also it doesn't reduce speed much and can use standard two phase clocking.

1.3. Pipeline ADC

Although simpler and manageable, as the number of bits/stage increase, the complexity of two steps ADC still grows exponentially. For resolution of 10 bits and above, the complexity reaches a maximum and hence the need for pipelining the sub ranging blocks arises.

Figure 5 shows the Pipeline ADC architecture. It looks similar to multi step ADC architecture except that every stage uses a separate Sample and Hold circuit.

Since Sample and Hold circuits are clocked by alternating clock phases, therefore, in every clock phase, a stage must perform the bit decision and amplify the difference signal to generate the residue for the next stage. Pipelining the residue greatly simplifies the ADC architectures. The complexity now grows linearly with the number of bits to resolve and hence is becoming popular. Here, the overall performance is limited by the accuracy of the residue amplifier. The potential error sources are

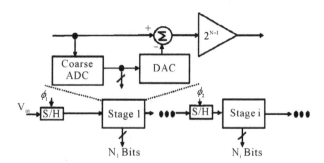

Figure 5. Pipeline ADC architecture.

the settling behavior of the amplifier, ADC/DAC resolution and gain error of residue amplifier.

2. Types of Pipelined ADCs

2.1. One Bit/Stage Pipeline ADC

The simplest case of Pipeline ADC is to resolve 1 bit per stage as shown in **Figure 6**.

Each stage here performs the following operations:

The sampled signal is compared with $V_{ref}/2$ and the output of each comparator becomes the converted bit for that stage.

If $V_{in} > V_{ref}/2$, the output of comparator = "1", then $V_{ref}/2$ is subtracted from the held input signal and the difference is passed to the amplifier with a gain of 2. The result is passed as input to Sample and Hold circuit of the next stage.

In Pipeline ADC architecture, the MSB stage must be carefully designed. A slight error in first stage propagates through the converter and hence can result in a much bigger error at the end of conversion. The succeeding stages can be less accurate. The comparator and summer offsets together must be less than 1/2 LSB to keep the ADC accurate.

2.2. Bits/Stage Pipeline ADC

Using cascaded lower resolution stages [2-4], the Pipelined ADCs get their final resolution. For example, a 12-bit ADC can use a cascade of four 3-bit stages. Many designers are comfortable with 3-bit flash ADCs. However, 1.5 bits/stage is also becoming increasingly popular. There is an advantage of going for minimum stage resolution for high speed converters. It minimizes the inter stage gain required, which in turn maximizes the bandwidth, since gain bandwidth product is a constant for a given technology.

A 1.5 bits/stage is a 1 bit/stage into which some redundancy is added to compensate for device tolerances and imperfections [5]. A digital error correction mechanism later eliminates this redundancy. The 1.5 bits/stage uses two analog comparison levels V_u & V_L instead of a single level as in 1 bit/stage. Because of the use of gain of two, they must lie between $+V_{ref}/2$ and $-V_{ref}/2$. A common choice is $V_L = -V_{ref}/4$ and $V_u = +V_{ref}/4$. The MDAC architecture and its voltage transfer characteristics are shown in **Figure 7** which is highly nonlinear. The input voltage range is divided into three sections. The low range (L) below V_L, mid range (M) between V_u and V_L and the upper range (U) above V_u, as shown in the **Table 1**. The implementation details of 1.5 bits/stage is shown in **Figure 7(a)**. A resistor string provides voltage division to create reference voltages V_u and V_L.

All other high accuracy operations such as multiply-by-two are achieved by capacitor ratios. The Sample and Hold circuit and multiply-by-two amplifier can be combined to form a Multiplying DAC (MDAC). The cascaded MDAC outputs are passed through latches before feeding them to the redundancy bit removal circuit as shown in **Figure 8**.

Redundancy Bit Removal Algorithm
The probable error sources in data converters include offset voltages in comparators and Op-Amps, gain error in amplifier, nonlinearity in converter and others. Many of these errors are compensated by this algorithm [3,4].

Each 1.5-bit pipelined stage produces a 2-bit output code B1B0. Using redundancy bit removal algorithm, this is reduced to final 1 bit per stage code. For a resolution of 3 bits, the input voltage range of +2 V is divided into 8 equal slots and **Table 2** shows input voltage, the code generation of each stage and corresponding stage residue voltages. To generate the final code, the two bit codes generated by each stage are added in a predetermined way. For example, as shown in **Table 2**, for $V_{in} = 0.8$ V, the codes generated by successive stages are 10, 01 and 00. These bits must be added as follows to generate the final 3-bit code.

Table 1. Implementation details of Figure 7(a).

V_{in}	Range	B_1	B_0	DAC output	Analog residue output
$V_{in} > V_u$	U	1	0	$+V_{ref}$	$2\,V_{in} - V_{ref}$
$V_L < V_{in} < V_u$	M	0	1	0	$2\,V_{in}$
$V_{in} < V_L$	L	0	0	$-V_{ref}$	$2\,V_{in} + V_{ref}$

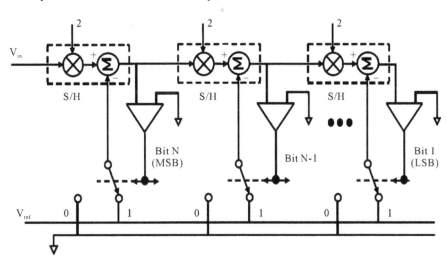

Figure 6. One bit/stage Pipeline ADC architecture.

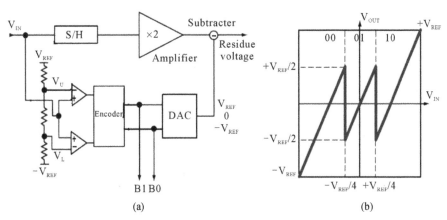

Figure 7. 1.5 Bit conversion technique. (a) MDAC; (b) Transfer characteristics.

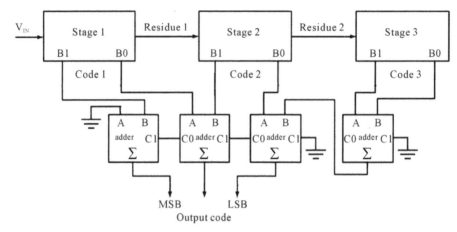

Figure 8. Implementation of redundancy bit removal algorithm.

Table 2. Development of error corrected output code.

V_{IN} (V)	RANGE (1)	CODE (1)	RES (1)	RANGE (2)	CODE (2)	RES (2)	RANGE (3)	CODE (3)	OUTPUT CODE
1.80	U	10	1.60	U	10	1.20	U	10	111
1.23	U	10	0.46	M	01	0.92	U	10	110
0.80	U	10	−0.40	M	01	−0.80	L	00	101
0.30	M	01	0.60	U	10	−0.80	L	00	100
−0.26	M	01	−0.52	L	00	0.96	U	10	011
−0.70	L	00	0.60	U	10	−0.80	L	00	010
−1.30	L	00	−0.60	L	00	0.80	U	10	001
−1.60	L	00	−1.20	L	00	−0.40	L	00	000

```
        1  0
  +        0  1
  +           0  0
     ─────────────
     1  0  1  0
```

Discard LSB and the final digital code is 101 for the case V_{in} = 0.8 V as shown in row 3 of **Table 2**.

The circuit implementation is shown in **Figure 8**.

2.3. Two Bits/Stage and Above

The 10-bit Pipelined ADC is implemented in 5 stages with 2 bits/stage, and in 4 stages using 3 bits/stage converting 3, 3, 3 and 1 bit respectively in consecutive stages [6]. Using 4 bits/stage conversion, the ADC is implemented in 3 stages converting 4, 4, 2 bits in successive stages and so on. All the sub converters are implemented using flash architectures already discussed.

3. Implementing the Pipelined ADC

The design issues of various building blocks are discussed in this section. The same blocks are used in dif-

ferent stages and the analysis is done with respect to area, speed of conversion, power dissipation and linearity.

3.1. Folded Cascode Op-Amp

Modern integrated CMOS Op-Amps are designed to drive capacitive loads. For capacitive loads, it is not necessary to use a buffer at the output (for providing a low impedance node). Therefore, it is possible to design Op-Amps at larger voltage swings and higher speeds than those which drive pure resistive loads [7-9]. These improvements are achieved with a single high impedance node at the output that drives only capacitive loads. For folded cascode Op-Amps the compensation is achieved by load capacitance C_L itself and it provides dominant pole compensation. As C_L increases, the Op-Amp stability improves but gets slowed down. The schematic of folded cascode Op-Amp is shown in **Figure 9**. The basic idea of folded cascode Op-Amp is to apply the opposite type PMOS cascode transistors to the input differential pair of NMOS type. The design of Op-Amp is becoming increasingly difficult as supply voltages and transistor channel lengths are scaled down. There are several

Optimizing the Stage Resolution of a 10-Bit, 50 Ms/Sec Pipelined A/D Converter & Its Impact on Speed, Power, Area, and Linearity

153

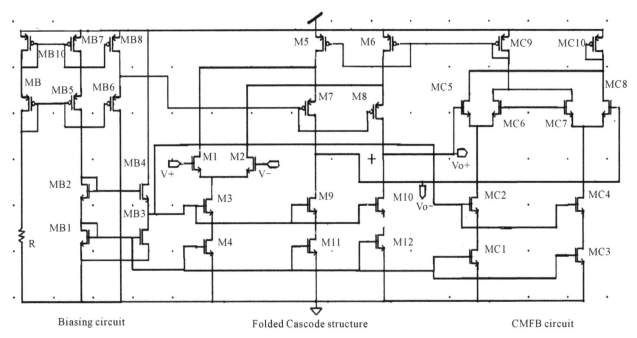

Figure 9. Folded cascode Op-Amp.

Op-Amp topologies possible viz. Two stage CMOS Op-Amp, regulated cascode Op-Amp, folded cascode Op-Amp and Telescopic cascode Op-Amp etc. A two stage CMOS Op-Amp is preferred where high gain and large output swing are required. However, the addition of second stage reduces unity gain frequency and hence speed of operation. A telescopic cascode Op-Amp offers better power and bandwidth criterion but has severe drawback of reduced output swing and hence not preferred for low voltage applications. Folded cascode Op-Amp provides higher output swing compared to telescopic cascode Op-Amp and better PSRR and speed over two stage Op-Amp. Hence folded cascode Op-Amp is used here.

This arrangement allows the output to be taken at the same bias levels as that of input signal. Even though it is a single stage, the gain is reasonable since the gain is decided by the product of input transconductance and the larger output impedance. The design uses band gap reference and common mode feedback circuit (CMFB). The Op-Amp results of **Figure 10** shows a unity gain frequency of 200 MHz at 88° phase margin and a gain of over 70 dB and 300 MHz at 72° phase margin for the same gain.

3.2. Sample and Hold Amplifier

The fully differential Sample and Hold implementation is shown in **Figure 11**. We can determine the input/output relationship of Sample and Hold circuit by evaluating the charge stored on Ci and Cf.

And the expression for output can be written as

$$V_{\text{out}} = V_{\text{out}+} - V_{\text{out}-}$$

$$= \left(1 + \frac{Ci}{Cf}\right)\left(V_{\text{in}+} - V_{\text{in}-}\right) - \frac{Ci}{Cf}\left(V_{ci+} - V_{ci-}\right) \quad (1)$$

If $Ci = Cf$, then a gain of two is achieved [10]. By connecting V_{ci+} and V_{ci-} to $+V_{\text{ref}}$ and $-V_{\text{ref}}$, we can get $2\,V_{\text{in}}$, $(2\,V_{\text{in}} + V_{\text{ref}})$ and $(2\,V_{\text{in}} - V_{\text{ref}})$ required for A/D Conversion. The simulated results of **Figure 12** show a sampling rate of 100 Msps. The power dissipation is seen to be 8 mW for 3.3 V supply.

3.3. Comparator

The comparator has three stages, the differential stage, decision making stage and the level restoring stage as shown in **Figure 13**. The simulation results of **Figure 14** show the comparator delay as 3.28 nS.

3.4. DAC Unit

The design uses a simple two way analog switch for 1-bit DAC and a current steering R-2R ladder DAC for higher number of bits. The resistor string is shared between the flash sub converter and the DAC to minimise the area [7].

4. Results

4.1. Effect of Bits/Stage on Area

If the total area of ADC is A_{tot} and area of one stage is As, then the total area is given by

$$A_{\text{tot}} = \left(\frac{N - r}{n - r}\right) As \quad (2)$$

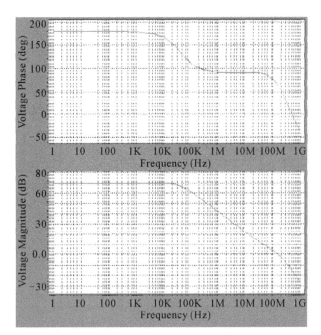

Figure 10. Gain & phase margin of FC Op-Amp.

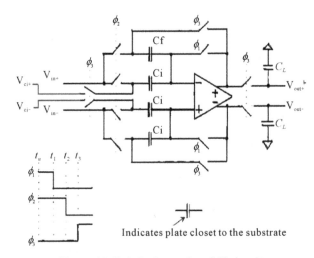

Figure 11. Switched capacitor S/H circuit.

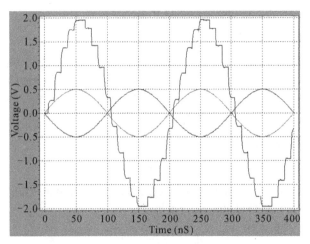

Figure 12. Sample and Hold output at 100 Msps.

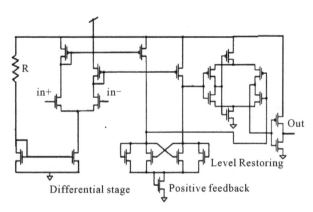

Figure 13. A high speed comparator.

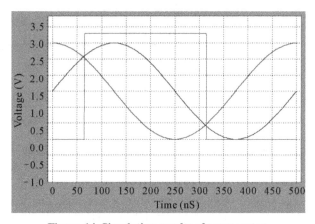

Figure 14. Simulation results of comparator.

where

N: Number of bits,

n: Number of bits converted per stage and,

r: Redundancy.

A_{tot} doesn't include the area occupied by the digital error correction, bias generation, clock generation and I/O pads. These areas are independent of n. The area of one stage includes the areas of comparator, DAC unit and that of sample & hold.

$$A_s = A_{\text{comp}}\left(2^{N-1}\right) + A_{\text{DAC}} + A_{SH} \qquad (3)$$

A_{SH} is observed to be almost proportional to $2n$. As n increases, the numbers of comparators increase and the delay increases. Therefore to reduce the settling time for the given load, the transconductance of the amplifier must be increased proportionally [4]. To increase the transconductance, the area of Sample and Hold and power dissipation must proportionally increase. If redundancy is introduced, then A_{SH} can be made independent of n (as incomplete settling is allowed). If n is decreased, then number of stages will increase and A_{SH} will increase. Therefore, A_{SH} will dominate for small values of n and if n is large, then A_{comp} dominates over A_{SH}. **Figure 15** shows the area distribution of Pipelined ADC.

The normalized area as a function of bits/stage is

Optimizing the Stage Resolution of a 10-Bit, 50 Ms/Sec Pipelined A/D Converter & Its Impact on Speed, Power, Area, and Linearity

155

shown in **Figure 16** where we see that the area reduces as we reduce the number of bits/stage showing a dip at 2 bits/stage.

4.2. Effect of Bits/Stage on Conversion Frequency

Since the sub ADCs use flash architectures, only two phase clocking is required for conversion. During phase 1, the first stage samples the input while the remaining odd stages samples the residue outputs of even stages. During phase 2, the even stages sample the outputs of odd stages. Therefore, the minimum duration of clock phase is set by the maximum settling time of the Sample and Hold amplifier [12].

If the two phases are of equal duration, then the maximum frequency of conversion F_c of ADC

$$F_{c\max} \leq \frac{1}{2(t_{s\max})} \qquad (4)$$

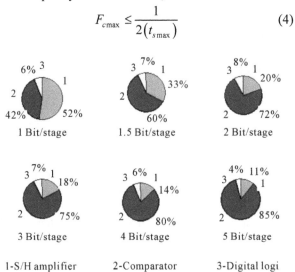

Figure 15. Area distributions among the blocks.

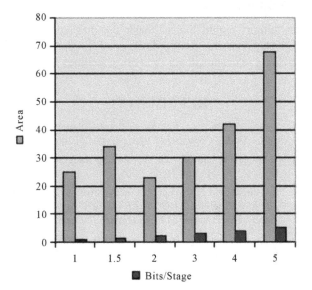

Figure 16. Normalized area vs bits/stage.

where $t_{s\max}$ is the maximum settling time of Sample and Hold amplifier.

If the Sample and Hold amplifier has a single pole transfer function (dominant pole compensation), and if unity gain frequency is fu, and if the input is a unit step function, then the gain of Sample and Hold amplifier is given by

$$A(t) = 2^{n-r}\left(1 - e^{-t/\tau}\right) \qquad (5)$$

where

$$\tau = \frac{2^{n-r}}{f_u} \qquad (6)$$

The first term of Equation (5) represents the ideal gain and the second term is because of incomplete settling. Even though Sample and Hold amplifiers are assumed to be identical, their settling times will not be identical and it is observed that the second stage Sample and Hold amplifier has maximum settling time $t_{s\max}$.

$$t_{s\max} = t_{s2} \approx (N - n + r)2^{n-r}\frac{\ln 2}{f_u} \qquad (7)$$

Substituting Equation (7) into Equation (6) gives

$$F_{c\max} \leq \frac{f_u}{(N - n + r)2^{n-r+1}\ln 2} \qquad (8)$$

Referring to Equation (8), the maximum frequency of conversion decreases for an increase in the bits/stage. Hence to increase the conversion frequency, the bits/stage must be minimized. The conversion frequency rates for the different bits/stage combinations are shown in **Figure 17**.

4.3. Effect of Bits/Stage on Power Dissipation

In ADCs the power is dissipated in Sample and Hold amplifier, sub converter, digital logic and biasing networks. The power dissipated in digital logic and biasing networks is much smaller than that in Sample and Hold amplifiers and sub converters. For reduced bits/stage, power dissipation in Sample and Hold amplifiers dominates while for increased bits/stage, the sub converter power dissipation dominates over Sample and Hold amplifiers. The power dissipation curves for various bits/stage conversions are shown in **Figure 18**.

4.4. Effect of Bits/Stage on Linearity

The error sources in Pipelined ADCs are offset, gain and non-linearity errors in Sample and Hold amplifiers, sub converters and DACs. The offset and gain errors can be compensated simply by scaling Rf/Ri or Ci/Cf in the amplifiers and offsetting the input to the ADC. Hence they are not so important in the determination of optimum

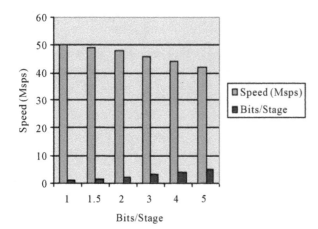

Figure 17. Frequency conversion rates vs bits/stage.

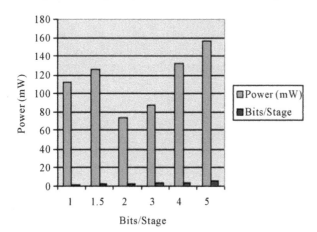

Figure 18. Power dissipation vs bits/stage.

number of bits/stage conversion. However, the non-linearity error is more difficult to compensate. **Figure 19** shows the signal flow model of a pipelined ADC with n stages and error sources $e_1 \cdots e_m \cdots e_n$. Here e_m represents the error of stage m and the error includes gain, offset, quantization and non-linearity errors.

The total error when reflected back into the input can be represented as

$$e_{\text{input}} = e1 + \sum_{m=1}^{n-1} \frac{e_{m+1}}{A^m} \qquad (9)$$

Equation (9) shows that as gain A increases, the effects of non-idealities of all stages after the first stage becomes smaller. Therefore, to limit the error of ADC to less than $\pm 1/2$ LSB,

$$e_m \le \frac{\text{Full Scaleoutput}}{2^{N+1}} A^{m-1} \qquad (10)$$

If the error in all stages are identical, *i.e.* $e = e_m$, then (9) becomes

$$e_m = e \left(1 + \sum_{m=1}^{n-1} \frac{1}{A^m} \right) = e \cdot M \qquad (11)$$

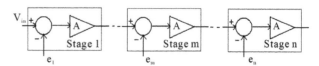

Figure 19. Signal flow graph of Pipelined ADC.

Referring to Equation (11), it is clear that the total error of all stages is equal to the first stage error multiplied by a factor M, which in turn depends on the gain A of the Sample and Hold amplifier. If $A = 1$ then $M = n$ and if $A \gg 1$ then $M = 1$. The boundary condition between these two cases is with $A = 2$ gives $M = 2$. Therefore, to make the first stage error to dominate over all other errors, the number of bits/stage must be chosen so that A is $>= 2$. Hence, more the number of bits/stage less is the non-linearity error in Pipelined ADCs. The sub converter and DAC errors can be eliminated by using redundancy and digital error correction mechanism and hence not considered here.

5. Conclusion

With pipelining, the maximum conversion frequency is seen to be almost independent of the number of stages. This allows the bit/stage is to be chosen to fulfill other requirements. This paper concludes that minimizing the bits/stage maximizes the conversion frequency and also minimizes the power dissipation and area requirements and the optimum value is 2 bits/stage. The effect of bits/stage on linearity is seen to be small but the linearity is seen to improve if we can increase the number of bits/stage. Confining the bits/stage to two, we get optimum results with respect to area, speed, power dissipation and linearity.

6. Acknowledgements

The authors would like to thank the management and principal, Varadha Reddy College of Engineering for providing relevant software and other facilities.

REFERENCES

[1] R. van de Plassey, "CMOS Analog-to-Digital and Digital-to-Analog Converters," Springer, Delhi, 2005.

[2] D. A. Johns and K. Martin, "Analog Integrated Circuit Design," Wiley, New Delhi, 2005.

[3] L. Brooks and H. S. Lee, "A Zero Crossing Based 8 b, 200 M/S Pipelined ADC," *IEEE ISSCC Digest Technical Papers*, San Francisco, 11-15 February 2007, pp. 460- 461.

[4] J. G. Peterson, "A Monolithic Video A/D Converter," *IEEE Journal of Solid-State Circuits*, Vol. 14, No. 6, 1979, pp. 932-937.

[5] K. Hadidi, G. C. Temes and K. W. Martin, "Error Analysis and Digital Correction Algorithms for Pipelined A/D

Optimizing the Stage Resolution of a 10-Bit, 50 Ms/Sec Pipelined A/D Converter & Its Impact on Speed, Power, Area, and Linearity

157

Converters," *Digest Technical Papers, IEEE International Symposium Circuits and Systems*, New Orleans, 1-3 May 1990, pp. 1709-1712.

[6] T. Matsuura, *et al.*, "An 8 b 20 MHz CMOS Half-Flash A/D Converter," *IEEE International Solid-State Circuits Conference*, San Francisco, 17-19 February 1988, pp. 220- 221.

[7] B. Razavi, "Design of Analog CMOS Integrated circuits," Tata McGraw-Hill, Bangalore, 2002.

[8] J. P. Li and U.-K. Moon, "A 1.8-V 67-mW 10-Bit 100-M/S Pipelined ADC Using Time-Shifted CDS Technique," *IEEE Journal of Solid-State Circuits*, Vol. 39, No. 9, 2004, pp. 1468-1476.

[9] T. B. Cho and P. R. Gray, "A 10-b, 20-Msample/s, 35 mW Pipeline A/D Converter," *IEEE Journal of Solid-State Circuits*, Vol. 30, No. 3, 1995, pp. 166-172.

[10] R. J. Baker, "CMOS Mixed-Signal Circuit Design," 2nd Edition, IEEE Press, Piscataway, 2009.

[11] J. K. Fiorenza, T. Sepke, P. Holloway, C. G. Sodini and H. S. Lee, "Comparator-Based Switched Capacitor Circuits for Scaled CMOS Technologies," *IEEE Solid-State Circuits*, Vol. 41, No. 12, 2006, pp. 2658-2668.

[12] S. H. Lewis, *et al.*, "A 10-b 20-Msample/s Analog-to-Digital Converter," *IEEE Journal Solid-state Circuits*, Vol. 27, No. 3, 1992, pp. 351-358.

21

Low Input and High Output Impedances Current-Mode First-Order Allpass Filter Employing Grounded Passive Components

Jiun-Wei Horng[*], **Chun-Li Hou, Yi-Sing Guo, Chih-Hou Hsu, Dun-Yih Yang, Min-Jie Ho**

Department of Electronic Engineering, Chung Yuan Christian University, Chung-Li, Chinese Taipei

ABSTRACT

A current-mode low input and high output impedances first-order allpass filter using two multiple output second-generation current conveyors (MOCCIIs), one grounded capacitor and one grounded resistor is presented. The suggested filter uses a canonical number of passive components without requiring any component matching condition. The frequency responses simulation results of the proposed filter confirm the theoretical analysis.

Keywords: Second-Generation Current Conveyor; First-Order Filter; Allpass; Current-Mode

1. Introduction

Current conveyors (CCs) are receiving much attention for their potential advantages such as inherent wider signal bandwidths, simpler circuitry and larger dynamic range [1,2]. Current-mode active filters with low input impedance and high output impedance are of great interest because they can be directly connected in cascade to implement higher order filters [3,4]. Besides the use of only grounded capacitor and resistor are beneficial from the point of view of integrated circuit fabrications [5,6]. Several current-mode first-order allpass filters using various active components have been reported. Some circuits use two current conveyors to realize such a first-order allpass filter function with high output impedance [7-9]. However, the passive components they used are not canonical and they require passive components matching conditions [7,8]. Moreover, these circuits [7-9] have not the advantage of low input impedance. The first-order allpass filters [10,11] each uses two current conveyors, one grounded capacitor and one grounded resistor with low input and high output impedances. The first-order allpass filter [12] uses one Z-copy current inverter transconductance amplifier and one grounded capacitor with low input and high output impedances. However, the output terminals of these circuits [10-12] require the connection of two current output terminals. This solution will degrade the final output impedance because of the parallel connection of two individual output impedances [13]. Some first-order allpass circuits

each use one active component [14] were presented. However, these circuits require passive matching conditions and the input impedances of are not low. Some first-order circuits use one active element, one capacitor and one resistor [15-17] were presented. However, these circuits have not the advantage of low input impedance. In 2009, a current-mode first-order allpass filter uses one current differencing transconductance amplifier (CDTA) and one grounded capacitor with low input impedance and high output impedance was presented [18]. As the CDTA is equivalent to the circuit composed of two second-generation current conveyors (CCIIs) with a transconductance amplifier [18], the CDTA is a relative complex device with respect to CCII.

In this paper, a new current-mode first-order allpass filter using two multiple output second-generation current conveyors (MOCCIIs), one grounded capacitor and one grounded resistor are presented. The proposed circuit has the advantages of low input and high output impedances and without requiring any element matching condition.

The rest of the paper is presented as follows. In Section 2 we present the proposed current-mode first-order allpass filter circuit. Section 3 discusses the active and passive sensitivities of the proposed filter. Section 4 discusses the influences of parasitic elements on the proposed circuit. The frequency responses simulation results are presented in Section 5. Section 6 concludes the paper.

2. Proposed Circuit

Using standard notation, the port relations of a MOCCII

---

[*]Corresponding author.

can be characterized by $v_x = v_y$, $i_{zk} = \pm i_x$ and $i_y = 0$. Considering the proposed current-mode circuit in **Figure 1**, the current transfer function can be expressed as

$$\frac{I_{out}}{I_{in}} = \frac{sCR-1}{sCR+1} \quad (1)$$

From (1) it can be seen that a first-order allpass response is obtained from I_{out}. Because the input terminal of the proposed first-order allpass filter is connected directly to the x terminal of MOCCII (1) and the y terminal of MOCCII (1) is grounded, the input terminal has the advantage of low input impedance. Because the I_{out} output terminal is taken out directly from the z_{22+} terminal of the MOCCII (2), the I_{out} output terminal has the advantage of high output impedance. The proposed circuit uses only one grounded resistor and one grounded capacitor, the use of only grounded capacitor and resistor are beneficial from the point of view of integrated circuit fabrications [5,6].

3. Non-Ideality Analysis of the MOCCIIs

Taking into consideration the MOCCII non-idealities, the port relations of MOCCII can be expressed as

$$v_x = \beta v_y \text{ and } i_z = \pm \alpha_k i_x \quad (2)$$

where $\alpha_k = 1 - \varepsilon_{ki}$ and $\varepsilon_{ki}(|\varepsilon_{ki}| \ll 1)$ denotes the current tracking error, $\beta = 1 - \varepsilon_v$ and $\varepsilon_v(|\varepsilon_v| \ll 1)$ is the input voltage tracking error of a MOCCII. Reanalysis of the filter circuit in **Figure 1** yields the following modified transfer functions:

$$\frac{I_{out}}{I_{in}} = \frac{sCR\alpha_{12}\alpha_{22} - \alpha_{11}\alpha_{22}\beta_2}{sCR + \alpha_{21}\beta_2} \quad (3)$$

The cutoff frequency is obtained by

$$\omega_c = \frac{\alpha_{21}\beta_2}{CR} \quad (4)$$

The active and passive sensitivities are low and obtained as $S_{C,R}^{\omega_c} = -1$; $S_{\alpha_{21},\beta_2}^{\omega_c} = 1$.

4. Influences of Parasitic Elements

A non-ideal MOCCII model is shown in **Figure 2** [19]. It is shown that the real MOCCII has parasitic resistors and capacitors from the y and z terminals to the ground, and also, a series resistor at the input terminal x. Taking into account the non-ideal MOCCIIs and assuming the circuits are working at frequencies much lower than the corner frequencies of $\alpha_k(s)$ and $\beta(s)$, namely, $\alpha_k \cong \beta \cong 1$. The transfer functions of **Figure 1** become

$$\frac{I_{out}}{I_{in}} = \frac{\left[s(C'-C_{z12})-(G'-G_a)\right]G_{x2}}{s^2 C'C_{z12} + s(C'G_{x2}+C'G'+C_{z12}G_a+C_{z12}G_{x2})+G'G_{x2}+G'G_a+G_aG_{x2}} \quad (5)$$

where $C' = C + C_{z11} + C_{y2} + C_{z21}$, $G' = G + G_{z12}$, $G_a = G_{z11} + G_{y2} + G_{z21}$.

In Equation (5), undesirable factors are yielded by the non-idealities of the MOCCIIs. The effects of capacitance C_{z12} become non-negligible at very high frequencies. To minimize the effects of the MOCCIIs' non-idealities, the operation angular frequency should restricted to the following condition

$$\omega \ll \sqrt{\frac{G'G_{x2}+G'G_a+G_aG_{x2}}{C'C_{z12}}} \quad (6)$$

5. Simulation Results

HSPICE simulations were carried out to demonstrate the feasibility of the proposed circuit in **Figure 1** using 0.18 μm, level 49 MOSFET from TSMC. The MOCCII was realized by the CMOS implementation in **Figure 3** [20] with the NMOS and PMOS transistor aspect ratios W/L = 4.5 u/0.9 u and W/L = 9 u/0.9 u, respectively.

Figure 4 represents the magnitude and phase responses of the first-order allpass filters, designed with $f_c = 3.979$ MHz: $C = 10$ pF and $R = 4$ kΩ. The power supply was ±1.25 V. The bias voltages are $V_b = -0.6$ V.

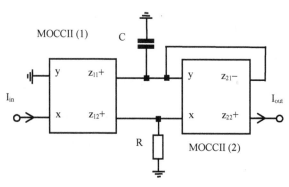

Figure 1. The proposed current-mode first-order filter.

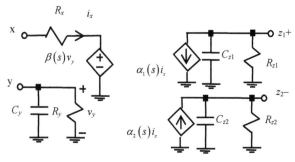

Figure 2. The non-ideal MOCCII model.

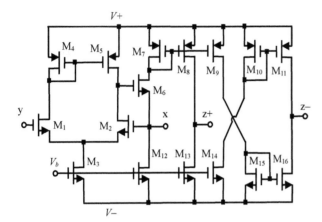

Figure 3. The CMOS MOCCII implementation.

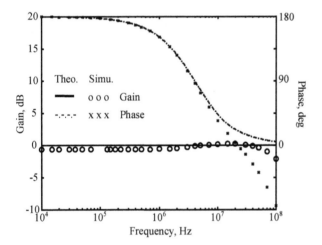

Figure 4. Simulation results of the proposed current-mode first-order allpass filter.

6. Conclusion

A new current-mode first-order filter configuration using two MOCCIIs, one grounded capacitor and one grounded resistor is presented. The proposed circuit has the advantages of low input and high output impedances, using grounded passive components and without requiring any element matching condition.

REFERENCES

[1]   C. Toumazou, F. J. Lidgey and D. G. Haigh, "Analog IC Design: The Current-Mode Approach," Peter Peregrinus, London, 1990.

[2]   J. W. Horng, Z. R. Wang and C. C. Liu, "Voltage-Mode Lowpass, Bandpass and Notch Filters Using Three Plus-Type CCIIs," *Circuits and Systems*, Vol. 2, No. 1, 2011, pp. 34-37.

[3]   A. M. Soliman, "Current Mode Universal Filter," *Electronics Letters*, Vol. 31, No. 17, 1995, pp. 1420-1421.

[4]   J. W. Horng, "Current-Mode and Transimpedance-Mode

Universal Biquadratic Filter Using Multiple Outputs CCIIs," *Indian Journal of Engineering & Materials Sciences*, Vol. 17, No. 3, 2010, pp. 169-174.

[5]   M. Bhushan and R. W. Newcomb, "Grounding of Capacitors in Integrated Circuits," *Electronic Letters*, Vol. 3, No. 4, 1967, pp. 148-149.

[6]   S. Minaei and E. Yuce, "All-Grounded Passive Elements Voltage-Mode DVCC-Based Universal Filters," *Circuits, Systems, and Signal Processing*, Vol. 29, No. 2, 2010, pp. 295-309.

[7]   J. W. Horng, C. L. Hou, C. M. Chang, W. Y. Chung, H. L. Liu and C. T. Lin, "High Output Impedance Current-Mode First-Order Allpass Networks with Four Grounded Components and Two CCIIs," *International Journal of Electronics*, Vol. 93, No. 9, 2006, pp. 613-621.

[8]   B. Metin, K. Pal and O. Ciceloglu, "All-Pass Filter for Rich Cascadability Options Easy IC Implementation and Tenability," *International Journal of Electronics*, Vol. 94, No. 11, 2007, pp. 1037-1045.

[9]   I. A. Khan, P. Beg and M. T. Ahmed, "First-Order Current Mode Filters and Multiphase Sinusoidal Oscillators Using CMOS MOCCIIs," *The Arabian Journal for Science and Engineering*, Vol. 32, No. 2C, 2007, pp. 119-126.

[10] S. Maheshwari, "Novel Cascadable Current-Mode First Order All-Pass Sections," *International Journal of Electronics*, Vol. 94, No. 11, 2007, pp. 995-1003.

[11] S. M. Al-Shahrani, "CMOS Wideband Auto-Tuning Phase Shifter Circuit," *Electronics Letters*, Vol. 43, No. 15, 2007, pp. 14-15.

[12] D. Biolek and V. Biolkova, "Allpass Filter Employing One Grounded Capacitor and One Active Element," *Electronics Letters*, Vol. 45, No. 16, 2009, pp. 807-808.

[13] J. W. Horng, "High Output Impedance Current-Mode Universal Biquadratic Filters with Five Inputs Using Multi-Output CCIIs," *Microelectronics Journal*, Vol. 42, No. 5, 2011, pp. 693-700.

[14] S. Minaei and M. A. Ibrahim, "General Configuration for Realizing Current-Mode First-Order All-Pass Filter Using DVCC," *International Journal of Electronics*, Vol. 92, No. 6, 2005, pp. 347-356.

[15] A. Toker, S. Ozoguz, O. Cicekoglu and C. Acar, "Current-Mode All-Pass Filters Using Current Differencing Buffered Amplifier and a New High-Q Bandpass Filter Configuration," *IEEE Transactions on Circuits and Systems-II: Analog and Digital Signal Processing*, Vol. 47, No. 9, 2000, pp. 949-954.

[16] S. Kilinc and U. Cam, "Current-Mode First-Order All-Pass Filter Employing Single Current Operational Amplifier," *Analog Integrated Circuits and Signal Processing*, Vol. 41, No. 1, 2004, pp. 47-53.

[17] S. Maheshwari, "A New Current-Mode Current-Controlled

All-Pass Section," *Journal of Circuits, Systems, and Computers*, Vol. 16, No. 2, 2007, pp. 181-189.

[18] A. Lahiri and A. Chowdhury, "A Novel First-Order Current-Mode All-Pass Filter Using CDTA," *Radioengineering*, Vol. 18, No. 3, 2009, pp. 300-305.

[19] E. Yuce, "Grounded Inductor Simulators with Improved

Low-frequency Performances," *IEEE Transactions on Instrumentation and Measurement*, Vol. 57, No. 5, 2008, pp. 1079-1084.

[20] W. Surakampontorm, V. Riewruja, K. Kumwachara and K. Dejhan, "Accurate CMOS-Based Current Conveyors," *IEEE Transactions on Instrumentation and Measurement*, Vol. 40, No. 4, 1991, pp. 699-702.

22

Power Efficient Battery Charger by Using Constant Current/Constant Voltage Controller

Falah Al Hassan

Department of Electrical and Electronics Engineering, Eastern Mediterranean University, Famagusta, North Cyprus

ABSTRACT

The Battery Charger Specification presents solution for rechargeable batteries used in portable electronic equipment such as laptop computer systems, cellular telephones and video cameras and the demands for low cost battery chargers are rising these days without give attention for the performance. The goal of the paper was combining high efficiency and versatility with low-cost design and this paper includes the design of the snubber cell, and the components of the current/voltage control charge method. This charger applies a relatively constant current and constant voltage to the battery indefinitely regardless of the AC input rang voltage all the equations described in this paper. The design of prototype converter is verified through an experimental result.

Keywords: Battery Charger; Flyback; Constant Currant; Constant Voltage; Snubber; Efficiency

1. Introduction

The main function of any battery charger is to cause current to flow back into a battery in the opposite direction from which current flowed during discharge. A battery on charge is not a fixed or static load. It has a voltage of its own and is connected to the charger so that the two voltages oppose each other. Thus, the current that flows is the result of the difference between the voltages of the charger and the battery and a function of the low ohmic resistance of the battery. The voltage of the battery itself rises during the charge, further opposing the flow of current as the charge progresses. The basic requirements of a charger as they relate to the battery are a safe value of charging current throughout the entire cycle, protection against conditions that would result in overcharge, and accurate termination of the charge when complete or reduction of the current to a level which provides a safe charge maintenance value. The desired characteristics of a charger as they relate to the user are Maximum reliability, Automatic operation to the degree practical in the application, Simplicity in design and construction, Good efficiency and power factor, Ease of operation, Reasonable cost and rapid charging.

Battery chargers are designed typically around two modes of operation, namely, constant-voltage charging and constant-current charging. The former utilizes a constant voltage source and an equivalent series resistance to control the amount of current that flows into the battery. As soon as the battery voltage is raised to the voltage sources, the converter must limit its current to prevent excessive dissipation. The latter, moreover, keeps the charging current constant until the battery voltage reaches a designated value [1].

Tiny switch reduces total component count, design size, weight and, at the same time increases efficiency when compared to MOSFET or RCC switch, **Figure 1** shows the schematic of the basic battery charger, which also serves as the reference circuit for the design proposes.

2. Proposed Battery Charger Topology

A charger drive circuit that consists of a flyback DC-DC converter with a snubber cell and a constant output current and voltage control as a driver for battery charger is proposed. With this drive circuit, the charger system becomes small size, and has a higher efficiency especially. The configuration for the circuit to charge battery by constant current and constant potential method is shown in **Figure 1**, where N_P and N_S winding is a high-frequency transformer, C_{DC} is the input filter capacitor, C_P is the output filter capacitor, V_{DC} is the DC input voltage generated by rectifying AC voltage using a bridge rectifier diode, V_o is the output voltage, I_o is the output current, D_R is a rectifier diode and U1 is a power management IC with a MOSFET incorporated in it connected to a photoelectrical coupler used for photo-electronic isolation. The proposed constant output current and voltage circuit is based on negative-feedback-control theory.

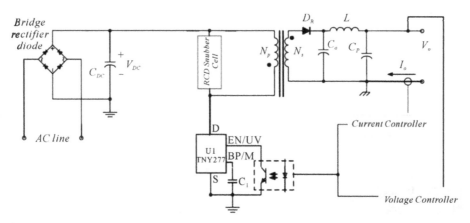

Figure 1. The basic battery charger circuit.

High-frequency transformer is used to transfer energy from input-end to output-end. During the "ON" period for the integrated MOSFET, transformer stores energy in its primary winding and the output current is supplied from the output filter capacity C_P only. When the MOSFET Turns "OFF", the energy stored in the power transformer is transferred to the battery load and to C_P as it replaces the charge it lost when it was alone delivering load current. Current controller and voltage controller generates a control signals by comparing the detected voltage with a predetermined reference voltage. U1 regulates the "ON/OFF" time of the integrated MOSFET according to the corresponding control signals, providing a constant output current and constant output voltage with high efficiency converting to the battery at last.

2.1. Power Management IC

A piece of power management IC-TNY277, a member of TinySwitch-III family produced by Power Integrations Inc., is used in the drive circuit. TNY277 incorporates a high-voltage power MOSFET with a power supply controller in one device, using an "ON/OFF" control scheme and offers a design flexible solution with a low system cost and extended power capability. The pin configuretion of TNY277 is shown in **Figure 1**, where D pin is the power MOSFET drain connection, providing internal operating current for both start-up and steady-state operation and S pin is internally connected to the output MOSFET source for high voltage power return and control circuit common. EN/UV pin has dual functions: enable input and line under-voltage sense. During normal operation, switching of the power MOSFET is controlled by this pin [2].

2.2. RCD Snubber Cell Selection

When the power MOSFET is turned off, there is a high voltage spike on the drain due to the transformer leakage inductance. This excessive voltage on the MOSFET may lead to an avalanche breakdown and eventually failure of the Tiny switch. Therefore, it is necessary to use an additional network to clamp the voltage. The RCD snubber circuit and MOSFET drain voltage waveform are shown in **Figures 2** and **3**, respectively. The RCD snubber network absorbs the current in the leakage inductance by turning on the snubber diode D_{sn} once the MOSFET drain voltage exceeds the voltage of node X as depicted in **Figure 2**. In the analysis of snubber network, it is assumed that the snubber capacitor is large enough that its voltage does not change significantly during one switching cycle. The snubber capacitor used should be ceramic or a ma- terial that offers low ESR. Electrolytic or tantalum capa- citors are unacceptable due to these reasons [3-5].

The first step in designing the snubber circuit is to determine the snubber capacitor voltage at the minimum input voltage and full load condition (V_{sn}). Once V_{sn} is determined, the power dissipated in the snubber network at the minimum input voltage and full load condition is obtained as

$$P_{sn} = \frac{\left(V_{ds}\right)^2}{R_{sn}} = \frac{1}{2} f_s L_{lK} \left(I_{ds\,Peak}\right)^2 \frac{V_{sn}}{V_{sn} - V_R} \qquad (1)$$

where $I_{ds\,peak}$ is the maximum peak current through the TNY277 at the minimum input voltage condition, f_s is the TNY277 switching frequency, L_{lK} is the leakage in-ductance, V_{sn} is the snubber capacitor voltage at the minimum input voltage and full load condition, V_R is the reflected output voltage and R_{sn} is the snubber resistor. V_{sn} Should be larger than V_R and it is typical to set V_{sn} to be 2.5 times V_R. Too small a V_{sn} results in a severe loss in the snubber network as shown in Equation (1). The leakage inductance is measured at the switching frequency on the primary winding with all other windings shorted. Then, the snubber resistor with proper rated wattage should be chosen based on the power loss. The maximum ripple of the snubber capacitor voltage is obtained as

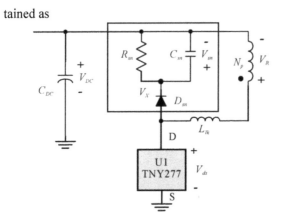

Figure 2. RCD snubber circuit.

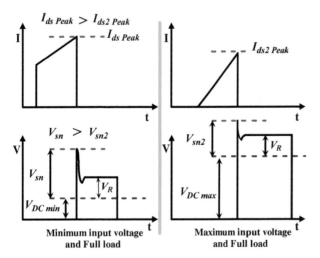

Figure 3. MOSFET drain voltage and snubber capacitor voltage.

$$\Delta V_{sn} = \frac{V_{sn}}{C_{sn} R_{sn} f_s} \tag{2}$$

where f_s is the TNY277 switching frequency. The snubber capacitor voltage (V_{sn}) of Equation (7) is for the minimum input voltage and full load condition, When the converter is designed to operate in CCM under this condition, the peak drain current together with the snubber capacitor voltage decrease as the input voltage increases as shown in **Figure 3**. The peak drain current at the maximum input voltage and full load condition ($I_{ds\,Peak}$) is obtained as

$$I_{ds\,Peak} = \sqrt{\frac{2 P_{in}}{f_s L_P}} \tag{3}$$

where the maximum input power P_{in}, is given by

$$P_{in} = \frac{P_o}{\eta} \tag{4}$$

where P_o is the output power and the η is the circuit efficiency.

And the transformer primary side inductance L_P is given by

$$L_P = \frac{\left(V_{DC\,min} D_{max}\right)^2}{2 P_{in} f_s k} \tag{5}$$

where k is the is the ripple factor in full load and minimum input voltage condition and $V_{DC\,min}$ is the minimum DC link voltage and the maximum duty cycle ratio D_{max} is given by

$$D_{max} = \frac{V_R}{V_{DC\,min} + V_R} \tag{6}$$

the snubber capacitor voltage under maximum input voltage and full load condition is obtained as

$$V_{sn2} = \left(\frac{V_R + \sqrt{\left(V_R\right)^2 + 2 R_{sn} f_s L_{IK} \left(I_{ds\,Peak}\right)^2}}{2} \right) \tag{7}$$

where f_s is the TNY277 switch frequency, L_{IK} is the primary side leakage inductance, V_R is the reflected output voltage and R_{sn} is the snubber resistor.

From Equation (7), the maximum voltage stress on the internal MOSFET is given by

$$V_{ds\,max} = V_{DC\,max} + V_{sn2} \tag{8}$$

where is maximum DC link voltage $V_{DC\,max}$ given by

$$V_{DC\,max} = \sqrt{2} V_{line\,max} \tag{9}$$

in this section the snubber cell elements selected successfully to improve the efficiency and performance of the proposed charger.

2.3. Analysis for the Constant-Output-Current and Constant-Output Voltage Circuit

In general, a battery charger employs constant current (CC)/constant voltage (CV) control circuit for an optimal charge of a battery. **Figure 4** shown a constant current (CC)/constant voltage (CV) circuit based on the flyback converter is proposed in this paper, a simple, low cost circuit using a comparator (U3) and shunt regulator (U4), being validated with a parametric detailed analysis provided in this section.

DC input voltage V_{DC} is generated by rectifying AC input voltage V_{AC} using a bridge rectifier, and its maximum $V_{DC\,max}$ is specified in Equation (9).

Assume that the switching frequency and the "ON" period for the power MOSFET are f_s and t_{on}, respectively. Then duty ratio D is defined according to the following equation:

$$D = f_s \cdot t_{on} \tag{10}$$

The input power P_i for the drive circuit is calculated by Equation (4) where P_o is the output power and the η is the circuit efficiency. Thus the average primary current I_i

is represented as follows:

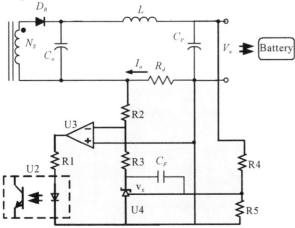

Figure 4. CC/CV control circuit for battery charger.

$$I_i = \frac{P_i}{V_{DC\,max}} = \frac{P_o}{\eta \cdot V_{DC\,max}} \quad (11)$$

Assume that the initial current in primary winding is zero ampere.

During the MOSFET "ON" period, there is a fixed voltage across primary winding and current in it ramps up linearly. At the end of the "ON" period, the primary current has ramped up to I_p, as shown in **Figure 5(a)**. The relationship between I_i and I_p can be represented as follows:

$$I_p = \frac{2I_i}{f \cdot t_{on}} \quad (12)$$

The power output of the flyback circuit is determined by the primary inductance L_P and the primary current I_p, where L_P can be calculated as

$$L_P = \frac{V_{DC\,max} \cdot t_{on}}{I_p} \quad (13)$$

When MOSFET turns "OFF", the current in the magnetizing inductance forces a reversal of polarities on primary winding. Since the current in an inductor cannot change instantaneously, at the instant of turn "OFF", the primary current transfers to the secondary at an amplitude

$$I_s = I_p \cdot \frac{N_p}{N_s} \quad (14)$$

where N_p, N_s, are the primary and secondary winding turns. During the MOSFET "OFF" period, the secondary current ramps down linearly, shown in **Figure 5(b)**, with an average value calculated as

$$I_{av} = \frac{I_s\left(1 - f \cdot t_{on}\right)}{2} \quad (15)$$

Finally, from (10)-(14) and by using Equation (4), the

circuit output voltage V_o can be represented as the following equation:

$$V_o = \eta \cdot \frac{V_{DC\,max}}{N} \cdot \left(\frac{f \cdot t_{on}}{1 - f \cdot t_{on}}\right) \quad (16)$$

where N is the primary/secondary turns ratio. Assume that the reference voltage in **Figure 4** is V_{ref}, the voltage detected by R_d is V_d and the voltage across the zener diode U4 is V_z, then the V_r and V_d is given by follwing equations:

$$V_r = V_z\left(\frac{R2}{R3 + R2}\right) \quad (17)$$

$$V_d = I_o \cdot R_d \quad (18)$$

when $V_d > V_r$ the photoelectrical coupler (U2) and the MOSFET turns "OFF" to reduce the output current. On the contrary, if $V_d < V_r$, the photoelectrical coupler leaves off work and the MOSFET turns "ON", helping increasing the output current.

Constant voltage (CV) control: The voltage divider network of R_4 and R_5 should be designed to provide V_z to the reference pin of the U4. The relationship between R_4 and R_5 is given by

$$R_5 = \frac{V_z \cdot R_4}{V_O - V_z} \quad (19)$$

where V_o is the output voltage. By Assuming R_4 it is easily to obtained R_5.

The feedback capacitor (C_F) introduces an integrator for CV control. To guarantee stable operation, C_F of 470 nF is chosen.

R_1 should be designed to provide proper operating current for the shunt regulator (U4) and to guarantee the full swing of the feedback voltage for the TINY 277 Switch.

Finally a snubber cell and constant output current and constant output voltage elements are obtained thus the final scheme of the proposed fly back converter is shown in **Figure 6**.

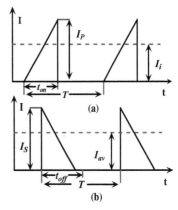

Figure 5. Current waveform in primary winding (a) and (b)

secondary winding.

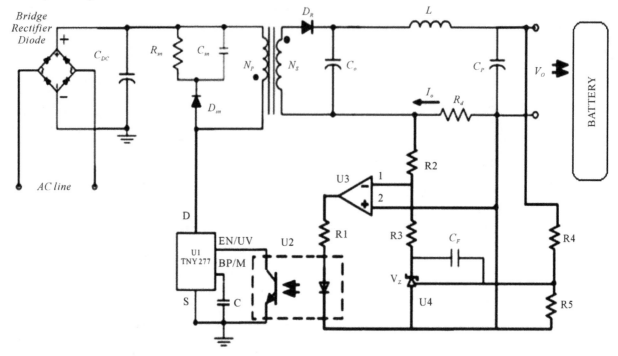

Figure 6. The final scheme of the proposed fly back converter.

3. Experimental Result of Proposed Charger

In order to show the validity of the proposed battery charger presented in this paper, the fly back converter with snubber cell and constant current/constant voltage controller has been built and fabricated with an input range of 85 - 256 AC voltage and the output of 5 V/1 A with 94% efficiency. All the circuit elements values and part number based on **Figure 6** are given in **Table 1** in Appendix.

Under a constant input of 85 V AC the output voltage vs the output currant is shown in **Figure 7** and **Figure 8** shows the TNY277 drain voltage V_{ds} and drain current I_{ds} waveforms under a constant input of 85 V AC.

Under an input range of 85 - 265 V AC the circuit output voltage approximately 5 V and the output current approximately 1 A as shown in **Figures 9** and **10** respectively also the proposed circuit efficiency according the input AC voltage range is clearly shown in **Figure 11**.

4. Conclusion

A constant output current and constant output voltage and snubber circuit based on the flyback converter is investigated and a circuit prototype with an output of 5 V/1 A is designed and fabricated the experiments results suggest that the proposed driving method has a high accuracy, good stability and high efficiency. The simulations and experimental results have proven good performances and verify the feasibility of the proposed

driving method, and it's most effective under different

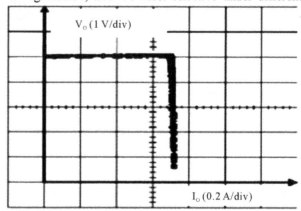

Figure 7. Output voltage vs output current.

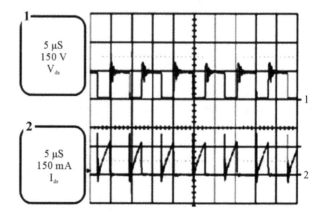

Figure 8. Waveforms of drain current and voltage at 85 AC voltage at full load condition.

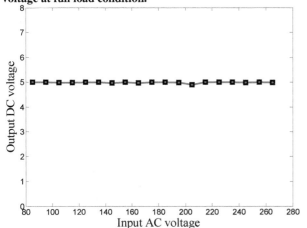

Figure 9. Output voltage vs input AC voltage.

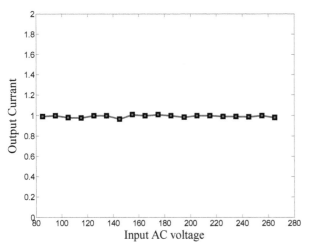

Figure 10. Output current vs input AC voltage.

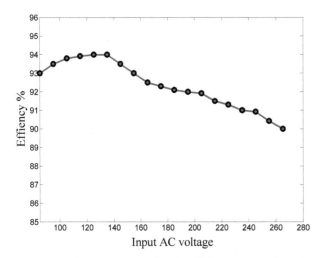

Figure 11. The proposed circuit efficiency according the input AC voltage range.

conditions of industrial applications.

5. Acknowledgements

I would like to express my sincere gratitude to Prof. Dr. Osman Kukrer for his invaluable help and support all over this work.

REFERENCES

[1] N. K. Poon, B. M. H. Pong and C. K. Tse, "A Constant-Power Battery Charger with Inherent Soft Switching and Power Factor Correction," *IEEE Transaction on Power Electronics*, Vol. 18, No. 6, 2003, pp. 1262-4269.

[2] T. Liu, S. Wang, S. Song and Y. Ai, "Research on High Efficiency Driving Technology for High Power LED Lighting," *Asia-Pacific of Power and Energy Engineering Conference*, Chengdu, 28-31 March 2010, pp. 1-4.

[3] P. C. Todd, "Snubber Circuits: Theory, Design and Applications," Texas Instrument, Dallas, 2001.

[4] S. J. Finney, B. W. Williams and T. C. Green "RCD Snubber Revisited," *IEEE Transaction on Industry Application*, Vol. 32, No. 1, 1996, pp. 155-160.

[5] S. Y. R. Hui and H. Chung, "Resonant and Soft-Switching Converters," In: M. H. Rashid, Ed., *Power Electronics Handbook*, Academic Press, Cambridge, 2000, pp. 271-304.

Appendix

The table bellow shows the elements values and part numbers of the proposed charger.

Table 1. The proposed circuit elements value and part numbers.

Circuit Elements	Values	Part number
C_{DC}	6.8 µF	Any
R_{sn}	270 KΩ	Any
C_{sn}	470 ρF	Any
C_o	330 µF	Any
C_p	330 µF	Any
C_F	470 µF	Any
C	1 nF	Any
L	1.8 µH	Any
R_1	56	Any
R_2	1 KΩ	Any
R_3	3.9 KΩ	Any
R_4	2 KΩ	Any
R_5	2 KΩ	Any
R_d	0.56 Ω	Any
D_{sn}	-	UF4007
D_R	-	SB360
U1 (switch)	-	TNY277 switch
U2 (photoelectrical coupler)	-	H11A817A
U3 (comparator)	-	KSP2222
U4 (zener diode)	-	KA431
Transformer winding	-	EER1616
Bridge rectifier diodes	-	1N4007

23

An Enhanced Bulk-Driven Folded-Cascode Amplifier in 0.18 μm CMOS Technology

Arash Ahmadpour[1,2], Pooya Torkzadeh[2]

[1]Department of Electronic Engineering, Islamic Azad University, Lahijan Branch, Lahijan, Iran
[2]Department of Electronic Engineering, Islamic Azad University, Science and Research Branch, Tehran, Iran

ABSTRACT

A new configuration of Bulk-Driven Folded-Cascode (BDFC) amplifier is presented in this paper. Due to this modifying, significant improvement in differential DC-Gain (more than 11 dB) is achieved in compare to the conventional structure. Settling behavior of proposed amplifier is also improved and accuracy more than 8 bit for 500 mV voltage swing is obtained. Simulation results using HSPICE Environment are included which validate the theoretical analysis. The amplifier is designed using standard 0.18 μm CMOS triple-well (level 49) process with supply voltage of 1.2 V. The correct functionality of this configuration is verified from –50°C to 100°C.

Keywords: Bulk-Driven Folded-Cascode (BDFC) Amplifier; DC-Gain; Bulk-Driven (BD); Folded-Cascode (FC); CMOS

1. Introduction

Design of high-performance integrated circuits is becoming increasingly challenging with the persistent trend toward reduced supply voltages, especially in analog part. This requires traditional analog circuit solutions to be replaced by new approaches to get the best performance and more flexible mixed-mode structure strategies that are compatible with future standard CMOS technology trends. This combination of the analog and digital parts should be done in an optimal way and the optimization process is application dependent [1-4]. The main bottleneck in analog circuits is the operational amplifier. Meanwhile, fully differential amplifiers have better performance compared to the single ended amplifiers. The single-stage amplifiers are inherently less prone to instability; most applications use the amplifier in a closed-loop feedback configuration which can result in instability. This possible instability is likely to manifest under high frequency operation. However, single-stage amplifiers suffer of lower voltage gain compare to the multi-stage amplifiers, especially in low-voltage applications and future deep sub-micron technologies. However multi-stage amplifiers introduce more low frequency poles and available compensation techniques limit the amplifier's speed; nevertheless, they consume much more power. On the other hand, achieving high gain/swing performance is hardly possible for single-stage amplifiers [5].

Fully differential folded-cascode (FC) amplifier is being used in many low-voltage and high bandwidth applications and does not suffer from "mirror pole" limitations. This structure is utilized in many cases and exhibits a superior performance because of its special features like potentially high gain, single parasitic pole, wide bandwidth, acceptable limitation of the common mode (CM) voltage range [5-8]. Besides, bulk-driven (BD) amplifiers or complex gain enhancement techniques are other techniques that have been already introduced to boost the voltage gain of amplifiers. Recently, a number of techniques for increase in the gain of BD amplifiers have been reported [9-11]; but for a sufficient gain, most of them utilize multi-stage or gain-boosting structures. This paper presents the design of a modified structure of single-stage BDFC amplifier that has significant performance in comparison with the conventional BDFC amplifier. It is shown that the proposed amplifier has higher DC-Gain, without degrading of the frequency and transient responses, due to the action of the new merge circuit topology. The proposed structure is done in 0.18 μm triple-well CMOS process for switched-capacitor applications. The design procedures of this paper are organized as follows. Section 2 analyses the small signal of conventional and proposed BDFC amplifiers and introduce the bias and common-mode feedback (CMFB) structures. Section 3 presents the simulation results. Finally the conclusion is given in Section 4.

2. Bulk-Driven Amplifier Circuits

2.1. Conventional Bulk-Driven Folded-Cascode Amplifier

A typical PMOS BDFC amplifier in differential mode capable of operating with low supply voltage is depicted in **Figure 1**. Because of high performance and wide applications, the detailed analysis of this structure has been explained in [5,6]. NMOS and PMOS transistors ac currents are derived by:

$$i_{ds} = g_m v_{gs} + g_{mb} v_{bs} + g_{ds} v_{ds} \qquad (1)$$

$$i_{sd} = g_m v_{sg} + g_{mb} v_{sb} + g_{ds} v_{sd} \qquad (2)$$

where g_m, g_{mb}, and g_{ds} are gate transconductance, bulk transconductance, and output conductance, respectively. By using Equations (1) and (2) and considering $V_{i-} = -V_{i+}$ and $V_{o-} = -V_{o+}$, the differential DC-Gain of corresponding amplifier is calculated by:

$$A_{v1} = -g_{mb1} \cdot R_{out} = -g_{mb1} \cdot \left(R_{o1} \| R_{o2} \right) \qquad (3)$$

$$R_{out} = \left[1 + r_{ds5} \left(g_{m5} + g_{mb5} \right) \left(r_{ds1} \| r_{ds3} \right) \right]$$
$$\quad \left\| \left[r_{ds7} + r_{ds9} \left(1 + r_{ds7} \left(g_{m7} + g_{m7} \right) \right) \right] \qquad (4)$$
$$\approx \left[g_{m5} r_{ds5} \left(r_{ds1} \| r_{ds3} \right) \right] \| g_{m7} r_{ds7} r_{ds9}$$

By applying good approximations, the differential DC-Gain of this amplifier is calculated as:

$$A_{v1} \approx -g_{mb1} \times \frac{g_{m5} r_{ds5} \left(r_{ds1} \| r_{ds3} \right) \times g_{m7} r_{ds7} r_{ds9}}{g_{m5} r_{ds5} \left(r_{ds1} \| r_{ds3} \right) + g_{m7} r_{ds7} r_{ds9}} \qquad (5)$$

In a typical 0.18 μm CMOS process, a voltage gain about of 39 dB and unity gain bandwidth (UGBW) of approximately 14.5 MHz with phase margin of 89.7° for a capacitive load of 1pF is achievable (bias current of branches is 40 μA). To increase the DC-Gain of conven-

tional FC amplifier, a new technique is proposed in Section B.

2.2. Proposed Structure

The To achieve high DC-Gain in amplifier, the bulk terminals of transistors M_5 to M_8 is used in new configuretion, which NMOS and PMOS devices are in opposite phases. These transistors are auxiliary transistors which increases the output resistance, so DC-Gain will boost. **Figure 2** shows the proposed amplifier without bias and CMFB circuits. Using Kirchhoff's Current Law at the node V_{o+}, the KCL Equation becomes:

$$i_{sd1} + i_{ds5} = i_{ds3} \qquad (6)$$

therefore, using Equations (1) and (2), result in:

$$-g_{mb1} \cdot v_{i+} = \frac{v_{D1}}{r_{ds1} \| r_{ds3}} + \frac{v_{D9}}{r_{ds9}} \qquad (7)$$

considering $i_{ds5} = i_{sd7} = i_{sd9}$ and $V_1 = -V_2$, and also using Equations (1) and (2), result in:

$$\left[r_{ds7} + r_{ds9} + r_{ds7} \cdot r_{ds9} \left(g_{m7} + g_{mb7} \right) \right] \cdot v_{D9}$$
$$= g_{mb7} \cdot r_{ds7} \cdot r_{ds9} \cdot v_1 + r_{ds9} \cdot v_{o+} \qquad (8)$$

$$r_{ds9} \cdot \left(1 + r_{ds5} \left(g_{m5} + g_{mb5} \right) \right) \cdot v_{D1} - r_{ds5} \cdot v_{D9}$$
$$= g_{mb5} \cdot r_{ds5} \cdot r_{ds9} \cdot v_1 - r_{ds9} \cdot v_{o+} \qquad (9)$$

$$r_{ds7} \cdot \left(1 + r_{ds5} \left(g_{m5} + g_{mb5} \right) \right) \cdot v_{D1}$$
$$+ r_{ds5} \cdot \left(1 + r_{ds7} \left(g_{m7} + g_{mb7} \right) \right) \cdot v_{D9} \qquad (10)$$
$$= \left(g_{m5} - g_{mb5} \right) \cdot r_{ds5} \cdot r_{ds7} \cdot v_1 + \left(r_{ds5} + r_{ds7} \right) \cdot v_{o+}$$

using (8) to (10), Equations are obtained as follows:

$$r_{ds7} \cdot r_{ds9} \cdot g_{mb7} \cdot \left(1 + r_{ds5} \left(g_{m5} + g_{mb5} \right) \right) \cdot v_{D1}$$
$$= r_{ds5} \cdot \left(1 + r_{ds7} \left(g_{m7} + g_{mb7} \right) \right) \cdot v_{D9} \qquad (11)$$

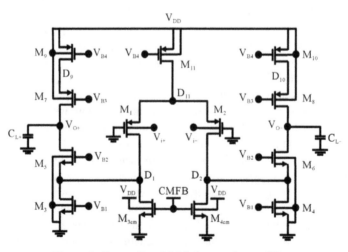

Figure 1. Conventional folded-cascode amplifier.

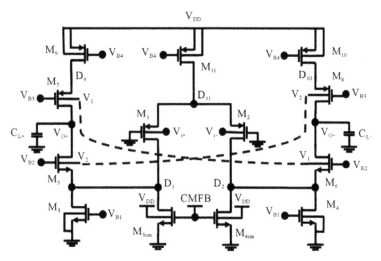

Figure 2. Proposed folded-cascode amplifier.

$$g_{mb7} \cdot r_{ds7} \cdot \left(1 + r_{ds5}\left(g_{m5} + g_{mb5}\right)\right) \cdot \left(g_{mb5} \cdot r_{ds9} - 1\right) \cdot v_{D1} \quad (12)$$
$$= \left(g_{mb5} \cdot r_{ds5} + g_{mb7} \cdot r_{ds7}\right) \cdot v_{o+}$$

$$r_{ds5} \cdot \left(1 + r_{ds7}\left(g_{m7} + g_{mb7}\right)\right) \cdot \left(g_{mb5} \cdot r_{ds9} - 1\right) \cdot v_{D9} \quad (13)$$
$$= r_{ds9} \cdot \left(g_{mb5} \cdot r_{ds5} + g_{mb7} \cdot r_{ds7}\right) \cdot v_{o+}$$

substituting (11) to (13) into (7) results in:

$$A_{v2} = -K_1 \cdot g_{mb1} \cdot R'_{out} = -K_1 \cdot g_{mb1} \cdot \left(R'_{o1} \| R'_{o2}\right) \quad (14)$$

$$R'_{out} = \left[K_2 \cdot \left(r_{ds1} \| r_{ds3}\right)\left(1 + r_{ds5}\left(g_{m5} + g_{mb5}\right)\right)\right]$$
$$\left\| \left[\left(r_{ds5}\left(1 + r_{ds7}\left(g_{m7} + g_{m7}\right)\right)\right)\right] \quad (15)\right.$$
$$\approx \left[K_2 \cdot g_{m5} r_{ds5}\left(r_{ds1} \| r_{ds3}\right)\right] \| g_{m7} r_{ds5} r_{ds7}$$

where K_1 and K_2 is

$$\begin{cases} K_1 = \dfrac{\left(g_{mb5} \cdot r_{ds9} - 1\right)}{\left(g_{mb5} \cdot r_{ds5} + g_{mb7} \cdot r_{ds7}\right)} > 1 \\ K_2 = g_{mb7} \cdot r_{ds7} \end{cases} \quad (16)$$

rewriting (14), so

$$A_{v2} \approx -g_{mb1} \times \frac{\left(g_{mb5} \cdot r_{ds9} - 1\right)}{\left(g_{mb5} \cdot r_{ds5} + g_{mb7} \cdot r_{ds7}\right)}$$
$$\times \frac{\left[g_{mb7} r_{ds7} \cdot g_{m5} r_{ds5}\left(r_{ds1} \| r_{ds3}\right)\right] \times g_{m7} r_{ds5} r_{ds7}}{\left[g_{mb7} r_{ds7} \cdot g_{m5} r_{ds5}\left(r_{ds1} \| r_{ds3}\right)\right] + g_{m7} r_{ds5} r_{ds7}} \quad (17)$$

It is clear that with increasing the K_1 and K_2, the output resistance will be boosted. A significant enhancement in the total value of A_{v2} is obtained conesquently. Indeed K_1 will be controlled by choosing appropriate biases and sizes of M_5 to M_8, especially controlling the bulk terminals of V_1 and V_2 of these transistors. However, $g_{mb5} r_{ds9}$ must be greater than 1, because excluding it might take K_1 to zero and decrease

the DC-Gain, so before fabrication, the proposed amplifier must be simulated in the corners of fabrication process and wide temperature ranges. In this design procedure, $K_1 = 1.33$ and $K_2 = 9.12$ are obtained, respectively. Bias circuit and CMFB block which utilized in the conventional and proposed structures is shown in **Figures 3** and **4**, respectively.

3. Simulation Results

In this section, simulation results of the proposed amplifier are shown and are compared with the conventional structure. Amplifiers have been designed in a typical 0.18 μm CMOS process with the same capacitor load and power consumption and then simulated by HSPICE environment using level 49 parameters. A closed-loop configuration with 1 pF capacitors is used to study the linearity and step response of the amplifiers, which is shown in **Figure 5**. With the mentioned value of capacitors, closed-loop gain of the amplifiers is approximately 0 dB.

HSPICE AC simulation results of the proposed and the conventional FC amplifiers are shown in **Figure 6**. The UGBW and phase margin of both structures are approximately equal. As demonstrated in **Figure 6**, the proposed amplifier achieves a DC-Gain about 50 dB which is 11 dB higher than DC-Gain of the conventional amplifier in the same power supply and process. It is considerable that by choosing a greater amount of both K_1 and K_2 in Equation (16) higher DC-Gain can be achieved. Total Harmonic Distortion (THD) of both amplifiers for input CM voltage up to 1.2 Vp-p was tested. For 50 KHz and 1.2 Vp-p input frequency, THD of conventional and proposed structures were –37.97 dB and –42.2 dB, respectively. **Figure 7** shows THD comparison of proposed and conventional amplifiers in different CM voltage swing. As demonstrated of these tests, the conventional FC amplifier achieves higher linearity in lower

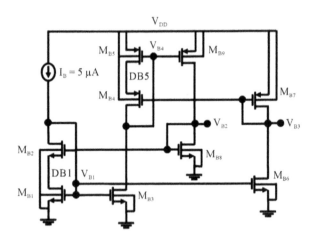

Figure 3. Bias circuit for both amplifiers.

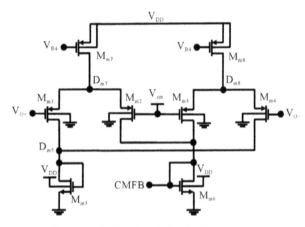

Figure 4. CMFB circuit for both amplifiers.

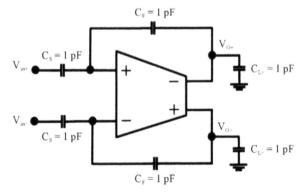

Figure 5. Closed-loop configuration.

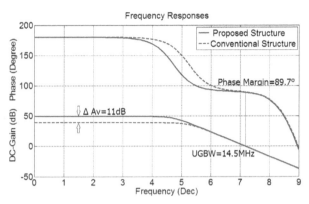

Figure 6. Open-loop frequency response of amplifiers.

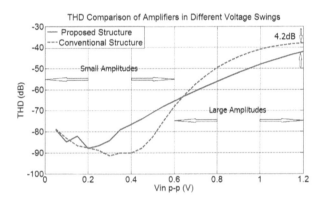

Figure 7. THD comparison of amplifiers in different voltage swing.

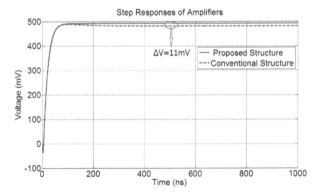

Figure 8. Step response of amplifiers for Vop-p = 500 mV.

output voltage amplitudes. However, in higher output voltage amplitudes, both amplifiers have acceptable linearity and eliminate undesirable harmonics. The accuracy of the amplifiers for different input step voltage amplitudes in unity gain configuration was also tested. The result of the step response simulation for 500 mV amplitude is illustrated in **Figure 8**, which demonstrate that the accuracy of the proposed amplifier is more than 8 bit for up to 500 mV output voltage swing.

Figure 9 illustrates the effective input transconductance of amplifiers as a function of the input CM voltage. It is obvious that both designs function correctly for rail-to-rail input CM voltage values with acceptable variations. Finally, the simulated performance of both amplifiers and its comparison with previous structures are summarized in **Table 1**. In order to compare the relative performance of structures, a new figure of merit (FOM) is used as follows:

$$\text{FOM} = 20\log\left\{\left(\frac{\text{UGBW} \times C_L}{P_{diss}}\right) \times \left(\frac{A_V \times V_{inp\text{-}p}}{THD}\right)\right\} \quad (18)$$

Table 1. Comparisons of characteristics of proposed amplifier with conventional and previous amplifiers.

Parameters	Conventional-BDFC	Proposed-BDFC	[7]	[8]	[9]	[10]	[11]
Technology	0.18 μm	0.18 μm	0.5 μm	0.18 μm	0.18 μm	0.18 μm	0.18 μm
Configuration/ Number of St.	Bulk-Driven Single-Stage	Bulk-Driven Single-Stage	Gate-Driven Single-Stage	Gate-Driven Single-Stage	Bulk-Driven Gain-Boosting	Bulk-Driven Two-Stage	Gate-Driven Single-Stage
V_{DD} (V)	1.2	1.2	3.3	1.8	0.8	0.5	1.2
DC-Gain (dB)	39	50	60	67	68	63	50.9
UGBW (MHz)	14.5	14.5	320	920	8.12	0.57	489.8
Phase-Margin(°)	89.7	89.7	82	67	89	50	77.2
THD (dB)	−37.97 (@1200 mV)	−42.2 (@1200 mV)	−58 (@26 mV)	NA	NA	−57.7 (@500 mV)	NA
Power (μW)	375	375	7500	3900	94	26	661.2
FOM (dB)	170	185	180	NA	NA	226.5	NA

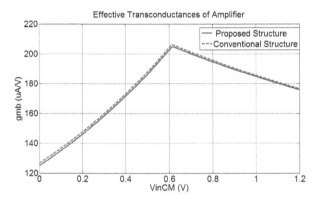

Figure 9. Effective bulk-transconductance of amplifiers from rail-to-rail.

The unit of proposed FOM is $(\text{MHz} \times \text{pF} \times \text{mV})/\text{mW}$, which this form the benchmark for the comparison with the results from this work.

4. Conclusions

In this paper, a novel approach to increase the DC-Gain of conventional BDFC amplifier is presented. With the presented method the DC-Gain of proposed amplifier increased more than 11 dB. All transistors in both amplifiers have same size and both designs consume 375 μW with 1 pF capacitive load.

Accuracy in the closed-loop configuration of amplifier in higher output voltage swings is the main advantage of the proposed structure. Step response simulations demonstrate that the accuracy of the proposed amplifier is more than 8 bit for up to 500 mV output voltages swing. Moreover, THD simulations show that proposed amplifier achieves reasonable linearity in comparison with conventional structure in different voltage swings, especially in large input signal swing.

REFERENCES

[1]   S. Chatterjee, Y. Tsvidis and P. Kinget, "Ultra-Low Voltage Analog Integrated Circuits," *IEICE Transactions on Electronics*, Vol. E89-C, No. 6, 2006, pp. 673-680.

[2]   S. Yan and E. Sanchez-Sinencio, "Low-Voltage Analog Circuit Design Techniques: A Tutorial," *IEICE Transactions*, Vol. E00-A, No. 2, 2000, pp. 179-196.

[3]   J. Ramirez-Angulo, R. G Carvajal and A. Torralba, "Low Supply Voltage High Performance CMOS Current Mirror with Low Input and Output Voltage Requirements," *IEEE Transactions on Circuits and Systems-II Express Briefs*, Vol. 51, No. 3, 2004, pp. 124-129.

[4]   ITRS, "The International Technology Roadmap for Semconductors," 2008. http://public.itrs.net

[5]   B. Razavi, "Design of Analog CMOS Integrated Circuits," McGraw Hill, New York, 2001.

[6]   P. R. Gray, P. J. Hurst, S. H. Lewis and R. G. Meyer, "Analysis and Design of Analog Integrated Circuits," 4th Edition, John Wiley & Sons, New York, 2001.

[7]   S. M. R. Hasan and N. Ula, "A Novel Feed-Forward Compensation Technique for Single-Stage Fully-Differential CMOS Folded-Cascode Rail-to-Rail Amplifier," *Electrical Engineering*, Vol. 88, No. 6, 2006, pp. 509-517.

[8]   B. Alizadeh and A. Dadashi, "An Enhanced Folded-Cascode Op-Amp in 0.18 μm CMOS Process with 67 dB DC-Gain," *IEEE International Conference, Faible Tension Faible Consummation*, 30 May-1 June 2011, pp. 87-90.

[9]   J. Rosenfeld, M. Kozak and E. G. Friedman "A Bulk-Driven CMOS OTA with 68-dB DC-Gain," *Proceedings of IEEE International Electronics Circuits Systems*, Tel-Aviv, 13-15 December 2004, pp. 5-8.

[10]   M. Trakimas and S. Sonkusale, "A 0.5 V Bulk-Input OTA with Improved Common-Mode Feedback for Low-Frequency Filtering Applications," *Analog Integrated Circuits and Signal Processing*, Vol. 59, No. 1, 2009, pp. 83- 89.

[11]   R. Assaad and J. Silva-Martinez, "Enhancing General Performance of Folded-Cascode Amplifier by Recycling Current," *Electronics Letters*, Vol. 43, No. 23, 2007, pp.

1243-1244.

24

Effect of Temperature & Supply Voltage Variation on Stability of 9T SRAM Cell at 45 nm Technology for Various Process Corners

Manisha Pattanaik[1], Shilpi Birla[2], Rakesh Kumar Singh[3]

[1]VLSI Group, Atal Bihari Vajpayee Indian Institute of Information Technology and Management, Gwalior, India
[2]Department of Electronics & Communications, Sir Padampat Singhania University, Udaipur, India
[3]Department of Electronics & Communications, Bipin Chandra Tripathi kumaon Engineering College, Dwarahat, India

ABSTRACT

Due to the continuous rising demand of handheld devices like iPods, mobile, tablets; specific applications like bio-medical applications like pacemakers, hearing aid machines and space applications which require stable digital systems with low power consumptions are required. As a main part in digital system the SRAM (Static Random Access Memory) should have low power consumption and stability. As we are continuously moving towards scaling for the last two decades the effect of this is process variations which have severe effect on stability, performance. Reducing the supply voltage to sub-threshold region, which helps in reducing the power consumption to an extent but side by side it raises the issue of the stability of the memory. Static Noise Margin of SRAM cell enforces great challenges to the sub threshold SRAM design. In this paper we have analyzed the cell stability of 9T SRAM Cell at various processes. The cell stability is checked at deep submicron (DSM) technology. In this paper we have analyzed the effect of temperature and supply voltage (Vdd) on the stability parameters of SRAM which is Static Noise Margin (SNM), Write Margin (WM) and Read Current. The effect has been observed at various process corners at 45 nm technology. The temperature has a significant effect on stability along with the Vdd. The Cell has been working efficiently at all process corners and has 50% more SNM from conventional 6T SRAM and 30% more WM from conventional 6T SRAM cell.

Keywords: DSM Technology; Process Corners; Write Margin; Read Current; Static Noise Margin

1. Introduction

With continuous scaling of the supply voltages, the SRAM cell does not function properly at sub-threshold supply voltage ranges as at theses voltages the SNM deteriorates and is not enough for reliable and stable operation. With the increased complexity of the microprocessors and digital signal processors on-chip register files and SRAMs are expected to increase significantly while maintaining the stability. SRAM caches represent an important part of modern processors as they have an increasingly large influence on the system speed and power consumption [1]. SRAMs are expected to increase significantly as the demands of handheld devices are increasing day by day but stability demand is rising.

Various SRAMs from 6T to 13T [2-5] has been proposed to improve the stability and performance along with low power consumption. In this paper we have analyzed the stability and leakage of our proposed SRAM PNN stack at various process corners. This cell is suitable and operational for deep sub-threshold technology and is op-erational at all the process corners. Process variation like dopant variation, temperature, and threshold affects the overall performance of the design at deep sub micron technology [6].

This paper is organized as follows: In Section 2 a brief overview is given about 6T SRAM cell, Section 3 deals with the proposed 9T SRAM cell whose analysis is to be done. Section 4 includes the Simulation & Analysis part and finally the conclusion.

2. Conventional 6T Sram Cell

In traditional 6T-SRAM as shown in **Figure 1**, it has one wordline and two bitlines which are required during a read and write operations. The cell must be both stable during a read event and writeable during a write event ignoring redundancy; such functionality must be preserved for each cell under worst-case variation. At the cell level, transistor strength ratios must be chosen such that cell static noise margin and write margin are both maintained, which presents conflicting constraints on the cell transistor strengths.

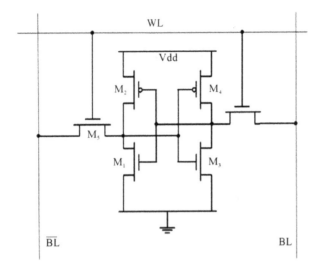

Figure 1. 6T SRAM cell.

For cell stability during a read, it is desirable to strengthen the storage inverters and weaken the pass-gates. The opposite is desired for cell write ability a weak storage inverter and strong pass-gates. This delicate balance of transistor strength ratios can be severely impacted by device variation, which dramatically degrades stability and write margins, especially in scaled technologies. Low supply voltages further exacerbate the problem as threshold voltage variation consumes a larger fraction of these voltage margins. Variability can thus limit the minimum operating voltage of SRAM.

3. 9T SRAM Cell-Working

The 9T SRAM cell is shown in **Figure 2**. This cell has 9T and it is like the conventional SRAM cell which has cross coupled inverters like the conventional cell. It is connected in PNN fashion that is one PMOS as Pull-up transistor and 2 NMOS one is for stacking purpose and the other Pull-down transistor. It has one discharging NMOS transistor ND. The RD signal is always connected to ground reference during the read operation. The data storage in the 9T cell is performed by the cross-couple inverters [7]. Two NMOS access transistors (PG) NA1 and NA2 connect to the virtual storage nodes (V1 & V2) to the write bitline pair when the write wordline (WDL) is on. N1 and N2 transistors are placed in between the pull-up PMOS transistors P1 and P2 and the pull-down NMOS transistors N3 and N4 of the cross-coupled inverters. RDL is read signal which controls the read port. N3 and N4 are the pull down transistors. During read the RDL signal is grounded so that there will be less power consumption. There is only one wordline for reading and writing. During write "1" keep BL as high and also WDL and RDL high. Similarly during write "0" we can keep BL as "0". During read keep WDL and RDL as "0".

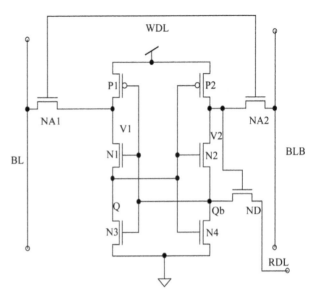

Figure 2. 9T SRAM cell.

4. Analysis of the Stablity of the Cell

In order to verify the robustness of an integrated circuit design, semiconductor manufacturers will fabricate corner lots, which are groups of wafers that have had process parameters adjusted according to these extremes, and will then test the devices made from these special wafers at varying increments of environmental conditions, such as voltage, clock frequency, and temperature, applied in combination (two or sometimes all three together) in a process called characterization. Corner-lot analysis is most effective in digital electronics because of the direct effect of process variations on the speed of transistor switching during transitions from one logic state to another, which is not relevant for analog circuits, such as amplifiers.

The stability of any SRAM cell is basically measure from the noise margin, write margin and read current of the cell [8]. We have analyzed the three parameters of stability at various process corners along with the temperature variation and voltage variations. We have mainly focused on three process variations which are of more concerned for digital applications. We have simulated the SRAM cell at 45 nm technology taking Vtn = 0.22 V and Vtp = |0.22| V.

4.1. Noise Margin Analysis

The Static Noise Margin (SNM) is the maximum amount of noise voltage that can be tolerated at the both inputs of the cross-coupled inverters in different directions while inverters still maintain bi-stable operating points and cell retains its data [8-10]. In other words, the Static Noise Margin (SNM) quantifies the amount of noise voltage required at the storage nodes of SRAM to flip the cell data. We have varied the temperature from –20°C to 125°C and the Vdd has been varied from 0.5 V to 1.0 V.

Reducing the Vdd will reduce the SNMAs the temperature is increased the SNM reduces in the three corners (TT, FF, FS) as shown in **Figures 3-5** respectively.

The highest SNM is 0.3949 V at 1.0 Vdd and at TT corner, for FF corner the highest SNM is 0.3649 V at 1.0 Vdd, and for FS corner the highest SNM is 0.3749 V at 1.0 Vdd. But the highest SNM is calculated at the lowest temperature. We have taken the temperature 50°C and varying Vdd and find the SNM which is given in **Table 1**.

4.2. Write Margin Analysis

Write Margin is an important parameter which ensures robust write operation. The Write Margin (WRM) is defined as the potential difference between the BL level at which the data is flipped and the end-point (e.g., GND). The effect of temperature and voltage variation is also analyzed for write margin. We have varied the temperature from –20°C to 125°C and the Vdd has been varied from 0.5 V to 1.0 V. The write margin increases exponentially with Vdd and also incraeses as temperature incareses as shown in **Figures 6-8**.

The highest WM is 0.4859 V at 1.0 Vdd and at FS corner, for FF corner the highest WM is 0.4379 V at 1.0 Vdd, and for TT corner the highest SNM is 0.3771 V at 1.0 Vdd. But the highest SNM is calculated at the highest temperature and highest Vdd. We have taken the tem-

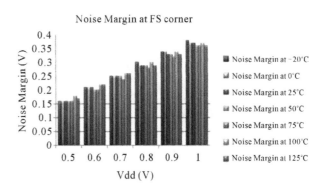

Figure 5. Noise margin at FS corner with respect to temperature variation.

Table 1. SNM at different process corners.

Vdd (V)	SNM at different corners (V)				
-	SS	TT	FF	SF	FS
0.5	0.184	0.184	0.174	0.184	0.124
0.6	0.234	0.224	0.214	0.224	0.174
0.7	0.274	0.264	0.254	0.274	0.214
0.8	0.324	0.304	0.284	0.314	0.254
0.9	0.364	0.344	0.314	0.354	0.294
1	0.404	0.374	0.334	0.394	0.324

perature 50°C and varying Vdd and find the WM which is given in **Table 2**.

4.3. Read Current Analysis

The read current in an SRAM memory cell is the current flowing from the precharged bit line (BL) along the conducting pass-gate (PG) transistor and the pull-down (PD) transistor to ground. We have varied the temperature from –20°C to 125°C and the Vdd has been varied from 0.5 V to 1.0 V. The read current decreases drastically with Vdd decreases and the effect of temperature is not very prominent as in **Figures 9-11**.

The highest read current is 31.6 μA at 1.0 Vdd and at FF corner, for FS corner the highest read current is 29.8 μA at 1.0 Vdd, and for TT corner the highest SNM is 23 μA at 1.0 Vdd. But the highest read current is calculated at the lower temperature and highest Vdd. We have taken the temperature 50°C and varying Vdd and find the read current which is given in **Table 3**.

5. Conclusion

In this paper we have anlaysed the stability parameters at various process corners to find the work ability of the cell and it has been successfully operative in all the process corners. It has been observed that cell is stable

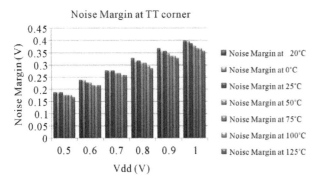

Figure 3. Noise margin at TT corner with respect to temperature variation.

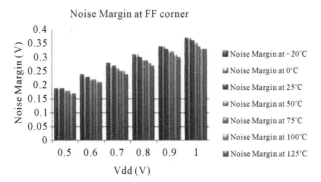

Figure 4. Noise margin at FF corner with respect to temperature variation.

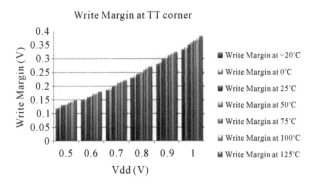

Figure 6. Write margin at TT corner with respect to temperature variation.

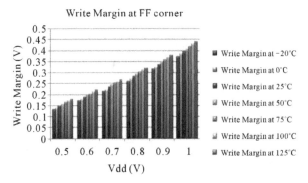

Figure 7. Write margin at FF corner with respect to temperature variation.

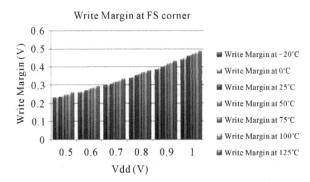

Figure 8. Write margin at FS corner with respect to temperature variation.

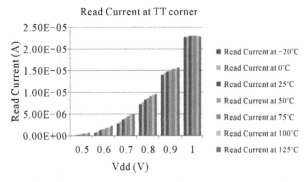

Figure 9. Read current at TT corner with respect to temperature variation.

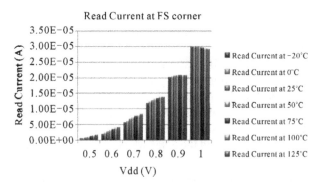

Figure 10. Read current at FS corner with respect to temperature variation.

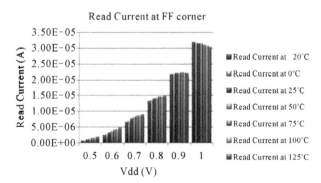

Figure 11. Read current at FF corner with respect to temperature variation.

Table 2. Write Margin at different process corners.

Vdd (V)	Write Margin at different corners (V)				
	SS	TT	FF	SF	FS
0.5	0.118	0.131	0.154	0.035	0.239
0.6	0.141	0.1618	0.194	0.066	0.271
0.7	0.172	0.2018	0.240	0.107	0.310
0.8	0.213	0.249	0.291	0.154	0.356
0.9	0.262	0.3010	0.346	0.206	0.406
1	0.314	0.3563	0.404	0.261	0.461

Table 3. Read current at different process corners.

Vdd (V)	Read current at different corners (A)				
	SS	TT	FF	SF	FS
0.5	7.59E−08	3.26E−07	1.22E−06	9.51E−08	9.68E−07
0.6	4.79E−07	1.43E−06	3.62E−06	5.58E−07	3.09E−06
0.7	1.88E−06	4.09E−06	7.91E−06	2.12E−06	7.06E−06
0.8	4.94E−06	8.67E−06	1.41E−05	5.45E−06	1.30E−05
0.9	9.85E−06	1.51E−05	2.20E−05	1.07E−05	2.06E−05
1	1.65E−05	2.30E−05	3.12E−05	1.76E−05	2.96E−05

Effect of Temperature & Supply Voltage Variation on Stability of 9T SRAM Cell at 45 nm Technology for Various Process Corners

179

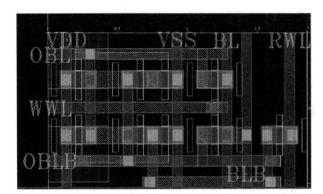

Figure 12. Layout of 9T SRAM cell.

with SNM at 0.8 V with 0.3 V which is higher by 50% from conventional 6T. The write ability of the cell at 0.8 V with temperature 50°C is also higher by the conventional 6T SRAM by 30%. The cell is also having low leakge current as the leakage current measure at 0.8 V at FF corner is 43 nA and the leakage current in the worst case is 68 nA. The cell area is 1.901 μm^2 which can be further optimized by sizing the cell. The cell layout is as shown in **Figure 12**. The cell is suitable for applications where stability and power are concerned.

6. Acknowledgements

The authors are grateful to their respective organizations for their encouragement and support.

REFERENCES

[1] B. H. Calhoun and A. P. Chandrakasan, "Static Noise Margin Variation for Sub-Threshold SRAM in 65 nm CMOS," *IEEE Journal of Solid-State Circuits*, Vol. 41, No. 7, 2006, pp. 1673-1679.

[2] M. Sinangil, N. Verma and A. P. Chandrakasan, "A Reconfigurable 8T Ultra-Dynamic Voltage Scalable (U-DVS) SRAM in 65 nm CMOS," *IEEE Journal of Solid-State Circuits*, Vol. 44, No. 11, 2009, pp. 3163-3173.

[3] Z. Y. Liu and V. Kursun, "Characterization of a Novel Nine-Transistor SRAM Cell," *IEEE Transaction of Very Large Scale Integration Systems*, Vol. 16, No. 4, 2008, pp. 488-492.

[4] S. Lin, Y.-B. Kim and F. Lombardi, "Design and Analysis of a 32 nm PVT Tolerant CMOS SRAM Cell for Low Leakage and High Stability," *Integration the VLSI Journal*, Vol. 43, No. 2, 2010, pp. 176-187.

[5] A. J. Bhavnagarwala, X. Tang and J. D. Meindl, "The Impact of Intrinsic Device Fluctuations on CMOS SRAM Cell Stability," *IEEE Journal of Solid-State Circuits*, Vol. 36, No. 4, 2001, pp. 658-665.

[6] Z. Guo, A. Carlson, L.-T. Pang, K. Duong, T.-J. K. Liu and B. Nikolic, "Large-Scale Read/Write Margin Measurement in 45 nm CMOS SRAM Arrays," *IEEE Symposium on VLSI Circuits Digest of Technical Papers*, Honolulu, 18-20 June 2008, pp. 42-43.

[7] R. K. Singh, S. Birla and M. Pattanaik, "Characterization of PNN Stack SRAM Cell at Deep Sub-Micron Technology with High Stability and Low Leakage for Multimedia Applications," *International Journal of Computer Applications*, Vol. 33, No. 1, 2011, pp. 13-17.

[8] J. J. Wang, S. Nalam and B. H. Calhoun, "Analyzing Static and Dynamic Write Margin for Nanometer SRAMs," *International Symposium on Low Power Electronics and Design*, Bangalore, 11-13 August 2008, pp. 129-134.

[9] E. Seevinck, *et al.*, "Static-Noise Margin Analysis of MOS SRAM Cells," *IEEE Journal of Solid-State Circuits*, Vol. 22, No. 5, 1987, pp. 748-754.

[10] S. Birla, M. Pattanaik and R. K. Singh, "Static Noise Margin Analysis of Various SRAM Topologies," *IACSIT International Journal of Engineering and Technology*, Vol. 3, No. 3, 2011, pp. 304-309.

25

Analytical and Numerical Model Confrontation for Transfer Impedance Extraction in Three-Dimensional Radio Frequency Circuits

Olivier Valorge[1], Fengyuan Sun[2], Jean-Etienne Lorival[2], Mohamed Abouelatta-Ebrahim[2,3],
Francis Calmon[2], Christian Gontrand[2]

[1]R3 Logic Inc., Monbonnot-Saint-Martin, France
[2]Université de Lyon, Villeurbanne, France
[3]Faculty of Engineering, Ain Shams University, Cairo, Egypt

ABSTRACT

3D chip stacking is considered known to overcome conventional 2D-IC issues, using through silicon vias to ensure vertical signal transmission. From any point source, embedded or not, we calculate the impedance spread out; our ultimate goal will to study substrate noise via impedance field method. For this, our approach is twofold: a compact Green function or a Transmission Line Model over a multi-layered substrate is derived by solving Poisson's equation analytically. The Discrete Cosine Transform (DCT) and its variations are used for rapid evaluation. Using this technique, the substrate coupling and loss in IC's can be analyzed. We implement our algorithm in MATLAB; it permits to extract impedances between any pair of embedded contacts. Comparisons are performed using finite element methods.

Keywords: Through Silicon Via (TSV); Green's Function; Transmission Line Model; Radio Frequency (RF); Transfer Impedance Extraction

1. Introduction

As the complexity of mixed digital-analog designs increases and the area of the current technologies decreases, substrate noise coupling in integrated circuits becomes a significant consideration in the design. Nowadays, nanotechnology and the development of semiconductor technology enable designers to integrate multiple systems into a single chip, not only in 2D (planar), but also in 3D (in the bulk). This design technology reduces cost, while improves performance and makes the system on chip possible. Through Silicon Vias (TSV) or through wafer interconnection is most likely the solution to go to 3D device stacking [1-3]. The potential benefits of 3D integration can vary depending on approach; they include multifunctionality, increased performance, reduced power, small form factor, reduced packaging, increased yield and reliability, flexible heterogeneous integration and reduced overall costs. A key study in a recent paper of ourselves [4] comes from the fact that, when, for instance, the MOS bulk-electrode is floating, the bulk potential becomes a function of the substrate perturbations and this affects, for instance, the value of the MOS threshold voltage which in turn varies the MOS drain current.

Also, the switching of the MOS drain current due to an applied square signal is a strong function of the MOS and the bulk capacitances. So, our aim was to de- termine the source of the bulk variation: the CMOS input voltage or the TSV HV (High Voltage: ~42 V) signal and hence evaluate the impact of the TSV on the CMOS inverter (**Figure 1**). The CMOS devices are implemented using the standard layers of the 0.35 μm BiCMOS ST Microelectronics-like technology and with threshold voltages of 0.65 V for nMOS and –0.6 V for pMOS.

2. CMOS Compact Model

To achieve this aim, basic simulations are performed using the SPICE models for the CMOS devices, the finite element method (FEM) for the bulk regions of the devices, and this mixed-mode simulation is performed using TCAD program packages. In the mixed mode simulation, we use the SPICE model parameters which are extracted by means of the ICCAP RF extraction program [5]. In this section the technological process steps of the CMOS in 0.35 μm BiCMOS technology is presented.

We start up with a lightly-doped P-type wafer (2E 15 cm^3) and form the buried N$^+$ layer by ion implantation of

Analytical and Numerical Model Confrontation for Transfer Impedance Extraction in Three-Dimensional
Radio Frequency Circuits

181

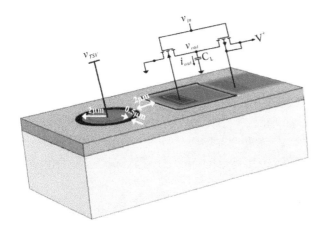

Figure 1. 3D cross-section of TSV-CMOS mixed mode coupling.

arsenic into the respective mask pattern. Afterwards, a high temperature anneal is performed to remove damage defects and to diffuse the arsenic into the substrate. During this anneal an oxide is grown in the buried N$^+$ windows to provide a silicon step for alignment of subsequent levels. Therefore, the nitride mask is selectively removed and the remaining oxide serves as blocking mask for the buried P$^+$ layer implant. After finishing the alignment of the buried layer and the deposition of the epitaxial-layer a twin well process is used to fabricate the N-well of the pMOS and the P-well of the nMOS. As compared to conventional CMOS a relatively short well drive-in (100 min) is performed at 1150°C. After the wells are fabricated, the whole wafer is planarized and a pad oxide is grown. The oxide is capped with a thick nitride. After patterning the active regions of the devices, an etch step is used to open up the field isolation regions. Prior to field oxidation, a blanket channel stop is implanted. Oxidation is used to fabricate a 300 nm thick field oxide. To minimize buried layer diffusion, the oxidation temperature is quite moderate (900°C). Then the nitride masks are removed from the active regions. We proceed with the resist strip and perform a pre-gate oxide etch to clean the oxide surface. A 7.6 nm thick gate oxide is grown on top. Then a polycrystalline silicon layer is deposited. This polysilicon layer is implanted with arsenic for the nMOS and boron for the pMOS; the dopants will diffuse out from the polysilicon layer at the final source-drain anneal. The polysilicon layer is patterned to define the CMOS gates. Phosphorus and boron are implanted to form shallow LDD regions for the nMOS and pMOS devices. Then the sidewall spacer formation is initiated. Therefore, an oxide layer is deposited and anisotropically etched back. Next, the source-drain regions are heavily doped by phosphorus and boron, which is depicted. Finally, the fabrication of the active regions is finished by the source-drain anneal. Hence, a 30 s long RTA anneal at 850°C is performed.

The schematic cross-section of the CMOS including the active area doping concentrations is shown in the **Figure 2**. The retrograde well utilizes high-energy implant to produce a self-aligned channel stop and an extremely shallow, low sheet-resistance while maintaining controllable, low channel threshold voltages. It shunts the vertical device which is the key to successfully harnessing the parasitic vertical bipolar transistor. Short channel effects can be minimized by increasing the background doping concentration and decreasing the gate oxide thickness. Shallow source/drain ($\approx$0.2 μm) is used to reduce short channel effects and overlap capacitance. The hot carrier effects are controlled by introducing the lightly-doped drains (LDD). In the light of the above mentioned technological steps, the simulated CMOS 2D cross-section is shown in **Figure 3** and the technological process steps are summarized in **Figure 4**. Extracted from typical characteristics (**Figure 5**) compact model electrical parameters for NMOS and PMOS are shown in **Table 1** (using LEVEL3 SPICE model). As an example, a 2D structure is shown in **Figure 6(a)**, with the TSV placed near the nMOS device with $T_{OXTSV} = 0.5$ μm and $V^+ = 1.2$ V. In this structure, the pMOS bulk and source electrodes are shorted and only the impact on the nMOS

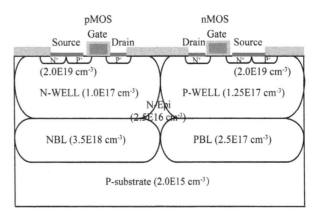

Figure 2. The schematic cross-section of the CMOS.

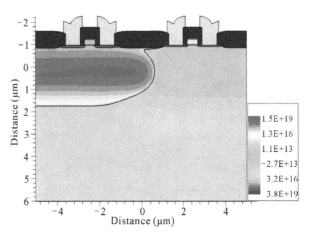

Figure 3. 2D cross-section of CMOS.

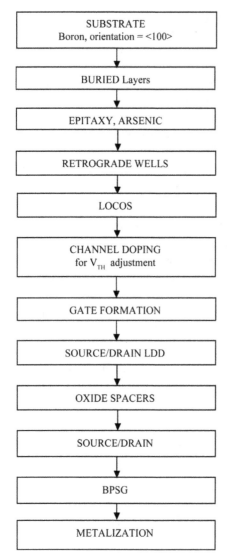

Figure 4. The process steps of a 0.35 μm BiCMOS technology.

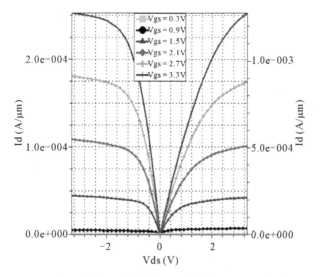

Figure 5. nMOS and pMOS; e.g. Id-Vd$_S$ characteristics.

Table 1. The SPICE model parameters of CMOS devices.

model nMOS (LEVEL = 3)	model pMOS (LEVEL 3)
+UO = 5.829856E+02	+UO = 95.7
+VTO = 5.362076E−01	+VTO = −5.593849E−01
+TOX = 7.600 n	+TOX = 7.600 n
+NSUB = 1.5E+17	+NSUB = 1.00E+17
+VMAX = 2.854458E+05	+VMAX = 3.067345E+04
+CJ = 5.0E−04	+CJ = 100.6 u
+MJ = 0.5	+MJ = 500.5 m
+CJSW = 5.0E−10	+CJSW = 50.30 p
+MJSW = 0.33	+MJSW = 500.5 m
+CGDO = 6.0E−09	+CGDO = 8.0E−09
+CGSO = 6.0E−09	+CGSO = 8.0E−09
+CGBO = 6.0E−09	+CGBO = 8.0E−09
+PB = 1	+PB = 982.3 m
+FC = 0.5	+FC = 500.0 m
+XJ = 200 n	+XJ = 200.00 n
+DELTA= 2.255185E−02	+DELTA = 3.291260E−02
+THETA = 0.08	+THETA = 36.9 m
+ETA = 0	+ETA = 100.0 m
+KAPPA = 0.6)	+KAPPA = 0.01)

is supposed as shown in **Figure 6(a)**. The potential distribution in the TSV-CMOS structure is shown in **Figure 6(a)**; it is clearly observed that nearly half of the TSV voltage is dropped across the TSV oxide (at the left) and the other half across the depleted region in the substrate and there is a few potential contours are observed in the active regions of the MOS devices. The waveforms of the TSV, CMOS input and output voltages and the output current wave form (the current through the load capacitor) are shown in **Figure 6(b)**. It is cleared from the figure that the current is switching w.r.t the CMOS input waveform and there is no effect of the digital HV signal of the TSV.

In order to accelerate the devices and circuit design without significant loss of accuracy and reliability, designer should not model the substrate with numerical methods.

Especially in the high-frequency cases, the loss of the circuit performance caused by the silicon substrate is very important. Considering the radio frequency (RF) range, the substrate could have, at some nodes of interest, an "RLC" behavior (approximately an "RC" one for low frequencies); it is important to prevent the whole system

Analytical and Numerical Model Confrontation for Transfer Impedance Extraction in Three-Dimensional
Radio Frequency Circuits

183

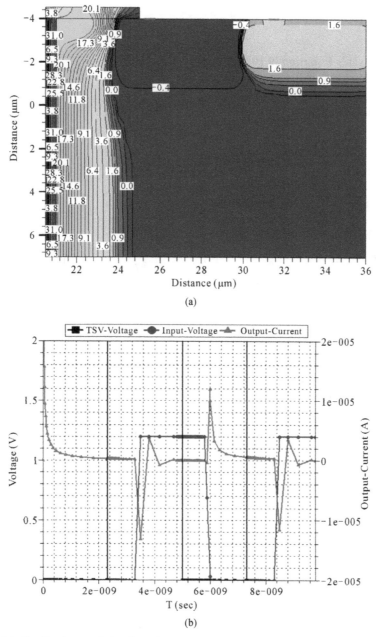

Figure 6. (a) The Potential distribution, and (b) the voltages and output-current waveforms for V_{in} = 0.0/1.2 V and V_{TSV} = 0.0/42.0 V.

(die, with its packaging) from surges, bounces, or parasitic oscillations. So we need effective tools to analyze the practical layout, to calculate the electric performance of the circuit. We need calculate the impedance matrix and partial inductance matrix to analyze the substrate coupling.

Here, Green function will be applied for homogeneous layers to the substrate circuit model extraction, as opposed to numerical method; the resolution speed of this method is much faster. Some basic recalls and concept are first introduced. The use of discrete cosine transforms (DCT) or Fast Fourier transforms (FFT) in this model

will accelerate the compute speed obviously. Then an improved model which can be applied on substrate with in-depth contacts is shown; it can treat the case of contacts lying in different layers. As a check, we compare with a FEM method [6].

3. Substrate Extraction

3.1. Green Kernels

In this paragraph, we present a technique for modeling the substrate. This algorithm relies on the electrostatic Green function in the substrate medium and the Fast

Fourier Transform; it is well known when contacts are on the die surface [7,8].

Green Function and Poisson's Equation [9,10]

Posing and solving problems that are described by the Poisson equation is one of the cornerstones of electrostatics. Poisson's equation is handled as:

$$\Delta V = -\frac{\rho}{\varepsilon} \qquad (1)$$

where, V is the electrical potential, ρ is the charge density and ε the dielectric permittivity of the medium.

The algorithm is the same for the electrostatic or quasi-static case where Poisson's equation is replaced by the Ohm's Law (neglecting the diffusion currents):

$$\boldsymbol{J} = \sigma \cdot \boldsymbol{E}, \qquad (2)$$

with $\sigma = \sigma_0 + j\omega\varepsilon$, for the harmonic domain.

Where, J is the current density in A·m^{-2}, E the electric field in V·m^{-1} and σ the conductivity of the medium in S·m^{-1}. A different form of the law's ohm is given by:

$$\Delta V = -\frac{\operatorname{div}(\boldsymbol{J})}{\sigma}, \qquad (3)$$

where V is the potential (V), div(J) is not null since an extent current (density) is imposed.

Finding V for some given $\rho(=1/\sigma)$ and ε is an important practical problem, since this is the usual way to derive the electric potential for a given charge distribution.

The above equation may be turned into an integral equation of the form:

$$\phi(r) = \int_V \rho(r')G(r,r')\mathrm{d}^3r' \qquad (4)$$

G is the potential due to a point charge placed at a point r' and G is known as Green function (or Kernel).

The Green function can be got by solving the following equation:

$$\nabla^2 G = -\frac{\delta(r-r')}{\varepsilon} \qquad (5)$$

If the Green function is known, this equation does provide a technique for determining the potential at any point in the volume V due to a known arbitrarily distributed charge density.

Consider a localized charge at the point P (x', y', z') in the upper layer of stacked dielectric layers as shown on the **Figure 7(a)**. Here, we assume the substrate as an equivalent system composed of stacked layers; each of them has a dielectric constant and a resistivity of the corresponding resistive substrate layer.

The potential in Q (x, y, z) induced by the charge in P is the solution of Poisson's equation and is given by:

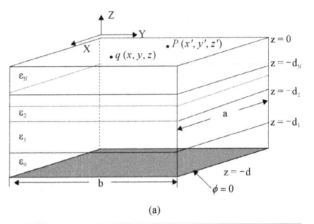

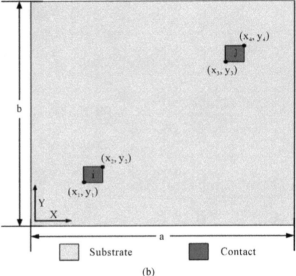

Figure 7. (a) Stacked layers model of the substrate and (b) Top view: contact altitudes: $-d < z_i, z_j < 0$.

$$\Delta G(x,y,z,x',y',z') = -\frac{\delta(x-x')\cdot\delta(y-y')\cdot\delta(z-z')}{\varepsilon_N} \qquad (6)$$

If we assume that $G = X(x, x') \cdot Y(y, y') \cdot Z(z, z')$, we can rewrite the Poisson's equation, thus resulting in:

$$Y \cdot Z \cdot \frac{\mathrm{d}^2 X}{\mathrm{d}x^2} + X \cdot Z \cdot \frac{\mathrm{d}^2 Y}{\mathrm{d}y^2} + X \cdot Y \cdot \frac{\mathrm{d}^2 Z}{\mathrm{d}z^2}$$
$$= -\frac{\delta(x-x')\cdot\delta(y-y')\cdot\delta(z-z')}{\varepsilon_N} \qquad (7)$$

Noting a and b the die dimensions, we get:

$$X = \cos\left(\frac{m\cdot\pi\cdot x}{a}\right); \quad Y = \cos\left(\frac{n\cdot\pi\cdot y}{b}\right) \qquad (8)$$
$$\text{with } m \in [0,\infty) \text{ and } n \in [0,\infty)$$

(m and n are integers)

The Green's function-equation-involves an infinite series of sinusoidal functions:

Analytical and Numerical Model Confrontation for Transfer Impedance Extraction in Three-Dimensional Radio Frequency Circuits

185

$$\sum_{m=0}^{\infty}\sum_{n=0}^{\infty}\cos\left(\frac{m\cdot\pi\cdot x}{a}\right)\cdot\cos\left(\frac{n\cdot\pi\cdot y}{b}\right)$$

$$\times\left[\frac{d^2Z}{dz^2}-\left(\left(\frac{m\cdot\pi\cdot x}{a}\right)^2+\left(\frac{n\cdot\pi\cdot y}{b}\right)^2\right)\cdot Z\right] \qquad (9)$$

$$=-\frac{\delta\left(x-x'\right)\cdot\delta\left(y-y'\right)\cdot\delta\left(z-z'\right)}{\varepsilon_N}$$

By defining:

$$Z(z,z')=Z'(z,z')\cdot\cos\left(\frac{m\cdot\pi\cdot x'}{a}\right)\cdot\cos\left(\frac{n\cdot\pi\cdot y'}{b}\right) \qquad (10)$$

we get a simple equation:

$$\frac{a\cdot b}{4}\cdot\left[\frac{d^2Z}{dz^2}-\gamma_{mn}^2\cdot Z\right]=-\frac{\delta\left(z-z'\right)}{\varepsilon_N} \qquad (11)$$

$$G(x,x',y,y',z,z')=\sum_{m=1}^{\infty}\sum_{n=1}^{\infty}\left[\frac{2\cdot\left(A_N\cdot e^{-\gamma_{mn}\cdot(d+z_l)}+B_N\cdot e^{\gamma_{mn}\cdot(d+z_l)}\right)\cdot\left(e^{-\gamma_{mn}\cdot z_h}+e^{\gamma_{mn}\cdot z_h}\right)}{a\cdot b\cdot\varepsilon_N\cdot\gamma_{mn}\cdot\left(B_N\cdot e^{\gamma\cdot d}-A_N\cdot e^{-\gamma\cdot d}\right)}\right]\cdot\cos\left(\frac{m\cdot\pi\cdot x}{a}\right)\cdot\cos\left(\frac{n\cdot\pi\cdot y}{b}\right) \qquad (13)$$

Then we can get, or instance, the expression of the capacities from the matrix of capacitive coefficients [C] by using this equation. In order to have [C] or [G] (conductance matrix), we only have to calculate [P], i.e.:

$$p_{ij}=\frac{1}{V_j\cdot V_i}\int\limits_{V_i}\int\limits_{V_j}G\cdot dv_j\cdot dv_i \qquad (14)$$

with $\gamma_{mn}=\sqrt{\left(\frac{m\cdot\pi\cdot x}{a}\right)^2+\left(\frac{n\cdot\pi\cdot y}{b}\right)^2}$.

For $z\neq z'$, $\delta\left(z-z'\right)=0$. The above equation has the well known general solution:

$$Z'=A\cdot e^{-\gamma_{mn}\cdot(d+z)}+B\cdot e^{\gamma_{mn}\cdot(d+z)} \qquad (12)$$

This equation invokes a transmitted wave and a reflected one. Then, after deriving formal mathematical solution for Equation (12), with boundary conditions, we will discuss hereafter on a more physical approach of the problem, using the so-called Transmission Lines Method (TLM).

A general solution, for $m>0$ and $n>0$ of the Green electrostatic function is given as:

Now, the Green function becomes the only unknown. As long as we get G, then the contact-to-contact capacitance (or admittance) will be easily calculated.

Here we only consider the case of both the point charge and the point of observation are in the same dielectric layer, on the surface with $z=z'=0$. The Green function then changes to,

$$G\left(x,y;x',y'\right)_{z=z'=0}=\left(G_0\right)_{z=z'=0}+\left(\sum_{m=0}^{\infty}\sum_{n=0}^{\infty}f_{mn}C_{mn}\cos\left(\frac{m\cdot\pi\cdot x}{a}\right)\cos\left(\frac{m\cdot\pi\cdot x'}{a}\right)\cos\left(\frac{n\cdot\pi\cdot x}{b}\right)\cos\left(\frac{n\cdot\pi\cdot x'}{b}\right)\right) \qquad (15)$$

where $C_{mn}=0$ for $(m=n=0)$, $C_{mn}=2$ for $m=0$ or $n=0$ but $m\neq n$ and $C_{mn}=4$ for all others mn $(m>0)$ and $(n>0)$.

The function f_{mn} is given by:

$$f_{mn}=\frac{1}{ab\gamma\varepsilon_N}\frac{\beta_N\tanh\left(\gamma_{mn}d\right)+\Gamma_N}{\beta_N+\Gamma_N\tanh\left(\gamma_{mn}d\right)} \qquad (16)$$

where

$$\gamma_{mn}=\sqrt{\left(\frac{m\cdot\pi\cdot x}{a}\right)^2+\left(\frac{n\cdot\pi\cdot y}{b}\right)^2} \qquad (17)$$

β_N and Γ_N can be computed recursively from:

$$\begin{bmatrix}\beta_k\\\Gamma_k\end{bmatrix}=\frac{1}{2}\cdot\begin{bmatrix}1+\frac{\varepsilon_{k-1}}{\varepsilon_k} & \left(1-\frac{\varepsilon_{k-1}}{\varepsilon_k}\right)e^{2\theta_k}\\1-\frac{\varepsilon_{k-1}}{\varepsilon_k}e^{-2\theta_k} & 1+\frac{\varepsilon_{k-1}}{\varepsilon_k}\end{bmatrix}\begin{bmatrix}\beta_{k-1}\\\Gamma_{k-1}\end{bmatrix} \qquad (18)$$

where $\theta_k=\gamma_{mn}\left(d-d_k\right)$, $\beta_0=1$, $\Gamma_0=-1$.

Substituting by the Green function and considering two rectangular contacts i and j whom the geometric data are given by x_1, x_2, y_1, y_2 and x_3, x_4, y_3, y_4.

The "coefficient-of-potential" matrix is calculated with the following equation, giving the potential of contact i, induced by an elementary charge spread all over the contact:

$$p_{ij}=\frac{\Gamma_N}{a\cdot b\cdot\varepsilon_N\cdot\beta_N}+\left\{\sum_{m=0}^{\infty}\sum_{n=0}^{\infty}f_{mn}\cdot C_{mn}\cdot\frac{a^2\cdot b^2}{m^2\cdot n^2\cdot\pi^4}\cdot\frac{\left(\sin\left(m\cdot\pi\cdot\frac{x_2}{a}\right)-\sin\left(m\cdot\pi\cdot\frac{x_1}{a}\right)\right)\cdot\left(\sin\left(m\cdot\pi\cdot\frac{x_4}{a}\right)-\sin\left(m\cdot\pi\cdot\frac{x_3}{a}\right)\right)}{\left(x_2-x_1\right)\cdot\left(x_4-x_3\right)}\right.$$

$$\left.\times\frac{\left(\sin\left(n\cdot\pi\cdot\frac{y_2}{b}\right)-\sin\left(n\cdot\pi\cdot\frac{y_1}{b}\right)\right)\cdot\left(\sin\left(n\cdot\pi\cdot\frac{y_4}{b}\right)-\sin\left(n\cdot\pi\cdot\frac{y_3}{b}\right)\right)}{\left(y_2-y_1\right)\cdot\left(y_4-y_3\right)}\right\}$$

$$(19)$$

And then we invert $[P]$ to generate $[C]$ and extract contact-to-contact parasitic.

In practice, we adjoin a new calculation grid to the initial one (of a M·N dimension), in such a way that we can apply directly a discrete cosine transform (DCT) to accelerate the algorithm resolution.

To calculate the substrate resistance, the Green's method is formally equivalent. We have only to replace ε by $1/\sigma\ (=\rho)$ in the former analytical expressions and to consider the admittance matrix $[G]$ replacing the capacitance matrix $[C]$ to determine the different substrate resistances. A current spreading along all the contact is then consider instead of a Q (charge).

For instance, stating from some region of interest of the 0.35 μm CMOS technology cited above, first we approximate the actual profile by uniformly doped stacked layers.

3.2. Transmission Line Analogy for Multilayered Media

In its simplest form, a transmission Line (TL) is a pair of conductors linking together two electrical systems (source and load, for instance), with a forward (f) and return (r) paths; for cases where the return path (and the forward) is floating, a third conductor (or more) is introduced as the grounding shield. For microwaves, they are waveguides. In our case, the propagation of EM waves, their interferences, through the silicon substrate, is among the most serious obstacles in the steady trend towards integration of present day microelectronics. In fact the TL method (TLM) is well established; it can be seen as a more physical interpretation of the mathematical developments presented above, but equivalent.

The principal strength of this method is it is well dedicated to embedded contacts, in any number; for instance in **Figure 7(b)**, keeping the same location of the contacts in the $< x, y >$ plane, we have been changing ad libitum their zi and zj contact altitudes. In practice, a region of interest of the 0.35 μm process is selected, and decomposed in twelve layers (see **Figure 8** and **Table 2**).

Let us consider a plane wave, which its plane of incidence parallel to the $<z', z>$ plane; the medium it is incident upon is multilayered.

Then, we consider the general case in which the line's impedance is not the same as that of the load. Wave front A hits the load Z_L: a part of its energy is absorbed by Z_L, the remaining energy is reflected; in this case, voltage and current wave-fronts are not in phase. This reflected wave can meet another incident wave form B.

The direction of current flow depends on the polarity of the waveform at the time of observation; if two positive directed waveforms (one forward an one reflected) meet, the current waveforms subtract but the voltage

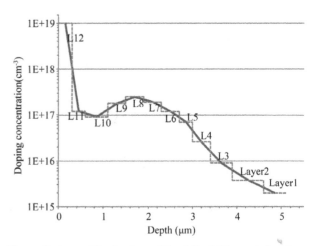

Figure 8. A specific depth profile of the 0.35 μm technology (p-region).

Table 2. Schematic doping profile values in the default p-region of the standard BiCMOS process.

Layer	Thickness (μm)	Concentration (cm⁻³)	Resistivity (Ω·m)	Conductivity (S/m)
12	0.3	1.00E+19	8.80963472E–05	11351.21
11	0.3	1.20E+17	1.70903883E–03	585.12
10	0.5	9.00E+16	2.13546702E–03	468.28
9	0.4	1.80E+17	1.26525401E–03	790.36
8	0.4	2.50E+17	1.00280455E–03	997.20
7	0.4	1.90E+17	1.21694516E–03	821.73
6	0.4	1.20E+17	1.70903883E–03	585.12
5	0.3	7.00E+16	2.61060351E–03	383.05
4	0.4	2.60E+ 16	6.06685659E–03	164.83
3	0.5	9.00E+15	1.60533251E–02	62.29
2	0.7	3.80E+15	3.65908063E–02	27.33
1	0.5	2.00E+15	6.83455581E–02	14.63

waveforms add. Likewise, if a positive directed waveform meets a negative directed waveform, the current will add and the voltage will subtract (**Figure 9**).

The expression for the apparent impedance is given below:

$$Z = \frac{V_{\text{total}}}{i_{\text{total}}} = \frac{V_f \pm V_r}{i_f \pm i_r} \qquad (20)$$

staring for the general solution for voltages and currents:

$$V(z) = V_f e^{\gamma z} + V_r e^{-\gamma z} \qquad (21)$$

$$I(z) = Y_c \left(V_f e^{-\gamma z} - V_r e^{\gamma z} \right) \qquad (22)$$

where the propagation coefficient is the square root of Z

Analytical and Numerical Model Confrontation for Transfer Impedance Extraction in Three-Dimensional
Radio Frequency Circuits

187

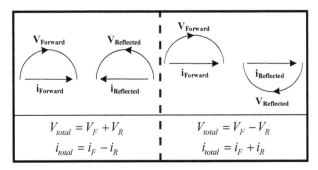

Figure 9. Two possible interactions between the voltage (current) of the forward wave and the voltage (current) of the reflected wave.

and Y product, respectively the linear impedance and admittance;

The $\gamma = \alpha + j\beta$; α attenuation, $\beta = 360°/\lambda_{si}$ are derived directly from the chain matrix:

$$\begin{bmatrix} V_1 \\ I_1 \end{bmatrix} = \begin{bmatrix} \cosh\gamma L & Z_c\sinh\gamma L \\ Y_c\sinh\gamma L & \cosh\gamma L \end{bmatrix}\begin{bmatrix} V_2 \\ -I_2 \end{bmatrix} \quad (23)$$

and from the output branch: $V_2 = -Z_L I_2$

$$\begin{bmatrix} V_1 \\ I_1 \end{bmatrix} = -I_2\begin{bmatrix} Z_L\cosh\gamma L & Z_c\sinh\gamma L \\ Z_L Y_c\sinh\gamma L & \cosh\gamma L \end{bmatrix} \quad (24)$$

where $Z_c = 1/Y_c$ (square root of Z and Y ratio) is the characteristics impedance (Electric and magnetic fields modulus ratio), Z_L is the charge impedance, L is the distance from the load. We can extract an input impedance, said Z_l ($= V_1/I_1$), function of the load impedance Z_{l+1} (l: layer number) as:

$$Z_l = Z_c\frac{Z_{l+1} + Z_c\tanh\gamma L}{Z_c + Z_{l+1}\tanh\gamma L} \quad (25)$$

This very well known (TLM) equation Z_l is directly related to Equation (16).

In fact, restarting from Equation (12), taking into account the limit or boundary conditions—continuity of potential, and the discontinuity of the electric field if there is a surface charge at the considered layer interface—it is quite easy to program this iterative solution (versus substrate depth, or layers) of Equation (12).

Regarding the injected current source point (contact), there are two classes of layers, upper (up) and lower (lo) ones. Then we introduce in our program [11] the derivation current (for instance, in the upper layer):

$$I = \frac{Z_{up}}{Z_{up} + Z_{lo}}V \quad (26)$$

In our simulator, we use a matricial formalism, extending the impedance and the current transmission from a layer l to its adjacent (cf. Equation (16) or Equation (25)), starting from a k layer:

$$\begin{bmatrix} Z_{k,l+1} \\ T_{k,l+1} \end{bmatrix} = \begin{bmatrix} A_k & -B_k \\ C_k & -D_k \end{bmatrix}\begin{bmatrix} Z_{k,l} \\ T_{k,l} \end{bmatrix} \quad (27)$$

4. First Green/TLM Results

First of all, we did some numerical experiences using COMSOL® [6], a well known multiphysics (cf. thermal, mechanical couplings) simulator; it is also a dedicated tool for full wave electromagnetic analysis. It uses essentially Galerkin-like algorithms. Typically a 3D simulation can use a few ten of minutes or hours.

For instance, we compare it, with a very good accuracy, with the analytical formula associated to an "R//C" filter (see, for instance: **Figure 10**; Resistivity bulk: 10 Ω·cm, 2 contacts: 50×50 μm^2, distant of 200 μm); we obtain the following extracted parameters: R = 2.3 KΩ, C = 4.5 fF.

Now it is very easy to calculate, by TLM method any transfer impedance. Possibly embedded in the substrate, contacts can be introduced into any layer; they can be real (metal like) or virtual. Presented is a two contacts example on the **Figure 11**; the he surface die is 30 μm × 30 μm, with M = N = 300, surface contact: 20 points × 20 points (the calculation point, M·N, are equidistributed).

The Green function $G(z, z')$ describing the electric field response to the unity current is identifiable to the transfer impedance between any two points; then we can calculate this impedance spreading. We can extract the potential, particularly between two contacts. This way, we use the inverse transform of the Kroneker matricial product of the impedance by the current DCT. For instance, as a first check, we present on the **Figure 12** the impedance module for two in-depth contacts, at the interfaces: L_5/L_6 and L_9/L_{10}; the comparison between "TLM/Green" and "COMSOL" is quite good.

5. Conclusions

An efficient and elegant technique to model substrate coupling, via frequency dependant impedance extraction,

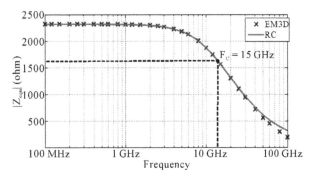

Figure 10. Impedance: comparison between COMSOL and the analytical result "R//C" (Resistivity bulk: 10 Ω·cm; 2 contacts: 50×50 μm^2, distant of 200 μm).

Zsub.Z_9__5.*(Ip1_d_c_t-Ip2_d_c_t)

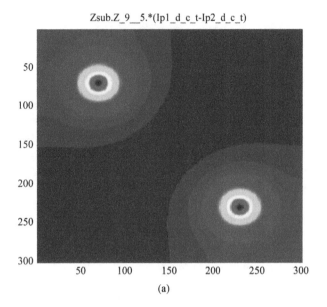

(a)

Zsub.Z_1__1_2.*(Ip1_d_c_t-Ip2_d_c_t)

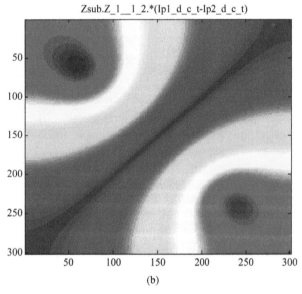

(b)

Figure 11. Potential distributions via transfer impedance (from red to dark blue: voltage decreasing). (a) Contacts embedded in the bulk; interfaces: L_5/L_6 and L_9/L_{10}; (b) Contacts at surface and bottom.

has been presented and programmed. The technique uses a combination of the classical Green function or transmission line method approach and the use of Fast Fourier Transform. The speed of this latter technique makes it suitable for optimization of circuit layout and for minimization of substrate coupling related effects. But the model is often limited to contact locations at the surface; in practice, in our work, the contacts can be placed anywhere in the substrate, so a new research should be enhanced in 3D.

For the near future, considering for instance our compatible 0.35 μm CMOS predilection technology, the digital part can attack any region from the substrate, the ana-

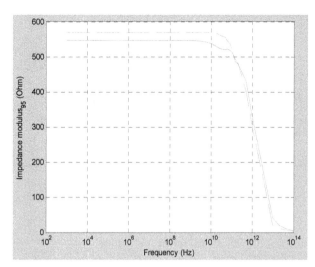

Figure 12. Comparison between finite element method (dashed-upper-line) and Green/TLM (solid-lower-line) (layer interfaces: L_5/L_6 and L_9/L_{10}).

logical CMOS or HBT devices, via a stochastic probability matrix derived from the switching activity [12]; the parasitic wave or impulsion aggressions can be derived via our transfer impedance methods; In fact, we could calculate a two point spectral density of current fluctuations, knowing that our method can handle any number of contacts. The ultimate goal will be to build a "whole" compact model dedicated to actual 3D circuits.

6. Acknowledgements

This work is supported by the Cluster for Application and Technology Research in Europe on NanoElectronics (CATRENE): 3D-TSV Integration for MultiMedia and Mobile applications (3DIM³).

REFERENCES

[1] L. Cadix, C. Bermond, C. Fuchs, A. Farcy, P. Leduc, L. DiCioccio, M. Assous, M. Rousseau, F. Lorut, L. L. Chapelon, B. Flechet, N. Sillon and P. Ancey, "RF Characterization and Modelling of High Density Through Silicon Vias for 3D Chip Stacking," *Microelectronic Engineering*, Vol. 87, No. 3, 2010, pp. 491-495.

[2] R. Gharpurey and S. Hosur, "Transform Domain Techniques for Efficient Extraction of Substrate Parasitics," *International Conference on Computer-Aided Design*, San Jose, 9-13 November 1997, pp. 461-467.

[3] P. S. Crovetti and F. L. Fiori, "Efficient BEM-Based Substrate Network Extraction in Silicon SoCs," *Microelectron Journal*, Vol. 39, No. 12, 2008, pp. 1774-1784.

[4] M. Abouelatta-Ebrahim, R. Dahmani, O. Valorge, F. Calmon and C. Gontrand, "Modelling of through Silicon via and Devices Electromagnetic Coupling," *Microelectron-*

Analytical and Numerical Model Confrontation for Transfer Impedance Extraction in Three-Dimensional
Radio Frequency Circuits

189

ics Journal, Vol. 42, No. 2, 2011, pp. 316-324.

[5]   W8511BP IC-CAP Wafer Professional Measurement Bundle, Agilent.

[6]   COMSOL Multiphysics. http://www.comsol.com

[7]   R. Gharpurey and R. G. Meyer, "Modeling and Analysis of Substrate Coupling in Integrated Circuits," *IEEE Journal of Solid State Circuits*, Vol. 31, No. 3, 1996, pp. 344-353.

[8]   A. M. Niknejad, R. Gharpurey and R. G. Meyer, "Numerically Stable Green Function for Modeling and Analysis of Substrate Coupling in Integrated Circuits," *IEEE Transactions on Computer-Aided Design of Integrated Circuits and Systems*, Vol. 17, No. 4, 1998, pp. 305-315.

[9]   N. Verghese, D. J. Allstot and S. Masui, "Rapid Simula-

tion of Substrate Coupling Effects in Mixed-Mode ICs," *IEEE Custom Integrated Circuits Conference*, San Diego, 9-12 May 1993, pp. 18.3.1-18.3.4.

[10]   N. K. Verghese, D. J. Allstot and M. A. Wolfe, "Fast Parasitic Extraction for Substrate Coupling in Mixed-Signal ICs," *IEEE Custom Integrated Circuits Conference*, Santa Clara, 1-4 May 1995, pp. 121-124.

[11]   Matlab. http://www.mathworks.com

[12]   C. Gontrand, S. Labiod, O. Valorge, P. Mary, J. C. N. Perez, P. J. Viverge, F. Calmon and S. Latreche, "Markov Chain Approach of Digital Flow Disturbances on Supplies via Heterogeneous Integrated Circuit Substrate," *International Journal of Numerical Modeling*, Vol. 30, No. 4, 2010, pp. 54-63.

26

Improved Evaluation Method for the SRAM Cell Write Margin by Word Line Voltage Acceleration[*]

**Hiroshi Makino[1], Naoya Okada[2], Tetsuya Matsumura[3], Koji Nii[4], Tsutomu Yoshimura[5],
Shuhei Iwade[1], Yoshio Matsuda[2]**

[1]Faculty of Information Science and Technology, Osaka Institute of Technology, Hirakata, Japan
[2]Graduate School of Natural Science, Kanazawa University, Kanazawa, Japan
[3]SoC Software Platform Division, Renesas Electronics Corporation, Itami, Japan
[4]Design Platform Development Division, Renesas Electronics Corporation, Kodaira, Japan
[5]Faculty of Engineering, Osaka Institute of Technology, Osaka, Japan

ABSTRACT

An accelerated evaluation method for the SRAM cell write margin is proposed using the conventional Write Noise Margin (WNM) definition based on the "butterfly curve". The WNM is measured under a lower word line voltage than the power supply voltage VDD. A lower word line voltage is chosen in order to make the access transistor operate in the saturation mode over a wide range of threshold voltage variation. The final WNM at the VDD word line voltage, the Accelerated Write Noise Margin (AWNM), is obtained by shifting the measured WNM at the lower word line voltage. The WNM shift amount is determined from the measured WNM dependence on the word line voltage. As a result, the cumulative frequency of the AWNM displays a normal distribution. Together with the maximum likelihood method, a normal distribution of the AWNM drastically improves development efficiency because the write failure probability can be estimated from a small number of samples. The effectiveness of the proposed method is verified using the Monte Carlo simulation.

Keywords: Static Random Access Memory (SRAM); Write Noise Margin (WNM); Vth Fluctuation; Variance; WNM Distribution

1. Introduction

The recent progress of process technology has caused various fluctuation problems in device characteristics due to transistor area reduction. The threshold voltage (Vth) fluctuation caused by dopant fluctuation strongly influences device characteristics [1,2]. Generally, this dopant induced Vth fluctuation is random and obeys a normal distribution.

The stability of SRAM cells is greatly affected by Vth fluctuation, because SRAM cells are usually designed using minimum design rules. Vth fluctuation degrades both the read and the write operation stabilities. It is said that the read operation is usually more critical than the write operation under Vth fluctuation. However, the write operation is also affected by a large Vth fluctuation. In addition, a recent paper indicates that write operation failure is more dominant than read operation failure under low supply voltage conditions [3]. Therefore, an accurate evaluation of write operation stability is as important as an evaluation of read operation stability.

Conventionally, the Write Noise Margin (WNM), based on the "butterfly curve", is used as a metric of write operation stability [4]. Since the write operation is strongly affected by the Vth of the SRAM cell access transistors, the conventional WNM is also expected to be sensitive to Vth variation of the SRAM cell access transistors. However, the WNM is not sensitive to Vth variation when the WNM is large. In addition, the WNM does not obey a normal distribution. Takeda *et al.* described these problems and maintained the importance of a normal distribution of the WNM [5]. They proposed a new write margin definition which is sensitive to Vth variation of the access transistors and follows a normal distribution. Recently, several new definitions have been proposed [6-9]. If the write margin obeys the normal distribution, the write margin distribution can be easily esti-

[*]Several parts of this paper are based on the authors' previous work presented in the 2011 13th International Symposium on Integrated Circuits (ISIC), which is described in Proceedings of ISIC 2011, pp. 67-70, December 2011.

mated by a small number of samples [5]. This drastically improves development efficiency, especially when combined with the maximum likelihood method.

In this paper, we propose an accelerated evaluation method for the SRAM cell write margin using the conventional butterfly curve based WNM definition. The WNM is measured at a lower word line voltage than the power supply voltage VDD and calibrated to the WNM of the VDD word line voltage. In the proposed method, the write margin obeys the normal distribution even under the conventional WNM definition.

In Section 2, the reason why the conventional WNM does not obey the normal distribution is analyzed. In Section 3, an accelerated evaluation method for the SRAM cell write margin is proposed based on the analysis in Section 2. In Section 4, the proposed method is verified using the Monte Carlo simulation. Finally, Section 5 provides the conclusion.

2. Conventional Write Noise Margin

A diagram of the SRAM write operation circuit is shown in **Figure 1**. Let us assume that the inverted data are written to the SRAM cell where "1" is stored on the internal node V1 and "0" on the V2. Then, the data "0" and "1" are given on bit lines BL and /BL, respectively, under the activated word line WL. If the voltages of nodes V1 and V2 are inverted, the write operation is successful. Hereupon, V1, V2, BL, /BL and WL represent the voltages.

The definition of the conventional Write Noise Margin (WNM) based on the butterfly curve is shown in **Figure 2**. We draw the DC transmission curves of inverter A (InvA in **Figure 1**) and inverter B (InvB in **Figure 1**) under WL = VDD, BL = 0 V and /BL = VDD. The VDD is the power supply voltage. The WNM is defined as the width of the smallest embedded square between the two DC transmission curves.

Generally, the write margin is a function of the threshold voltage Vth's of the six transistors in a SRAM cell. If the write margin is linear on the Vth's, the write margin is expected to obey the normal distribution, allowing us to predict the write margin distribution accurately from a small number of samples. Furthermore, if the write margin distribution is the normal distribution, the write yield can also be easily estimated [10].

The dependence of the WNM on the Vth is examined using the SPICE simulation. The transistor parameter of 45-nm process technology [11] is used with the power supply voltage of VDD = 1.0 V. The threshold voltages are the typical values of Vthn = 0.404 V for the NMOS transistors and Vthp = –0.384 V for the PMOS transistors. The transistor sizes are L = 45 nm and W = 55 nm, 83 nm, and 55 nm with for the access, driver, and load transistors, respectively.

The simulation results are shown in **Figure 3**. We set ΔVth = 0, a typical threshold voltage. The WNM is not linear on the Vth of the access transistor N1. However, the WNM is almost linear on the other transistors. The nonlinearity on access transistor N1 causes the WNM to deviate from the normal distribution [10]. In the lower Vth region, the load transistor P1 determines WNM = 0, that is, the write limit. In the higher Vth region, the access transistor N1 determines the write limit. The slope of the WNM for the N1 changes significantly near ΔVth = 0.1 V. The WNM is completely linear for ΔVth > 0.1 V. We call this area the linear section of the WNM for the N1. WNM = 0 is on this straight line. When ΔVth < 0.1 V, the slope of the WNM is almost equal to 0. This means that the WNM is not sensitive to Vth variation of the N1 when the WNM is large. This is consistent with previous research [5]. The access transistors only affect the WNM in the case of a large Vth variation. In other words, the WNM distribution has a tail at the side of the small margin. A large number of samples is needed in order to estimate the distribution. If we estimate the distribution with a small number of samples, with many appearing around ΔVth = 0, the predicted distribution is very sharp. This results in an overestimation of ΔVth for WNM = 0, because the slope of the WNM is nearly equal to 0 around ΔVth = 0.

The reason why the WNM has different slopes around

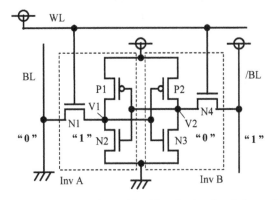

Figure 1. Diagram of the SRAM cell circuit of the write operation.

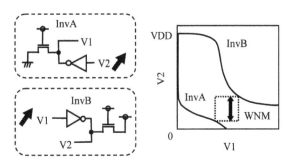

Figure 2. Definition of the Write Noise Margin (WNM).

ΔVth = 0.1 V can be explained by a change in the operation mode of the access transistors when the WNM is evaluated. The dependence of the V1 on the ΔVth of N1 in **Figure 1** is examined using the SPICE simulation at V2 = 0 V. The results are shown, together with the WNM, in **Figure 4**. The dashed line, which is determined by the equation V1 = VDD-Vth, represents the boundary of the operation mode of the access transistor N1. In the region to the left of the dashed line, the N1 operates in the linear mode and to the right of the dashed line, it operates in the saturation mode. Therefore, the operation mode of the access transistor changes around the point where the V1 curve intersects with the dashed line. The changing point

of the WNM slope, which is around ΔVth = 0.1 V, closely corresponds to the changing point of the operation mode of the access transistor. Thus, a change in the slope of the WNM is strongly related to a change in the operation mode of access transistor N1.

In the AC write operation of a SRAM cell, access transistor N1 is always in the saturation mode at the beginning of the write operation because the V1 is not lower than the WL. Write failure occurs when the N1 stays in the saturation mode during the write operation. Therefore, the write margin should be evaluated in the saturation mode of access transistor N1. Contrary to the actual AC write operation, the conventional WNM is

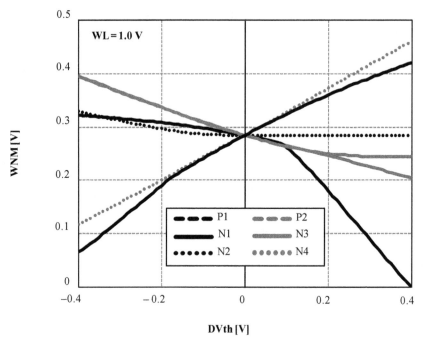

Figure 3. Dependence of the WNM on the ΔVth at WL = VDD.

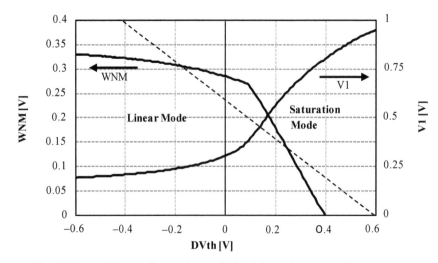

Figure 4. Dependence of the WNM and V1 at a fixed voltage of V2 = 0 V on the threshold voltage variation of the access transistor N1 in the write operation.

evaluated in the linear mode of the access transistor when the write margin is large. Using the conventional WNM definition, therefore, is not an effective way to evaluate the stability of a SRAM cell.

3. Accelerated Evaluation Method

In this section, we propose an accelerated evaluation method for the SRAM cell write margin based on the conventional WNM definition. In the proposed method, the access transistor is forced to operate in the saturation mode by lowering the word line voltage from the VDD. The WNM is then measured under the lower word line voltage. The word line voltage is chosen from a range which causes the access transistor to operate in the saturation mode. The WNM at the word line voltage of the VDD is calibrated from the measured WNM at the lower word line voltage. This calibrated WNM is called the Accelerated WNM (AWNM).

First, we measure the dependence of the WNM on the word line voltage. The WNM given by the SPICE simulation is shown in **Figure 5**. The power supply voltage is VDD = 1.0 V. The solid line represents the simulation results. The WNM is linear for a word line voltage of less than 0.9 V, meaning that the access transistor N1 operates in the saturation mode in this range of word line voltages, the equivalent of a high ΔVth. The slope change of the WNM at the word line voltage of 0.9 V corresponds to a change in the operation mode of the access transistor N1 around the threshold voltage of ΔVth = 0.1 V in **Figure 4**. The operation mode of the N1 moves to the linear mode in WL > 0.9 V.

Although the accelerated evaluation method using a word line voltage below 0.9 V gives a good linearity for the WNM, the value of the WNM itself is small when compared to the WNM at WL = 1.0 V. This is because

the WNM is evaluated at a lower word line voltage. Therefore, this value is calibrated to the WNM at WL = 1.0 V. The dashed line in **Figure 5** represents the extrapolated line. The extrapolated value of the WNM using the straight line is 0.35 V, the WNM at WL = 1.0 V, which is the AWNM in the proposed method.

In the accelerated evaluation method, the AWNM at WL = 1.0 V, denoted as AWNM (WL$_{1.0}$), is obtained from the measured WNM at a low word line voltage, the WNM (WL$_{m}$), as:

$$AWNM\left(WL_{1.0}\right) = WNM\left(WL_{m}\right) + \alpha\left(WL_{1.0} - WL_{m}\right),$$
(1)

where α is the slope of the WNM for the WL voltage in the linear section. This AWNM is considered to be the write margin corresponding to the AC write operation.

Figure 6 shows the dependence of the WNM on the ΔVth at the word line voltage of 0.8 V. A negative value is defined as the maximum length of an embedded square in the crossed curves, as shown in **Figure 7**. This means that the data are not inverted. In **Figure 6**, the slope changing point of the WNM for the N1 moves to the left when compared to the slope changing point under the word line voltage of 1.0 V (**Figure 3**). As a result, the measured samples around ΔVth = 0 V are in the linear section. In **Figure 8**, the dependence of the WNM and AWNM on the ΔVth's is shown for access transistor N1 and load transistor P1. The solid lines are the AWNM and the dashed lines are the WNM. The extrapolated lines are drawn from the AWNMs around ΔVth = 0 V. The extrapolated line for access transistor N1 gives the correct write limit because the threshold voltage ΔVth at AWNM = 0 predicted by the extrapolated line is the same as the ΔVth at WNM = 0. This means that measured samples around ΔVth = 0 V for the N1 predict the

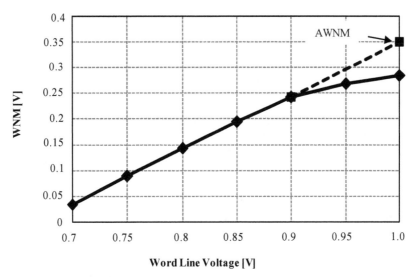

Figure 5. Dependence of the WNM on the word line voltage.

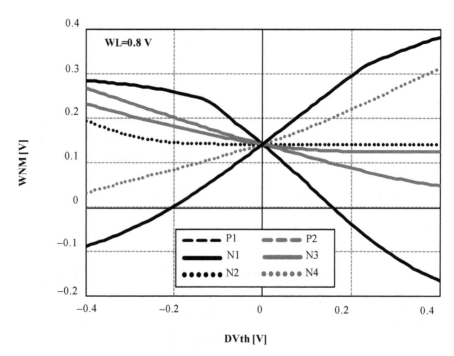

Figure 6. Dependence of the WNM on ΔVth under WL = 0.8 V.

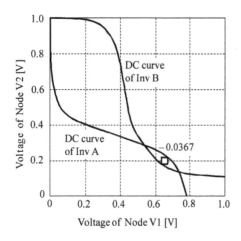

Figure 7. The butterfly curve with a negative write margin when ΔVth = 0.2 V for the N1 and ΔVth = 0 V for other transistors (see Figure 6).

correct write limit if the AWNM is used as a metric. As for load transistor P1, there is a slight difference between the write limit of the WNM and the write limit predicted from the AWNM around ΔVth = 0. The extrapolated line for the P1 gives about a 0.1 V higher ΔVth value than the WNM for the write limit. This means that the AWNM predicts a slightly lower write limit for the Vth variation of the P1. The absolute value of the predicted ΔVth at AWNM = 0 for access transistor N1 is smaller than the absolute value for load transistor P1. Therefore, when the AWNM is used as a metric, the Vth variation of the N1 has the strongest influence on the write operation while the influence of the P1 is relatively small. Furthermore,

the write limit predicted by the AWNM is always in the safer side, because the absolute value of the predicted write limit for the P1 variation is always lower than the write limit in the WNM.

The AWNM and the WNM are shown for the other transistors in **Figure 9**. These transistors have only a small influence on the write limit because the absolute ΔVth values at AWNM = 0 are far larger than those for the N1 and the P1 shown in **Figure 8**.

4. Monte Carlo Simulation

The proposed method is verified using the Monte Carlo simulation. The Vth's are assumed to follow the normal distribution with a variance of σ_{Vth} = 50 mV and a mean of Vthn = 0.404 V and Vthp = −0.384 V. In the Monte Carlo simulation, we make the Vth's of six SRAM cell transistors independently change at random. The number of samples is 100,000. For simplicity, we set the same variance for every transistor.

In this simulation, the threshold voltage Vth is set to a typical value. In the actual measurement of real devices, however, the threshold voltages of the SRAM cell transistors are not known. By measuring the dependence of the WNM on the word line voltages of several samples, it is relatively easy to find a word line voltage that allows the access transistor to operate in the saturation mode. If the measured samples include those with a very low Vth, in which the access transistor operates in the linear mode in the WNM measurements, they can be excluded when determining the word line voltage. This does not affect the simulation, because the probability of encountering

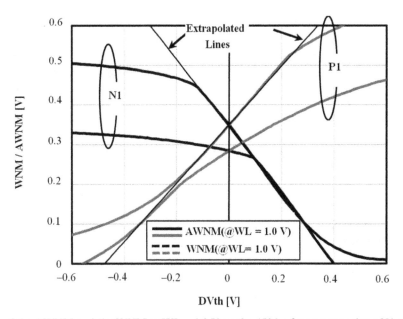

Figure 8. Dependence of the AWNM and the WNM at WL = 1.0 V on the ΔVth of access transistor N1 and load transistor P1.

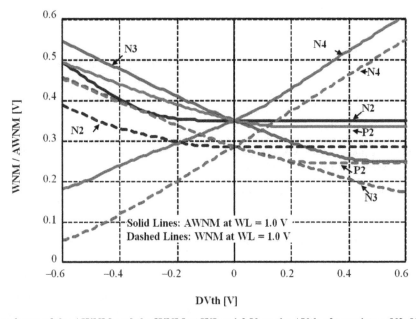

Figure 9. Dependence of the AWNM and the WNM at WL = 1.0 V on the ΔVth of transistors N2, N3, N4, and P2.

such devices is very small. The dependence of the WNM on the word line voltage is shown for the first ten samples in **Figure 10**. The slopes $\alpha = \Delta WNM/\Delta WL$ are almost the same for the ten samples in each linear section. A word line voltage can be chosen, such as 0.7 V or 0.8 V, from these data. The cumulative frequency scaled by the variance σ is shown in **Figure 11**. A straight line for the cumulative frequency indicates a normal distribution of the write margin. Lines I, II, and III are the WNM at WL = 0.7 V, 0.8 V, and 1.0 V, respectively. Line IV is the AWNM corresponding to WL = 1.0 V calibrated from line I, that is, the WSNM at WL = 0.7 V. Line V is

the AWNM corresponding to WL = 1.0 V calibrated from line II, that is, the AWNM at WL = 0.8 V. For the calibration, we use $\alpha = 1.060$, which is the mean value of the ten samples. The mean values of the WNM and AWNM, μ_{WNM} and μ_{AWNM}, are summarized in **Table 1**. The two means of the AWNM at WL = 1.0 V, calibrated from the WNM at WL = 0.7 V and WL = 0.8 V, are very similar. Lines IV and V of the AWNMs at WL = 1.0 V, calibrated from I and II, respectively, almost overlap, demonstrating the validity of the proposed method.

The slope of the cumulative frequency of the conventional WNM at WL = 1.0 V (line III in **Figure 11**)

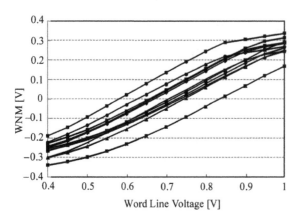

Figure 10. Dependence of the WNM on the word line voltage for the first ten samples in the Monte Carlo simulation.

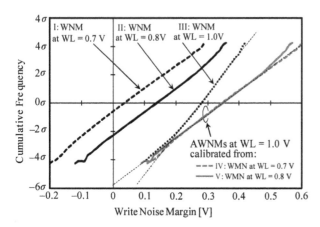

Figure 11. The cumulative frequency of the AWNM and the WNM. Lines I, II and III are the WNM at WL = 0.7 V, 0.8 V, and 1.0 V, respectively. Lines IV and V are the AWNM at WL = 1.0 V calibrated from lines I and II, respectively. The IV and V lines almost overlap.

Table 1. The mean values of the WNM and AWNM.

	μ_{WNM} [V]	μ_{AWNM} [V]
WL = 0.7 V	0.0355	0.354
WL = 0.8 V	0.144	0.356
WL = 1.0 V	0.284	

changes at about WNM = 0.2 V. There are two slopes corresponding to the two operation modes of access transistor N1, as discussed in Section 2. Obviously, the conventional WNM does not obey the normal distribution. Therefore, the WNM at WL = 1.0 V gives a low write failure probability if the probability is estimated from a slope in the vicinity of ΔVth = 0 V. On the other hand, the cumulative frequency of the WNM at WL = 0.7 V and WL = 0.8 V are straight lines. This means that the frequencies follow the normal distribution. The slopes of the extrapolated lines are almost the same. As a result, both the AWNMs (lines IV and V) follow the normal

distribution. Their slopes are the same as that of the conventional WNM in the small WNM region below 0.2 V, because the access transistor operates in the saturation mode in this region. The extrapolated σ values at AWNM = 0 of the cumulative frequency of the AWNMs coincide with the σ value at WNM = 0 extrapolated from the linear section in the small WNM region, as shown in **Figure 11**. **Table 2** summarizes the values of $-\mu_{WM}/\sigma_{WM}$ which correspond to the extrapolated cumulative frequency at WM = 0 in the scale of σ. Hereupon, we will use write margin (WM) as a general designation. There are two $-\mu_{WM}/\sigma_{WM}$'s in the conventional WNM based on the two slopes in the cumulative frequency. Because the cumulative frequencies, IV and V in **Figure 11**, nearly overlap, the $-\mu_{WM}/\sigma_{WM}$'s for the two AWNMs calibrated from WL = 0.7 V and WL = 0.8 V are almost the same.

If the WM obeys the normal distribution, the write failure probability P_{WF} of writing "0" to the left-side storage node V1 in **Figure 1** is given as:

$$P_{WF} = \int_{-\infty}^{-\mu_{WM}/\sigma_{WM}} \frac{1}{\sqrt{2\pi}\sigma_{WM}} \exp\left(-\frac{(WM-\mu_{WM})^2}{2\sigma_{WM}^2}\right) dWM \tag{2}$$

μ_{WM} and σ_{WM} are the mean and the variance of the WM distribution, respectively. By using the variable transformation $x = (WM - \mu_{WM})/\sigma_{WM}$, we obtain the following equation:

$$P_{WF} = \int_{-\infty}^{-\mu_{WM}/\sigma_{WM}} \frac{1}{\sqrt{2\pi}} \exp\left(-\frac{x^2}{2}\right) dx \tag{3}$$

The write failure probability of writing "1" is equal to the write failure probability of writing "0" due to SRAM cell symmetry. Furthermore, the cases of writing "0" error and writing "1" error are considered to be almost exclusive to each other. Thus, write yield Y_W is given as:

$$Y_W = 1 - 2P_{WF} \tag{4}$$

If the distribution of the WM is not guaranteed to be the normal distribution, it is very difficult to estimate the write yield because the distribution cannot be generally determined by only the measured data.

Table 3 shows the linearly extrapolated $-\mu_{WM}/\sigma_{WM}$ and

Table 2. Extrapolated values of $-\mu_{WM}/\sigma_{WM}$ giving WM = 0 in Figure 11.

	$-\mu_{WM}/\sigma_{WM}$
WNM	−8.58[*]/−6.08[**]
AWNM at WL = 1.0 V from WL = 0.7 V	−5.72
AWNM at WL = 1.0 V from WL = 0.8 V	−5.78

[*]The extrapolated value as a straight line with the slope of the WNM around the mean value of 0.28 V. [**]The extrapolated value as a straight line with the slope of the WNM around the mean value of 0.15 V.

Table 3. Extrapolated write limits and P_{WF}'s of the WNM and the AWNMs.

| | WNM | AWNM | | CWLM [10] |
		from 0.7 V	from 0.8 V	
$-\mu_{WM}/\sigma_{WM}$	−8.24	−5.72	−5.78	−5.71
P_{WF} [ppm]	8.61×10^{-11}	5.33×10^{-3}	3.74×10^{-3}	5.65×10^{-3}

the write failure probability (P_{WF}) for the data in **Figure 11**. P_{WF}'s are calculated from each $-\mu_{WM}/\sigma_{WM}$ using Equation (3). In **Table 3**, the $-\mu_{WM}/\sigma_{WM}$ and P_{WF} values in the definition proposed by Gierczynski *et al.* [6] are also shown as a reference [10]. We call this write margin the CWLM (Combined Word Line Margin). The CWLM not only gives the correct write limit, but also displays good linearity in the cumulative frequency and, therefore, obeys the normal distribution, as discussed in detail in [10].

The extrapolated $-\mu_{WM}/\sigma_{WM}$ values of the AWNM from the WNM at WL = 0.7 V and WL = 0.8 V are nearly equal within a deviation of 1.05%. Therefore, the predicted P_{WF}'s are very similar to each other within a factor of 1.43. Furthermore, the extrapolated $-\mu_{WM}/\sigma_{WM}$ values in the AWNMs also clearly match the values in the CWLM. This means that the AWNMs calibrated from the WNM at WL = 0.7 V and WL = 0.8 V give suf-

ficiently accurate P_{WF}'s. In SRAM design, predicting the order of the P_{WF} is important for determining the redundancy circuit. Therefore, obtaining an accurate P_{WF} using the AWNM is valuable. Thus, the butterfly curve based WNM is still effective when used for the proposed accelerated evaluation method.

Figure 12 shows the dependence of the μ_{WM}/σ_{WM} of AWNM and the calculated P_{WF} on the word line voltage at which the WNM is measured. The μ_{WM}/σ_{WM} value stays almost constant for a word line voltage higher than 0.65 V, resulting in similar P_{WF} values within the same order of magnitude in this word line voltage region. However, the μ_{WM}/σ_{WM} increases for a word line voltage below 0.65 V, resulting in a rapid decrease in the P_{WF}. This is because the off-state access transistor appears at the low word line voltage. If the Vth of the access transistor deviates to high, it turns off at the low word line voltage. When the access transistor turns off, the linearity of the WNM for the word line voltage is lost. Therefore, a WNM measured with an off-state access transistor does not follow the normal distribution. As the word line voltage decreases below 0.65 V, the number of samples with such off-state access transistors rapidly increases. As a result, the μ_{WM}/σ_{WM} and P_{WF} values deviate from the correct value. In this case, a word line voltage from 0.65 V to 0.8 V is suitable to evaluate the AWNM.

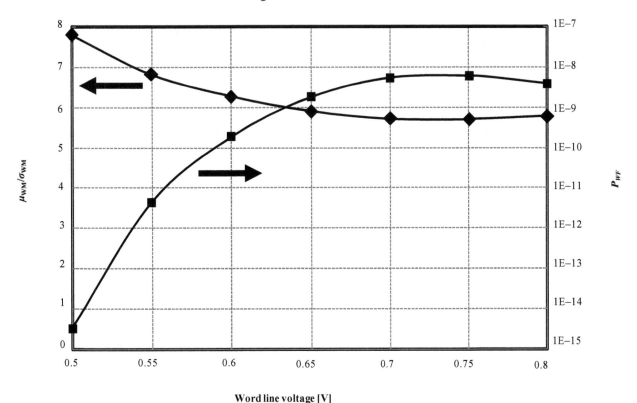

Figure 12. Dependence of the μ_{WM}/σ_{WM} of the AWNM and the calculated P_{WF} on the word line voltage at which the WNM is measured.

If the WM is guaranteed to obey the normal distribution, the variance and the mean can be easily estimated from a small amount of data. According to the maximum likelihood method, the mean μ_{WM} and the variance σ_{WM} are obtained from the write margin WM_j data, with an error of order $1/\sqrt{N}$ as:

$$\mu_{WM} = \frac{1}{N} \sum_j WM_j \qquad (5)$$

$$\sigma_{WM}^2 = \frac{1}{N} \sum_j \left(WM_j - \mu_{WM} \right)^2. \qquad (6)$$

In **Tables 4-6**, the variance and the mean obtained from (5) and (6) using the Monte Carlo simulation data are summarized. **Table 4** shows the case of a conven-

Table 4. The mean and variance of the WNM at V = 1.0 V in the Monte Carlo simulation.

	μ_{WM} [V]	σ_{WM} [V]	μ_{WM}/σ_{WM}	P_{WF} [ppm]
N = 100	0.305	0.0395	7.73	5.38×10^{-9}
N = 300	0.302	0.0368	8.19	1.31×10^{-10}
N = 1000	0.305	0.0385	7.93	1.10×10^{-9}
N = 3000	0.306	0.0369	8.20	1.20×10^{-10}
N = 10,000	0.306	0.0374	8.12	2.33×10^{-10}
N = 30,000	0.306	0.0376	8.14	1.98×10^{-10}
N = 100,000	0.306	0.0374	8.18	1.42×10^{-10}

Table 5. The mean and variance of the AWNM at WL = 1.0 V calibrated from the WNM at WL = 0.7 V in the Monte Carlo simulation.

	μ_{WM} [V]	σ_{WM} [V]	μ_{WM}/σ_{WM}	P_{WF} [ppm]
N = 100	0.340	0.0591	5.76	4.21×10^{-3}
N = 300	0.342	0.0588	5.81	3.12×10^{-3}
N = 1000	0.345	0.0603	5.72	5.33×10^{-3}
N = 3000	0.345	0.0596	5.79	3.52×10^{-3}
N = 10,000	0.346	0.0602	5.75	4.46×10^{-3}
N = 30,000	0.346	0.0607	5.70	5.99×10^{-3}
N = 100,000	0.347	0.0606	5.72	5.33×10^{-3}

Table 6. The mean and variance of the AWNM at WL = 1.0 V calibrated from the WNM at WL = 0.8 V in the Monte Carlo simulation.

	μ_{WM} [V]	σ_{WM} [V]	μ_{WM}/σ_{WM}	P_{WF} [ppm]
N = 100	0.348	0.0607	5.74	4.46×10^{-3}
N = 300	0.349	0.0589	5.92	1.61×10^{-3}
N = 1000	0.352	0.0602	5.85	2.46×10^{-3}
N = 3000	0.352	0.0591	5.95	1.34×10^{-3}
N = 10,000	0.353	0.0597	5.92	1.61×10^{-3}
N = 30,000	0.353	0.0603	5.86	2.31×10^{-3}
N = 100,000	0.354	0.0600	5.89	1.93×10^{-3}

tional WNM at WL = 1.0 V. In this table, the μ_{WM}/σ_{WM} is large, even at N = 100,000, when compared to the other extrapolated values in **Table 3**. This shows that the write failure probability is underestimated in the conventional WNM, even when N = 100,000 is used. **Table 5** shows the case of the AWNM at WL = 1.0 V calibrated from the WNM at WL = 0.7 V. Because the AWNM obeys the normal distribution, a close agreement is observed between a value with a small N, for example, N = 100, 300, etc., and a value with N = 100,000 or an extrapolated value in **Table 3**. Also, the calculated P_{WF} for every N is close to that of the CWLM in **Table 3** within a factor of 1.81. This means that a sufficiently accurate write failure probability can be easily predicted from a small number of measured samples. **Table 6** shows the AWNM at WL = 1.0 V calibrated from the WNM at WL = 0.8 V. In this case, although the μ_{WM}/σ_{WM} is close to the extrapolated value in **Table 3** for only N = 100, it becomes slightly larger for N > 100. As a result, the calculated P_{WF}'s for N > 100 are smaller than the values in **Table 5**, creating an increase in the deviation from the P_{WF}'s of the CWLM in **Table 3**. The reason for such deviation can be explained by the sample which is produced when the access transistor is operating in the linear mode. When the Vth of an access transistor becomes low, the access transistor operates in the linear mode under a relatively lower word line voltage. In **Figure 10**, we can see that one of the ten samples begins to deviate from the linear section above the word line voltage of 0.85 V. This sample is thought to have a low-Vth access transistor. If the number of samples increases, samples with access transistors operating in the linear mode under a word line voltage of less than 0.8 V will appear. Such samples deviate from the normal distribution. We can observe this phenomenon in **Figure 11** as a deviation from the linearity of Line V in the high WM region.

Although the P_{WF}'s in **Table 6** are still useful for predicting the write failure probability because they are in the same order as the write failure probability of the CWLM in **Table 3**, the P_{WF}'s in **Table 5** are more accurate. Therefore, 0.7 V should be chosen as the word line voltage at which the WNM is measured. This can be easily done by finding the center of the word line voltage region in which every sample is in the linear section, in **Figure 10**. By using an appropriate word line voltage, the proposed method allows us to predict the correct write failure probability from a small number of measured samples. This provides a drastic improvement in development efficiency.

5. Conclusion

We have proposed an accelerated evaluation method for the SRAM cell write margin based on the conventional WNM definition. The WNM is measured under a lower word line voltage than the VDD of the power supply voltage, forcing the access transistor to operate in the saturation mode. The Accelerated Write Noise Margin (AWNM), the WNM at WL = VDD in this method, is obtained by shifting the WNM at the lower word line voltage. The extent of the shift is determined from the WNM dependence on the word line voltage. The effectiveness of the proposed accelerated evaluation method for the write margin is verified using the Monte Carlo simulation. The cumulative frequency of the AWNM is linear, indicating a normal distribution. Together with the maximum likelihood method, the normal distribution of the AWNM dramatically improves development efficiency, because the write failure probability can be estimated using a small number of samples.

REFERENCES

[1] M. J. M. Pelgrom, A. C. J. Duinmaijer and A. P. G. Welbers, "Matching Properties of MOS Transistors," *IEEE Journal of Solid-State Circuits*, Vol. 24, No. 5, 1989, pp. 1433-1440.

[2] P. A. Stolk, F. P. Widdershoven and D. B. M. Klaassen, "Modeling Statistical Dopant Fluctuations in MOS Transistors," *IEEE Transactions on Electron Devices*, Vol. 45, No. 9, 1998, pp. 1960-1971.

[3] O. Hirabayashi, A. Kawasumi, A. Suzuki, Y. Takeyama, K. Kushida, T. Sasaki, A. Katayama, G. Fukano, Y. Fujimura, T. Nakazato, Y. Shizuki, N. Kushiyama and T. Yabe, "A Process-Variation-Tolerant Dual-Power-Supply SRAM with 0.179 um^2 Cell in 40 nm CMOS Using Level Programmable Wordline Driver," *ISSCC Digg Technology Papers*, 2009, pp. 458-459.

[4] A. Bhavnagarwala, S. Kosonocky, C. Radens, K. Stawiasz, R. Mann, Q. Ye and K. Chin, "Fluctuation Limits & Scaling Opportunities for CMOS SRAM Cells," *ISSCC Digg Technology Papers*, 2005, pp. 659-662.

[5] K. Takeda, H. Ikeda, Y. Hagihara, M. Nomura and H. Kobatake, "Redefinition of Write Margin for Next-Generation SRAM and Write-Margin Monitoring Circuit," *IEEE ISSCC, Digest of Technology Papers*, 2006, pp. 630-631.

[6] N. Gierczynski, B. Borot, N. Planes and H. Brut, "A New Combined Methodology for Write-Margin Extraction of Advanced SRAM," *IEEE International Conferences on Microelectronic Test Structure*, 19-22 March 2007, pp. 97-100.

[7] K. Zhang, U. Bhattacharya, Z. Chen, F. Hamzaoglu, D. Murray, N. Vallepalli, Y. Wang, B. Zheng and M. Bohr, "A 3-GHz 70-Mb SRAM in 65-nm CMOS Technology with Integrated Column-Based Dynamic Power Supply," *IEEE Journal of Solid-State Circuits*, Vol. 41, No. 1, 2006, pp. 146-151.

[8] C. Wann, R. Wong, D. Frank, R. Mann, S.-B. Ko, P. Croce, D. Lea, D. Hoyniak, Y.-M. Lee, J. Toomey, M. Weybright and J. Sudijono, "SRAM Cell Design for Stability Methodology," 2005 *IEEE VLSI-TSA International Symposium on VLSI Technology*, April 2005, pp. 21-22.

[9] E. Grossar, M. Stucchi, K. Maex and W. Dehaene, "Read Stability and Write-Ability Analysis of SRAM Cells for Nanometer Technologies," *IEEE Journal of Solid-State Circuits*, Vol. 41, No. 11, 2006, pp. 2577-2588.

[10] H. Makino, S. Nakata, H. Suzuki, S. Mutoh, M. Miyama, T. Yoshimura, S. Iwade and Y. Matsuda, "Reexamination of SRAM Cell Write Margin Definitions in View of Predicting Distribution," *Transactions on Circuits and Systems II: Brief Express*, Vol. 58, No. 4, 2011, pp. 230-234.

[11] Visit, "45 nm PTM HP Model: V2.1." http://www.eas.asu.edu/~ptm/

27

High-Frequency Heating for Soldering in Electronics

Vladimir L. Lanin

Electronic Technique and Technology Department, Belarus State University of Informatics and Radioelectronics, Minsk, Belarus

ABSTRACT

Processes of high-frequency (HF) heating are examined and its parameters for the soldering of electronic modules are optimized. The advantages of HF heating are the following: selectivity by skin-effect; high density of energy; processing in any environment, including vacuum or inert gas; high ecological cleanliness, improvement solder flowing by electrodynamics forces increase the quality of soldering connections. Investigation of HF electromagnetic heating has allowed to optimize heating speed in local zones of soldering connections formation and to improve their quality due to joint action of superficial effects and electromagnetic forces.

Keywords: HF Heating; Inductor; Soldering; Electronic Modules

1. Introduction

Importance of energy saving in technology forces to address to high-frequency (HF) electromagnetic heating providing of local high speed heating of conducting materials in any environment. The choice of heating frequency, induction design and optimization of heating modes is necessary for formation of qualitative soldering connections in electronics products [1]. HF electromagnetic heating allows to activate solder and to improve wetting solderable surfaces. There is a big variety of induction heating devices designs [2]. To through heating conducting bodies of round, square and rectangular section, solder balls in electronics modules apply circular type inductor, flat bodies—inductors with magnetic gap or as flat spirals [3]. For heating rings, small payments, wires use induction devices with closed and unclosed magnetic circuit. Quality of soldering connections depends on HF frequency, speed of heating, adjustability of heating in time and on section solderable details [4].

2. HF Heating Parameters Modeling

The soldering in electronics is characterized by small specific capacity of heating, small dimensions of modules and their sensitivity to electromagnetic fields [5]. Therefore, it is necessary to optimize effective HF heating power and heating efficiency. Effective HF heating power is generally equal

$$P = \frac{U^2 \cos\varphi \cdot \eta}{R_h},\qquad(1)$$

where: U—effective voltage on inductor, $\cos\varphi$—power factor, η—heating efficiency, R_h—electric resistance in heating zone.

The factor of HF heating power depends on size of a gap h between a surface of body and inductor, and also from electric and magnetic properties of a heated material:

$$\cos\varphi = \frac{1}{\sqrt{1 + \left(1 + \sqrt{2\mu_0}\, h \sqrt{\dfrac{f}{\rho_d \cdot \mu}}\right)^2}}.\qquad(2)$$

For a circular inductor the increase in a gap h from 1 up to 10 mm on frequencies from 400 up to 2000 kHz causes decrease $\cos\varphi$ for diamagnetic materials almost in 10 times, and for ferromagnetic in 3 - 4 times. HF heating efficiency is determined by ratio of the inductor's electric resistance R_i, current-carrying trunks R_t and a detail material in heating zone R_d:

$$\eta = \frac{R_d}{R_d + R_i + R_t}.\qquad(3)$$

At R_i calculations it is supposed, that HF current in the inductor proceeds in a layer with the depth δ_u, and the inductor length depends on coil diameter D_i and number of coils N [6]

$$R_i = \frac{N D_i \sqrt{\rho_i \mu_0 \cdot f}}{d_i},\qquad(4)$$

where d_i—diameter of inductor tube.

Electric resistance to HF currents can be defined from the assumption, that the width of a heating zone at small gap sizes h is equal to a projection of inductor diameter, and the length—to a ring $\pi \cdot ND_d$

$$R_d = \frac{\pi ND_d}{d_i}\sqrt{\frac{\rho_d}{\mu_0 \rho f}}. \tag{5}$$

Electric resistance in the HF heating zone linearly decreases with the reduction of inductor coils number and detail diameter. The maximum values of efficiency for magnetic materials up to 0.9 - 0.95 are reached at $D_d \leq 0.01$ m. After substitute expressions (2), (4), (5) in (1) and make the transformations we will receive expression for effective HF heating power [7] (Equation (6)).

Depending on the type of HF generator, effective voltage on inductor is 50 - 500 V. According to that, the heating power changes from 1 to 20 kW depending on magnetic and electric properties of materials (**Figure 1**).

In equal conditions magnetic materials require smaller specific power. The general law is nonlinear decrease in heating power depending on HF currents frequency that is connected with display of superficial effect. However decrease in frequency increases electrodynamics effect of the fused solder hashing and raises its' spreading.

Thus the electronic devices soldering sensitive to an electric field, the choice of frequency is necessary out from a condition $\delta < H/4$, where H—thickness of a package wall. In this case intensity of field inside the package will be decreased in 100 times that excludes degradation of electronic components [8].

3. Experimental Techniques

For induction heating systems effects of affinity, ring and concentration of a magnetic field are common. But it is possible to create power lines concentration of a field on the set heating surface of a conducting body using magnetic conductor of the certain design. Two types of inductors were investigated: circular with internal (**Figure 2(a)**) and open-ended magnetic conductor (**Figure 2(b)**). The first scheme contained HF generator 1, circular inductor 2 with the cylindrical magnetic core 3, and pyrometer 4. The soldering details 5 placed on thermal insulator 6. In the second scheme the generator 1 was connected to a winding inductor with conductor 2 of ferromagnetic material. In a gap of magnetic conductor details 4 were heated. The winding of inductor is connected by a direct current to an input of regulating rectifier 3.

Frequency was controlled on an output of generator with accuracy 0.1 kHz; amplitudes of a voltage and a current—by universal digital voltmeter; time—by the timer with accuracy 0.1 s; temperature—by the device 6 with accuracy 1°C. Intensity of HF field in a gap was perceived by a measuring framework and estimated by the device 7. Appearance of HF equipment for soldering is resulted on **Figure 3**.

4. Experimental Results and Discussion

Thermal dependences for the soldering of integrated circuits cases have shown influence of inductor's circular design. Two inductor coils (2) in one plane owing to linear site of heating creates more uniform heating of package of the integrated circuit, assembly by soldering (**Figure 4**). It promotes greater full efficiency in 1.6 - 1.8

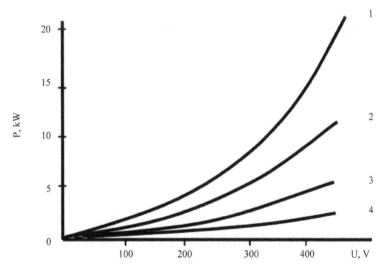

Figure 1. Heating power vs voltage and materials: 1. Copper; 2. Aluminum; 3. Iron; 4. Kovar.

$$P = \frac{U^2}{\sqrt{1+\left(1+1.4h\sqrt{\frac{\mu_0 f}{\rho_d \mu}}\right)^2}\left(1+\frac{(0.15ND_i+0.1L_t)f}{\pi ND_d}\sqrt{\frac{\rho\mu\mu_0}{\rho_d}}\right)} \tag{6}$$

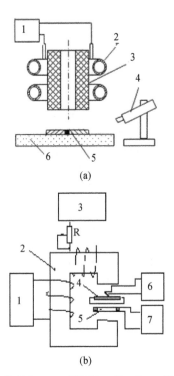

(a)

(b)

Figure 2. Schemes of EM heating for soldering.

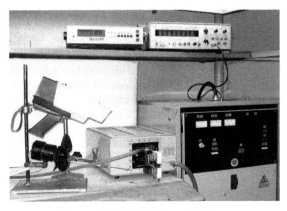

Figure 3. HF soldering equipment.

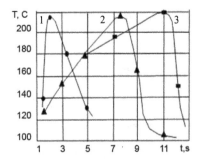

Figure 4. Thermal relationships in soldering zone.

times in comparison with two coils (1) and in 4 times with one coil (3). For the second heating scheme the analysis has shown that at the first stage (up to 10 s) speed of heating was 60°C/s, and further has decreased up to

20°C/s, in connection with increase in losses of energy due to radiation. When factor of overlapping of gap K > 1, dispersion of heat occurs with greater speed.

Materials with low electrical conductivity at overlapping gap optimum are heated up with a speed up to 50°C/s. Heating speed of details in a magnetic gap falls with growth of frequency, because the intensity of an electromagnetic field decreases.

For improvement quality of soldering connections due to increase of the solder spreading area and fuller filling of capillary gaps with it in connection from the moment of the beginning solders spreading before the termination of the soldering details informed low-frequency vibrations by submission of an alternating current by frequency of 50 - 400 Hz and amplitude 1 - 10 A in inducing winding. The amplitude of vibrations of details made 0.5 - 1.0 mm.

The optimal parameters of HF heating with inductor with open-ended magnetic conductor: $f = 300$ kHz, $H = 2.5 \times 10^4$ A/m, current amplitude 1 - 10 A in inducing winding.

HF heating in frequency band 1000 - 2000 kHz has the greater dependence on size of capacity and electrophysical characteristics of materials. At capacity of heating of 1 kW intensity of a field makes 4.5×10^4 A/m, and time of the soldering of magnetic materials—5 sec (**Figure 5**).

5. Conclusions

Modeling and investigation of HF electromagnetic heating has allowed to optimize heating speed in local zones of formation of soldering connections and to improve their quality due to joint action of superficial effects and electromagnetic forces. To small-sized details from non-magnetic materials it is preferable to use inductor with a

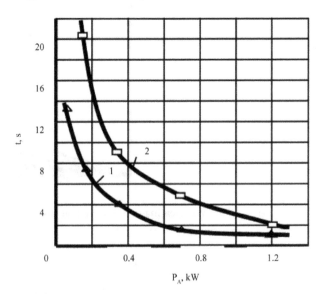

Figure 5. Soldering time—HF heating power relationship.

magnetic backlash as its' working frequency much below, so it increases inductor's efficiency.

Magnetic materials require smaller specific power of HF heating. The general law for all magnetic materials is nonlinear decrease in heating power depending on frequency of HF currents that is connected to display of superficial effect.

The optimal parameters of HF heating by inductor with open-ended magnetic conductor: frequency 300 - 400 kHz, intensity of magnetic field $H = (2.5 - 4.5) \times 10^4$ A/m, current amplitude 1 - 10 A in inducing winding.

REFERENCES

[1]   S. Lupi, Ed., "Induction Heating. Industrial Applications," U.I.E., Paris, 1992, p. 142.

[2]   S. Zinn and S. L. Semiatin, "Elements of Induction Heating: Design, Control, and Application," ASM International, 1988, p. 335.

[3]   M. Li, H. Xu, S.-W. R. Lee, J. Kim and D. Kim, "Eddy Current Induced Heating for the Soldering Reflow of Area Array Packages," *IEEE Transactions on Advanced Packaging*, Vol. 2, No. 31, 2008, pp. 399-403.

[4]   E. Rapoport and Y. Pleshivseva, "Optimal Control of Induction Heating Processes," CRS Press, New York, 2007.

[5]   V. L. Lanin, "Efficiency of Heating by Concentrated Flow of Energy in the Process of Soldering in Electronics," *Electronnaya Obrabotka Materialov*, No. 2, 2002. pp. 17-20.

[6]   V. L. Lanin, "High Frequency Electro-Magnetic Heating in Electronic Systems Soldering Processing," *Electronnaya Obrabotka Materialov*, No. 5, 2004. pp. 79-84.

[7]   V. L. Lanin, "Modeling of HF Electro-Magnetic Heating during the Soldering of Electronic Devices," *News of the Belarus Engineering Academy*, Vol. 2, No. 14, 2002, pp. 167-168.

[8]   V. L. Lanin, A. P. Dostanko and E. V. Telesh, "Formation of Current-Carrying Connections in Electronics Products," Publication Center of the BSU, Minsk, 2007, p. 574.

Permissions

The contributors of this book come from diverse backgrounds, making this book a truly international effort. This book will bring forth new frontiers with its revolutionizing research information and detailed analysis of the nascent developments around the world.

We would like to thank all the contributing authors for lending their expertise to make the book truly unique. They have played a crucial role in the development of this book. Without their invaluable contributions this book wouldn't have been possible. They have made vital efforts to compile up to date information on the varied aspects of this subject to make this book a valuable addition to the collection of many professionals and students.

This book was conceptualized with the vision of imparting up-to-date information and advanced data in this field. To ensure the same, a matchless editorial board was set up. Every individual on the board went through rigorous rounds of assessment to prove their worth. After which they invested a large part of their time researching and compiling the most relevant data for our readers. Conferences and sessions were held from time to time between the editorial board and the contributing authors to present the data in the most comprehensible form. The editorial team has worked tirelessly to provide valuable and valid information to help people across the globe.

Every chapter published in this book has been scrutinized by our experts. Their significance has been extensively debated. The topics covered herein carry significant findings which will fuel the growth of the discipline. They may even be implemented as practical applications or may be referred to as a beginning point for another development. Chapters in this book were first published by Scientific Research Publishing Inc.; hereby published with permission under the Creative Commons Attribution License or equivalent.

The editorial board has been involved in producing this book since its inception. They have spent rigorous hours researching and exploring the diverse topics which have resulted in the successful publishing of this book. They have passed on their knowledge of decades through this book. To expedite this challenging task, the publisher supported the team at every step. A small team of assistant editors was also appointed to further simplify the editing procedure and attain best results for the readers.

Our editorial team has been hand-picked from every corner of the world. Their multi-ethnicity adds dynamic inputs to the discussions which result in innovative outcomes. These outcomes are then further discussed with the researchers and contributors who give their valuable feedback and opinion regarding the same. The feedback is then collaborated with the researches and they are edited in a comprehensive manner to aid the understanding of the subject.

Apart from the editorial board, the designing team has also invested a significant amount of their time in understanding the subject and creating the most relevant covers. They scrutinized every image to scout for the most suitable representation of the subject and create an appropriate cover for the book.

The publishing team has been involved in this book since its early stages. They were actively engaged in every process, be it collecting the data, connecting with the contributors or procuring relevant information. The team has been an ardent support to the editorial, designing and production team. Their endless efforts to recruit the best for this project, has resulted in the accomplishment of this book. They are a veteran in the field of academics and their pool of knowledge is as vast as their experience in printing. Their expertise and guidance has proved useful at every step. Their uncompromising quality standards have made this book an exceptional effort. Their encouragement from time to time has been an inspiration for everyone.

The publisher and the editorial board hope that this book will prove to be a valuable piece of knowledge for researchers, students, practitioners and scholars across the globe.

List of Contributors

Marcel Siadjine Njinowa and Hung Tien Bui
Department of Applied Sciences, Université du Québec à Chicoutimi, Chicoutimi, Canada

François-Raymond Boyer
Department of Computer Engineering, École Polytechnique de Montréal, Montréal, Canada

Rakesh Kumar Singh
Department of E & CE, BT-Kumaon Engineering College, Dwarahat, India

Manisha Pattanaik
Department of Information Technology, VLSI Group, ABV-IIITM Gwalior, Gwalior, India

Neeraj Kr. Shukla
Department of EECE, ITM University, Gurgaon, India

Manish Tiwari and Amit Dhawan
Electronics and Communication Engineering Department, Motilal Nehru National Institute of Technology, Allahabad, India

Takashi Kambe
Department of Electrical and Electronic Engineering, Kinki University, Higashi-Osaka, Japan

Nobuyuki Araki
Graduate School of Science and Technology, Kinki University, Higashi-Osaka, Japan

Nima Ahmadpoor and Ebrahim Farshidi
Department of Electrical Engineering, Shahid Chamran University, Ahvaz, Iran

Wagah F. Mohammad
Communications & Electronics Department, Faculty of Engineering, Philadelphia University, Amman, Jordan

Jose-Ignacio Izpura and Javier Malo
Group of Microsystems and Electronic Materials (GMME-CEMDATIC), Universidad Politécnica de Madrid (UPM), Madrid, Spain

Fabrizio Palma and Stefano Perticaroli
Department of Information Engineering, Electronics and Telecommunications, Sapienza Università di Roma, Rome, Italy

Magdi S. Mahmoud
Systems Engineering Department, King Fahd University of Petroleum and Minerals (KFUPM), Dhahran, Saudi Arabia

Hisham M. Soliman
Electrical Engineering Department, Cairo University, Giza, Egypt

Firas Yengui and Nacer Abouchi
Lyon Institute of Nanotechnology (INL-UMR5270), University of Lyon, Lyon, France

Sophie Taupin
ST Microelectronics, Grenoble, France

Patrice Russo and Gael Pillonnet
Lyon Institute of Nanotechnology (INL-UMR5270), University of Lyon, Lyon, France
ST Microelectronics, Grenoble, France

Vijaya Bhadauria
Electronics and Communication Engineering Department, Motilal Nehru National Institute of Technology, Allahabad, India

Krishna Kant
Department of Computer Engineering and Application, GLA University, Mathura, India

Swapna Banerjee
Electronics and Electrical Communication Engineering Department, Indian Institute of Technology, Kharagpur, India

Erdal Oruklu, Richard Hanley, Christophe Desmouliers and Jafar Saniie
Department of Electrical and Computer Engineering, Illinois Institute of Technology, Chicago, USA

Semih Aslan
Ingram School of Engineering, Texas State University, San Marcos, USA

Fernando M. Vallina
Xilinx Inc., San Jose, USA

Lea Mo
Department of Biotechnology Engineering, Ort Braude College, Karmiel, Israel

Zeev Rubin
Physics Unit, Ort Braude College, Karmiel, Israel

Jen-Yu Shieh
Department of Electro-Optics Engineering, National Formosa University, Yunlin County, Chinese Taipei

Luke K. Wang
Department of Electrical Engineering, National Kaohsiung University of Applied Sciences, Kaohsiung, Chinese Taipei

Ming-Lei Chiu
Chung Hua-Chin Kong Optoelectronics Co. Ltd., Chung Hwa County, Chinese Taipei

Jin Young Choi
Electronic & Electrical Engineering Department, Hongik University, Jochiwon, South Korea

Firas Yengui, Lioua Labrak, Felipe Frantz, Renaud Daviot, Nacer Abouchi and Ian O'Connor
The Lyon Institute of Nanotechnology (INL), University of Lyon, Lyon, France

Taiki Hashizume and Masahiro Fukui
Department of VLSI System Design, Ritsumeikan University, Kusatsu, Japan

Masaya Yoshikawa
Department of Information Engineering, Meijo University, Nagoya, Japan

Adisak Monpapassorn
Department of Electronic Engineering, South-East Asia University, Bangkok, Thailand

Perala Prasad Rao and Kondepudi Lal Kishore
Department of Electronics and Communication Engineering, Jawaharlal Nehru Technological University, Hyderabad, India

Falah Al Hassan
Department of Electrical and Electronics Engineering, Eastern Mediterranean University, Famagusta, North Cyprus

Arash Ahmadpour
Department of Electronic Engineering, Islamic Azad University, Lahijan Branch, Lahijan, Iran
Department of Electronic Engineering, Islamic Azad University, Science and Research Branch, Tehran, Iran

Pooya Torkzadeh
Department of Electronic Engineering, Islamic Azad University, Science and Research Branch, Tehran, Iran

Shilpi Birla
Department of Electronics & Communications, Sir Padampat Singhania University, Udaipur, India

Olivier Valorge
R3 Logic Inc., Monbonnot-Saint-Martin, France

Mohamed Abouelatta-Ebrahim
Université de Lyon, Villeurbanne, France
Faculty of Engineering, Ain Shams University, Cairo, Egypt

Fengyuan Sun, Jean-Etienne Lorival, Francis Calmon and Christian Gontrand
Université de Lyon, Villeurbanne, France

Hiroshi Makino and huhei Iwade
Faculty of Information Science and Technology, Osaka Institute of Technology, Hirakata, Japan

Yoshio Matsuda and Naoya Okada
Graduate School of Natural Science, Kanazawa University, Kanazawa, Japan

Tetsuya Matsumura
SoC Software Platform Division, Renesas Electronics Corporation, Itami, Japan

Koji Nii
Design Platform Development Division, Renesas Electronics Corporation, Kodaira, Japan

Tsutomu Yoshimura
Faculty of Engineering, Osaka Institute of Technology, Osaka, Japan

Vladimir L. Lanin
Electronic Technique and Technology Department, Belarus State University of Informatics and Radioelectronics, Minsk, Belarus

Printed in the USA
CPSIA information can be obtained
at www.ICGtesting.com
JSHW051438221024
72173JS00006B/1507